STANLEY B. BAKER
The Pennsylvania State University

MERVILLE C. SHAW
California State University, Chico

Improving Counseling Through
PRIMARY PREVENTION

Merrill Publishing Company
A Bell & Howell Company

COLUMBUS • TORONTO • LONDON • MELBOURNE

To our students, whom we teach
and from whom we learn

Published by Merrill Publishing Company
A Bell & Howell Information Company
Columbus, Ohio 43216

This book was set in Palatino.

Administrative Editor: Vicki Knight
Production Coordinator: Jeffrey Putnam
Cover Designer: Jim Wiese

Photo credits (All photos copyrighted by the
individuals or companies listed.): Merrill
Publishing/photographs by Lloyd Lemmerman,
25; Jean Greenwald, 68; Mary Hagler, 253, Larry
Hamill, 262; photographs by Harvey Phillips, 92;
Strix Pix, 112, 134; Alan Cliburn, 168; Charles J.
Quinlan, 205.

Library of Congress Catalog Card Number: 86-62077
International Standard Book Number: 0-675-20512-3
Printed in the United States of America
1 2 3 4 5 6 7 8 9—92 91 90 89 88 87

CONTENTS

PREFACE

Primary prevention is a promising approach to guidance and counseling for several reasons. It may help move guidance into the main stream of education; it can help bring counseling to more students; and it can increase both the effectiveness and visibility of services. It is not intended to replace what exists, but to augment it. The concepts and techniques of primary prevention can also help reduce the number of students who require specialized attention to existing personal, interpersonal, or academic problems because its aim is to prevent such problems from occurring.

The primary preventive approach also promotes effective relationships between guidance specialists, and teachers and parents. The need for such effective relationships has always been assumed; at the same time, there has been a tendency for cooperation to occur only after a problem has been identified. The ideas presented here provide the basis for effective, ongoing relationships rather than relationships that occur only at low points in a child's movement through the educational system.

The seasoned professional reading this book may notice that what is included is not all new. Primary prevention has long been effective in public health. Applying the concept to behavior, as opposed to physical illness, has been adopted by community mental health professionals. Guidance specialists have flirted with a number of primary preventive ideas without calling them by that name. *Psychological eduction, moral development, career development,* and *communications skills* all fit comfortably within the primary-preventive framework. What is new is not the specific tactics used to accomplish primary preventive goals, but the focus on primary prevention as a legitimate, organized, and necessary component of any balanced guidance program.

The major purposes of this book are to introduce the techniques of primary prevention, to illustrate how such techniques can be used, and to demonstrate the essential role of primary prevention in schools. The term *guidance specialist* is used throughout as a generic term that includes school counselors, school psychologists, and school social workers. In our view, all these professionals can play a significant role in the implementation of primary-preventive programs.

The book is organized to provide, first, an introduction to the concept of primary prevention. This is followed by a series of chapters that discuss major strategies used to achieve primary-preventive goals in schools. Outlines of sample primary preventive units are included. The final two chapters address the considerable problem of how to go about making changes that will permit the inclusion of primary prevention in an ongoing school program and indicate what might be included in an integrated primary-prevention program. Readers are encouraged to use these ideas when designing their own prevention programs.

We are grateful to several people who have helped us to translate our ideas into a finished product. Vicki Knight saw potential in our ideas. At two universities separated by three time zones, we received unselfish support from colleagues, students, and secretarial staffs. For their especially important contributions, we wish to acknowledge, Larry Clayton, Ed Herr, Don Keat, Mark Kiselica, and Claire Markham at Penn State; and Vernie Bishop, Susan Percira and Suzette Gibb at California State University, Chico. Several chapters in this book would be much less informative if we had been unable to include case study materials based on the preventive efforts of Barbara Baeckert, Patricia Best, Jim Butler, Marie Cini, Diane Baneker, Patricia Day-Shomburg, Diana Durbin, Sandi Hay-Manos, Jan Miller, Katie Scalise, Sally Stabb, Betsy Stano, Ron Thomas, and RoseAnn Tunall. Finally, several important ideas were contributed by our five discerning reviewers: David J. Drum, University of Texas at Austin; Stephen G. Weinrach, Villanova University; Michael Waldo, University of Maryland; Dick Dustin, University of Iowa; and Leroy Baruth, University of South Carolina.

S.B.B.
M.C.S.

FOREWORD

Throughout the history of the mental health professions, there has been an enduring tension between those public policies and institutional goals which argue for serving all persons and those policies and goals which single out only some persons, typically those most distressed, as deserving treatment. Such has been the seeming dichotomy between *prevention* of mental illness and other emotional problems of living, and the *treatment* of such maladies.

Baker and Shaw in *Improving Counseling Through Primary Prevention* have effectively refocused the attention of guidance specialists on the importance of primary prevention as a therapeutic strategy, the advantages of which outweigh awaiting a future need for remediation or therapy of "at-risk populations." Such a position is consistent with a growing national awareness that placing all of one's mental health resources into secondary and tertiary mental health care is not likely to resolve the problems of emotional, behavioral, and social distress that are so prevalent in the population.

Economic, as well as humanitarian reasons , argue for a shift in the philosophy of mental health services provided in schools and in community settings. For example, recent estimates suggest that 96 percent of federal expenditures in health care, including mental health care, are for treatment and only 4 percent for prevention of unhealthy lifestyles. However, a variety of federal reports of the last decade, including the Surgeon General's Report on Health Promotion and Disease Prevention in 1979, indicate that 50 percent of all deaths and seven of the ten leading causes of death are behaviorally determined. In young people ages 15 to 24, 75 percent of deaths are the results of accidents, homicides, and suicides. These statistics suggest that unhealthy life styles and many of their corollaries, such as ineffective interpersonal skills, lack of self-esteem, and inappropriate responses to anger, are preventable. If they are not prevented, treatment is either very expensive, relatively ineffective, or only palliative.

Primary prevention is, as Baker and Shaw suggest, an adjunct to the promotion of mental wellness, as well as to the reduction of mental illness or other interpersonal and intrapsychic difficulties. Applying the competencies of guidance specialists to primary prevention includes helping persons develop problem-solving skills, manage anxiety and stress more consciously and with more control, assume personal responsibility for their lives, gain an internal locus of control, and increase their feelings of power or reduce their feelings of powerlessness. These targets of primary prevention involve such skills as interpersonal communications, anger management, assertiveness training, decision-making, values clarification, systematic relaxation, cognitive restructuring of belief systems, and others that help individuals anticipate and cope more effectively with challenges and stresses.

If national support for primary prevention historically has been more rhetorical than real, the cause is, at least partially, an inability by many counselors to translate the philosophy of primary prevention into practice. Telling how counselors can actually practice primary prevention is a major strength of this book. In addition to defining terms and discussing theory, this book addresses directly and completely the tactics that comprise primary prevention for various purposes. The chapters on communication skills training, psychological education, cognitive behavioral approaches, and career education, for example, contain detailed descriptions of techniques and their implementation.

Improving Counseling Through Primary Prevention also addresses the importance of the environment. The organizational and structural aspects of the learning environments in schools are discussed in relation to the effects of their various physical properties on learning and behavior; so, too, are such matters as classroom reward structures, ability groupings, open versus self-contained classrooms, and incentives for learning for indiviuals and groups.

Chapter eight covers another important emphasis: the assessment of specific children at risk in relation to school readiness and sociometric status. This part of the book is unique in several ways. First, it deals at some length with several major groups of children at risk because of abuse, family disruption, death in the family, lack of support networks, or stress. Second, however important are both identification of and primary prevention provided to such children, the chapter deals with the identification of ineffective adults (parents and teachers) and of non-facilitative environments for children.

The final two chapters are equally unique and useful. Chapter nine discusses the guidance specialist as an agent for change and how change can be planned and implemented. The reader receives a mini-course on organizational behavior as it relates to the influence of administrative structure, power bases, and other dimensions of system analysis. The chapter concludes with a comprehensive discussion of program development, from the formulation of a rationale for primary prevention, the relating of functions to goals and objectives, to the creation of an evaluation strategy.

Improving Counseling Through Primary Prevention concludes with a chapter that summarizes the preceding nine chapters, but does so by developing a menu of suggestions for K to 12 primary prevention programming. The menu connects primary prevention purposes appropriate to the needs of students at different educational levels to the tactics and programs described in the various chapters of the book.

In sum, *Improving Counseling Through Primary Prevention*, is a readable, practical, and useful text. I learned much from reading it. Certainly, any guidance specialist (counselor, school psychologist, or social worker) interested in primary prevention in the schools should start with this text.

Edwin L. Herr, Ed.D.
Professor and Head,
Division of Counseling and
   Educational Psychology, and
   Career Studies
The Pennsylvania State University

1

AN INTRODUCTION
TO PRIMARY PREVENTION

Tremendous changes have taken place in school guidance over the past 30 years. While a guidance specialist who retired a generation ago would certainly recognize some aspects of what guidance specialists do today, there is much that would be new to such a person. In the area of specific techniques there have been major shifts. Group counseling, barely considered in the early 50s, is in common use. Tests of various kinds, very much in vogue throughout the first 15 years of our arbitrary 30-year period, have not only had their use diminished significantly, but are being seriously questioned by lay persons and professionals alike. Only in the area of special education does testing appear to have maintained its popularity. Career development, known 30 years ago as vocational guidance, has assumed an increasingly broader role, both in terms of the time at which it is introduced into the school setting and also in terms of the areas of an individual's life with which it concerns itself. A wide variety of standard programs dealing with various aspects of guidance are now available including, for example, values clarification, magic circles, teacher effectiveness training, and many others.

In addition to changes in techniques, a series of even more fundamental kinds of change have occurred in guidance. Our mythical specialist of 30 years ago could say, comfortably, that the outcomes of guidance are intangible. This is no longer the case; the idea of accountability has apparently arrived and is not likely to disappear. Paralleling the idea of accountability has been the concept of program development with its emphasis on establishing goals and objectives and on assessing the outcomes of guidance services.

The emphasis of guidance also appears to be changing. Almost from the beginning guidance has professed the importance of providing service to all children. Realistically, however, it appears to have concerned itself more with children whom teachers, administrators and parents have believed were in need of special help. Perhaps this emphasis reached its zenith with the passage of Public Law (PL) 94-142, the Education for All Handicapped Children Act. Recently, however, a renewed concern for the provision of guidance services to all children appears to have come about. This shift may be occurring in part as a reaction to what some feel is an overemphasis on special education and also, in part, as a return to the original philosophical assumption that guidance services are for all children. One aspect of this renewed commitment to all children is an increased emphasis on the prevention of problems, as opposed to their remediation. This emphasis, called primary prevention, has become a major focus of community psychology and, in a variety of ways, has been manifest in the public school context.

WHAT PRIMARY PREVENTION IS

Over the years it has been assumed that when professionals used the word *prevention* they have been talking about the same thing. Any study of the prevention literature will reveal that this is not the case. It is necessary, therefore, to define more precisely what primary prevention means as it is used in this book. Although specific primary-preventive techniques in schools can be identified as far back as 1941 (Bullis, 1941), it was not until 1964, so far as we can determine, that specific attempts were made to define *primary prevention* as it relates to behavior and to establish its place in a hierarchy of human services (Caplan, 1964). In spite of Caplan's efforts there continues to be considerable misunderstanding and disagreement about what primary prevention is.

For present purposes, a definition proposed by Shaw and Goodyear (1984) will be used. The first three statements are taken from Cowen (1982).

1. It must be group- or mass-, rather than individually-oriented (even though some of its activities may involve individual contacts).
2. It must have a before-the-fact quality, i.e., be targeted to groups not yet experiencing significant maladjustment (even though they may, because of their life situations or recent experiences, be at risk for such outcomes).
3. It must be intentional, i.e., rest on a solid, knowledge-base suggesting that the program holds potential for either improving psychological health or preventing maladaptation.
4. School learning problems and behavior problems that contribute to school learning problems are also appropriate targets for primary-preventive activities. (p. 444)

The direction implied by this definition differs somewhat from what appears to be the current practice of guidance specialists. First, the definition suggests that children who should receive guidance services include those who do *not* currently manifest problems. It appears that guidance specialists are presently most often involved after a problem has been identified in a specific individual. A second difference resides in the emphasis on the application of primary-preventive techniques to entire groups. This is meant to include not only the now-accepted small group approach, but also to include larger groups of children; in terms of intended outcomes the application of primary-preventive techniques includes whole school populations.

There are two basic assumptions with respect to applications of primary-preventive techniques in schools. The first is that all children can benefit from certain kinds of professional guidance services. The second is that all children are entitled to such services. These assumptions are the historic philosophical undergirding for guidance services but they do not appear to be met by the present emphasis on problem children and special education. The addition of primary-preventive components to guidance efforts will result in better balanced programs that have the potential to provide practical and effective ways to reach all children.

The addition of the fourth criterion to Cowen's definition of primary prevention seems quite necessary in the school setting. In spite of almost 50 years of emphasis on the role of mental health in schools, teachers, administrators, parents, and school boards, although willing to give lip service, seem to remain unconvinced. As a matter of fact, a review of specific books on the general topic of mental health in schools indicates that they reached a peak of popularity in the 50s and have declined precipitously in number until the present time.

There can certainly be little dispute that there is an interactive effect between mental health and school achievement variables. Neither is there any attempt to deny the importance of mental health in children. On the other hand, the guidance efforts that schools are most likely to support are those aimed at the accomplishment of fundamental educational goals held by those groups which basically determine school practices. Without the support of people in these groups guidance workers can hope to accomplish little. If guidance specialists wish to be included as central to the educational mission of the schools, rather than being considered as ancillary to that mission, then guidance goals must more closely approximate the more broadly accepted goals of education.

THE RELATIONSHIP OF PRIMARY PREVENTION TO OTHER ASPECTS OF THE GUIDANCE PROGRAM

It is possible to see the relationship of primary prevention to other aspects of the guidance program through use of a simple model (see figure 1-1). The model represents the full spectrum of basic components of guidance services. It is assumed that guidance services may provide services which are basically of three types. These are: (a) primary prevention, (b) the remediation of normal developmental problems encountered by many children, and (c) the provision of more intensive diagnostic and therapeutic services for a relatively small fraction of children with more serious problems.

Each of these three approaches represents a broad, general goal of guidance. Caplan (1964) refers to these approaches as primary, secondary, and tertiary prevention. While this labeling provides a certain symmetry that may be appealing, it is fundamentally misleading and confusing. Secondary and tertiary "prevention" are not preventive, but remedial. In schools, the third goal is currently dealt with mainly under the rubric of PL 94-142 responsibilities and activities. School psychologists and some school social workers tend to be more heavily involved, although school counselors are increasingly called upon to provide services relevant to this general goal. The second goal has been largely the focus of school counselors although school psychologists and school social workers are at times involved in these kinds of activities. All three of these professional groups, however, have a role to play with respect to the first goal, namely that of primary prevention.

There are two basic ways of providing services to accomplish the goals of these three general approaches. The first of these is the more traditional way, the provision of services directly to children. The second is a less common but by no means rare approach, that of providing services to those who stand in relationships of basic responsibility to children. The two groups that have received the most attention are parents and teachers. School administrators should probably be added as a third important group, and a few bold professionals have moved in this direction (Watson, 1969).

It should be noted that the difference between direct and indirect services is deeper than the issue of how the services are provided. There is also a basic conceptual and philosophical difference between services provided directly to a child who has a problem and, as in primary prevention, those provided to children who have not yet been identified as having problems. In the former case, there is an assumption, usually unrecognized, that it is the child who must change, that it is the child who must adapt to the existing situation, and that the situation itself either is unchangeable or does not need to change.

This phenomenon has been discussed by others including Hersch (1972), Rappaport, Davidson, Wilson and Mitchell (1975), and Ryan (1971). These authors suggest that the provision of remedial services to children may result from blaming the victim rather than the cause. Such traditional methods of providing services directly to those assumed to be in need of them tend to overlook the possibly more effective and realistic approach of improving the environment in which children live and learn. The approach of providing services to adults (indirect services) makes the assumption that the environments in which children learn are important in determining the extent to which they develop and learn without unnecessary problems.

The indirect approach also helps to answer the question of how a small number of guidance specialists can reach a large number of children in an

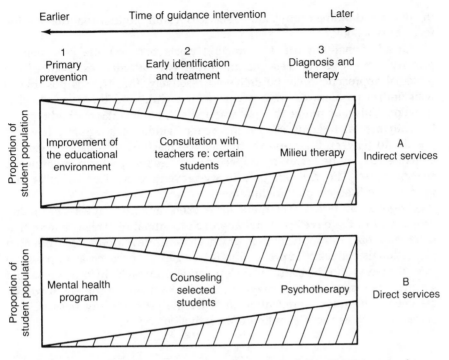

Figure 1-1 *A general model for guidance services.* The horizontal dimension represents the time at which guidance intervention takes place. The two different rectangles represent two basic techniques for achieving objectives—directly through working with students or indirectly through working with significant adults in the learning environment. The proportion of the population that can be reached through a given technique initiated at a given time is indicated by the white areas. Crosshatched areas represent the proportion of the population *not* reached by a given program.

effective manner. This approach is especially relevant to primary prevention since teaching parents and teachers to be more effective should help them to work preventively over the span of their careers as parents and teachers. Figure 1-1 indicates that primary prevention is aimed at large numbers of children while the remedial and therapeutic approaches focus on smaller proportions of the population: Primary prevention is for all, while remediation and therapy are for those who need it.

The combination of three basic goals and two different service modes outlined in figure 1-1 results in six identifiable program types. Within the direct services mode, primary prevention will tend to focus on the provision of services that can roughly be considered mental health–oriented; early identification and treatment will focus on counseling with identified students; the therapeutic mode will focus on the more intensive diagnosis and treatment of more seriously disabled students. Within the indirect services mode, primary prevention will focus on improving the educational environment; the remedial approach will focus on consultation with teachers about identified students; the therapeutic approach will focus on change through the use of therapeutic environments. It is the primary prevention goal and the direct and indirect provision of services leading to this goal that are the focus of this book.

An additional important distinction exists between the provision of primary-preventive services and the other two alternatives. Both of the remedial approaches may be delivered reactively, that is, it is possible to wait until a problem or crisis occurs with a child and then react to that situation. This may not be the best way to do it, but it is the method typified by both mental hygiene clinics and school guidance programs. It is *not* possible to deliver primary-preventive services reactively. Primary-preventive activities require the planning of specific activities for specific populations at specific times. The delivery of primary-preventive services is active and preplanning is an absolute requirement.

It should be noted that there have been, and continue to be, many proponents of the developmental approach to guidance. This is a term that has been more philosophical than practical. Some developmentally oriented professionals believe that prevention is a negative approach as opposed to the (allegedly) more positive developmental approach. In order to avoid getting sidetracked on what may be basically a semantic problem, it will be assumed that primary prevention includes the promotion of positive outcomes, as well as the prevention of negative outcomes.

THE CONCEPT OF A BALANCED GUIDANCE PROGRAM

It appears that in practice most schools do not employ primary-preventive strategies to any substantial extent. It is impossible to speak definitively on this issue since research that would provide a basis for this assertion has either not been done or has not been reported, although studies of how guidance personnel use their professional time reveal little in the way of primary-preventive activities. If the assertion is true, then it appears that current professional efforts focus primarily on remediation and therapy and this emphasis has certainly increased since the advent of PL 94-142. These speculations suggest that school guidance programs tend to be out of balance, that they tend to focus on the provision of services to smaller numbers of students already identified as having problems.

Most guidance programs are probably out of balance in another sense as well. It has been asserted for many years that students should be the direct recipients of services from guidance specialists and it appears that, in the main, this has been the favored mode of service delivery. The large number of articles appearing in professional journals within the last 10 years that recommend the use of indirect services suggests that this situation may be changing and that guidance specialists are beginning to view indirect services as a means of reaching larger numbers of students in an effective way.

What is being suggested is that guidance programs should be balanced in terms of both the general thrust of services (i.e., primary prevention, remediation, and therapy) and in terms of the mode of service delivery (direct and indirect services). Balanced programs would reach larger numbers of students in more effective kinds of ways, they would include significant adults as well as children, they would provide higher visibility to guidance specialists, and they would provide services more directly in line with the expectations of our various publics and thus generate greater support.

PRIMARY PREVENTION IN SCHOOLS: A PERSPECTIVE

Many school personnel may not be familiar with the term *primary prevention*. The term itself is not new. It has a long history in the area of public health. Everyone will recognize the application of Salk vaccine in the virtual eradication of polio in the United States and the work of the World Health Organization in the total eradication of small pox as examples of primary prevention. As a matter of fact, it does not seem inappropriate to assert that the greatest advances in the field of human health have come about more as a result of primary-preventive efforts than as a result of the more journalistically obvious medical approaches such as heart transplants.

There is a faint trail of primary-preventive effort in education going at least as far back as 1941. In that year, Bullis published an article in which he described a human relations class in which the attempt was to assist children to interact more effectively with others. These children were not defined as problem children and this approach seems to have met the criteria established for primary prevention earlier in this chapter. In 1955, Ralph Ojemann and his colleagues (Ojemann, Levitt, Lyle, & Whiteside) published the results of an approach which they labeled "causal understanding." It is clear from the work described in this article that Ojemann had begun his thought and work on this approach at a time much earlier than the 1955 publication date. Ojemann's basic tactic was to teach teachers how to teach children to understand that behavior has causes and is not random. Ojemann's findings suggest that improved interpersonal relationships resulted from this approach. His work differed from that of Bullis in several ways. First, he specifically identified his approach as preventive. Second, he developed specific curricula for the entire range of elementary grades, and third, his work was continued over a period of years rather than being a single experiment. It should also be noted that Ojemann (1971) later expanded his approach from its direct services thrust to include changing teacher behavior, an indirect services mode. This pioneering work in primary prevention in schools deserves a great deal more attention than it appears to have received.

Other early contributions to the primary-preventive approach in schools were made by Barbara Biber and her associates at Bank Street School. They reported (Biber, Gilkeson, & Winsor, undated) on methods intended to achieve improved mental health in children by including mental health concepts in the total school curriculum. Later, Biber (1961) reported on attempts to implement these methods. These efforts focused specifically on the development of ego strength in children.

Although the work of Gerald Caplan is not directly related to schools, he does appear to be the individual who drew the greatest attention to the idea of primary prevention in the area of mental health. His *Principles of Preventive Psychiatry* (1964) focused the attention of mental health workers on the specific topic of primary prevention, which had previously drawn little interest. Since 1964 primary prevention has become an important focus of professional writing in psychiatry and, even more so, in community psychology.

Perhaps the major professional group to respond to the preventive challenge has been community psychology. Nonexistent prior to 1965 when, according to Adelson and Kallis (1970), it came into being at a meeting in Swampscott, Massachusetts, community psychology quickly adopted primary prevention as its own. The interests of this group have not remained confined to the community at large, but have also broadened to include the school. By and large, however, community psychologists have restricted their efforts, even in the schools, to the prevention of mental health problems. The specific prevention of school learning problems has been largely ignored by this group.

Developments in primary-preventive approaches applicable in schools by guidance experts have largely ignored the use of the term *primary prevention*. While the concept has apparently not had widespread use among guidance specialists, the techniques of primary prevention applicable to schools have developed rapidly since the late 60s. It is difficult to pinpoint specific individuals or groups responsible for the burgeoning of primary-preventive activities in schools. Attempts by Ryans (1960) to determine the characteristics of good teaching and good teachers, although largely unsuccessful, began to draw attention to learning environments as an area in need of further exploration. The more scientific attempts of Flanders (1965) to assess learning environments also drew attention to the idea that problems that children had in learning might be avoidable. His system, of demonstrated utility, has not been widely adopted, possibly due to its complexity. The early work of Carkhuff in attempting to expand and quantify Rogerian principles (Carkhuff & Berenson, 1967) eventually led to the development of a means to both teach and assess what has come to be known as "communication skills," a group of behaviors important not only in counseling but also in teaching (Aspy, Roebuck, & Aspy, 1984). These developments provided a basis for an improved technology that others could use to improve learning environments, a primary-preventive activity.

In the early 70s, the idea of psychological education or affective education, originated in part by Ojemann at an earlier date, received a new impetus beginning with the work of Mosher and Sprinthall (1970). Since that time, large numbers of different tactics leading to the general goal of personal and social growth for children have been developed. It is these types of activities for implementation directly with children and the indirect types of activities focusing on the learning environment that will be discussed in subsequent chapters.

A Broadening of Primary-Preventive Goals in Schools

The primary-preventive approach in schools has tended to retain an emphasis on mental health (or personal and social development) although increasing attention is being given to the prevention of school-oriented problems. Generally speaking, it seems fair to state that direct approaches (e.g., affective education, cognitive interpersonal problem solving skills, magic circles, etc.) tend to retain a focus on mental health concerns. Indirect approaches focusing on environments, (e.g., communication skills for teachers and parents, behavior management skills for teachers and parents, interpersonal process recall techniques, etc.) tend to target school learning as the major concern. This difference is reflected in figure 1-1.

Both direct and indirect approaches are important and necessary in the provision of primary-preventive services. The indirect approach does appear to have advantages which makes its greater use desirable. Its emphasis on school learning seems more likely to obtain the support of significant education role groups such as teachers, parents, school boards and the general public, than the mental health emphasis. Further, the investment of time with teachers who may spend a professional lifetime in a classroom and with parents who are likely to have more than a single child helps to spread the effect of the guidance specialist's efforts. An emphasis of this sort could be helpful in moving guidance specialists from the periphery of education, where they seem often to be, into the mainstream.

Emphasizing delivery of services to adults, as suggested above, through the indirect service mode should be pointed up as a substantial change in direction for guidance specialists. This shift appears to have come about as a result of increasing recognition of the importance of environment, both at school and at home, in determining how well a child learns, with a concomitant recognition that the provision of remedial services to children with problems may be neither effective nor philosophically justifiable. This approach, sometimes called an ecological approach (Carroll, Bell, Brecher, & Minor, 1971; Lapides, 1977), has served to emphasize teaching as an important skill in the repertoire of guidance specialists.

The idea that school guidance personnel should be concerned about learning outcomes can be traced, in part, to Wrenn (1962) who, in his influential book *The Counselor in a Changing World,* suggested that guidance goals be broadened to include cognitive outcomes. This position was reiterated by Lipsman (1969) who suggested that cognitive goals should be a major focus of school counselor efforts. Others who have made similar suggestions include Grunwald (1971), Hayes and Clair (1978) and Pielstick (1963). Primary prevention in schools must be considered to include both cognitive and affective emphases.

Still more recently, another concept, not classifiable either as affective or cognitive, has made its appearance. This is the concept of competence. It stems mainly from the research of Burton White (1975) on the development of competence in very young children. White's work, which began as a series of naturalistic research studies and continued over a period of years, has

tremendous implications for both the manner and the time at which guidance interventions can most effectively be made. White asserts, based on his research, that the first three years of life are of crucial importance in determining the extent to which a child will perform in a competent manner at school age and, even more narrowly, that the period between approximately 8 and 24 months is the time at which competence either develops or fails to develop. His research suggests the conditions under which children develop competence and therefore has a direct bearing on the delivery of primary-preventive services to the parents of very young children.

THE PRESENT STATUS OF PRIMARY PREVENTION IN SCHOOLS

A number of laudatory articles on the role of primary prevention have been written for school psychologists (Evans, 1971; Gray, 1960; Kennedy, 1971; Trachtman, 1961; Wonderly, 1979), school social workers (Rowen, 1970), and school counselors (Christensen, 1969; Gerler, 1976; Goodyear, 1976; Menacker, 1976; Shaw, 1986; White & Mitchell, 1976), but there is real question about the extent to which these clarion calls to the troops have had an impact on actual practice. A study of the journal literature suggests that school psychologists, more than the other two professional groups, have paid attention to the broad issue of primary prevention. On the other hand, the same study of the literature suggests that it is the school counselors who have written the most about the techniques of primary prevention, usually without labeling them as primary prevention. There is no shortage of articles on primary prevention or on the techniques of primary prevention as they relate to schools.

Despite a surfeit of articles in the area of primary prevention, there appears to be considerable doubt of the extent to which such programs and procedures are currently being implemented in schools. Even the numerous studies available as to how guidance specialists use their professional time are of little help in answering this question due to the fact that most studies are not structured in such a way that distinctions among primary, secondary, and tertiary prevention are possible. There is, of course, little doubt that primary-preventive activities are occurring in some settings. The state of Oregon, for example, has defined, certified, and placed in the schools a new professional specialist called the child development specialist. The basic responsibilities of this specialist are defined, by statute, as primary-preventive ones. On the other hand, impressions gained from studies, albeit inadequate, of how guidance specialists use their professional time, as well as impressions gained from attendance at professional meetings, discussions with colleagues in the schools, and other sources providing a basis for informed opinion suggest that the term *primary prevention* is essentially unknown at the school level and that primary-preventive activities do not have a high priority with most school guidance personnel. The reasons for this demand examination.

Barriers to Primary Prevention in Schools

While there have been many articles extolling the virtues of primary prevention, there have also been a substantial number that have raised serious questions about this approach. A sampling of such writing includes Adler (1978), Broskowski and Baker (1974), Clarizio (1979), Garmezy (1971), and Hagin (1980). Although a number of specifics in each of these articles are idiosyncratic, there are also certain commonalities.

Perhaps one of the most fundamental problems resides in the question of what primary prevention actually is. A reading of articles dealing with primary prevention (whether they are basically philosophical or research-oriented) shows clearly that what one author and what another author call primary prevention are not equivalent. The great variation in definition of *primary prevention* prompted Cowen (1982) to say, "An *author's* decision to call something primary prevention may be the single most important determinant of whether it is so classified and cited" (p. 134). Some define it very narrowly so that primary-preventive services are intended only for groups that are neither experiencing problems at a given time nor are expected to have such problems; the "at-risk" populations are not included as part of the definition. Others include the at-risk groups in their definition of populations that may legitimately be served by primary prevention. A significant number of others define *primary prevention* in the way that we defined remediation and in the way that Caplan (1964) has defined secondary prevention, that is, provision of service in the early stages of development to individuals who have been detected to have problems. Perhaps the best (or worst) example of this misclassification, certainly the most "official" mistake of its kind, occurred in California in 1982 when the state legislature, with the alleged intent of providing primary-preventive services, actually described services which appropriately belong in the remedial category. Fortunately, it appears that consensus may be developing on what primary prevention is and that consensus appears to favor more conservative definitions such as the one proposed by Cowen (1982) and by Shaw and Goodyear (1984), which we have chosen to use.

A second deterrent to the adoption of primary prevention programs is the apparent preoccupation of all groups of guidance specialists with remedial populations and the parallel devotion of these groups to one-on-one counseling or treatment. Over the last 30 years, such individual treatment has assumed the level of a sacred rite, and most guidance professionals consider it the sine qua non of professionalism. Even group counseling, which has been waiting in the wings for the last 30 years, has had a difficult time gaining the center of the stage due to the preference for individual counseling. This emphasis has grown, particularly in school counseling, as the trend to emphasize "counseling," a specific function, has diminished the earlier emphasis on "guidance," which is not a specific professional activity, but rather a generic term implying services to all children. The overemphasis on individual counseling has helped to remove guidance specialists from the mainstream of education and placed them in the backwaters. Without a return to an emphasis on services with the potential for reaching all children, the guidance professions are likely to remain in the backwater, where they may gradually slip under the surface and disappear.[1]

A third hindrance is the preoccupation of each of the three major groups of guidance professionals with certain traditional tasks. For example, study after study (so many that they will not be cited) has indicated that school counselors spend substantial amounts of their time doing what, in some places, is called programming and in others scheduling, but consists mainly in getting secondary school students into classes. Many, and possibly most, counselors consider this to be a form of "educational guidance" and justify it on that basis. Regardless of whether or not it is justifiable, it consumes about half of the time of school counselors in most situations. School psychologists have a similar historic preoccupation, as everyone will know, with testing and assessment. Since the passage of PL 94-142, school psychologists have undoubtedly increased the amount of time spent in assessment, as demands for the identification, diagnosis and placement of children entitled to the "free and appropriate public education" specified by federal

---

1. The Bureau of School Climate of the California State Department of Education reported in fall, 1982 that in the preceding two years one-third of all school counseling positions in the state had disappeared.

law have increased. School social workers, like their counseling and psychology compatriots, also have a professional preoccupation. This is with the home visit. Indeed, school social workers have at times asserted that the home is turf which belongs to them, and others are forewarned to keep out. The home visit often involves the completion of an interview schedule and is intended, in the main, to result in the collection of diagnostic information. The value of these various activities is not at issue here. Rather, the point is that until each of these professions is willing or able to give up some of the traditional roles that they have assumed, it is unlikely that primary prevention will gain a significant foothold in the schools.

Philosophical Considerations

There are also philosophical issues in relation to primary prevention that must be resolved. There are two in particular that should be discussed. The first relates to the unresolved issue of whom guidance services are for. As pointed out previously, guidance specialists have typically avowed, but not practiced, the philosophy that guidance services are for all children. The fact is that there is only a limited amount of guidance service available. If remedial services are diminished in order to provide primary-preventive services there is the concern that those who need such remedial services may not receive them, at least not to the same extent. To offset this councern, two points can be made. The first is that the implementation of primary-preventive functions should, over time, decrease the subsequent need for remedial ones. The second is that with the advent of PL 94-142 many additional resources that did not previously exist have become available for assisting children with special problems.

Since the decision as to how a finite quantity of guidance services should be divided between prevention and remediation is a value question, there are no right or wrong answers. But putting the decision into this format demands that *however* limited resources are used, they must be used effectively. Further, guidance services rendered should be examined in the light of whether they are both professional (i.e., require 2 to 4 years of specialized graduate training) and unique (i.e., are a speciality of a given profession which could not be performed by another type of educator). This holds particularly true for activities that consume the greatest amount of time, and some of these activities might not withstand this type of scrutiny.

The second philosophical issue is equally complex. The question has been raised as to whether the provision of primary-preventive guidance services represents a violation of civil liberties (Clarizio, 1979). Specifically, the question is whether or not the provision of certain kinds of primary-preventive interventions may constitute an invasion of privacy. For example, is the provision of psychological or affective education the business of public schools? If it is, and if some aspects of providing this affective educational process are interpreted by some to include revelations about personal feelings or family life in a group situation, can participation in such process be required of all students at some given grade level? It is quite likely that a majority of any professional group would agree that *requiring* discussion of personal or family issues is inappropriate, even if it were agreed that personal and social development is an appropriate part of the school's function. It seems clear that such goals would need to be sought through means other than techniques of group counseling and other methods often employed to promote personal or social growth.

In spite of many years of exposure to the importance of mental health, or affective growth, neither the public at large nor the educational establishment appears fully to have accepted these goals as *prime* responsibilities of the school nor do they seem ready to do so. If one examines situations in which mental health, affective education, personal growth or other noncognitive goals are a matter of concern, it will frequently be found that such programs operate within the school system on the basis of soft money. The history of such programs appears to be that when special funding disappears, so does the program. The implication is that those who view affective development as important are peripheral to the operation of the school enterprise—which, indeed, appears to describe the current status of school counselors, school psychologists, and school social workers. Professionals in those groups who want to be viewed as central to the functioning of schools are likely to have to alter their goals (and functioning) to parallel those of the public and of the broader educational establishment.

What are the implications of this situation? Does this mean that those who have a legitimate expertise and concern about personal development and who recognize that it is related to cognitive growth must resign themselves to being on the periphery? Our answer is a firm no. The implication is rather that the responsibility for demonstrating how affective growth and cognitive growth are related falls on guidance professionals. The concept of mental health cannot stand alone in the school setting. It must be emphasized that cognitive development is improved when mental health variables are taken into account. As an important adjunct to this, it is also possible to demonstrate that when the conditions promoting the affective development of children are maximal, teaching becomes easier for teachers (Aspy & Roebuck, 1977).

Some Practical Considerations

A concern of many guidance specialists, when confronted with the desirability of implementing some primary-preventive activities, is that they do not have the skills required to carry out such functions. Assuming that a given professional has skills in group and individual counseling and consulting, it is reasonable to assume that the basic skills necessary for the provision of primary-preventive services are present. To leave it at that, however, would be to minimize the problem. There are at least three areas that deserve further consideration. First, the manner in which skills are used in primary prevention will be different. Individual counseling will be minimal; the use of teaching skills is likely to be maximal. At the same time, it should be emphasized that the basic interpersonal skills that make for success in counseling also appear to be those that make for success in teaching (Flanders, 1965; Aspy & Roebuck, 1977).

A second area of difference between primary prevention and other program emphases lies in the requirement for organizing activities. It has been mentioned that remedial programs can be run on a reactive basis, that is, one waits for the fire and then puts it out. Primary-preventive programs cannot be run adequately in this fashion. The fact that groups of children, teachers, parents, or others will be the typical units dealt with, the before-the-fact quality of primary prevention, and its ongoing nature all demand serious and detailed planning. Experience suggests that this is not an activity either valued by or engaged in by a majority of guidance professionals. In primary-preventive programs, it is mandatory. The shift from a reactive to an active mode may be a difficult one to make.

Another legitimate concern of those considering the initiation of primary prevention activities relates to the availability of useful material. Individual counseling in particular and group counseling in general do not require a great deal in the nature of specific materials or prespecified content. It is clear that much of what goes on in primary prevention does require these things. The fact is, that there is a great deal in the way of professionally prepared material available to guidance specialists interested in primary-preventive activities. This is made as an assertion at this point; the justification for the assertion will become evident as materials are referred to in later chapters.

The Problem of Change

In contrast to the issues presented above, the issue of change is not specific to primary prevention. It has been well documented (Carlson, 1965; Miles, 1964) that bringing about planned and lasting change in educational systems is a difficult undertaking. It should be emphasized that the difficulty of initiating change and of ensuring its longevity is not unique to education but affects almost any large bureaucratic structure. It should also be emphasized that failure to change does not necessarily imply intransigence or incompetence on the part of those who resist change. Resistance to change, except under pressure, seems to be an almost normal human response.

Change in the educational system seems to come about mainly under one of two conditions. The first is social demand that results in change being legislated. The second is funds for change becoming available. These two conditions are not unrelated. The most salient recent example of both is the passage of PL 94-142, which mandated a free and appropriate public education for all children. Whether the educational system should lead in or follow social change is a long-standing philosophical issue in education. History suggests that major educational changes have come about as the result of social change, rather than education leading the way to social change. If change is to be introduced successfully, special steps will need to be taken to ensure its acceptance. This topic will be discussed more fully in chapter 9.

WHY PRIMARY PREVENTION IS IMPORTANT

Considering the current limited status of primary prevention in schools, the barriers to its use, and the difficulties of change in general, what are the reasons for attempting to introduce primary-preventive approaches in schools? What advantages would accrue to students and to guidance specialists if primary-preventive activities were added to existing programs? Perhaps the most fundamental is that primary-preventive approaches are intended to reach *all* students and, in addition, to provide the means through which services can be provided effectively to all students. Guidance began as a service intended for all students and it is only in recent years that the focus has changed from all to only a fraction of the students in school. It is suggested that a guidance program should be a *balanced* program, designed to provide a range of effective services, including services to the typical as well as to the atypical student.

In providing guidance services designed to reach all students, the guidance specialist comes more into line with the basic school philosophy that all children should be served. Further, when the emphasis is on services aiming at cognitive development, the guidance specialist, in the eyes of other educators, moves guidance from the periphery of education into the center, overcoming one of the most serious obstacles to the acceptance of guidance specialists as genuine members of the educational team. Such support from teachers, administrators, and parents is vital to the effectiveness, and perhaps even to the continued existence, of the guidance specialities. We would recognize a sign of such acceptance if budget-cutting groups were to start with areas of education other than guidance.

Using an economic model, Harper and Balch (1975) argue that primary prevention will return a great deal for each guidance dollar invested. This is true for a variety of reasons. First, the typical unit dealt with in primary prevention is the group rather than the individual; groups of teachers, groups of parents, or groups of children up to and including classroom-sized groups. Further, when services are provided to teachers or to parents, these services are capable of being generalized beyond the present class or, in the case of parents, beyond a single child. Remedial services, on the other hand, generally apply to specific children with specific problems which afford little opportunity for teachers or parents to generalize beyond the specific case. A final economic consideration is that successful primary-preventive programs should diminish the need for high-cost remedial programs.

An important adjunct to this approach is the level of interest and participation of others in the guidance process. When a child has a problem and is referred to a guidance specialist for help by a teacher, it is generally assumed by that teacher that it is the responsibility of the guidance specialist to bring about change. Teachers usually assume, and indeed often insist, that they need play no part in the remedial process. They may not see that as their job. This places a difficult and often impossible burden on the guidance specialist who realizes that teachers and parents must often cooperate in attempts to bring about change in the behaviors of children. On the other hand, teachers are usually interested in getting practical help in improving their teaching just as parents are interested in getting practical help in raising and managing their children. The motivation of teachers with respect to participating in a remedial process may be low while the motivation of teachers and parents for participating in preventively oriented functions is likely to be considerably higher.

An additional benefit of primary-preventive approaches is heightened visibility. Guidance specialists are often relatively invisible in terms of what they do. Counselors may stick to their offices, psychologists to their testing rooms, and school social workers to functions outside the school itself. Indeed, teachers often complain about such isolation. Primary-preventive services are, almost by definition, services provided in highly public and visible settings. Assuming that such services are viewed as effective, heightened visibility will improve the image of guidance specialists.

CONDITIONS NECESSARY FOR PRIMARY PREVENTION IN SCHOOLS

It is possible to specify some of the broad conditions necessary to the successful implementation of primary-preventive guidance services in schools. The first is that there needs to be a commitment on the part of both guidance staff and administration to the delivery of effective guidance services to all children. Second, there must be a willingness to forego some traditional activities which do not achieve any particular purpose or which can be achieved equally well through other means. Third, there must be a willingness to invest time in planning. Fourth, there must be personnel belonging to the school who have the necessary skills to provide primary-preventive services. A serious problem in many places is the fact that primary-preventive services are delivered either on the basis of special project monies or by outside agencies, such as the community mental health service. Unless personnel who deliver guidance services are members of the permanent staff, both the personnel and the services they provide are likely to be viewed as ancillary to the basic purposes of the schools by other members of the school staff. This perception may be fatal to the success of such services and will normally result in their early demise. Finally, the staff, in addition to basic skills, must have some specific knowledge of primary-preventive materials and techniques.

TYPES OF PRIMARY-PREVENTIVE TECHNIQUES

The most important purpose of this book is to provide information on primary prevention that will have utility in the school setting. What follows is a brief outline of major techniques with very brief descriptions of each. A chapter will be devoted to each of these topics.

1. Communication skills: This approach aims to improve the listening, and responding skills of individuals. It is likely to be used, in the main, in an indirect fashion with teachers, parents, or others with the purpose of improving their teaching or parenting effectiveness. It may be used directly with children for the purpose of improving their interpersonal skills.

2. Psychological education (a broad descriptive term covering, actually, a variety of approaches): Psychological education is normally used directly with populations of children, rather than with adults. Purposes and procedures may vary widely, and goals may range from improved understanding of self or improved understanding of others to greater cognitive knowledge of interpersonal principles.

3. Behavioral approaches: For the purposes of this volume it is necessary to adapt generally remedial behavioral approaches to meet preventive goals. The emphasis is on prevention of stress with special attention to training for assertiveness, social problem solving, cognitive restructuring, emotive imagery, meditation, and progressive muscle relaxation.

4. Career education: This is the modern version of one of the original bases of the guidance movement. Broader in scope than the original thrust of vocational guidance and aimed at children from elementary through high school, the concern of career education for all children and its emphasis on the promotion of skills qualify this strategy as belonging under the primary prevention umbrella.

5. Developing competence in children: The basic idea in this approach stems from the work of Burton White (1975) with infants and young children. The focus of most competence training is on populations who either have, or who it is anticipated will have, young children.

6. Approaches focusing on the nonhuman environment: This approach to primary prevention focuses on variables that may enhance or inhibit children's performance. These range from the relatively simple, such as lighting and wall color, to considerably more complex variables, such as class structure, class size, or classroom reward structures.

7. The use of assessment in primary prevention: The use of psychometrics in primary prevention is extremely limited. They are basically used for only two purposes. One is the identification of at-risk groups and individuals; the other use of psychometrics is for the analysis of learning environments.

There is a caveat, already noted by others (Kessler & Albee, 1975), which should be observed. It would easily be possible to construe *any* activity aimed at the improvement of humanity's condition as "primary prevention." In order to avoid a dispersion of functions so great that effectiveness is lost, guidance personnel need to ask themselves two questions. First, what are the appropriate goals of the school? This question can be answered in a wide variety of ways, but two purposes are likely to be generally agreed upon. One is that schools must foster cognitive development. The other is that schools must provide a situation or learning environment where cognitive development can take place optimally. There are, of course, a number of other possible answers, but it is likely that these two will find general agreement.

The second question to be asked is: What are the proper contributions of a guidance specialist (school counselor, school psychologist, or school social worker) to children in the school setting? Again, a wide variety of answers is possible but, in the main, there is likely to be agreement that helping to optimize children's learning and their personal/social development are appropriate goals. This approach will help guidance specialists to rule out a number of less appropriate activities and to rule in those which are appropriate. We have more than enough to do without taking on roles that others can perform more effectively. The balance of the material in this book will illustrate that even if guidance specialists were to provide *only* primary preventive services, a circumstance unlikely to occur, they would be able to spend all of their time doing so.

THE ORGANIZATION OF THIS BOOK

This chapter has been intended to provide the reader with a brief understanding of the background of primary prevention, a definition of what it is, and an understanding of how it fits into a balanced human services program. The next seven chapters deal with the specific techniques and approaches to the provision of primary prevention. Following discussion of these techniques is chapter 9, which provides information on how to initiate and implement programs of primary prevention. The feeling of the authors is that it is necessary to know something about primary prevention before discussion of how to implement primary-preventive programs can make sense. The final chapter pulls together all of the prior material and presents a prototypical K–12 primary-preventive program. The "menu" concept is used in this chapter so that the reader can select the techniques most appropriate to a particular situation from those which are available.

REFERENCES

Adelson, D., & Kallis, B. L. (Eds.). (1970). *Community psychology and mental health.* Scranton, PA: Chandler.

Adler, P. T. (1978). A prevention parable revisited. *American Journal of Orthopsychiatry, 48,* 394–395.

Aspy, D. N., & Roebuck, F. M. (1977). *Kids don't learn from people they don't like.* Amherst, MA: Human Resource Development Press.

Aspy, D. N., Roebuck, F. M., & Aspy, C. B. (1984). Tomorrow's resources are in today's classroom. *Personnel and Guidance Journal, 62,* 455–459.

Biber, B. (1961). Integration of mental health principles in the school setting. In G. Caplan (Ed.) *Prevention of Mental Disorders in Children.* pp. 323–352. New York: Basic Books.

Biber, B., Gilkeson, E., & Winsor, C. (undated). Teacher education at Bank Street College. In J. Samler (Ed.) *Basic approaches to mental health in the schools.* (pp. 48–58). Washington, DC: American Personnel and Guidance Association.

Broskowski, A., & Baker, F. (1974). Professional, organizational, and social barriers to primary prevention. *American Journal of Orthopsychiatry, 44,* 707–719.

Bullis, H. E. (1941). How the human relations class works. *Understanding the Child, 10,* 5–10.

Caplan, G. (1964). *Principles of preventive psychiatry.* New York: Basic Books.

Carkhuff, R. R., & Berenson, B. (1967). *Beyond counseling and therapy.* New York: Holt, Rinehart, & Winston.

Carlson, R. O. (1965). *Adoption of educational innovations.* Eugene, OR: The Center for the Advanced Study of Educational Administration, University of Oregon.

Carroll, J., Bell, A. A., Brecher, H., & Minor, M. (1971). Psychoeducational services for elementary schools: A preventive systems approach. *Journal of the National Medical Association, 63,* 450–454.

Christensen, O. C. (1969). Education: A model for counseling in the elementary school. *Elementary School Guidance and Counseling, 4,* 12–19.

Clarizio, H. G. (1979). Primary prevention of behavioral disorders in schools. *School Psychology Digest, 8,* 434–445.

Cowen, E. L. (1982). Primary prevention research: Barriers, needs, and opportunities. *Journal of Primary Prevention, 2,* 131–137.

Evans, D. R. (1971). New directions in school psychology. *Western Psychologist, 2,* 69–73.

Flanders, N. A. (1965). *Teacher influence, pupil attitudes, and achievement.* Washington, DC: U.S. Department of Health, Education, and Welfare, Office of Education.

Gerler, E. R., Jr. (1976). New directions for school counseling. *School Counselor, 23,* 247–251.

Garmezy, N. (1971). Vulnerability research and the issue of primary prevention. *American Journal of Orthopsychiatry, 41,* 101–116.

Goodyear, R. K. (1976). Counselors as community psychologists. *Personnel and Guidance Journal, 54,* 513–516.

Gray, S. W. (1960). Broader rules for school psychologists. *Educational Leadership, 27,* 226–229.

Grunwald, B. (1971). Strategies for behavior change in schools. *Counseling Psychologist, 3,* 55–57.

Hagin, R. A. (1980). *Prediction, prevention, presumption.* Address given at the convention of the American Psychological Association, Montreal, Quebec, Canada.

Harper, R., & Balch, P. (1975). Some economic arguments in favor of primary prevention. *Professional Psychology, 6,* 17–25.

Hayes, M. E., & Clair, T. N. (1978). School psychology—Why is the profession dying? *Psychology in the Schools, 15,* 518–521.

Hersch, C. (1972). Social history, mental health, and community control. *American Psychologist, 27,* 749–754.

Kennedy, D. A. (1971). A practical approach to school psychology. *Journal of School Psychology, 9,* 484–489.

Kessler, M., & Albee, G. W. (1975). Primary prevention. *Annual Review of Psychology,* *26,* 557–591.

Lapides, J. (1977). The school psychologist and early education: An ecological view. *Journal of School Psychology, 15,* 184–189.

Lipsman, C. (1969). Revolution and prophecy: Community involvement for counselors. *Personnel and Guidance Journal, 48,* 97–100.

Menacker, J. (1976). Toward a theory of activist guidance. *Personnel and Guidance Journal, 54,* 318–322.

Miles, M. E. (1964). *Innovation in Education.* New York: Bureau of Publication, Teachers College, Columbia University.

Mosher, R. L., & Sprinthall, N. A. (1970). Psychological education in secondary schools: A program to promote individual and human development. *American Psychologist, 25,* 911–924.

Ojemann, R. H. (1971). Humanizing the school. *The N. E. Principal,* vol. 50.

Ojemann, R. H., Levitt, E. E., Lyle, W. H., & Whiteside, M. F. (1955). Effects of a "causal" teacher training program and certain curriculm changes on grade school children. *Journal of Experimental Education, 24,* 95–114.

Pielstick, N. L. (1963). School psychology, a focus on learning. *Journal of School Psychology, 1,* 14–19.

Rappaport, J., Davidson, W. S., Wilson, M. N., & Mitchell, A. (1975). Alternatives to blaming the victim or the environment: Our places to stand have not moved the earth. *American Psychologist, 30,* 525–528.

Rowen, R. B. (1970). Model for service delivery in school social work. *Journal of the International Association of Pupil Personnel Workers, 14,* 173, 180.

Ryan, W. (1971). *Blaming the victim.* New York: Random House.

Ryans, D. G. (1960). *Characteristics of teachers, their description, comparison, and appraisal: A research study.* Washington, DC: American Council on Education.

Shaw, M. C. (1986). The prevention of learning and interpersonal problems. *Journal of Counseling and Development, 64,* 624–627.

Shaw, M. C., & Goodyear, R. K. (1984). Introduction to the special issues on primary prevention. *Personnel and Guidance Journal, 62,* 444–445.

Trachtman, G. M. (1961). New directions for school psychologists. *Journal of Exceptional Children, 28,* 159–162.

Watson, D. H. (1969). Group work with principals: Implications for elementary counselors. *Elementary School Guidance and Counseling, 3,* 234–242.

White, B. L. (1975). *The first three years of life.* Englewood Cliffs, New Jersey: Prentice–Hall.

White, R. G., & Mitchell, K. R. (1976). The role of the school counselor in the prevention and management of psychoeducational problems in the school community. *Australian Journal of Education, 20,* 306–315.

Wonderly, D. M. (1979). Primary prevention in school psychology: Past, present, and proposed future. *Child Study Journal, 9,* 163–179.

Wrenn, C. G. (1962). *The counselor in a changing world.* Washington, DC: American Personnel and Guidance Association.

2

COMMUNICATION SKILLS TRAINING

ROLE IN PRIMARY PREVENTION

In chapter 1, the communication skills approach was defined as one in which individuals are taught to improve their listening and responding skills. As such, communication skills training programs provide a vehicle for large scale dissemination of psychological skills because the requisite skills are portable, efficient, and replicable. Earlier proponents of prevention suggested that giving the principles and skills of psychology away would be a means of enhancing the effectiveness of helpers and the masses (Hobbs, 1964; Miller, 1969). Converting psychological principles to teachable communication skills that can be disseminated by systematic methods and programs has become a popular paradigm in such fields as community mental health, counselor education, and counseling and clinical psychology.

Communication skills training programs share common assumptions that help to identify them also as primary prevention programs in terms of the criteria cited in chapter 1. First, they all emphasize the importance of the facilitative conditions of empathy, genuineness, and regard (Levant, 1983). Second, they all are founded on an assumption that acquisition of new or improved communication skills will have a positive impact on the social systems in which the recipients are embedded (Levant, 1983). Third, program developers know what communication competencies people need in order to master life's challenges (Egan & Cowan, 1979). These assumptions have been translated into similar goals and objectives across various independently developed communication skills programs.

According to Levant (1983), communication skills training can be focused toward three different objectives: it can be training *for* treatment, training, *as* treatment, or training for enhancement. We view the communication skills programs from the viewpoint of their potential for achieving primary prevention goals, that is, as training for enhancement. Accordingly, we view communication skills training programs as having potential for indirect enhancement through training teachers, parents, or other adults in order to improve their communications with and influence on students and for direct enhancement through assisting individual students to improve their interpersonal communications.

BACKGROUND AND CURRENT STATUS

The common importance of empathy, genuineness, and regard across communication skills training programs lends credence to a conclusion that these programs evolved from the client-centered psychology movement thought to have started with the early work of Carl Rogers (1951, 1957). In the intervening years, client-centered counseling and therapy grew in popularity while the importance of prevention in mental health and of making operational the concepts of empathy, genuineness, and regard gradually evolved too. Realizing that the clientele was outstripping the number of available counselors and therapists (Levant, 1983) and that prevention might be more promising than remediation, Truax & Carkhuff (1967), Carkhuff (1969a, 1969b), Gordon (1970), and Ivey (1971), among others, noted the need for action and published early efforts to translate the facilitative conditions into skills that could be taught systematically.

Since the early 1970s, a number of communication skills training programs have been published, each focusing on a set of skills for an audience that the authors thought would be receptive. Some, such as Ivey (1971), were quite general in the audience they addressed, while others, such as Gordon (1970), were more specific. Nevertheless, all of these programs have three basic ingredients: identification of specific skills or competencies, systematic methods for teaching the skills, and programs for skill dissemination (Larson, 1983).

Several prominent examples of the communication skills approach are cited in this chapter because they have withstood the test of time, and they clearly have something to offer relative to primary prevention. Others for which there was not enough room or about which we were less certain will be cited as well. What seems to be common across all of these materials is that most programs depend on specially prepared trainers, and most are more advanced as a popular training vehicle than as an empirically evaluated body of knowledge. One might conclude that the generation of psychologists who developed these programs busied themselves with translating theory into operations, and the next generation will need better to assess the effects.

PROGRAMS HAVING POTENTIAL FOR INDIRECT ENHANCEMENT THROUGH TRAINING SIGNIFICANT ADULTS

Human Resource Development (Criterion-Referenced Instruction–Based Approach)

■ *Goals.* Dissatisfied with existing theories and training programs (Carkhuff & Berenson, 1967; Truax & Carkhuff, 1967), R. R. Carkhuff gradually developed an eclectic counseling model and a corresponding technology for teaching communication skills (cf. Carkhuff, 1969a, 1969b, 1971; Carkhuff & Anthony, 1979). Known as the Human Resource Development (HRD) model, core conditions of empathy, unconditional positive regard, congruence, concreteness, confrontation, initiative, problem solving, and program development were gradually conceptualized and systematically presented to trainees in a three-step program: self-exploration, understanding, and action. Much of the work on HRD has evolved from the Carkhuff Institute of Human Technology in Amherst, Massachusetts.

Since 1974, the general conceptual form of the HRD program has been redesigned and incorporated into a criterion-referenced instruction–based approach (CRI) (Cash, 1983). Consequently, behaviorally designed skills were added to the HRD model, and the three-stage program became one of four stages: prehelping, responding, personalizing, and initiating. Among the many groups who have received HRD training are adult school personnel such as teachers. The basic goal is to improve the trainees' (e.g., teachers') communication skills so that they will improve the mental health climate for those with whom they communicate (e.g., students). It appears as if some HRD proponents are considering life skills training in order to help trainees cope with everyday living needs (Cash, 1983). The life skills approach appears to be focused on direct enhancement through training programs for students.

■ *Tactics.* According to Cash (1983), the CRI approach presents the HRD model in a format that includes clearly defined goals, objectives, and training activities that are presented in observable and measurable performance terms. Cash (1983) presents a 45-hour training program consisting of six modules, although as few as 20 to 30 hours are deemed necessary to acquire comprehension, performance, execution, and transfer of responding skills to a natural environment. As many as 50 to 60 hours are thought to be needed in order to acquire the problem solving and program development skills that are necessary for completing the entire series. The six modules in the 45-hour program are: (a) introduction and overview, (b) prehelping skills (attending, observing, and listening), (c) responding skills (accurate response to feeling and to reasons for the feeling), (d) personalizing skills (personalizing the problem situation, defining the problem and deficits causing the problem, responding to new feelings, and identifying personalized goals), (e) helper initiating through problem-solving processes, and (f) helper initiating through program development steps (planning skills that can provide direction toward personalized goals).

A group training mode is recommended with the number of trainees limited by the number of available qualified trainers. Ten to 12 trainees per trainer is the prescribed size for practice sessions, although larger groups of unlimited size can be gathered for didactic presentations, demonstrations, and some assessment. Qualified trainers are an all-important ingredient of the HRD program. They should have completed an approved training program that would ensure their possessing effective interpersonal skills themselves while also being familiar with the HRD program.

While successful completion of the minimal HRD training program seems acceptable, a more comprehensive program covering theory, research, rater training, instruction in small group delivery skills, and successful small group experience seems to be preferred. Cash (1983) describes a pyramid approach for gradually developing trainers within an institution. Actually, a national pyramid approach seems to be in effect because all trainers can trace their training through various levels of previously trained persons to those who initiated the HRD program.

What Cash (1983) refers to as the tell-show-do approach includes a sequential program of preassessment, didactic presentation, demonstration, guided practice, and postassessment. In general, the training format moves from teaching and practicing prescribed verbal responses to individualizing the natural use of the skills by each trainee. Trainers apply social learning principles (e.g., positive reinforcement, modeling, feedback, prompting, and shaping) and are supported by video or audio tapes of models and of the trainees' performance in practice. In addition, there is a trainer's manual (Cash, Sherba, & Mills, 1975) and a trainees' workbook (Cash, 1981). Homework assignments are built into the program, and trainees keep individual logs or journals of their daily subjective experiences in relation to the training program.

The assessment measures mentioned above are given before the program begins in order to make necessary training strategy adjustments and to acquire a baseline measure of trainee competence. They are also given after the program in order to measure trainee gains. The most common rating index is Carkhuff's (1971) Communication Discrimination Indexes (CDI). In the CDI, trainee responses to standardized stimulus statements are rated by trained judges on a 5-point set of ordinally ranked criteria (levels). Actually, there are nine levels since midpoints are established at 1.5, 2.5, 3.5, and 4.5 with corresponding predetermined criteria. The minimum acceptable level of functioning/responding in the CDI system is 3.0. This scale provides trainee gains upon completion of the program and after a period of follow-up time during which there is no training, if so desired.

Since competency at empathic responding appears to be a goal of most communications skills training programs, we thought it appropriate to provide examples of the different levels of functioning as categorized by the CDI system. Taken from Cormier and Cormier (1985, p. 23), each sample is offered as a response to the same *helpee* (person helped) lead, that being "I've tried to get along with my father, but it doesn't work out. He's too hard on me." The example of a minimum acceptable response (i.e., a 3.0-rated response) is "You feel discouraged because your attempts to get along with your father have not been very acceptable." The rationale for rating this response as 3.0 is:

Level 3 has understanding but no direction; it is a reflection of feeling and meaning based on the client's explicit message. In other words, a Level 3 response reflects both the feeling and the situation. In this response, "You feel discouraged" is the reflection of the feeling, and "because of not getting along" is the reflection of the situation.

Table 2-1
Examples of response categories on the Communication Discrimination Index

---

Level 1

Helper: I'm sure it will all work out in time (reassurance and denial).
or
You ought to try harder to see his point of view (advice).
or
Why can't you two get along (question)?

Level 1 is question, reassurance, denial, or advice.

Level 2

Helper: You're having a hard time getting along with your father.

Level 2 is a response to only the *content,* or cognitive portion, of the message; feelings are ignored.

Level 4

Helper: You feel discouraged because you can't seem to reach your father. You want him to let up on you.

Level 4 has understanding and some direction. A Level 4 response identifies not only the client's feelings but also the client's deficit that is implied. In a Level 4 response, the client's deficit is personalized, meaning the client accepts responsibility for the deficit, as in "You can't reach" in this response.

Level 5

Helper: You feel discouraged because you can't seem to reach your father. You want him to let up on you. One step could be to express your feelings about this to your father.

A Level 5 response contains all of a Level 4 response plus at least one action step the person can take to master the deficit and attain the goal. In this example, the action step is "One step could be to express your feelings about this to your father."

Note. From *Interviewing Strategies For Helpers* (2nd ed.) by W. H. Cormier and L. S. Cormier, 1985, Monterey, CA: Brooks/Cole Copyright 1985, by Wadsworth Inc. Reprinted by permission.

Table 2-1 presents examples of responses to the same helpee statement that is given above, each representing one of the four remaining CDI categories. Corresponding statements of the rationale behind the ratings follow each example.

Since the CRI approach espouses the concept of trainee mastery, the general rule of thumb for trainers is to achieve mastery of a skill by at least 90% of the trainees before moving ahead in the training program. This necessitates careful attention to the performance of each trainee during the program and requires that trainers be able mentally to rate trainees on an index like the CDI while observing their practice performance. In addition, audio and/or video equipment seems to be a necessity during the practice component in order to give the trainer assistance in supervising and rating the trainees.

■ *Evaluation of Effects.* Carkhuff (1972) reviewed 30 studies that he thought rather conclusively provided evidence of strength for the HRD model. However, Lambert and DeJulio (1977) reviewed the same 30 studies and concluded that the value of HRD had yet to be established empirically, citing several common experimental design faults across the studies in question.

Cash (1983) presented a brief narrative review of research conducted prior to implementation of the CRI approach as well as studies conducted since CRI was introduced. Difficulty in drawing narrative conclusions was attributed to variance in training time across studies, variety in dependent variables deemed as important by each researcher, different time intervals between posttesting and follow-up testing across studies, and variance in sample sizes. Within his review, Cash (1983) stated that where post-CRI research was involved: "Over 45 studies report significant pre-to-post gains by trainees in an average training program" (p. 255). Since all but one of these studies (Cash & Vellema, 1979) were either unpublished reports or master's theses, it is currently an impossible task to judge their quality and that of Cash's conclusions against criteria similar to those applied by Lambert and DeJulio (1977) to the HRD model. Although other researchers have studied with mixed results the effect of HRD on variables such as academic achievement, attendance, behavior, attitude toward school, and interpersonal communication skills, Cash and colleagues seem to favor level of functioning in the helping relationship as measured by the CDI. Thus, level of discrimination and level of communication are their favored dependent variables while effects of videotaped interviews, effects of written instruments, level of attending behaviors, and self-reports about training have also received attention.

Person-Centered Education

■ *Goals.* Drawing heavily from Carkhuff's HRD model, David Aspy and Flora Roebuck set out to humanize interpersonal relations in the schools by training teachers to respond better to children, to understand them better, and to do a better job of teaching them course content. Their National Consortium for Humanizing Education (NCHE) has trained thousands of teachers for over two decades.

■ *Tactics.* The best single presentation of the NCHE training program is found in *The Skills of Teaching* (Carkhuff, Berenson, & Pierce, 1976). Using the HRD model as a foundation, Aspy and Roebuck (1977) adapted some twists of their own based on earlier research in order to appeal to teacher sensibilities. For example, the training program is introduced as one that will increase student learning rather than improving human relations because teachers, particularly secondary teachers, tend to view content acquisition as the most important concern. Flanders' Interaction Analysis (Flanders, 1965) and Bloom's Taxonomy of Educational Objectives (Bloom, Englehart, Furst, Hill, & Kratwohl, 1956) are used initially as a means of providing teachers with nonthreatening feedback about their pretraining levels of classroom interactions and cognitive presentation.

As with HRD, the basic NCHE training program systematically teaches specific interpersonal communication skills slanted toward classroom teaching. Independent skill modules found in the program are: accepting feelings, increasing praise, accepting student ideas, questioning skills, increasing student involvement, problem solving, program development, planning for learning, organization for learning, working with small groups, and customary experiences. Because the modules are independent, adaptations of the program can be made to fit the training needs of teacher trainees as determined by a preliminary analysis. Since the training includes didactic presentations of requisite information, associating skills with teachers' daily tasks and goals, guided practice, guided experiential applications of skills, and self-testing, skilled and appropriately prepared trainers are important. As is the case with HRD, Aspy and Roebuck (1977) have a specialized training method and program for trainers.

▪ *Evaluation of Effects.*   The NCHE program was founded on a researchable training schematic, and numerous evaluation studies, many correlational, have been conducted. In Aspy and Roebuck (1977, 1983), and Aspy, Roebuck, and Aspy (1984), a case for the efficacy of Person-Centered Education is stated quite strongly, citing positive effects on attitudes toward self, school, and others; discipline problems; physical health; attendance; IQ changes; and cognitive growth across studies of teachers (direct effects) and their students (indirect effects). On the other hand, several of the pre-1972 NCHE studies were included among those cited as lacking in experimental rigor by Lambert and DeJulio (1977). Perhaps the best approach is to view the effects of the NCHE program with more caution and less enthusiasm than that expressed by Aspy and Roebuck for the time being until independent reviews are reported.

Relationship Enhancement

▪ *Goals.*   Relationship Enhancement (RE) can be traced to an earlier family therapy program developed by Bernard Guerney, Jr. which was the first transformation of therapeutic method to a systematic, programmed educational model (Guerney, 1983). Current RE efforts are centered in Guerney's Institute for the Development of Emotional and Life Skills (IDE-ALS) at the Pennsylvania State University. The goals of RE are rather broad in that they focus on therapy, problem prevention, and personal/vocational enrichment concerns. Examples would be: to help individuals improve their personal and interpersonal adjustment, to help individuals change in desired therapeutic directions, and to help groups achieve their goals. More specifically, Guerney (1983) cites such goals as: to understand and acknowledge one's own emotions and desires; to communicate one's self-understanding to others; consciously to control one's interpersonal behavior; to learn to generate understanding, appreciation, and trust in others; and to solve problems and resolve conflicts in realistic, sustainable ways.

By his own admission, Guerney (1983) has been influenced by Rogers, Freud, Horney, Sullivan, Skinner, Bandura, and Timothy Leary. Thus, the RE program is a blend of cognitive instruction (principles, attitudes, and values) and behavioral instruction (guided practice and rehearsal).

■ *Tactics.* There is a modified paradigm for RE when used for training professionals (e.g., teachers) or paraprofessionals that is very much like the general approach, differing only at the outset where trainees are asked to establish goals that allow them to generalize learning to the real world, are asked to arrange the goals in a hierarchy in order to provide simulations for training applications, and are given a pretraining assessment of their RE skills. The remainder of the systematic RE training program is as follows: motivation, explanation, demonstration, modeling/prompting, supervised practice, supervised homework, in vivo applications of acquired skills, and supervision of skills maintenance.

Success of RE training is quite dependent on the existence of competent, genuine, and empathic trainers. Consequently, like HRD, expansion of the RE program is dependent on a pyramidlike system of training persons who eventually become trainers of others. Emphasis is placed on selection of persons who are agreeable and empathic, teaching them the basic principles, values, and format of RE, and teaching them social learning principles (e.g., positive reinforcement, modeling, prompting, feedback, simulating).

Although modifiable, the typical RE training format is 20 hours of classroom instruction, in vivo practice, and homework assignments. A three-day workshop is followed by one or more advanced training workshops, each lasting a day or two. These, in turn, may be followed for those desirous to become trainers by participation as group coleaders with supervision by certified trainers (Guerney, 1983). The best source of detailed information about the RE program is Guerney (1977).

Guerney (1983) provides an interesting overview of the basic components of RE. Readers should note that RE is designed to assist people to either improve their one-way communications or to help enhance mutual communications among two or more persons. In the expressive component, trainees are taught to increase their self-sensitivity and to communicate it to others (e.g., when expressing one's point of view, to show understanding of the feelings and views of others). Skills embedded within the empathic component are there to help trainees to elicit self-revealing information from others, to increase personal attractiveness to others, and to achieve self-understanding (e.g., listen intently, put oneself in the other person's place, and accept corrections readily). Mode switching is a component designed to teach trainees to control the flow of expressor and empathic modes beneficially for all persons involved in a given set of interpersonal communications. The interpersonal conflict/problem resolution component provides trainees with skills that will aid them in resolving internal and external problems and conflicts. In so doing, trainees learn how to satisfy as closely as possible the goals of all concerned parties. A facilitator component is included in order to help trainees to elicit responses that will prevent conflict and problems, enrich relationships, and foster mutual personal growth (e.g., using expressive skills to indicate appreciation of any sincere attempt at compliance with your goals). Lastly, a generalization and maintenance component is designed to help trainees use their skills in natural settings (e.g., having trainees set aside specific times when they practice their skills).

▪ *Evaluation of Effects.* Most research that has evaluated effects of RE has been devoted to its efficacy in marriage and family therapy, premarital enrichment and problem prevention programs, and divorce adjustment. Five or six controlled studies abstracted in Guerney (1983) and Levant (1983) covered applications of RE derivatives to parent education (two studies), training of residence hall workers (one study), training of drug rehabilitation paraprofessionals (one study), and training school personnel (two studies). Results of these studies are mixed or favorable to RE. Where results were favorable, attention was primarily focused on improvement of the trainees' levels of communication and student perception of the classroom climate created by trainees versus that created by nontrainees.

Obviously, six studies do not make a body of knowledge about the efficacy of RE as a primary prevention program. RE's current influence is due primarily to its use in therapeutic and secondary prevention settings. As RE becomes increasingly popular as a training-for-enhancement program, there will be a corresponding need for controlled outcome studies.

Parent and Teacher Effectiveness Training

▪ *Goals.* After having earlier developed Leadership Effectiveness Training (LET) programs to help business administrators and executives develop democratic, group-centered leadership styles, Thomas Gordon concluded that many families who retained his services as a clinical psychologist primarily needed human relations training in order to improve their communications (Gordon, 1983). Hence, Parent Effectiveness Training (PET) and, later, Youth Effectiveness Training (YET), Teacher Effectiveness Training (TET), and Effectiveness Training for Women were born. A student and colleague of Carl Rogers, Gordon has attempted to make Rogerian theory operational in his programs by adopting the same pedagogical techniques as Rogers espoused in the 1940s and 1950s. In so doing, Gordon has carefully chosen the language of education rather than that of therapy in order to develop an educational training model.

Due to the emphasis on indirect enhancement in this section, our attention will be devoted to PET and TET here. Since Gordon (1983) views the desire for power and coercion over children to be quite prevalent among parents and teachers, his general goal is to replace power-based methods with democratic ones. As a result, children are expected to take on responsibility for ownership of their own problems and for their solutions.

▪ *Tactics.* All of Gordon's programs have a core of common components: empathic, nonevaluative listening; mutual problem solving; no-lose conflict resolution; and dealing with values and collisions. PET and TET have their own texts: and Gordon (1975) and Gordon (1977), respectively. As in the programs cited earlier in the chapter, trained leaders are important to the success of PET and TET. In PET and TET's first decade, thousands of persons were taught as trainees and trainers. Through his Effectiveness Training Corporation, Gordon has created an international organization for delivering training programs and trainer workshops. Thus, a pyramidlike approach is also operating here. One reviewer of the training workshops thought that they were insufficient for those with previous training similar to that of counselors when sophisticated trainees were mixed with those having a less sophisticated background (Weinrach, 1977).

The training programs are about 24 hours in length and can be spread out over as many as eight weeks. Beyond the core components, PET emphasizes greater respect among parents for their own needs and their right to have those needs met if they express them more openly, honestly, and directly. Featured skills are I-messages (rather than you-messages), self-disclosure, no-lose decision making, learning to model desired behaviors, and an analysis of problem ownership.

Although very much like PET, TET focuses on non-power methods to help teachers cope with unacceptable behavior. In addition to the nonblaming I-messages and mutual problem solving skills mentioned above, TET has what Gordon (1983) refers to as skills for involving entire classes in the establishment of rules and procedures and drawing students into class discussions.

■ *Evaluation of Effects.* At least 23 studies are known to exist in which the efficacy of PET has been tested (Levant, 1983) while TET has apparently been independently evaluated only once, and that study was an unpublished report with absenteeism serving as the only dependent variable (Gordon, 1983). With regard to PET, there seem to be mixed conclusions. Gordon (1983) himself identified six positive changes in parent trainees that occurred in three or more independent studies (e.g., increased self-confidence, increased acceptance of children, and increased trust in children) and some evidence of indirect effects on children of parent trainees, for example, increased self-esteem (two studies) increased perception by children of parental acceptance of them (one study), and decreased instances of inappropriate and disruptive behavior (one study).

Of three independent narrative reviews, two were not supportive (Doherty & Ryder, 1980; Rinn & Markle, 1977) and one offered modest support for PET (Levant, 1983). Serious methodological problems are reported to effect many of the evaluation studies and seem to cause independent reviewers to be unenthusiastic or moderate in their assessments. These reviews indicate not that PET and/or TET are ineffective, but that little methodologically acceptable evidence of effectiveness is currently available.

Interpersonal Process Recall

■ *Goals.* A distinctive feature of Interpersonal Process Recall (IPR) is its emphasis on discovery learning. This, in turn, differentiates it somewhat from the other approaches cited in this chapter because they appear to be more prescriptive and more closely associated with clearly defined skills that are to be presented and learned systematically. IPR evolved from its beginnings as a graduate practicum in counselor education at Michigan State University in the early 1960s into an international interpersonal relations training program for mental health professionals, health care professionals, teachers, military personnel, and others.

The founder of IPR is Norman Kagan who believes that trainees should develop a sense of responsibility for their own behaviors. Consequently, they will become better able to talk openly about the ongoing interpersonal relations process. A very basic tenet of IPR and the reason for the R in the acronym is Kagan's position that people understand much more of each other's communications than they admit to themselves or others. IPR is designed to develop better awareness of interpersonal communications. Finally, Kagan presents IPR as an educational program that will add a dimension to the trainees' current set of abilities rather than a new set of behaviors to replace undesirable ones (Kagan, 1983).

■ *Tactics.*   Kagan's emphasis on discovery learning and the recall concept make IPR quite different from other communication skills programs. We think it is fair to say that while the program has structure and is systematic, there is more subjectivity in the operations and, thus, in the outcomes than is true with other programs.

IPR consists of seven sequential units that are accompanied by instructor and student manuals and a professionally produced instructional film series. As a result, IPR is considered independent of a need for specially prepared trainers although educational workshops are available for prospects (Kagan, 1983). Training may vary from 2 to 50 hours (Ford, 1979).

The most popular format of IPR is a 30- to 50-hour training program. Each of the seven units is accompanied by a 16 mm color film in which an instructor presents and directs related exercises. The seven units are: (a) Elements of Facilitating Communication, (b) Affect Simulation, (c) Trainee (Counselor) Recall, (d) Inquirer Training, (e) Client/Student Recall, (f) Mutual Recall, and (g) Transfer of Training.

According to Kagan (1983), Elements of Facilitating Communication is the only pure skill-related unit having specific behaviors and programmed responses. Presented within a philosophical context that the skills will help sometimes but not always, and that they have worked in the past for the more successful mental health professionals, the four response modes in this unit are (a) exploratory questions, (b) listening intently and paraphrasing, (c) focusing on subtle affective themes, and (d) honest, gentle labeling.

Affect Simulation is a unique component of IPR that Kagan (1983) traces to some discovery learning encountered early in his professional career. Hypothesizing that trainees may have concerns about engaging in intimate communications as the IPR training progresses, Kagan attempts to diffuse those feelings by presenting trainees with filmed vignettes portraying actors speaking directly into the camera about any one of 70 personal concerns that range from general to those for specific audiences of trainees. An example is:

"You're a good teacher . . . but you know Smith in English—her classes are just great. I just love them. They're so enjoyable and so interesting. Your classes are good, too. I really like them" (Kagan, 1983, p. 233). Trainees are requested to imagine themselves responding to the filmed affect stimulus and are encouraged to talk about their reactions. Followed by a brief didactic presentation on interpersonal theory, the purpose of this unit is to help trainees discover their feelings of vulnerability and become less fearful of interpersonal communications, especially the ones to come in the remainder of the IPR training program.

The next three components involve different configurations of the recall phenomenon. First, Trainee Recall begins with a video or audiotaped interview between a trainee and a client or student focusing on some legitimate concern that they share. This is followed by trainee/inquirer review of the tape in which the trainee controls the switches, and the inquirer is restricted to encouraging responses.

Inquirer Training may be either the third or fourth unit in the sequence. Each trainee is taught to ask probing but noninterpretive open-ended questions when serving as the inquirer during the various recall phases of IPR. Thereafter, all trainees are capable of alternating as inquirers or trainees during the recall units.

The next step is called Client/Student Recall. Shifts in assignments are made in order to have trainees previously taught to be inquirers serve in that capacity for students or clients of trainee colleagues. Thereafter, the inquirers share summaries of the student/client comments during the tape review with the trainees who originally interviewed those students/clients.

Mutual Recall brings the trainee and student/client together in a recall session with an inquirer. Both are encouraged to mutually share their thoughts and feelings about the interview.

Transfer of Learning is the seventh IPR unit. During this module, a second didactic presentation is offered in order to provide information based on Horney's (1945) theory of interpersonal behavioral styles. This information is predicated on an assumption that trainees will need assistance with the transfer-of-learning process. Thereafter, trainees may be encouraged to engage independently in interview-recall follow-up interviews with others or may be given specific assignments. For instance, teachers have been assigned to do recall sessions with an entire classroom.

■ *Evaluation of Effects.* In Kagan's (1983) opinion, IPR is by its nature difficult to evaluate via traditional experimental research techniques because discovery learning encourages individualization of outcome criteria. Thus, assessment of predetermined outcome criteria may miss the point.

Where experimental research has been conducted, much of it was related to counseling practica, counselor training, and educating medical students. In 11 studies where significant outcomes favoring IPR occurred, the dependent variables of interest were differential trainee gains in interview behavior, differences in client and roommate evaluations of trainees, ability successfully to train others to be facilitative, self-actualization of trainees, and differential gains in depth of exploration by clients of trainees (Kagan, 1983). Nonsignificant findings occurred in at least four studies where the dependent measures were affective sensitivity, interview behavior, ego development, and internality of the trainees. Kagan (1983) points out that nonsignificant findings resulted in two cases where the trainees lacked motivation and where indirect effects of the trainees on clients were measured. Ford (1979) suggests that results of a study by Spivack (1972) may mean that IPR may be more effective when preceded by a program teaching basic skills (e.g., attending, responding).

IPR has received favorable evaluations in the majority of the few studies that have been conducted. However, more research is in order, especially where teacher training is involved. There is one study that reported effects on teacher training, and the results are promising. Burke and Kagan (1976) found that it was feasible to offer a system-wide implementation of IPR training on a large scale and, as a result, students of teachers who were trained rated those teachers as being more human and likable.

PROGRAMS HAVING POTENTIAL FOR DIRECT ENHANCEMENT THROUGH TRAINING STUDENTS

Microcounseling

■ *Goals.* Microcounseling (MC) could have also been categorized as a program with potential for *indirect* enhancement because it has been used in training adults. We decided to place it in the direct enhancement category because MC is so flexible yet comprehensive that it appears to be the best vehicle for counselors who wish to develop their own hybrid communication skills programs. Thus, counselors may use the MC approach to develop peer helping or similar programs for direct delivery of communication skills training to youth and children. Other models seem to require training and adaptation of a highly specific program. Readers should understand that we think that using good highly specific programs is an excellent idea if the outcomes are beneficial. Consequently, we will also present several highly specific communication skills programs for client enhancement of children and youth in this Direct Enhancement section of the chapter.

Allan E. Ivey of the University of Massachusetts is credited with conceiving the microcounseling program. Defined as the ability to generate multiple alternative responses to given situations, intentionality is the basic goal of microcounseling. Intentionality is achieved through systematic, supervised acquisition of individual microskills that are gradually incorporated into a broad-based repertoire of skills in which one is competent and from which one can select as occasion dictates. Of course, education for understanding of the conceptual bases of interpersonal functioning and communications is also an important ingredient of MC training. Trainees also need to have responsible reasons for their responses and an awareness of their potential influence (Ivey & Galvin, 1983).

Intentionality, the goal, also reflects Ivey's philosophy of demystifying psychology and making its benefits more available to laypersons. This includes the trainer function, making it possible for numerous persons to learn and share interpersonal functioning competencies (Ivey & Authier, 1978).

MC began with an attempt to make the well-known concepts of empathy, respect, genuineness, and concreteness operational by translating ideas into behaviors (microskills) and teaching those behaviors systematically in order to make the recipients more empathic, respectful, genuine, and concrete in their interpersonal communications (Ivey, 1971). The earliest microskills included primarily what are commonly referred to as the basic listening and attending skills. With time, the microskill hierarchy increased (Ivey & Galvin, 1983). Early applications of MC were directed toward counselor trainees. However, in time, the MC approach was used to train others, such as nurses, business executives, social workers, and paraprofessionals. MC is viewed as a transferable program because recipients may apply their skills repertoire differentially, and trainers are invited to adapt the basic model to their own needs. This is possible because it is the skills themselves that are basic, not rigid adherence to a specific training format.

■ *Tactics.* Although not viewed as a rigid necessity for training success, an MC format does exist, from which individuals may depart if they wish. The basic components of the MC program are some form of instruction, demonstration, supervised practice, and feedback. Approximately 45 hours of training are recommended for preparation to engage competently in a broad repertoire of response sets, yet programs of as few as 2 and as many as 60 or more hours are known to have been conducted. Size of training groups has varied from less than 10 to more than 60. Even numbers of trainees are often preferred because of the advantages often associated with being able to have trainees practice in dyads.

The classic MC format proceeds as follows. First, following the program introduction, trainees are shown a videotaped vignette of someone presenting a personal problem by talking to the screen in a manner that causes the trainees to feel it is directed toward them. When the tape stops, trainees are asked to offer a response to the taped commentary. Since this request precedes any information dissemination or skills acquisition, the trainees are informed that many different responses may indeed be appropriate under the right circumstances. Second, trainees begin to examine specific responses that are known to have worked for successful therapists and counselors so they may be better prepared for situations similar to that simulated by the videotape. Third, the process is continued with a brief introduction of the skill to be taught (e.g., paraphrasing). The skills are taught individually and gradually blended into a repertoire of skills. Fourth, trainees view a videotaped expert model demonstrating the skill. Fifth, trainees receive reading material elaborating on the concepts just viewed on videotape. Sixth, immediate supervised practice of the skills is conducted in small groups using audio- or videotapes to record the practice efforts for feedback purposes.

Last, trainees are encouraged to apply their skills extemporaneously to in vivo situations.

The current hierarchy of microskills that have been identified for application of the MC technique is much more comprehensive than that which was first introduced by Ivey (1971). The current hierarchy begins with attending behaviors (eye contact, verbal tracking, body language, and vocal qualities) and continues from the simple to the more complex. Next in the hierarchy are client observation skills; open and closed questions; encouraging, paraphrasing, and summarizing; reflection of feeling; and reflection of meaning. The series from "open and closed questions" to "reflection of meaning" is classified as the basic listening sequence. There follow focusing (on client, problem, others, us, interviewer, or cultural/environmental context); influencing (direction, logical consequences, interpretation, self-disclosure, advice/information/exploration/instruction, feedback, and influencing summary); and confrontation (of discrepancies, of incongruities). Skill sequencing and structuring an interview into stages of rapport/structuring, defining the problem, defining the goal, exploring alternatives and confronting incongruities, and generalizing the daily life are next. The final sequence is skill integration (different applications related to theoretical, situational, and cultural variations). For a detailed presentation of the current MC training program, see Ivey (1983).

■ *Evaluation of Effects.* Comprehensive reviews by Ford (1979) and Kasdorf and Gustafson (1978) of over 150 studies offer ample evidence that MC may be used in a variety of configurations, and that trainees acquire the skills being taught, doing so rather quickly. These studies seem to be limited to simple skills found on the lower half of the MC hierarchy. Baker, Scofield, Clayton, and Munson (1984) and Baker, Johnson, Kopala, and Strout (1985), offer evidence that microskills training can be used successfully to teach higher-order skills as well (in these cases, decision making counseling and test interpretation skills). There is much less evidence of the indirect effects of MC although Ivey and Galvin (1983) cite some evidence that views of others toward trainees have improved after training was completed.

Pupil Relationship Enhancement Programs

■ *Goals.* Derived from Guerney's (1977) RE approach, Pupil Relationship Enhancement Programs (PREP) have been reported by Avery, Rider, and Haynes-Clement (1981), Haynes and Avery (1979), Hatch and Guerney (1975), and Vogelsong (1978). The foundational influences and resultant goals remain the same as those stated above in the RE section. Changes in the basic RE model have been made to adapt for the younger ages and earlier developmental stages of those receiving PREP training.

■ *Tactics.* Programs have been established for adolescents (Avery, et al. 1981; Haynes & Avery, 1979; Hatch & Guerney, 1975) and for children as young as 10 years (Vogelsong, 1978).

Conducted in English classes, the Haynes and Avery (1979) and Avery et al. (1981) program was 16 hours in length and occupied 1 hour per day. Content for this program seems to have been based on a model described in Hatch and Guerney (1975). In this version of PREP, attention was devoted to enhancing adolescent trainees' skills as speakers and listeners in dyadic interactions.

Basic tactics in the PREP program include leader explanations, demonstrations, and intensive skills practice. In the early stages, trainees remain in dyads in a specific mode for 5 to 10 minutes. Gradually, they switch modes more frequently in order to simulate natural mutual conversations. An example of the specific mode concept is for one trainee in a dyad to remain as a speaker while the other remains a responder.

Trainees are taught to be speakers, responders, and facilitators. As speakers, they are taught to precede expressive statements with empathic ones, to express things in terms of their own self-perceptions, to include statements of feelings when affect is involved, to associate their statements with specific behaviors, and to state messages explicitly. As responders, they are instructed to set personal feelings aside, clarify and reflect the speaker's feelings, seek out latent feeling messages, remain nonjudgmental, avoid questions, and attend to speakers physically (e.g., good eye contact). As facilitators, trainees are taught to use their expressive (speaker) and empathic (responder) skills in new situations and to train others to use those skills. To accomplish this, trainees work in small groups where those alternating as facilitators covertly practice while watching others overtly serve as speaker and responder. Facilitators are also asked to provide feedback with the speaker in their training dyad. As is the case with RE, specially qualified and trained leaders are recommended to assure successful PREP programs.

Vogelsong's (1978) application of RE to an elementary school setting incorporated only the first stage of Guerney's (1977) RE program—empathic acceptance of others. The general format of this program included introduction of the concept via the best available tactic for catching the trainees' attention (e.g., analogies, simulations, explanations), demonstrations, structured training exercises, supervised practice, and brief discussions at the close of each training session. The program was divided into five stages, each consisting of two 45-minute sessions. Thus, the program had a duration of 7½ hours.

The first stage of Vogelsong's program consisted of leader-directed instruction in showing and recognizing emotions. In the second stage, trainees learned to identify those feelings expressed by others and to express that understanding verbally in declarative sentences. Stage 3 found the trainees alternating as partners in dyads where they practiced responding empathically to stimuli provided by the trainer. In the fourth stage, trainees formed double dyads and added three dimensions to the training format—thinking of their own topics, reversing the speaker and responder roles, and discussing whether or not they felt the other understood their feelings. The final stage brought a dimension where trainees shared their current feelings and discussed the importance of being aware of one's own feelings.

■ *Evaluation of Effects.* To our knowledge, little direct empirical evidence of the effects of PREP programs is available. However, some generalizations from studies of other RE programs may be in order. In an application where the trainees were adolescents, Haynes and Avery (1979) found that the trainees scored significantly higher than nontrainees on measures of self-disclosure and empathy skills. In a 5-month follow-up on a sample of the same subjects, Avery et al. (1981) found that the significant differences had been maintained. Vogelsong's (1978) evaluation of effects of a modified PREP program on 10-year-olds led him to conclude that the trainees increased more in empathic acceptance than nontrainees. In addition, anecdotal reports led to a conclusion that the trainees enjoyed the program and were highly motivated to see it continue after the planned conclusion.

Youth Effectiveness Training

■ *Goals.* One of Gordon's (1983) several communication skills programs based on enhancing democratic human relations, Youth Effectiveness Training (YET) is designed for direct implementation with youthful trainees. The desired result is that youths who receive YET will accept ownership of their problems and responsibility for resolving them.

■ *Tactics.* YET tactics are founded on the same principles as those delineated above in the sections on PET and TET. Practical alterations have been made to adapt Gordon's ideas to an audience of youths.

Gordon (1983) recommends class sizes ranging from 8 to 15 persons and a 28-hour training program, preferably presented in two 14-hour segments. A broad range of suggested leader techniques includes didactic leader presentations, group discussions, demonstrations of skills, visual aids, role play simulations, games, workbook exercises, and homework. Topics included in the YET program are: influence of authority and power on human relationships, typical unproductive youth responses to adult authority, and youth self-defeating behaviors. Skills taught in the YET program are: understanding one's own feelings, communicating one's feelings to others, assessing one's own strengths, setting goals for achieving success, empathic listening, no-lose problem solving and conflict resolution strategies, and appreciating the viewpoints of others (Gordon, 1983).

■ *Evaluation of Effects.* Since there is no body of research on YET, most evidence of the effects of YET will have to be carefully generalized from the studies of PET reported above. Direct evidence of the potential for YET is reported in an experimental dissertation study by Bennison (1979) who found that when compared to those receiving no training, YET-trained students demonstrated stronger leadership potential, more positive attitudes toward their mothers, higher self-sentiment, and greater ability to function in both group and interpersonal relationships. In addition, they perceived their parents as more caring for and accepting of them.

Peer Helping Programs

■ *Goals.* Synonymous with *peer counseling* and *peer facilitator* programs, *peer helping* serves as a descriptor for a group of training programs with common as well as differential goals and tactics. Basic communication skills are a common ingredient of these peer helping programs while additional skills are tailored to specific projects that may be directed toward training students to be tutors, special friends to other students, small group leaders, or counselor/teacher assistants.

Common goals for peer helping programs are focused on helping both the children who are trained to be peer helpers and those who receive the benefits of their training. Peer helpers should acquire improved attending and responding skills as well as a variety of higher-order skills that are peculiar to specialized training they received (e.g., tutorial skills or small group leadership skills). In addition, peer helpers should learn to act responsibly and to feel good about themselves because of their helping accomplishments and the peer relationships generated by the experience (Keat, 1976). Children and others who are served by trained peer helpers should become better able to think about their ideas and feelings and more able to make responsible decisions (Myrick & Bowman, 1981). Joint personal and academic growth through experiencing positive interpersonal relationships should be experienced by peer helpers and helpees (Myrick & Bowman, 1983).

Although peer helping is not identified with one spokesperson or organization, Robert Bowman and Robert Myrick of the counselor education program at the University of Florida stand out as being significant contributors to the peer helping literature. Their book, *Children helping children: Teaching students to become friendly helpers* (Myrick & Bowman, 1981) seems to be a very important printed resource in the peer helping literature.

■ *Tactics.* The basic peer helper training model contains a selection procedure, training in basic helping skills, training in specialized helping skills where applicable (e.g., contingency management skills, leading class discussions), and supervised in vivo applications of acquired knowledge and skills. Examples of the basic helping skills are listening skills, nonverbal communication, self-disclosure, reflective listening skills, clarifying, giving feedback, being aware of one's own feelings, and developing alternative courses of action (Campbell, 1983).

All writers who discuss tactics seem to emphasize the importance of being systematic and organized in conducting training programs for peer helpers. Although not a hard-and-fast rule, school counselors or other pupil personnel/guidance staffers (e.g., school psychologists) are the most likely candidates to serve as trainers and supervisors. Of course, teachers are often quite capable of training peer helpers. In general, trainers are encouraged to begin with close supervision and then gradually reduce the closeness of supervision as the peer helpers become more able to reach out spontaneously and help others (Myrick & Bowman, 1983).

Table 2-2
Similarities and differences across six peer helper training programs

Reference	Description	Length of Training	Grade Level
Allan & Dyck (1983)	Cross-Grade Helpers		7
Bowman & Myrick (1980)	Junior Counselor Program	10.5 hrs.	3–6
Edwards (1976)	Student Helper Program	7.5 hrs.	5, 6
Gumaer (1976)	Peer Facilitator Training	9.0 hrs.	5, 6
Hoffman (1976)	Peer Models Training	10 hrs.	5
Mitchum (1983)	Total Involvement Program	7.5 hrs.	6–8

References for this table are listed in the reference section at the end of this chapter.

Several examples of reported peer helper training programs serve to highlight their similarities and differences. Table 2-2 provides comparative information about program descriptors, length of training, and grade level of trainees for six peer helping programs.

■ *Evaluation of Effects.* Several years ago, Scott and Warner (1974) were able to identify seven studies that experimentally assessed the effects of peer counseling, and they concluded that the effects were limited. More recently, Dougherty and Taylor (1983) supplied limited evidence of promising effects from four controlled studies that evaluated peer helper empathy scores, self-concepts, academic performance, attitudes toward others, and helpee self-concepts. Obviously, peer helping programs are in need of a body of empirical research to assess effects in a controlled manner.

OTHER PROGRAMS

Beyond those described and analyzed above, there are other communication skills training programs about which published reports and/or manuals are available. Although less well known, these programs may merit the attention of some readers. Space limitations prevent our making reviews as comprehensive as those above. However, we will list them here and in the reference section while encouraging readers to keep them in mind. Listed alphabetically, they are: Burka, Hubbell, Preble, Spinelli, and Winter (1972); Danish and Hauer (1973); D'Augelli and Weener (1978); Gazda, Asbury, Balzer, Childers, and Walters (1984); Goldstein (1981); Goodman (1983); Johnson (1978); Levant, Slattery, and Slobodian (1981); and Miller, Nunnally, and Wachman (1975).

CASE STUDIES

In this section and in several following chapters, we are presenting examples of programs designed and implemented in the field. In so doing, we are providing information about the designers' efforts in planning, implementing, and evaluating their programs, thinking that readers will find the information inspiring and helpful. These are not perfect programs. Various problems occurred during implementation, and some of those problems are documented from anecdotal comments by the designers. All of the program implementers acquired information while conducting the programs that led them to plan on incorporating changes in future efforts. Examples of the lessons they learned are presented in the evaluation sections of the summaries. It seems apparent to us that individuals who desire to implement primary prevention programs must first have a plan, must then implement it as well as they can, must objectively evaluate their efforts, and must bravely "go back to the drawing board" in order to improve on their designs and begin planning new, improved models.

ECHO: Effective Communication for Helping Others

Scheduling the Program and Selecting Participants. The ECHO [1] program was designed for a special audience. However, it could easily have been presented to a general audience. Thus, we are presenting it here as a program with potential for primary prevention programming. The special audience for which the ECHO program was designed was the student council and honor society members of a rural senior high school. The primary goal of the ECHO program was improved communications between the student leaders and their student constituents. One group of 10 and another group of 6 10th and 11th grade volunteers met once weekly for nine weeks.

First Session. After speaking to the groups about the purpose of the training program and the importance of effective communications, the leader used an icebreaker activity known as "What's My Line?" to help the participants to become acquainted while also illustrating the importance of listening and of observing nonverbal clues. Following a leader presentation of group rules (e.g., regular attendance, confidentiality, appropriate feedback behaviors), the groups were encouraged to discuss thoughts generated by the activities of the first session. One group appeared to be cohesive and eager to participate while the other, generally older group was competitive and appeared suspicious of the leader.

Second Session: Eighty-six Percent of Communication. A charadelike body language game was introduced in order to stress the importance of body language and to help the trainees realize that inaccurate interpretations may lead to communication problems. In the game, the participants had stickers placed on their foreheads containing descriptive adjectives (e.g., *ferocious, confused, excited*). Not knowing the word themselves, they were to try to guess it from nonverbal cues provided by other group members.

The leader then introduced the concept of attending behaviors using Egan's (1982) SOLER model: Face others *s*quarely in an *o*pen position *l*eaning slightly forward, while maintaining *e*ye contact and remaining *r*elaxed. After the leader had demonstrated appropriate use of the SOLER position, group members rehearsed it in dyads, receiving feedback from their partners. The session closed with a discussion of trainee reactions to the exercises in which they had engaged. Both groups responded in a positive manner with the second group no longer openly displaying competitiveness.

---

1. This program was designed and implemented by Diane L. Daneker.

Third Session: Games People Play. This session opened with a leader presentation on the importance of nonjudgmental and value-free communications. This was followed by an exercise in which group members acted out simulated roles for the group which they had been assigned during the previous session. Entitled "Masks for Halloween," the roles represented instances where persons lacked genuineness and congruence (e.g., adolescent girl upset over losing boyfriend acting as if all was well). The role plays were followed by group discussions of insights gained from the exercises.

Fourth Session: Please Hear What I'm Not Saying. Using herself as a simulated model, the leader concurrently informed the group about superficial masks people present for themselves for ego protection and the importance of helping others to become less dependent on those masks by communicating acceptance to them. This was followed by an exercise in which the group completed a 12-item "Hidden Assumption Test" (e.g., "Some months have 30 days. Some have 31. How many have 28?"). Again, the session closed with a discussion of acquired insights. Most members responded well and demonstrated their having added the SOLER attending responses to their behavior repertoire.

Fifth Session: Understanding the Problem. Group members were paired into dyads and asked to take turns playing two roles. In one role, they asked "How do you think you would approach this problem?" in response to a problem shared by their partners. In the second role, each responded "What do you want me to do about it?" to the same problem statement. This exercise was accompanied by a group discussion of differential feelings generated by the two different response approaches. The leader then distributed a three-page handout with examples of different ways to respond (e.g., advice, analysis, reassurance, questioning, clarification, and reflection). In their dyads, group members watched the leader model various attending behaviors, then rehearsed them. This was followed by a discussion of their observations. The dyadic technique was very productive.

Sixth Session: Problem Solving. The session opened with a leader presentation of a four-step problem solving model: (a) Using communication skills already acquired to identify the problem, (b) brainstorming alternate solutions, (c) identifying advantages and disadvantages associated with each alternative, and (d) ranking alternatives and making a tentative choice. Following a demonstration by the leader, group members divided into triads in order to rehearse the technique. In the triads, they took turns as helper, helpee, and observer. A group discussion followed. One group was confused about the process while, in the other group, one member shared a personal problem and received assistance with it.

Seventh Session: Referral—Knowing Others and Where. Discussion of this topic was initiated by asking the groups to brainstorm when and where to refer simulated helpees presented to them by the leader. The leader then demonstrated how the trainees could use the previously learned problem solving model in order to make the referral decision. After some leader comments about responsibilities and limitations, a group discussion took place. Those members with the best attendance records showed evidence of having acquired and developed the target skills.

Eighth Session: Growing Up Ain't Easy. All group members were first to be asked to read a poem by a 14-year-old girl depicting a realization that her outer-directedness had made her miserable. As was the case in the third session, group members were to act out simulated roles assigned to them in the previous session.

The roles represented typical adolescent problems (e.g., "the rebel," "the drug user," "Who am I?"). The groups were then to discuss ways to use their communication skills in responding to similar persons. Due to scheduling conflicts, the leader used this session to continue to practice skills and discuss problems, rather than introducing a new topic.

Ninth Session.　In this session, the trainees were first asked to complete a questionnaire on their attitudes toward the training program. They then engaged in a closing discussion of the ECHO program and how they might use the skills and knowledge acquired from it.

Evaluation.　All participants indicated that they enjoyed the program but thought time pressures attributed to shortened meeting times restrained their progress. The leader thought that more time could be devoted to the practice of skills by lengthening the program. The participants especially appreciated the opportunity to have their practices videotaped with subsequent opportunities to review their own videotapes.

A Social Communication Skills Training Program

Scheduling the Program and Selecting Participants.　The program [2] was conducted at a junior high school (grades 7 and 8) in a community dominated by a large land grant university. Volunteers and referrals were solicited for a program designed to enhance self-expression, questioning, attending, and acquaintanceship skills. When under way, the program had four consistently attending trainees. As such, it was experimental in nature. Yet, we think it has potential for primary prevention programming. Ten sessions were held during weekly 47-minute activity periods designed within the school's master schedule.

First Session: Introductions.　During this introductory session, the trainer introduced group members to each other, conducted an ice-breaking exercise, and reviewed the specific communication skills to be included in the program. This was followed by a discussion of the importance of communication and social skills in the trainees' lives.

Second Session: Self-Expression.　After opening the session with an explanation of how self-expression is an important factor in helping others get to know one another better and in enhancing friendships, the leader provided examples of several real-life situations where self-expression skills are important and encouraged the trainees to offer additional examples. Following demonstrations of suggested behavior by the trainer, the trainees practiced in simulated dyads. Examples of situations on which such exercises could focus are: telling others about one's interest, about the members of one's family, and about one's feelings on a specific issue.

Third Session: Questioning.　A brief review of the previous session was followed by a leader explanation of why questioning is an important part of good conversation—to find out more about others and to acquire additional information. The leader then provided examples of open and closed questions in conversations about families, hobbies, and school. After the trainees generated several examples of their own, they again practiced the skills in simulated exercises while divided

2.　This program was designed and implemented by Sally D. Stabb.

into training dyads. This practice strategy was followed throughout the training program with the leader making observations and offering positive reinforcement and feedback.

Fourth Session: Initiating Conversations.   After a brief review of the third session, the leader explained that leads such as invitations to talk, suggestions, or ideas help those engaged in a conversation to continue successfully and improve the probability that those engaged in the conversation will get along well. The leader gave examples of situations where such purposeful behavior would be useful and helped the trainees to generate ideas about additional situations in which they thought such skills were important (e.g., when working in committees, engaging in a game, or seeking to become better acquainted with others). This session closed, like the previous ones with the trainees engaged in the simulated practice exercise format.

Fifth Session: Nonverbal Attending Skills.   Brief review was followed by a leader demonstration of eye contact and body posture as elements of good nonverbal attending behavior. The group then discussed the importance of informing others that one is paying attention and is willing to listen if good communications are desired. Trainee practice followed the usual format.

Sixth Session: Verbal Following Skills.   After briefly reviewing the previous session, the leader explained how verbal following behavior is also an important component of good attending—for the same reasons that nonverbal attending behaviors are important—and presented verbal attending behaviors as techniques that allow respondees to demonstrate their understanding of what is being communicated to them. The leader identified skills such as paraphrasing, reflecting feelings, and verbal reinforcers (e.g., "uh-huh"), generated written responses, and monitored rehearsal of the skills.

Seventh Session: Synthesizing Skills Acquired in Previous Sessions.   In a more comprehensive review than was the case in earlier sessions, the leader covered all of the skills taught in the earlier lessons, asking the trainees to consider the importance of each. The trainees then described conversations as a mutual listening and responding process. Following this, the group divided into two subgroups in order to discuss a mutually acceptable topic while the leader observed and reinforced acts of skillful communication.

Eighth Session: Synthesizing Skills.   This session was a continuation of the exercise initiated in the previous session. More time was available for a discussion of trainee observations.

Ninth Session: Blocks to Effective Communication.   The leader offered a rationale for including this topic in the training program, namely the necessity of being able to recognize behaviors that inhibit good mutual interpersonal communications. The trainer and the trainees generated examples such as advice giving, prying, lecturing, devaluating, and judging. In a discussion of typical blocks to effective communication. The leader then demonstrated examples of such ineffective behaviors and encouraged the trainees to share their responses as observers.

Tenth Session: Review and Termination.   All skills covered in the training program were reviewed, and the trainer made comments on her observations about the progress made by the trainees. In closing, she suggested ways that the trainees might continue to enhance their acquisition of mutual communication skills.

Evaluation.   A trained observer sat in on all sessions observing trainees' performance of the skills being taught. Observation of a graphic recording of the summarized behavioral counts led to the conclusion that an overall increase in skilled behaviors occurred, but that progress was up-and-down rather than steadily upward over the duration of the training program. On days that particular skills were practiced, the incidence of their use was high, but this level was not maintained throughout all sessions.

On an objective measure of knowledge about the training program, there was a statistically significant improvement in the average group score from pretest to posttest. Overall, the trainer felt that the junior high school-aged trainees found the program acceptable and the content easy to understand. However, she thought that a larger program might be more effective and decided that, the next time the program was conducted the trainer should provide more structure.

A High School Communication Skills Unit

Scheduling the Program and Selecting the Participants. This program[3] was designed by two high school counselors as a unit that they offer to present during scheduled English classes in the high school curriculum (grades 11 and 12). Thus, the unit is presented to students assigned to academic classes at the invitation of the classroom teachers. Beyond that, the counselors hoped that the department would schedule the unit systematically in the curriculum across one grade level, and that the classroom teachers would eventually take charge of the instruction. Group size will vary according to the number of students enrolled in the classes. The usual arrangements are for training during ten class periods over two weeks, meeting five days per week.

First Session: Introduction. The unit is opened with a didactic leader presentation about the importance of good communications in careers and in interpersonal relationships. After a brief overview of unit content, activities are initiated in order to demonstrate the points made in the didactic presentation. The activities are an analysis of interpersonal communications that took place while class members were attempting to arrange themselves according to height and age; Pfeiffer and Jones's (1973–1974) two-way communication skills exercise; and an analysis of what happened during the two previous exercises according to questions designed by the trainers. As a homework assignment, the trainees are asked to complete a 40-item "Interpersonal Communication Inventory" by Bienvenu reproduced in Pfeiffer and Jones (1973–1974).

Second Session. This session opens with a discussion of responses to selected items on the inventory in the homework assignment. Individual scores are then compared with published averages. All trainees are then asked to participate in an exercise called the T square puzzle. The class is divided into two subgroups known as senders and receivers, and the two subgroups are asked to sit with their backs to one another. Each sender verbally instructs a corresponding receiver on how to assemble five differently colored and shaped pieces of paper into a T-shaped design without informing him/her of its shape. This is followed by a leader-directed class discussion of how the participants felt when attempting to communicate under the restrictions of the exercise, what problems were encountered, and what listening and responding failures prevented successful communications.

---

3. This class was designed and has been taught by Patricia L. Best and Katie Scalise.

Third Session. This session begins by finishing the previous exercise if necessary. The trainees are then asked to begin individual journals by either describing a situation in which they were misunderstood by another person or listing some of their communication strengths and weaknesses. Selected examples are then shared with the class. In an attempt to process reflections from the activities in the first two sessions, the class is divided into groups of six to eight trainees who then take an inventory of problems they encountered while trying to communicate with others, behaviors they engaged in that were successful, and feelings they experienced. Depending on how much time remains, a two-part filmstrip may be shown. Part 1 is entitled *Coping with Emotions* and part 2 is *The Art of Human Interaction*. Thought questions have been developed by the trainers to accompany the filmstrip.

Fourth Session. The opening exercise consists of a "Here-and-Now Wheel" which is a circle divided into four parts. Trainees are asked to write one word that describes their current feelings in a quadrant and single words describing their feelings on the previous weekend, during the previous week, and when feeling misunderstood in the other quadrants. Related discussion focuses on difficulties people experience when expressing feelings.

In a second exercise, a list of feeling words is distributed, and the group discusses definitions where necessary. Trainees are then asked to check those feelings that are easily expressed. This is followed by a discussion of feelings and emotions that are difficult to express and corresponding thoughts about reasons for said difficulties. Finally, the group discusses the advantages that may result from expressing one's feelings and the verbal ingredients of a statement accurately describing those feelings. Each person is asked to complete in their journal the statement "I feel _____ when _____," and to enter a specified number of feeling statements. If time remains, a filmstrip entitled *Emotions: The Coping Process* is shown.

Fifth Session. The fifth session opens with a journal writing exercise in which the participants are asked to write a description of their feelings about some important upcoming event (e.g., the holidays). In an ensuing discussion, participants are challenged to think of various ways in which people express their feelings and common responses that are made when feelings are expressed. Next, the group is divided into triads for an exercise in which they are presented with a listing of statements and asked to determine whether feelings are described or conveyed but not described. Again, depending on time constraints in this session or in the previous one, the film strip, *Emotions: The Coping Process*, may be shown.

Sixth Session. Using content from the previous session as foundation, the leader focuses discussion on ways in which feelings are conveyed nonverbally. Remarks are then made about the important impact nonverbal behaviors have on interpersonal communications. In the first of two exercises, four volunteers are asked to leave the room where they are to choose feeling words and then return to the group and act them out nonverbally with the remaining class members attempting to guess the feelings. The class is then divided into two teams, which in turn select feeling words and act them out nonverbally while the other team attempts to guess them. If there is time, the second exercise is a game of charades using feeling words as the stimulus. In either or both cases, related discussion is focused on types of body language used by the demonstrators and the number of guesses required before a successful response is achieved.

Seventh Session.   After asking trainees to write in their journals about messages their nonverbal behaviors communicate in classrooms, discussion is focused on what makes nonverbal messages congruent with verbal ones, and ways to understand the meaning intended by senders of verbal remarks. This session closes with an exercise in which several volunteers are asked to leave the room. While they are out of the room, a picture of an action scene is presented in some manner (e.g., an overhead projector) to the remaining trainees, who then view it for several minutes. One viewer is then selected to describe the events in the picture to the first student who returns from the hallway who, in turn, describes it to the next returnee. The process continues until all volunteers have reentered the room. Related leader-directed discussion is directed toward distortions that occurred over time, questions used to help clarify the descriptions, and the usefulness of paraphrasing as a means of checking out one's perceptions.

Eighth Session.   After reviewing material previously covered on body language and paraphrasing, the leader introduces information about and examples of open invitations to talk and reflective listening. This is followed by a discussion of how useful such communication behaviors are in the students' everyday lives. A related activity is then presented to the group in which the trainer reads prepared materials to the trainees and asks them to write paraphrases of what was read and descriptions of the feeling underlying the content of the statement. After asking some members to share their responses, the leader asks each participant to write a description of a situation in which someone has shared a problem with him or her. This information is used to design vignettes wherein each member of the class takes a turn as a sender and a receiver while the remainder of the group act as observers, giving constructive feedback to receivers when they attempt to use communication skills identified previously during the simulation.

Ninth Session.   The group exercise started at the close of session 8 is continued until completed. Afterward, the leader distributes previously prepared handouts containing varied examples of responses to the concerns of others. This stimulus is used to initiate a group discussion about which responses are and which are not appropriate reflective listening behaviors. If time remains, dyads are formed, and each couple engages in a simulated communication skills exercise with each partner attempting to engage in effective reflective listening and responding behaviors.

Tenth Session.   After finishing the simulation exercise initiated during the previous session, the leader introduces an exercise in which the class is divided into groups of four persons and each group is asked to define effective communication and list the skills required of good listeners and responders. Each group is then asked to share its conclusions with the entire class. The trainer closes by verbally reviewing all skills and related terms that have been introduced during the unit.

Evaluation.   At the time this manuscript was first prepared, the unit had been offered approximately four times per year for about five years. Results of a pre–post test of knowledge acquisition indicate that trainees adequately learn a sufficient amount of the content. Leader observations of trainee behaviors during simulation exercises led to a general conclusion that the skills are being successfully acquired during in-class rehearsal activities. While many students have indicated confidence in their ability to generalize the practiced skills to real-life situations, there is no formal evidence to either reject or support their beliefs.

SUMMARY

Although developed independently by professionals interested in prevention, the communication skills training programs in this chapter share three important ingredients. First, an emphasis on the importance of empathy, genuineness, and regard—the facilitative conditions; second, a belief that persons who achieve improved communications through the acquisition of new skills will have a positive impact on their social environments; and third, the confidence of program developers that the competencies being taught are needed in order for recipients to meet life's challenges successfully.

The roots of these communication skills training programs can be traced back to the client-centered psychology movement with the emphasis changing from therapy for individuals to skills training for prevention and therapy for individuals. This development is attributed to a gradual realization by some professions that the clientele was overwhelming the number of available therapists.

Several of the more prominent communication skills training programs have been reviewed and critiqued in this chapter. They all seem to be well-documented programmatically, being advanced as training paradigms but in need of increased attention to empirical experimentation in order to assess the effects on trainees.

Readers may notice that many of the established programs cited in this chapter fit into the indirect services category in that they are developed for training professionals (e.g., teachers, paraprofessionals, and parents). We believe that the communication skills training approach also has potential for direct services to children and adolescents and we have provided evidence in support of that belief in three case studies.

PUBLISHED RESOURCES

Adams, L. (1979). *Effectiveness training for women.* New York: Peter Wyden Books.

Egan, G. (1985). *The skilled helper.* Monterey, CA: Brooks/Cole.

Evans, D. R., Hearn, M. T., Uhlemann, M. R., & Ivey, A. E. (1979). *Essential interviewing: A programmed approach to effective communication.* Monterey, CA: Brooks/Cole.

Gordon, T. C. (1970). *Parent effectiveness training: Leader's guide.* Santa Barbara, CA: Effectiveness Training Associates.

Gordon, T. C. (1970). *Parent effectiveness training: Parent's workbook.* New York: Peter Wyden.

Guerney, B. G., Jr., & Vogelsong, E. (1981). *Relationship enhancement cassette tapes.* University Park, PA: Individual and Family Consultation Center.

Guerney, L. (1979). *Parenting: A skills training manual.* University Park, PA: Individual and Family Consultation Center.

REFERENCES

Allan, J., & Dyck, P. (1983). Improving school climate through cross-grade interactions. *Elementary School Guidance and Counseling, 18,* 137–146.

Aspy, D. N., & Roebuck, F. N. (1977). *Kids don't learn from people they don't like.* Amherst, MA: Human Resource Development Press.

Aspy, D. N., & Roebuck, F. N. (1983). Our research and our findings. In C. R. Rogers (Ed.), *Freedom to learn for the 80's* (pp. 199–217). Columbus, OH: C. E. Merrill.

Aspy, D. N., Roebuck, F. N., & Aspy, C. B (1984). Tomorrow's resources are in today's classrooms. *Personnel and Guidance Journal, 62,* 455–459.

Avery, A. W., Rider, K., & Haynes-Clements, L. A. (1981). Communication skills training for adolescents: A five-month follow-up. *Adolescence, 16,* 289–298.

Baker, S. B., Johnson, E., Kopala, M., & Strout, N. (1985). Test interpretation competence: A comparison of microskills and mental practice training. *Counselor Education and Supervision, 25,* 31–43.

Baker, S. B., Scofield, M. E., Clayton, L. T., & Munson, W. W. (1984). Microskills versus mental practice training for competence in decision making counseling. *Journal of Counseling Psychology, 31,* 104–107.

Bennison, W. M. (1979). The relationship of Youth Effectiveness Training to perceived locus of control, attitude toward parents and school, report of parental behavior, and selected personality dimensions of male and female adolescents (Doctoral dissertation, St. John's University, Jamaica, NY.) *Dissertation Abstracts International, 40,* 1392B.

Bloom, B. S., Englehart, M. D., Furst, E. J., Hill, W. H., & Kratwohl, D. R. (Eds.). (1956). *A taxonomy of educational objectives: Handbook 1, the cognitive domain.* New York: Longmans, Green.

Bowman, R. P., & Myrick, R. D. (1980). "I'm a junior counselor, having lots of fun." *School Counselor, 28,* 31–38.

Burka, J., Hubbell, R., Preble, M., Spinelli, R., & Winter, N. (1971). *Communication skills workshop manual.* Ft. Collins CO: Colorado State University Counseling Center.

Burke, J. B., & Kagan, N. (1976). *Influencing human interaction in schools.* (NIMH Grant MH 13526-03, final report). Chicago: National Institute of Mental Health.

Campbell, C. (1983). Successful training for elementary and middle school helpers. *Elementary School Guidance and Counseling, 18,* 118–123.

Carkhuff, R. R. (1969a). *Helping and human relations: Vol. 1. Selection and training.* New York: Holt, Rinehart, & Winston.

Carkhuff, R. R. (1969b). *Helping and human relations: Vol. 2. Practice and research.* New York: Holt, Rinehart, & Winston.

Carkhuff, R. R. (1971). *The development of human resources.* New York: Holt, Rinehart, & Winston.

Carkhuff, R. R. (1972). Major contributions to the development of systematic human resource development models. *Counseling Psychologist, 3* (3), 4–11.

Carkhuff, R. R., & Anthony, W. A. (1979). *The skills of helping: An introduction to helping skills.* Amherst, MA: Human Resource Development Press.

Carkhuff, R. R. & Berenson, B. G. (1967). *Beyond counseling and therapy.* New York: Holt, Rinehart, & Winston.

Carkhuff, R. R., Berenson, B. G., & Pierce, R. M. (1976). *The skills of teaching: Interpersonal skills.* Amherst, MA: Human Resource Development Press.

Carkhuff, R. R., Pierce, R. M., & Cannon, J. R. (1977). *The art of helping III.* Amherst, MA: Human Resource Development Press.

Cash, R. W. (1981). *Human resources development: Trainee's workbook.* Long Beach, CA: Fortyniner Bookstore.

Cash, R. W. (1983). The human resource development model. In D. Larson (Ed.), *Teaching psychological skills: Models for giving psychology away* (pp. 245–270). Monterey, CA: Brooks/Cole.

Cash, R. W., Sherba, D. S., & Mills, S. S. (1975). *Human resources development: A competency based training program.* Pasadena: Associates in Human Communication.

Cash, R. W., & Vellema, C. K. (1979). Conceptual versus competency approach in human relations training programs. *Personnel and Guidance Journal, 58,* 91–94.

Cormier, W. H., & Cormier, L. S. (1985). *Interviewing strategies for helpers: Fundamental skills and cognitive behavioral interventions* (2nd ed.). Monterey, CA: Brooks/Cole.

Danish, S. J., & Hauer, A. L. (1973). *Helping skills: A basic training program.* New York: Behavioral Publications.

D'Augelli, F. J., & Weener, J. M. (1978). Training parents as mental health agents. *Community Mental Health Journal, 14*(1), 14–25.

Doherty, W. J., & Ryder, R. G. (1980). Parent effectiveness training (PET): Criticisms and caveats. *Journal of Marital and Family Therapy, 6*(4), 409–419.

Dougherty, A. M., & Taylor, B. L. B. (1983). Evaluation of peer helper programs. *Elementary School Guidance and Counseling, 18,* 130–136.

Edwards, S. S. (1976). Student helpers: A multilevel facilitation program. *Elementary School Guidance and Counseling, 11,* 53–58.

Egan, G. (1982). *Training manual for the skilled helper.* Monterey, CA: Brooks/Cole.

Egan, G., & Cowan, M. A. (1979). *People in systems: A model for development in human service professions and education.* Monterey, CA: Brooks/Cole.

Flanders, N. A. (1965). *Interaction analysis in the classroom—A manual for observers.* Ann Arbor: University of Michigan.

Ford, J. D. (1979). Research on training counselors and clinicians. *Review of Educational Research, 49*(1), 87–130.

Gazda, G. M., Asbury, F. S., Balzer, F. J., Childers, W. C., & Walters, R. P. (1984). *Human relations development: A manual for educators* (2nd ed.). Boston: Allyn & Bacon.

Goldstein, A. P. (1981). *Psychological skill training: The structured learning technique.* New York: Pergamon Press.

Goodman, G. (1983). SASHA tapes: Expanding options for help-intended communication. In D. Larson (Ed.), *Teaching psychological skills: Models for giving psychology away* (pp. 271–286). Monterey, CA: Brooks/Cole.

Gordon, T. (1970). *P.E.T.: Parent effectiveness training.* New York: Peter Wyden.

Gordon, T. (1975). *Parent effectiveness training.* New York: New American Library.

Gordon, T. (1977). *Teacher effectiveness training.* New York: McKay.

Gordon, T. (1983). Three decades of democratizing relationships through training. In D. Larson (Ed.), *Teaching psychological skills: Models for giving psychology away* (pp. 151–170). Monterey, CA: Brooks/Cole.

Guerney, B. G., Jr. (1977). *Relationship enhancement: Skill-training programs for therapy, problem prevention, and enrichment.* San Francisco: Jossey–Bass.

Guerney, B. G., Jr. (1983). Relationship enhancement therapy and training. In D. Larson (Ed.), *Teaching psychological skills: Models for giving psychology away* (pp. 171–206). Monterey, CA: Brooks/Cole.

Gumaer, J. (1976). Training peer facilitators. *Elementary School Guidance and Counseling, 11,* 27–36.

Hatch, E. J., & Guerney, B., Jr. (1975). A pupil relationship enhancement program. *Personnel and Guidance Journal, 54,* 102–105.

Haynes, L. A., & Avery, A. W. (1979). Training adolescents in self-disclosure and empathy skills. *Journal of Counseling Psychology, 26,* 526–530.

Hobbs, N. (1964). Mental health's third revolution. *American Journal of Orthopsychiatry, 34,* 822–833.

Hoffman, L. R. (1976). Peers as group counseling models. *Elementary School Guidance and Counseling, 11,* 37–46.

Horney, K. (1945). *Our inner conflicts: A constructive theory of neurosis.* New York: Norton.

Ivey, A. E. (1971). *Microcounseling: Innovations in interviewing training.* Springfield, IL: Charles C. Thomas.

Ivey, A. E. (1983). *Intentional interviewing and counseling.* Monterey, CA: Brooks/Cole.

Ivey, A. E., & Authier, J. (1978). *Microcounseling: Innovations in interviewing, counseling, psychotherapy, and psychoeducation* (2nd ed.). Springfield, IL: Charles C. Thomas.

Ivey, A. E., & Galvin, M. (1983). Microcounseling: A metamodel for counseling, therapy, business, and medical interviews. In D. Larson (Ed.), *Teaching psychological skills: Models for giving psychology away* (pp. 207–228). Monterey, CA: Brooks/Cole.

Johnson, D. W. (1978). *Human relations and your career: A guide to interpersonal skills.* Englewood Cliffs, NJ: Prentice–Hall.

Kagan, N. (1983). Interpersonal process recall: Basic methods and recent research. In D. Larson (Ed.), *Teaching psychological skills: Models for giving psychology away.* Monterey, CA: Brooks/Cole.

Kasdorf, J., & Gustafson, K. (1978). Research related to microtraining. In A. Ivey & J. Authier, *Microcounseling: Innovations in interviewing, counseling, psychotherapy, and psychoeducation* (2nd ed., pp. 323–376). Springfield, IL: Charles C. Thomas.

Keat, D. B. (1976). Training as multimodal treatment for peers. *Elementary School Guidance and Counseling, 11,* 7–15.

Lambert, M. J., & DeJulio, S. S. (1977). Human resource development training programs: Where is the donut? *Counseling Psychologist, 6* (4), 79–86.

Larson, D. (1983). Giving psychology away: The skills training paradigm. In D. Larson (Ed.), *Teaching psychological skills: Models for giving psychology away* (pp. 1–14). Monterey, CA: Brooks/Cole.

Levant, R. F. (1983). Client-centered skills-training programs for the family: A review of the literature. *Counseling Psychologist, 11* (3), 29–46.

Levant, R. F., Slattery, S. C., & Slobodian, S. E. (1981). A systematic skills approach to the selection and training of foster parents as mental health para-professionals, II: Training. *Journal of Community Psychology, 9,* 231–238.

Miller, G. (1969). Psychology as a means of promoting human welfare. *American Psychologist, 24,* 1063–1075.

Miller, S., Nunnally, E. W., & Wachman, D. B. (1975). *Alive and aware: Improving communication in relationships.* Minneapolis: Interpersonal Communications Programs.

Mitchum, N. T. (1983). Introducing TIP: The Total Involvement Program for peer facilitators. *School Counselor, 31,* 146–149.

Myrick, R. D., & Bowman, R. P. (1981). *Children helping children: Teaching students to become friendly helpers.* Minneapolis: Educational Media Corporation.

Myrick, R. D., & Bowman, R. P. (1983). Peer helpers and the learning process. *Elementary School Guidance and Counseling, 18,* 111–117.

Pfeiffer, J. W., & Jones, J. E. (Eds.). (1973-1974). *A handbook of structured experiences for human relations training* (Vols. 1-4). La Jolla, CA: University Associates.

Rinn, R. C., & Markle, A. (1977). Parent effectiveness training: A review. *Psychological Reports, 41,* 95–109

Rogers, C. R. (1951). *Client-centered therapy: Its current practice, implications, and theory.* Boston: Houghton Mifflin.

Rogers, C. R. (1957). The necessary and sufficient conditions of therapeutic personality change. *Journal of Consulting Psychology, 21,* 95–103

Spivack, J. D. (1972). Laboratory to classroom: The practical application of IPR in a Master's level prepracticum counselor education program. *Counselor Education and Supervision, 12,* 3–16.

Truax, C. B., & Carkhuff, R. R. (1967). *Toward effective counseling and psychotherapy: Training and practice.* Chicago: Aldine.

Vogelsong, E. L. (1978). Relationship enhancement training for children. *Elementary School Guidance and Counseling, 12,* 272–279.

Weinrach, S. (1977). Re: Views. *Personnel and Guidance Journal, 55,* 556–559.

3

PSYCHOLOGICAL EDUCATION

ROLE IN PRIMARY PREVENTION

As defined in chapter 1, psychological education is viewed as a broad descriptive term covering a variety of approaches. From our vantage point, psychological education programs are delivered to populations of children and adolescents as either direct or indirect guidance services. Purposes and procedures of independently developed programs vary widely, and the goals appear to be stated differentially. However, these programs have common ingredients, which appear to be as follows: theoretical underpinnings that may lead to a better understanding of human behavior and cognitive development; a desire to enhance development in the affective domain (e.g., understanding causes of behavior, ego development, normal development, a sense of belonging to one's social group); and a desire to improve or enhance school environments for students by supplementing cognitive instructional influences with important, planned affective programs.

BACKGROUND AND CURRENT STATUS

Psychological education seemed to have become a vital concept in the minds of leaders in counseling and guidance when special issues of the *Personnel and Guidance Journal* and the *School Counselor* highlighting that concept were published in 1973. Carroll (1973), Cottingham (1973), Ivey and Alschuler

(1973), and others attempted to give form and substance to the idea through conceptual papers and examples. Others have followed suit over the intervening years, and the concepts remain much the same although new practices have been introduced. As Skovholt (1977) points out, psychological education is essentially founded on principles of humanistic and developmental psychology applied to educational settings in order to integrate intellectual and affective material via a process of demystifying psychological knowledge for the purpose of enhancing human development and mental health—translating professional knowledge about human behavior into programs that are useful to lay persons.

Authier, Gustafson, Guerney, and Kasdorf (1975) provided a foundation for helping counselors to view the role of psychological educator as a logical alternative to the traditional role of remediator. A perusal of the program descriptions that follow should lead readers to conclude that several individuals and groups have successfully used that alternative, translating concepts into action. Although the nature and content of these programs differ, their attention to primary prevention goals remains constant. In our viewpoint, successes in program conceptualization and development outstrip accomplishments in the area of evaluating program effects. Consequently, more and better research is necessary. Unfortunately, at present, consumers are often left with their own judgment as the best source for decision making about adopting or adapting psychological education programs reported in the literature.

We have reviewed several programs that seem to belong in the psychological education category. Although the Causal Understanding program predates the arrival of psychological education terminology, we think that it rightfully belongs among those programs reviewed in this chapter both as an equal and a precursor.

PROGRAMS THAT ARE ADAPTABLE TO CLASSROOM SETTINGS

Causal Understanding Training

■ *Goals.* Causal Understanding Training was introduced in the preventive psychiatry programs at the State University of Iowa (Ojemann, 1958). The concept of causal learning is founded on the belief that emotional conflicts may be reduced and mutually satisfying relationships enhanced if children and youth learn to appreciate the causes of behavior and apply that knowledge to their own behaviors. From this viewpoint, understanding and appreciation of the multiple, complex, interacting nature of the variables that influence human behavior will lead to a greater willingness to understand circumstances from the viewpoint of others, an increased realization that one's behavior has consequences, and a willingness to suspend judgment until sufficient logical information is available (Muus, 1960a). Ojemann (1958) suggested that inoculation with a causal orientation may lead to mutually satisfying relationships and reduced emotional conflicts because trainees learn to appreciate the causes of behavior and develop ideas for creative, satisfying use of their own energy.

■ *Tactics.*   Causal understanding training is provided through planned human relations classes that are founded on common incidents that occur in school. Although the incidents may vary, a common model for conducting the classes exists. First, the leader sets the stage, briefly explaining underlying principles. Second, the typical situation (incident) is described. Third, trainees are encouraged to share their feelings. Next, trainees are asked to attempt explanations of the behavior involved. Last, trainees are asked to suggest satisfactory solutions. As a secondary tactic, leaders are encouraged to use spontaneous incidents that occur. Throughout, teacher and administrator understanding and support are imperative for program success.

Ojemann (1958) suggested several tactics that have been implemented and studied. First, teachers can model desired behaviors in classrooms. Second, teachers can read to primary-aged children narrative accounts (e.g., a fight on the playground or someone left out of play activities) in which causal and noncausal responses are described. Similar narratives can be read by older children. In all cases, discussion is encouraged by the teacher in order to enhance understanding while not imposing adult values. A third tactic suggested by Ojemann is the reading of expositions about behaviors of adults toward children and youth, accompanied by related causal discussion. Finally, Ojemann suggests incorporating causal questions into academic topics (e.g., asking causal questions about behaviors of historical or literary characters or looking at reasons why social and political decisions are made). Whenever leader-directed training is initiated, it is suggested that the following stages to causal learning be practiced. First, set the stage by explaining how people tend to interact. Second, describe a typical situation. Third, encourage trainees to respond initially according to their feelings. Fourth, eventually, ask trainees to explain and understand the behavior in question. Last, encourage trainees to discuss satisfactory solutions to the situation.

■ *Evaluation of Effects.*   Those associated with the Preventive Psychiatry Research Program engaged in a commendable series of empirical evaluation studies (Levitt, 1955; Muus, 1960a, 1960b, 1960c, 1961; Ojemann, Levitt, Lyle, & Whiteside, 1955; Ojemann & Snider, 1964; and Snider, 1957). The most prominent results reported in these studies were with later elementary-aged subjects (grades 4, 5, and 6) who were trained by specially prepared teachers. The results were promising, especially on measures of various aspects of the nature of causality. Significant training effects were also noted on classroom behavior observational measures and self-report mental health measures. In general, program effects increased as the magnitude of training increased. For example, children experiencing two years of exposure to causal learning demonstrated a greater assessed impact than those who were exposed to one year (Muus, 1960a).

Positive clinical observations were reported as well. Young children were highly positive and surprisingly understanding in their responses, and counselors and teachers were very positive in their accolades after completion of structured training programs (Ojemann, 1958).

Deliberate Psychological Education

■ *Goals.* Conceptualized by Mosher and Sprinthall (1970), Deliberate Psychological Education (DPE) began as a U.S. Office of Education–sponsored training project conducted in the Harvard Graduate School of Education (Mosher & Sprinthall, 1971). Kolhberg (1975) associates DPE with the "cognitive development approach" which, in turn, can be traced to the work of John Dewey and, more recently, Jean Piaget. As such, DPE is based on a developmental theory in which cognitive reorganization of experiences is to be enhanced through successively higher levels or stages. The general goal of DPE is to create an environment that facilitates the coping and ego development of children and teenagers. Perhaps the most ambitious goal statement for DPE has been the stated desire to reorder the quality of classroom learning experiences through a deliberate focus on curriculum change (Sprinthall, 1973).

In actuality, DPE programs have most often been delivered to adolescents. Consequently, specific goals relevant to cognitive developmental needs of adolescents have been stated in the DPE literature. Bernier and Rustad (1977) stress the importance of promoting nonstereotypical thinking and of moving adolescents toward a richer and more differential perception of themselves and others. Carrying that idea further, Cognetta (1977) cites the need to enhance the adopting of a social perspective—moving from self-concerns to focusing on thoughts and feelings of others. DPE goals also include encouraging of cognitive restructuring by adolescents when they experience dissonance over circumstances that they do not fully understand (Bernier & Rustad, 1977).

■ *Tactics.* The most general description of DPE is that it represents learning psychology by doing psychology (Sprinthall, 1973). In deliberately attempting to affect personal and psychological development of adolescents through curriculum intervention, DPE advocates focus on psychological issues with an emphasis on reason and on unique and immediate circumstances as representative of the universal elements of human development (Kohlberg, 1975).

Specific DPE tactics have been delivered as guidance and counseling interventions through the school curriculum. Sprinthall (1981) reports three rounds of curriculum tactics thought at the time to be most appropriate interventions for achieving DPE goals. The earliest tactics consisted of T groups, lectures, field experiences, Gestalt exercises, films, and interviews; much of this is reported in Mosher and Sprinthall (1971).

A second round of programs evolved from lessons learned in the first, and a DPE model emerged as one-or two-term high school classes in which sequential topic seminars were blended with experimental practica. One example reported in the DPE literature was an active action/reflection–

seminar/reflection format combined with cross-age teaching of junior high school students for high school seniors enrolled in a social studies elective course (Cognetta, 1977). In this situation, the 12th-graders received comprehensive structured psychological training in a seminar (e.g., interpersonal communication skills training and related readings) accompanied by constant attention to considering and internalizing what they were thinking and experiencing. In addition to the seminar experiences, these students acted on their training by serving as cross-age teachers for junior high students enrolled in an ungraded elective course, the content of which focused on interests and socialization activities.

Erickson (1977) reports another example of the second round DPE programs. This intervention was delivered through a high school English elective for young women and had a seminar/reflection mode similar to the one reported in Cognetta (1977). However, the action/reflection idea was the field interviewing of adult women by students using Piaget-type questioning.

Sprinthall (1981) reports that the second round evolved as a careful balance between action learning and guided reflection and describes plans for a third round in the development of DPE programs. Based on evidence that DPE has had differential effects across groups of student recipients, third round efforts are being devoted to identifying methods of differential delivery of training, differential degrees of responsibility, matching of different learning environments and the like within what are essentially the same programs that evolved from round two.

■ *Evaluation of Effects.*   Advocates have diligently evaluated field studies during the three stages of DPE. Standardized measures of ego development, moral reasoning, affective learning, and communication skills acquisition have been used in addition to clinical measure of personal growth such as comments recorded in journals, class climate checks, student interviews, tape recordings of counseling interviews, class attendance, unsolicited comments, and parent reactions. Lockwood (1980) has pointed out that the multifaceted nature of DPE treatments makes determination of effects and of the source of those effects difficult to determine.

Sprinthall (1981) reported that results across all evaluation measures of the first round of DPE programs failed to uncover evidence that the programs had affected students in the desired direction. However, evidence acquired during the second round of DPE programs was much more promising. Using the metaanalysis approach of statistically integrating results across several related studies into a cumulative summary of treatment effects, Sprinthall (1981) demonstrated that DPE has effected significant change in the desired direction over time (pretraining to posttraining) on measures using interval scales (ego development and moral reasoning). Results on the clinical measure of personal growth were reported as being consistent with the interval data outcomes. The deliberately designed balance between action learning and guided reflection evolving from the second round of DPE programming has been proven to be effective on specifically defined measures. According to Sprinthall (1981), preliminary data indicate that third stage ideas for DPE programming may be on the right track.

Moral Education

■ *Goals.* Lockwood (1978) has described moral education as a "relatively coherent, measurable outcome in search of a clear treatment that will promote it" (p. 345). In that vein, perhaps the best place to begin coverage on moral education is with the measurable outcome—Kohlberg's model of moral development stages as it is made operational through the Moral Maturity Score (MMS) (Kohlberg & Turiel, 1971). Kohlberg's system is a refinement of earlier work by John Dewey and Jean Piaget and represents the so-called *cognitive-developmental* approach (Kohlberg & Wasserman, 1980). The word *cognitive* represents simulation of active thinking, and *developmental* implies movement through stages. Kohlberg has identified six overlapping ego and moral stages, and the goal of ego or moral development is to stimulate growth upward through the respective stages. Believing that children and adolescents may often be Presocial, Symbiotic, Impulsive; Self-protective; or Conformist (stages 1–3) in their ego development, teachers and counselors will attempt interventions designed to move students' moral development upward toward Conscientious, Autonomous, and Integrated stages (4–6). Related training is predicated on the belief that planned interventions to enhance moral development are both possible and (because individual and societal benefits will accrue) desirable to accomplish.

■ *Tactics.* As noted earlier, Lockwood (1978) considers moral education, the implementation of interventions based on moral development theory, to be somewhat unclear. One reason for this may be that DPE advocates also use Kohlberg's measure to evaluate their programs. Indeed, because the boundaries are not always clear, DPE and Planned Moral Education (PME) may easily be confused by laypersons as well as by reviewers of research.

In an attempt to achieve clarity, this section will begin with coverage of the tactics used by persons associated with Harvard's Center for Moral Education who originally trained teachers to conduct moral discussions in their classes and who later implemented a "just community" alternative school and a school-wide "fairness committee" within a cooperating high school. These early efforts led to further involvement by counselors, teachers, administrators, students, parents, and community in a teacher/advisor program, student service projects, and a student service center.

The classic PME intervention tactic seems to be the so-called moral discussion technique. The original thrust of the Center for Moral Education was to train social studies and English teachers and, conceivably, counselors and other teachers, to lead moral discussions among their students that consisted of conflict-laden hypothetical moral dilemmas. Colangelo (1982) and Colangelo and Dettman (1985) offer ideas on what form the moral dilemmas should take. In leading the moral discussions, the leaders exposed students to problems that contained contradictions for their current moral stage or structure, hoping to cause dissatisfaction with the current level at which they were operating. To do this successfully, it was believed that leaders had to create an atmosphere of interchange and dialogue so that conflicting moral views could be compared in an open manner. During the resulting interaction, leaders were originally to support students at the higher moral development stages. Known as the "plus-one matching" method, the next step was for the leader to challenge all students to use new higher order structures and clarification techniques when all appeared to understand the current level of thinking (Kohlberg & Wasserman, 1980). According to Lockwood (1978) consistent use of the "plus-one matching" technique across group leaders is quite difficult to achieve. This, in turn, makes generalization of evaluation efforts equally difficult to achieve.

Evaluation and replication of the "just community" alternative school, the "fairness committee," the teacher/advisor program, the student service project, and the student service center are even more difficult to achieve because, as a group, these programs involved practical applications of moral development principles through participatory governance, resolution of conflicts through mutual hearings and group decision making, and expanded opportunities to provide and to receive interpersonal helping services. These ever-growing applied moral education services did include such concrete tactics as advocacy and communication skills training for participants, however. More specifically, the training cited above included enhancement of listening, clarifying, and perspective taking skills.

Lapsley and Quintana (1985) and Nucci (1985) report on a more recent convention for the moral education approach. Known as transactive discussion, the more recent approach is founded on the idea that moral development may be promoted through interactions with peers (Berkowitz & Gibbs, 1983). Transactive behavior may take the form of discussion groups without leaders in which the goal is cooperative construction of resolutions and conciliation of differences. The goal of this approach is to achieve a dialogue in which peers engage in discursive reasoning with each other so that an interaction occurs between one's own reasoning and that of the others. It is argued that this process may enhance the moral development of the participants through efforts to extend the logic of others' arguments, refute the assumptions behind others' arguments, provide a common viewpoint, or resolve conflicting views.

■ *Evaluation of Effects.* As Lockwood (1978) pointed out, PME has a clearly defined set of outcome measures. In so stating, Lockwood cited MMSs taken from the Moral Judgment Interview (Kohlberg, Colby, Gibbs, & Speicher-Dubin, 1978). More recently, Rest (1979) has introduced the Defining Issues Test (DIT) also derived from Kohlberg's theory but using a multiple choice format. These two measures serve as the current criteria for measuring effects of PME programs, and both provide information about a person's relative positions on the stepped moral development scale. Since moral development stage scores are so central to the evaluation of PME program effects, it should be noted that there are some who strongly argue that the Kohlberg system is inappropriate (e.g., Kurtrines & Grief, 1974).

In that effects reported by the Kohlberg camp and refutations cited by the Kurtrines/Grief camp possibly represent polemic extremes, reviews by Lockwood (1978) and Rest (1980) will be cited with hopes that their positions are relatively objective. In the earlier of those two reviews, Lockwood (1978) focused only on MMSs and surmised that, on the average (across mixed results), direct discussion of moral issues and dilemmas can effectively promote growth of 1/3 to 1/2 of a stage on the 6-stage moral reasoning scale.

Having the advantage of additional time to review empirical results of related moral education research, including measured results from the DIT, Rest (1980) asserts that Kohlberg's theory is supportable, but the stage concept and other attributes need further verification. In general, Rest thinks that moral judgment is clearly related to behavior, but is also complicated, mediated, or modified by other variables.

With regard to his review of moral education intervention studies, Rest (1980) reports several conclusions: First, the most productive interventions in terms of change in moral judgment have a heavy emphasis on moral reasoning rather than broadly emphasizing psychological growth objectives; second, there is no evidence that the "plus-one matching" technique is effective; third, interventions of up to several months or more are necessary to produce change, and even then the changes are slight; and last, where effects accrue, it is difficult to determine which intervention is most effective or how much is needed.

Values Clarification

■ *Goals.* According to Glaser and Kirschenbaum (1980), current values clarification programs and materials generated by the National Center for Humanistic Education in Saratoga Springs, New York can be traced to earlier work by Louis E. Raths who drew on John Dewey's work to develop a nonjudgmental Socratic questioning technique (clarifying questions) to counsel apathetic, flighty, overconforming, and overdissenting individuals. Raths and students developed many strategies to carry out this clarifying process, and their procedures became known as Values Clarification programs (Raths, Harmon, & Simon, 1978).

Proponents of Values Clarification believe that persons are capable of working through inner conflict and moving toward greater fulfillment. Correspondingly, they believe that this process is enhanced when people are encouraged to reflect on their values, to consider alternatives and consequences, to act in ways consistent with their values positions, and to be aware of their feelings and behaviors. To accomplish these general outcomes, Values Clarification proponents seek to help trainees to learn the valuing processes and apply them to their own lives.

Group tactics are promoted because they provide opportunities to affirm one's own values while also hearing others' viewpoints, increase one's repertoire of alternatives, and learn important communication skills. The group mode is promoted for school settings because of a belief that factual and conceptual foci need to be balanced with a values focus.

■ *Tactics.* Hundreds of Values Clarification tactics have been developed over the years. According to Glaser and Kirschenbaum (1980), tactics often evolve from good clarifying questions that become elaborated into something more focused. An example they cited was the possible evolution of the "Twenty Things I Love to Do" tactic from a clarifying question such as "What are some things you love to do in life?"

Apparently there are some recommended commonalities across Values Clarification tactics. According to Glaser and Kirschenbaum (1980), four conditions are necessary to enhance effectiveness. First, the Values Clarification approach should be consistent with user philosophy and method. Second, the Values Clarification process should be part of the user's life style. Third, familiarity through experience should precede introducing Values Clarification tactics to others. Fourth, Values Clarification tactics should only be used when the occasion is right (e.g., when values exploration, career exploration, or problem solving are in order). Specific guidelines for leading groups engaging in Values Clarification tactics have also been suggested. They are: group members have the right to pass on questions or exercises, participants should listen to each other carefully, and each participant should have periods of time when he or she receives the group's undivided attention.

Several detailed sources of Values Clarification tactics are in print. Among those that evolve from the ideas of Raths and colleagues are work by the following authors: Harmin, Kirschenbaum and Simon (1973), Howe and Howe (1975), Kirschenbaum and Glaser (1978), Morrison and Havens (1976), Simon (1974), Simon, Howe, and Kirschenbaum (1972), and Smith (1977). Lockwood (1978) notes that Values Clarification tactics are generally presented more explicitly than the related goals. Consequently, there is a danger that users may pursue a variety of personal objectives or that they may be unclear about their objectives.

■ *Evaluation of Effects.* Lockwood (1978, 1980) and Kirschenbaum (1977) report that research on the effects of Values Clarification has been conducted. According to Lockwood (1980), research has followed a clear set of practices, and results of a second generation of studies indicate that the tactics seem workable with school age students. However, demonstrations of long-term effects are still needed.

In an earlier review, Lockwood (1978) lamented circumstances that led Values Clarification researchers to evaluate highly specific tactics that were based on relatively abstract goals. These circumstances apparently led researchers to use diverse, difficult to measure, affective variables such as self-esteem, self-concept, personal adjustment, and intraclass relations. At best, their findings have been very modest. In fairness to the Values Clarification users, there is a need for proponents to state clearer goals and identify reliable and valid measures before concluding that what is known from the research is conclusive (Lockwood, 1978).

The Human Development Program

■ *Goals.* The Human Development Program (HDP) was created by Harold Bessell and Ulvado Palomares who formed the Institute for Effectiveness in Children in San Diego, California from which to conduct their programs. HDP draws its major theoretical underpinnings from the work of Karen Horney who believed that children would be highly motivated and effective if they knew how to increase their powers, gain approval of adults and peers, and develop stable feelings about themselves (Bessell, 1970). In order to achieve these goals, HDP evolves from three major themes: Awareness (knowing what one's feelings, thoughts, and actions really are), Mastery (self-confidence via knowing one's abilities and how to use them and via controlling one's environment), and Social Interaction (knowing other people and understanding the element of causality in human relationships) (Palomares & Rubini, 1973). The program is sequential with levels of training evolving from earlier training topics and tactics.

■ *Tactics.* HDP has been used with all ages by social workers and mental health personnel in government agencies and in correctional institutions. However, it was originally established for elementary school teachers to use with their children, with Magic Circle being the basic tactic. The process by which leaders manage the Magic Circle is considered the most important factor for success in the HDP.

The Magic Circle technique is a structured group activity where the leader attempts to create an atmosphere of acceptance. Awareness of positive and negative feelings is encouraged in order to keep them from being bottled up through activities such as "I had a scary dream," "One way I wish I could be different," or "Something I wish for that is impossible." Mastery is encouraged by activities such as "I can relax," "Something I do well," and "A promise I made and kept." Social interaction activities allow trainees to explore their effects on others. An example is: "Something that you can do to make me feel good or bad." In addition to a well-defined curriculum, Bessell and Palomares have developed a set of criteria or recommendations for leading the Magic Circle, believing that a comprehensive training program is imperative. Implementation materials can be found in Bessell (1970, 1969–72), Bessell and Palomares (1971), and Palomares (1971, 1972). Lesson guides have been prepared for leaders that have 180 daily activities for each level of the program as well as objectives, procedures, needed materials, and the problem area of each day's lesson. Supportive materials reflecting principles of good practice and good mental health are also included. Bessell and Palomares believe that meetings should be conducted at approximately the same time every day because the sequential presentation of planned tasks will enhance gradual development of positive behavior patterns.

The principal rules of Magic Circle are that everyone should sit reasonably still, one person can talk at a time, and everyone must listen and be able to show that they have been listening. It is recommended that those who are overly disruptive or who refuse to participate be removed from the group and referred for individual help. With younger children, a concentric, tight circle is recommended consisting of assigned places with sexes alternated. Group membership should be considered carefully and homogeneity of developmental stages is preferred with those known to have more personal problems than others being spread across all groups. Once organized, group membership should be held constant. Tight circles of no more than 10 and no less than 7 are recommended for the youngest participants (e.g., 4- to 6-year-olds) with groups getting larger and circles more varied as the members get older. When one segment of a larger group is involved in Magic Circle, someone else must keep the others constructively occupied. Twenty-five minutes is the recommended time limit.

Leaders will introduce tasks from the lesson guides and will model active listening as well as other positive behaviors. Leadership is gradually to be shared with trainees so that they can practice the same positive behavior patterns. As a result of participation in Magic Circle, trainees should learn to become better listeners, group cohesiveness should be strengthened, and trainees should be more involved with their leaders (e.g., students with teachers).

▪ *Evaluation of Effects.* HDP trainees are taught to use an adaptation of the Fels Rating Scale to acquire a Developmental Profile for each person in their Magic Circle. Consisting of scales for awareness, mastery, and social interaction, the Fels scale may be used to report the progress of individual participants because the trait descriptions and descriptive cues apply to HDP training. To our knowledge, summaries of such ratings have not been published, however.

Cantor and Helfat (1976) offer an assessment of HDP that is apparently independent of the influence of the originators. Selecting HDP as the vehicle for their school-based primary prevention program, they learned that adaptations such as experiential exercise for nonverbal children and slowing down of the planned curriculum for verbal youngsters were necessary. They also found that many teachers had to redefine their roles to add the necessary affective dimensions to their repertoire. Yet, it was generally agreed that training of the classroom teacher is basic to HDP's success.

Cantor and Helfat (1976) report individual gains for isolated and new students, improved attendance, greater participation in other areas of learning, and increases in verbal solutions in place of acting out behaviors. Teachers have also reported improved morale. One such empirical study led to the conclusion that kindergarten children exposed to HDP demonstrated increased reading readiness scores more significantly than those exposed to story telling (Brett, 1973).

Schools Without Failure—Reality Therapy

▪ *Goals.* William Glasser, who runs the Institute for Reality Therapy in Los Angeles, California, suggested the ideas for this program in his book, *Schools Without Failure* (1969). Glasser believes that our single greatest need is for *identity*, which he defines as a personal realization that we are each someone who is distinguished from others, both important and worthwhile. Love and self-worth are viewed as pathways to identity, and home and school are the most important places for children to achieve identity. Glasser thinks that schools can have a direct effect on helping to fulfill the need for self-worth and can have an indirect effect on the need for love because persons who are made to feel worthwhile can tolerate some of the negative rejection associated with trying to love. According to Glasser (1969), self-worth is derived through knowledge and thinking and love is derived from learning to be responsible for each other, to care for each other, and to help each other (for their sake and one's own sake). More recently, Glasser supplemented these thoughts by stating that schools should ensure that their students have a supportive environment in which they have an opportunity to succeed and help others to succeed. He went on to state that when schools promote relevance and involvement, discipline is reduced, and that failure is closely related to disciplinary problems (Evans, 1982).

- *Tactics.* Glasser (1969) seems to espouse a general plan for educational reform, some part of which is pertinent to primary prevention strategies. The tactic that Glasser promotes having primary prevention potential is the classroom meeting. Three kinds of classroom meetings are identified, each of which has a different purpose and some different techniques, and all of which can be conducted according to a general set of tactics. The three types of classroom meetings identified by Glasser are social problem–solving meetings where the goal is to solve individual and social problems of the class and school, open-ended meetings where the goal is to discuss intellectually important subjects, and educational-diagnostic meetings in which the goals reflect concern over how well students understand the curriculum.

Leaders of social problem–solving meetings attempt to discover factual answers while those leading open-ended meetings do not. Educational-diagnostic meetings are sometimes best led by someone other than the regular classroom teacher, such as another teacher or a counselor, in order to increase the probability of evaluating the effectiveness of classroom teaching procedures objectively. On the other hand, there are several Glasser-recommended tactics that are common across all types of classroom meetings. They are: sitting in a tight circle with the leader moving elsewhere every meeting; exposing problems for open, honest discussion; encouraging identification of personal values that are associated with the topic; avoiding solutions that involve punishment of fault finding; and moving from open-ended questions to factual material. Specific suggestions offered in conjunction with social problem–solving meetings are supposed to encourage joint identification of alternative solutions and to direct discussions toward problem resolution. Glasser thinks that if students increase their decision making competence through involvement in a relevant process such as those class meetings, then self-confidence (self-worth) will result from successes.

■ *Evaluation of Effects.* No formal experimental research program has been conducted to evaluate the classroom meeting technique. However, Glasser states that data collected on school discipline shows that discipline problems drop between 80 and 90% in schools that use his programs (Evans, 1982).

Children: The Challenge Program

■ *Goals.* Rudolph Dreikurs has developed what is essentially a parenting program based on the theoretical principles of Alfred Adler. As a primary prevention program for students, the focus could be on both preparation for parenting and on application of Dreikurs's ideas about achieving a sense of belonging in one's social group. Believing that changing social conditions have led to circumstances in which children were increasingly demanding more freedom, decision making power, and responsibility, Dreikurs was determined to help parents understand the purpose of children's behavior and learn techniques for encouraging responsible participation in the family group. According to Adler's theory, behavior is purposeful and goal-directed, and the primary goal is to achieve a sense of belonging in one's social group (Dreikurs & Stolz, 1964).

■ *Tactics.* Dreikurs and Stolz (1964) consider the key element of Dreikurs's training program to be encouragement—giving it to trainees and teaching them to give it to others. Without encouragement, discouragement sets in. With encouragement come self-respect and a sense of accomplishment. In order to be good encouragers, people must first understand that security depends upon a feeling of belonging within the group, that skilled observers can misinterpret what they see and draw incorrect conclusions, that people are influenced by their environment (e.g., biological makeup, bodily functions, family atmosphere, and family constellation), and that people have different ways of responding to situations, relationships, and other people.

Recognition of mistaken goals children have is believed to be a source of understanding and of planning appropriate responses. Dreikurs cites the desire for undue attention, the struggle for power, retaliation and revenge, and the purposeful demonstration of one's own inadequacy as examples of mistaken goals that need to be changed.

A key principle of the Dreikurs idea is that the responsibility for change rests with the child. To pursue this end, Dreikurs advocates teaching children to understand the natural and logical consequences of their acts, being firm without being dominating, showing respect, eliminating criticism, and being consistent.

The Family Council technique has been proposed as a vehicle for simulating a democratic process wherein the desired skills can be developed through participation. Family Council technique operates according to specific rules such as every member present has equal voting power, absent members have no voting power, all must abide by group decisions, leader-

ship responsibilities are shared alternatingly, all members can present problems and solutions, and natural and logical consequences of alternatives must be considered.

■ *Evaluation of Effects.* Research on Dreikurs's ideas has focused on effects of parenting groups for parents, and Davis (1977) laments that much of it is in the form of self-reports acquired at the end of training. Three studies do have experimental characteristics, however. Agati and Iovino (1974), Frazier and Mattes (1975), and Hillman and Perry (1975) reported effects favoring the Dreikurs approach on variables such as more positive attitudes toward adult–child behavior, increased improvement in adjustment of subjects' children as perceived by parents, less restrictive attitudes toward children, and greater use of logical consequences thinking and logical consequences discipline techniques in line with the Dreikurs model. Although these outcomes are sparse and the subjects studied were parents, it may be reasonable cautiously to assume that similar effects could be achieved with school-aged subjects.

GUIDANCE CURRICULA

The programs cited above were developed with classroom settings in mind and with classroom teachers perceived as the persons who will deliver primary prevention services to students. That is not to say that adaptations could not be made in order to substitute counselors for teachers or that counselors could not serve as consultants to teachers. Another delivery approach that has received some support is to establish a place for guidance in the curriculum (cf. Carroll, 1973; Cottingham, 1973; Martin, 1983). In this configuration, counselors could be responsible for the direct delivery of primary prevention programs to students or for systematically consulting with teachers who are directly delivering components of the guidance curriculum. Martin (1983) suggests that advantages that may accrue for guidance are dissipation of alienation from teachers, greater counselor accountability, and increased likelihood of responding to the demands created by high school student-to-counselor ratios. The Salem Guidance Curriculum and the Developing Understanding of Self and Others program (Dinkmeyer, 1973) represent published applications of the guidance curriculum idea.

The Salem Guidance Curriculum

■ *Goals.* The Salem, Oregon school district and the Marion County Community Mental Health Program cooperatively developed a guidance curriculum that was then mandated as a curriculum area for all elementary students by the school board (Morgan, 1984; Morgan & Jackson, 1980). A minimum of 50 minutes per week was to be devoted to the curriculum. The general goal upon which the curriculum was based was to reduce mental health problems and emotional disturbances by systematically emphasizing efforts to assist children with goal development and future planning, learning to trust in themselves and others, and acquiring confidence and security through acquisition of feelings of competence and self-esteem.

Eight clusters of general goals were identified, those being: (a) awareness of feelings, (b) valuing, (c) decision making, (d) behavior, (e) listening, (f) cooperation and conflict resolution, (g) occupational/educational decision making, and (h) classroom management. Sets of related objectives were derived from each goal, leading to a system of objectives for grade levels that built upon those designed for earlier grade levels.

■ *Tactics.* Teaching units and instructional guides were established from the goals and objectives according to the following premises: guidance is a curriculum program; the scope and sequence of the guidance curriculum can be described; students are entitled to guidance and affective instruction, and said instruction is essential for efficient learning; and teachers are competent to deliver these services if given training and support. Content for the instruction guides has been taken from a variety of sources and blended into a hybrid program known as the Salem Guidance Curriculum. Several commercial resources used in the curriculum are listed in Morgan's (1984) article. They include Values Clarification, self-concept enhancing, and affective development materials.

■ *Evaluation of Effects.* All known evaluation efforts have been conducted internally. Morgan (1984) briefly describes a 30-item self-report questionnaire that has been used to assess student skill level growth in each of the eight major goal categories. Data indicating that average student scores are modestly increasing as they advance across grade levels has been interpreted as evidence of increases in affective skill level that may be attributed to the program. In addition, teachers responded positively to the program and, in some cases, offered anecdotal evidence of student skill acquisition and attitudinal change as well as an improved classroom environment.

Developing Understanding of Self and Others
■ *Goals.* Developing Understanding of Self and Others (DUSO) is the name of a structured format for counseling primary-aged students. The DUSO kits contain materials such as manuals, cassettes, puppets, and suggested activities. Having determined that effective counseling can be conducted at the primary level in a group context (Dinkmeyer & Caldwell, 1970), Dinkmeyer and colleagues developed the DUSO program in order to provide counselors and teachers with the necessary resources. The purposes of the DUSO program are to stimulate affective and social development through systematic exploration of individual's feelings, values, and attitudes. DUSO offers guided activities that are supposed to encourage children to experience success while also developing feelings of adequacy (Dinkmeyer, 1973).

■ *Tactics.* Although DUSO kits are viewed as important resources for achieving the goals cited above, counselors and teachers who implement the suggested activities are the key to success for the program. Realizing this, Dinkmeyer (1973) devotes space to motivating teachers and counselors to have appropriate attitudes and to create an atmosphere that encourages all children to participate and express themselves. Recommended leader tactics include valuing children as they are, showing faith in the children in order to enhance self-confidence, rewarding effort and accomplishment, integrating the group, pacing skill development in order to permit success, and focusing on strengths and assets (Dinkmeyer & Carlson, 1973; Dinkmeyer & Dreikurs, 1979).

Designed for implementation without special training by either counselors or teachers, there are two DUSO kits. DUSO D-1 is for grades 1 to 3 and DUSO D-2 is designed primarily for upper elementary level grades. Structured so that it can be implemented for a full school year on a daily basis, the DUSO program and materials are housed in a metal carrying case. All units are organized around eight major themes: (a) Toward Self-Identity: Developing

Self-Awareness and a Positive Self-Concept; (b) Toward Friendship: Understanding Peers; (c) Toward Responsible Interdependence: Understanding Growth from Self-Centeredness to Social Interest; (d) Toward Self-Reliance: Understanding Personal Responsibility; (e) Toward Resourcefulness and Purposefulness: Understanding Personal Motivation; (f) Toward Competence: Understanding Accomplishment; (g) Toward Emotional Stability: Understanding Stress; and (h) Toward Responsible Choice Making: Understanding Values. To be effective, program leaders must create an environment that encourages participation and open discussion within a group setting in response to the structure of the DUSO activities and materials.

■ *Evaluation of Effects.* Dinkmeyer (1973) reports that the DUSO program was field-tested during development with over 5,100 students in 175 classrooms across 36 states, including various economic, racial, and ethnic groups. Independent evaluations of DUSO have been reported by Salend (1983), who found simulations and discussions of hypothetical examples of handicapped persons to be successful in sensitizing nonhandicapped students and Larabee (1983), who supported using simulations with adolescents to foster understanding of aging.

CASE STUDIES

A Brief Peer Tutor Training Program

Scheduling the program and selecting participants. Students in grades 7 through 12 were encouraged to enlist for training as cross-aged tutors.[1] Volunteers were solicited and teachers were canvassed for referral suggestions. Adequate knowledge of subject matter served as an important selection criterion beyond an expressed interest to serve as a tutor. Nineteen volunteers ranging from grades 7 through 10 were assigned to four training groups during their study halls. Three 45-minute training sessions were conducted. Tutees were to be solicited by referrals from elementary school teachers.

First Session. All participants were asked to introduce themselves and share their reasons for volunteering. The leader then offered a brief lecture on the goals of the training and tutoring programs and the meaning and importance of confidentiality. A handout entitled "Study Skills Problems—Who Should Help?" was introduced as an aid for clarifying problems that are appropriately suited to tutorial intervention and used to generate group discussion. In conjunction with the handout, group members were asked to identify the appropriate source of help from among tutors, teachers, and counselors. Students with previous tutorial experience were able to enhance the discussion by sharing their insights. Where a tenth grader with tutorial experience was mixed with inexperienced seventh graders, the leader sensed that the younger participants seemed intimidated. To alleviate this condition without inappropriately modifying helpful sharing behavior by the tenth grader, the leader encouraged the seventh graders to offer comments and directed questions to them she was certain they could answer.

---

1. This program was designed and implemented by Elizabeth Stano.

Second Session. This session opened with a review of the first session and an introduction to the content and purpose of the second session. The leader then asked the trainees cooperatively to list qualities found in a good helper/tutor. A handout entitled "Being a Good Helper" was distributed and used as a stimulus for identifying important helping skills (e.g., "Quality: A good helper shows he/she cares. Skill: A good helper listens like [sic] a friend would listen.").

The leader then demonstrated appropriate listening, reflecting, summarizing, open-ended questioning, and complimenting skills to the trainees. They were then subdivided into dyads in which they took turns practicing all the demonstrated skills in a simulated manner while their partners played the roles of tutees. Too little practice time was available in one session, leading the trainer to conclude that at least one additional session should follow this one in order to continue with the skills training more proficiently.

Third Session. A leader-initiated review of the earlier sessions was followed by a lecture on such topics as motivation, self-monitoring, study methods, test taking, and time management. A two-page handout outlining major points in the lecture was distributed concurrently. The lecture was followed by presentation of a outline called "A Personal Skills Plan" on which the trainees were encouraged to set goals for their own self-monitoring; list study methods they use well, ones they need practice with, and ones they would like to learn; list test taking skills they possess, ones they need practice with, and ones they would like to learn; and create a 24-hour personal time schedule.

Again, the leader thought there was not enough time to cover the desired topics in her lesson plan. In addition, she felt that the lecture may have been perceived as dull. When examples of related research were cited and personal examples added discussion to the lecture atmosphere, the session was more successful.

Evaluation. Insights acquired from anecdotal observations by the group leader and cited above indicate that more time was probably needed to accomplish the goals established for this training program. In addition, activities that led to active trainee involvement and interaction seemed superior to activities, such as lectures, that did not. A more formal follow-up evaluation via an objectively scored survey format supported the leader's conclusions and provided evidence that, even with these shortcomings, the trainees thought the training was worthwhile and would help them to become better tutors.

A Program Designed to Enhance the Self-Concepts of Sixth-Grade Girls

Scheduling the program and selecting participants. A sixth-grade teacher recommended several girls for participation in a self-concept enhancement group.[2] Therefore, this particular group may have been involved in a *secondary* prevention program. However, we have included this program among our case studies because it has potential for primary as well as secondary prevention programming.

All candidates were screened by the trainer via a personal interview in order to explain the purpose of the program and assess their readiness. In order to help

2. This program was designed and implemented by Diana M. Durbin. A detailed report was published in the April, 1982 issue of *Elementary School Guidance and Counseling*. (Durbin, 1982).

participants to achieve improved levels of self-concept and self understanding, the program was designed so that each of Keat's (1979) HELPING modes (Health, Emotions, Learning, Personal Relations, Imagery, Need to Know, and Guidance) was introduced. During each session, one of the modes was introduced. The participants then stated their own concerns relative to that mode, developed their own treatment plan for the intervening week, and also determined a reward system for achieved treatment goals.

When the program was under way, each session began with members sharing with the group their progress on their individual plans. The leader then directed the group through an activity that introduced the next mode, encouraged discussion, and helped the participants to develop individual plans. In all, there were nine weekly 35-minute sessions. Four girls attended.

First Session. The leader reviewed the purpose of the groups and stated three rules for the members to follow: (a) One person talks at a time, (b) everything stated in the group stays within the group, and (c) feelings and thoughts should be expressed honestly. After a get-acquainted activity known as "clues," where participants try to identify each other from self-descriptive statements written and pooled, the leader spoke about individual similarities and differences and about how the HELPING model focused their attention on different important areas of their lives.

Second Session. The first mode was introduced, Health. Each participant was asked to look into the Magic Box (Canfield & Wells, 1976) and describe what she saw. Since each girl saw her own face, the leader was able to direct them to discussing individual physical differences. The leader then led a short discussion on the important relationships among diet, balanced meals, exercise, and health. She then presented a chart on which each member could keep a daily log of their diet, physical activities, and feelings about their appearance during the intervening week.

Third Session. In order to be able to discuss individual contracting, goal setting, and reward menus, the leader selected Guidance as the second mode, even though it was the last letter of the HELPING acronym. After opening the session with each member sharing the data on their Health logs, the leader was able to point out that engaging in physical activities or maintaining good dietary habits is sometimes challenging, and people need encouragement. This allowed her to introduce the concept of rewarding appropriate goal-directed behaviors and suggest some examples. A reward survey (Keat, 1979) was then used to help the members generate ideas for their own reward menus.

Noting that rewards may be used to diminish undesired behaviors and enhance desired ones, the leader introduced contracting as a means of clarifying goals, monitoring behaviors, and determining what rewards were in order. Each member was then given a multimodal contract form for their use during the remainder of the program. In addition to descriptive information (e.g., name and date), each contract contained seven rows (one for each of the HELPING modes) and four columns. The columns were entitled Concerns, Treatment, Progress, and Reward. Each represented an important stimulus category for the girls when planning, recording, and monitoring their weekly individualized self-improvement programs.

Fourth Session. After reviewing information about contracting, the leader introduced Learning as the next mode of interest by suggesting that the contracting method could be used to enhance their study habits. Keat and Guerney's (1980) restructuring-the-environment technique was introduced in order to offer ideas for acquiring improved study habits. The session closed with each member individually filling in the Health, Guidance, and Learning areas of their logs.

Fifth Session.   Progress on the logs was discussed as was the appropriateness of the rewards selected by the girls. To introduce the Emotions mode, the leader asked the group to experience as many emotions as they could and label them. Attention was then focused on appropriate ways to cope with anger. Ideas were generated by using Keat's (1980a) *Madness Management* booklet. Each member was then asked to read Wilt's (1979) *Handling Your Ups and Downs* during the intervening week because there had not been enough time to do so during the meeting.

Sixth Session.   To focus attention on the importance of healthy Personal Relations, an audiotape entitled *Friendship Training* (Keat, 1980b) was played. Following a leader-directed discussion of the information presented on the tape, instruction about the mechanics and usefulness of behavioral rehearsal was provided. Again, due to time constraints, all members of the group were asked to complete a related reading assignment during the intervening week, Wilt's (1978) *A Kid's Guide to Making Friends.*

Seventh Session.   Following individual reports of their progress on contracts, the group briefly discussed reactions to Wilt's (1978) ideas. The Need to Know mode was then introduced by the leader's outlining and explaining a five-step paradigm for making decisions: (a) State the problem; (b) brainstorm all possible alternatives; (c) examine advantages and disadvantages associated with each alternative; (d) rank-order the alternatives; (e) make a tentative choice from among the alternatives. The leader then attempted to assist the group in taking an inventory of areas about which they appeared to need further knowledge (e.g., sex, career planning).

Eighth Session.   The Imagery mode was introduced by a story from Simon's (1973) *I Am Lovable and Capable* (IALAC). This was followed by group brainstorming of ways to support and build up others' IALAC thoughts. Keat's (1979) idea of using hero imagery when confronted with a difficult task or assignment was introduced, and the leader provided an example.

Ninth Session.   The leader directed each individual through a review of the HELP-ING modes and collected evaluation data.

Evaluation.   All participants recorded an increase in positive responses and a decrease in negative responses from pre- to posttraining on a modified version of the Piers–Harris (1969) Self-Concept Scale. It should be noted that these were descriptive differences not subjected to a test of statistical significance and that there was no control group against which to compare the effects. All members expressed positive feelings about the group on an evaluation form. Improved academic achievement occurred for each girl in all areas except language arts.

Anecdotal comments by the leader indicate that she thought the program could be improved in several ways. They were: lengthening the meeting time to at least 45 minutes, scheduling more than one session for each mode—lengthening the program, and including responsibility training in order to promote the establishment of realistic goals.

An Affective Education Program for Second-Graders.

Scheduling the program and selecting participants.   Twenty-two second-grade children met weekly with the leader for 30 minutes over a period of 10 weeks.[3] They were all below average, academically. Thus, this program may also be

---

3. This program was designed and implemented by Jan L. Miller.

classified as one with secondary prevention goals. However, as was the case with the previous case study, this program is also viewed as having merit for primary prevention programming.

In the program, the six most often explored areas of self-concept cited in Dinkmeyer's (1970) *Developing Understanding of Self and Others* were used as the foci for individual sessions. Dinkmeyer's (1970) most often explored areas are: Uniqueness, Similarities, Likes and Dislikes, Feelings, Strengths, and Career Awareness. In each session, the leader attempted to facilitate related discussions and distributed a handout or assigned an art activity, allowing time to complete them at the end of the session. The children's work was then placed in individual cumulative folders until the program was completed.

First Session. After making introductory comments, the leader asked the students as a group, "What is so special about you?", and generated discussion about features that make people special. The group members were then asked to draw pictures or write words indicating ways in which they were unique. The closing exercise contained incomplete sentences with two options that were designated in words and pictures (e.g., "I am a" was followed by a drawing of a boy's and a girl's face with the words "boy" and "girl" beneath the appropriate drawings). The students were requested to create a story from the incomplete sentences. All seemed responsive to the activities.

Second Session. Each student was asked to talk about those self-characteristics that make them similar and dissimilar to others. Following this, each child drew a self-portrait while looking into a mirror and placed their thumbprint (in ink) below the portrait. Then, they tried to identify each other from the self-portraits. The exercise seemed popular, and the self-portraits were deemed to be quite accurate.

Third Session. Eight questions were presented to the children and, in response to each, they were asked to draw a picture with crayons (e.g., "What is your favorite food?", "What scares you?", "Whom do you like to be with the most?"). With regard to each question, the students were asked to locate others in the group who had the same answers. The leader then summarized some of the ways in which the group members were alike and different.

Fourth Session. Initially, the group members viewed a filmstrip entitled *Circle of Feelings* from the first part of a series entitled *Focus on Self-Development* (Science Research Associates, 1970) and discussed how they felt inside when being happy, sad, mad, and scared. This was followed by a drawing exercise in which the children were asked to place expressions on four blank oval faces below which were the words "happy," "sad," "scared," and "angry." Although the children could readily name all the feelings demonstrated in the filmstrip, the discussion apparently became too abstract. The leader thought the discussion could have been improved by using aids such as puppetry or role-played simulations.

Fifth Session. The session opened with a discussion about how feelings can be displayed in facial expressions. Cards with single words identifying feelings were placed face down on a table in front of the children and they were each asked to pick one and express the corresponding feeling with a facial expression while not telling the group what it was. The other children then attempted to guess what feeling was being expressed. Next, a worksheet containing incomplete sentences was distributed. Each sentence was to be completed with one of four feeling words: "happy," "sad," "mad," or "scared." The children were also encouraged to draw a picture on the reverse side, telling about a time when they felt important or proud. The students enjoyed playing fish with the feeling cards and guessing the feeling depicted in the facial expressions of their classmates.

Sixth Session. A story entitled "Warm Fuzzies" (Freed, 1971) was read to the group by the leader. Upon being told what warm fuzzies and cold pricklies represent, the group discussed reasons why people give or receive either warm fuzzies or cold pricklies. Each child was then asked to give a warm fuzzy response to one of the other group members. Cotton balls representing warm fuzzies were distributed to each student, and they were asked to give them to someone during the intervening week. The children became very involved in this program and were quite pleased about being able to give and receive warm fuzzies. Their teacher mentioned having overheard some of the children expressing positive comments about others.

Seventh Session. To open the session, the leader asked the children to think of words their teacher used in order to compliment them, printing those words on the blackboard. Each student was then asked to act out something they do well while the others tried to guess what it was. Finally, the group was asked to draw a picture about something they do well in crayon on art paper. The students were excited about citing things they do well and, as an afterthought, the leader felt those items should have been printed on the blackboard too.

Eight Session. All seats were arranged in a circle with one chair in the center. Selected children were asked to sit in the center while the others sat in the surrounding circle taking turns at stating complimentary things about the child in the center chair. The leader then initiated a discussion on how it feels to hear others say complimentary things. The children were pleased and enjoyed receiving compliments. There was considerable similarity in compliments across the group, and the children had to be encouraged to try to think of original things to say. Next time, the leader would prefer to make two smaller groups and assist the children more actively in their expression of compliments.

Ninth Session. In a group exercise, all students were asked to name jobs that begin with letters of the alphabet suggested by the leader. They were then asked to think about a job they would like to perform when they got older. The leader then spoke to them about ways to plan for achieving their job-related goals and asked them to draw a crayon picture of someone they would like to be. While, at first, the children seemed to consider future jobs thoughtfully, eventually they seemed to make choices that were similar to what their parents were doing.

Tenth Session. Each child was given a packet of seven, three-by-five cards. There was a letter on one side, and the reverse side was blank. The letter across the seven cards in each packet spelled out "I'm great." The children were directed to place the seven cards with the blank side facing upward. They were then asked to print answers to seven leader-directed questions on the blank side of their cards (e.g., "Name something that is fun for you," "Name something that you do well."). Answers were shared with classmates. The children were told to turn the cards over and try to unscramble the seven letters. The session and program concluded with a discussion on whether or not the statement "I'm great" is true. Each child seemed to feel good about him-/herself at the close of this session.

Evaluation. Observational data reported by the leader throughout the program painted a picture of receptive, active, and appreciative children participating in the program.

SUMMARY

Psychological education programs vary in content and design, yet seem to have common theoretical underpinnings. These programs appear to lead to a better understanding of human behavior and cognitive development, enhance affective development, and provide a means for balancing the cognitive instructional environment of the schools with affective programming. Founded on the principles of humanistic and developmental psychology, psychological education programming reflects efforts of various professionals to transfer their knowledge about human behavior into programs that will enhance human development and mental health. These programs have been given descriptive names such as Causal Understanding Training, Deliberate Psychological Education, Moral Education, Values Clarification, the Human Development Program, Reality Therapy, Children: The Challenge Program, the Salem Guidance Curriculum, and Developing an Understanding of Self and Others. Each has its supporters and disciples. All have their merits but require further development and evaluation.

Enough has been accomplished in each of these programs for us to advocate that practitioners find out more about them and assess suitability for local programming. Three case studies were offered as examples of where professionals applied some of the ideas presented in this chapter and reported on the perceived effects. One case study involved the preparation of junior high school students for cross-aged tutoring experiences. A second case study was designed to enhance the self-concept. Presented to sixth-grade girls, the self-concept enhancement program contained tactics that may be attributed to several of the programs presented in this chapter. The third case study described an affective education program for second-grade children that was derived from Dinkmeyer's work. It offered useful suggestions for helping young children to find meaning in the program.

Like the formal programs described in this chapter, the case study efforts represent first-generation efforts by the practitioners reporting about them. The practitioners shared information about efforts that needed improvement and about those that worked well. Before conducting similar efforts in the future, they will make revisions. Readers are encouraged to extract ideas, develop and implement programmatic efforts, assess efforts objectively, and make improvements willingly while continuing to design and implement preventive programs.

PUBLISHED RESOURCES

Aubrey, R. (1981). *A bibliography on programs in deliberate psychological education.* Nashville: Vanderbilt University.

Dinkmeyer, D., & Dinkmeyer, D., Jr. (1982). *Developing understanding of self and others.* (Rev. ed.). Circle Pines, MN: American Guidance Services.

Dreikurs, R., Grunwald, B. B., & Pepper, F. C. (1971). *Maintaining sanity in the classroom.* New York: Harper & Row.

Dupont, H., Gardner, O., & Brody, D. (1974). *Toward affective development.* Circle Pines, MN: American Guidance Services.

Hennesy, T. (1979). The counselor applies the Kohlberg moral development model. In T. Hennesy (Ed.), *Value/moral education: Schools and teachers* (pp. 145–165). New York: Paulist Press.

McElmurry, M. A., & Tom, D. N. (1981). *Feelings: Understanding our feelings of sadness, happiness, love, and loneliness.* Carthage, IL: Good Apple.

Rubin, A. (1980). *Children's friendships.* Cambridge, MA: Harvard University Press.

Schaefer, C. E., & Millman, H. L. (1981). *How to help children with common problems.* New York: Litton.

Wilt, J. (1978). *Making up your own mind.* Waco, TX: Word.

REFERENCES

Agati, G. J., & Iovino, J. W. (1974). Implementation of a parent counseling program. *School Counselor, 22,* 126–129.

Authier, J., Gustafson, L., Guerney, B., & Kasdorf, J. (1975). The psychological practitioner as teacher: A theoretical historical and practical review. *Counseling Psychologist, 5* (2), 31–50.

Berkowitz, M., & Gibbs, J. (1983). Measuring the developmental features of moral discussion. *Merrill–Palmer Quarterly, 24,* 399–410.

Bernier, J. E., & Rustad, K. (1977). Psychology of counseling curriculum: A follow-up study. *Counseling Psychologist, 6* (4), 18–22.

Bessell, H. (1969–1972). *Human development program: Activity guides—Levels BI, II, III, IV.* El Cajon, CA: Human Development Training Institute.

Bessell, H. (1970). *Methods in human development: Theory manual.* El Cajon, CA: Human Development Training Institute.

Bessell, H., & Palomares, U. (1971). *Human development program for institutionalized teenagers.* El Cajon, CA: Human Development Training Institute.

Brett, A. (1973). The influence of affective education on the cognitive performance of children (Doctoral dissertation, University of Miami). *Dissertation Abstracts International, 34,* 2454A

Canfield, J., & Wells, H. C. (1976). *One hundred ways to enhance self-esteem in the classroom.* Englewood Cliffs, NJ: Prentice–Hall.

Cantor, C. L., & Helfat, L. (1976). Training for affective education: A model for change in the schools. *Journal of Clinical Child Psychology,* 5–8.

Carroll, M. R. (1973). The regeneration of guidance. *School Counselor, 20,* 355–360.

Cognetta, P. (1977). Deliberate psychological education: A high school cross-age teaching model. *Counseling Psychologist, 6* (4), 23–25.

Colangelo, N. (1982). Characteristics of moral problems as formulated by gifted adolescents. *Journal of Moral Education, 11,* 219–232.

Colangelo, N., & Dettman, D. F. (1985). Characteristics of moral problems and solutions formed by students in grades 3 to 8. *Elementary School Guidance & Counseling, 19,* 260–271.

Cottingham, H. F. (1973). Psychological education, the guidance function, and the school counselor. *School Counselor, 20,* 40–45.

Davis, A. (1977). *Parenting programs and a literature review of selected studies.* Harrisburg, PA: Governor's Council on Drug and Alcohol Abuse.

Dinkmeyer, D. (1970). *Developing understanding of self and others.* Circle Pines, MN: American Guidance Services.

Dinkmeyer, D. (1973). *Developing understanding of self and others (DUSO D-2) manual.* Circle Pines, MN: American Guidance Services.

Dinkmeyer, D., & Caldwell, E. (1970). *Developmental counseling and guidance: A comprehensive school approach.* New York: McGraw–Hill.

Dinkmeyer, D., & Carlson, J. (1973). *Consulting: Facilitating human potential and change process.* Columbus, OH: Charles E. Merrill.

Dinkmeyer, D., & Dreikurs, R. (1979). *Encouraging children to learn: The encouragement process.* Englewood Cliffs, NJ: Prentice–Hall.

Dreikurs, R., & Stolz, V. (1964). *Children: The challenge.* New York: Hawthorn Books.

Durbin, D. M. (1982). Multimodal group sessions to enhance self-concept. *Elementary School Guidance & Counseling, 16,* 288–295.

Erickson, V. L. (1977). Deliberate psychological education for women: A curriculum follow-up study. *Counseling Psychologist, 6* (4), 25–29.

Evans, D. B. (1982). What are you doing? [An interview with William Glasser]. *Personnel and Guidance Journal, 60,* 460–465.

Frazier, F., & Mattes, W. A. (1975). Parent education: A comparison of Adlerian and behavioral approaches. *Elementary School Guidance & Counseling, 10,* 31–38.

Freed, A. M. (1971). *T. A. for kids.* Sacramento, CA: Alvyn–Freed.

Glaser, B., & Kirschenbaum, H. (1980). Using values clarification in counseling settings. *Personnel and Guidance Journal, 58,* 569–575.

Glasser, W. (1969). *Schools without failure.* New York: Harper & Row.

Harmin, M., Kirschenbaum, H., & Simon, S. B. (1973) *Clarifying values through subject matter.* Minneapolis: Winston.

Hillman, B. W., & Perry, T. (1975). The parent–teacher education center: Evaluation of a program for improving relations. *Journal of Family Counseling, 3* (1), 11–16.

Howe, L., & Howe, M. M. (1975). *Personalizing education: Values clarification and beyond.* New York: Hart.

Ivey, A. E., & Alschuler, A. A. (1973). An introduction to the field. *Personnel and Guidance Journal, 51,* 591–597.

Keat, D. B. (1979). *Multimodal therapy with children.* New York: Pergamon.

Keat, D. B. (1980a). *Madness management.* Harrisburg, PA: Professional Associates.

Keat, D. B. (1980b). *Friendship training* [audiotape]. Harrisburg, PA: Professional Associates.

Keat, D. B., & Guerney, L. (1980). *HELPING your child.* Falls Church, VA: AACD Press.

Kirschenbaum, H. (1977). *Advanced value clarification.* La Jolla, CA: University Associates.

Kirschenbaum, H., & Glaser, B. (1978). *The skills for living curriculum.* Findley, OH: Quest.

Kohlberg, L. (1975). Counseling and counselor education: A developmental approach. *Counselor Education and Supervision, 14,* 250–256.

Kohlberg, L., Colby, A., Gibbs, J., & Speicher-Dubin, B. (1978). *Standard form scoring manual.* Cambridge, MA: Center for Moral Education, Harvard University.

Kohlberg, L., & Turiel, E. (1971). Moral development and moral education. In G. S. Lesser (Ed.), *Psychology and educational practice* (pp. 410–465). Glenview, IL: Scott, Foreman.

Kohlberg, L., & Wasserman, E. R. (1980). The cognitive-developmental approach and the practicing counselor: An opportunity for counselors to rethink their roles. *Personnel and Guidance Journal, 58,* 559–567.

Kurtrines, W., & Grief, E. (1979). The development of moral thought: Review and evaluation of Kohlberg's approach. *Psychological Bulletin, 81,* 453–470.

Lapsley, D. K., & Quintana, S. M. (1985). Recent approaches to the moral and social education of children. *Elementary School Guidance & Counseling, 19,* 246–259.

Larabee, M. V. (1983). Using simulations to foster understanding of aging. *School Counselor, 30,* 261–268.

Levitt, E. E. (1955). Effect of "causal" teacher training programs on authoritarianism and responsibility in grade school children. *Psychological Reports, 1,* 449–458.

Lockwood, A. L. (1978). The effects of values clarification and moral development curricula on school-age subjects: A critical review of recent research. *Review of Educational Research, 48,* 325–364.

Lockwood, A. L. (1980). Notes on research associated with values clarification and value therapy. *Personnel and Guidance Journal, 58,* 606–608.

Martin, J. (1983). Curriculum development in school counseling. *Personnel and Guidance Journal, 61,* 406–409.

Morgan, C. (1984). A curricular approach to primary prevention. *Personnel and Guidance Journal, 62,* 467–469.

Morgan, C., & Jackson, W. (1980). Guidance as a curriculum. *Elementary School Guidance and Counseling, 15,* 99–103.

Morrison, K., & Havens, R. I. (1976). *Values clarification in counseling.* Madison, WI: Educational Media.

Mosher, R. L., & Sprinthall, N. A. (1970). Psychological education in secondary schools. *American Psychologist, 25* (10), 911–924.

Mosher, R. L., & Sprinthall, N. A. (1971). Deliberate psychological education. *Counseling Psychologist, 2* (4), 3–82.

Muus, R. E. (1960a). The effects of a one- and two-year causal learning program. *Journal of Personality, 28,* 479–491.

Muus, R. E. (1960b). The relationship between "causal" orientation, anxiety, and insecurity in elementary school children. *Journal of Educational Psychology, 51,* 122–129.

Muus, R. E. (1960c). A comparison of high causality and low causality oriented sixth grade children in respect to a perceptual intolerance of ambiguity test. *Child Development, 31,* 521–536.

Muus, R. E. (1961). The transfer effect on learning programs in social causality on an understanding of physical causality. *Journal of Experimental Education, 29* (3), 231–247.

Nucci, L. (1985) Future directions in research on children's moral reasoning and moral education. *Elementary School Guidance & Counseling, 19,* 272–282.

Ojemann, R. E. (1958). The human relations programs at the State University of Iowa. *Personnel and Guidance Journal, 37,* 198–206.

Ojemann, R. E., Levitt, E. E., Lyle, W. H., Jr., & Whiteside, M. F. (1955). The effects of a "causal" teacher training program and certain curriculum changes on grade school children. *Journal of Experimental Education, 24* (2), 95–114.

Ojemann, R. E., & Snider, B. C. F. (1964). The effect of a teaching program in behavioral sciences on changes in causal behavior scores. *Journal of Educational Research, 57,* 255–260.

Palomares, U. (1971). A place to come from. In J. Ballard (Ed.), *Dare to care/dare to act: Racism and education.* Washington, DC: Association for Supervision and Curriculum Development.

Palomares, U. (1972). Communication begins with attitude. In Joint Committee on Educational Goals and Evaluation (Eds.), *Education for the people.* Sacramento, CA: California State Education Department.

Palomares, U., & Rubini, T. (1973). Human development in the classroom. *Personnel and Guidance Journal, 51,* 653–659.

Piers, E., & Harris, D. B. (1969). *The Piers–Harris self-concept scale.* Nashville, TN: Counselor Recordings & Tests.

Raths, L. E., Harmin, M., & Simon, S. B. (1978). *Values and teaching* (2nd ed.). Columbus, OH: Charles Merrill.

Rest, J. R. (1979). *Developments in judging moral issues.* Minneapolis: University of Minnesota Press.

Rest, J. R. (1980). Moral judgment research and the cognitive-developmental approach to moral education. *Personnel and Guidance Journal, 58,* 602–605.

Salend, S. (1983). Using hypothetical examples to sensitize nonhandicapped students to their handicapped peers. *School Counselor, 30,* 306–310.

Simon, S. B. (1973). *I am loveable and capable.* Niles, IL: Argus Communications.

Simon, S. B. (1974). *Meeting yourself halfway.* Niles, IL: Argus Communications.

Simon, S. B., Howe, L., & Kirschenbaum, H. (1972). *Values clarification: A handbook of practices and strategies for teachers and students.* New York: Hart.

Skovholt, T. (1977). Issues in psychological education. *Personnel and Guidance Journal, 55,* 472–476.

Smith, M. B. (1977). *An introduction to value clarification.* La Jolla, CA: University Associates.

Snider, B. C. F. (1957). Relation of growth in causal orientation to insecurity in elementary school children. *Psychological Reports, 3,* 631–634.

Sprinthall, N. A. (1973). A curriculum for secondary schools: Counselors as teachers for psychological growth. *School Counselor, 20,* 361–369.

Sprinthall, N. A. (1981). A new model for research in the service of guidance and counseling. *Personnel and Guidance Journal, 59,* 487–493.

Science Research Associates. (1970). *Focus on self-development: Stage I.* Chicago, IL: Author.

Wilt, J. A. (1978). *A kid's guide to making friends.* Waco, TX: Word.

Wilt, J. (1979). *Handling your ups and downs.* Waco, TX: Word.

4

COGNITIVE-BEHAVIORAL
APPROACHES

ROLE IN PRIMARY PREVENTION

The source for cognitive-behavioral tactics in primary prevention programs has been the field of behavior therapy or behavior modification. Although the distinctions have become less clear in recent years, several characteristics are cited as sources of differences between behavior therapy and other therapeutic approaches. Prominent among those characteristics are the importance of the psychology of learning, consistent theory, and scientific research based on objective, measurable data (Eysenck, 1959; Jason & Bogat, 1983; Kazdin, 1978). Consequently, cognitive-behavioral approaches tend to include or highlight tactics derived from learning theory approaches such as counterconditioning, operant conditioning, social modeling, and cognitive restructuring.

Whereas cognitive-behavioral therapy goals focus on changing maladaptive behaviors, cognitive-behavioral approaches in primary prevention focus on preventing maladaptive responses to life's stressful situations. Cognitive-behaviorally derived primary prevention tactics take the form of coping skills training, the goal of which is to teach skills in advance of problematic situations so that recipients will be less vulnerable to psychological stress (Stone & Noce, 1980). In both cases, all behaviors are viewed as having developed according to the same principles.

When used in primary prevention programming, cognitive-behaviorally derived coping skills are presented to recipients in advance of, or in conjunction with, life circumstances that necessitate their use. In that way, the cognitive-behavioral approaches are used to promote good mental health. Persons who acquire a repertoire of cognitive-behavioral coping skills will enhance their chances for successfully coping with life's stresses—increasing their chances for good mental health. In this manner, wellness is promoted through cognitive-behavioral coping skills training.

In their general plans for stress management, Stensrud and Stensrud (1983) stated that individuals need to learn to assess stressful situations in order to choose the most appropriate coping responses for themselves, suggesting that there is a menu of choices from which individuals may choose if they have been appropriately prepared (i.e., trained). Stensrud and Stensrud (1983) suggested that there are three categories of common coping responses to stress, each linked to physiological symptoms that may occur if responses in that group of strategies are overused. The three general areas are passive–avoidant responses (overuse leading to respiratory troubles), cognitive–palliative responses (overuse leading to digestive disorders), and active responses (overuse leading to circulatory disorders). Stensrud and Stensrud (1983) concluded that it is better to use tactics that represent all three categories in response to stressful situations in order to prevent occurrence of the concomitant disorders associated with overuse of one set of responses.

Viewing coping skills training for stress reduction and better mental health as the focus of cognitive-behavioral approaches to primary prevention, this chapter has an organizational structure based on the Stensrud and Stensrud (1983) plan. Assertiveness and social problem–solving training will be presented as tactics for preventing overuse of passive–avoidant responses to stress. Cognitive restructuring and emotive imagery training will be offered as tactics for preventing overuse of cognitive–palliative responses to stress. Finally, meditation and progressive muscle relaxation training will be reviewed as tactics for preventing overreliance on active responses to stress. Together, these tactics offer a menu of cognitive-behaviorally based coping skills prevention programs.

BACKGROUND AND CURRENT STATUS

Whereas some cognitive-behaviorally oriented writers are known to advocate the importance of prevention, little has been done yet that has been reported in the professional literature. Consequently, most of the tactics reported in this chapter have been taken from programs that were used to treat maladaptive behaviors. We are assuming that the same programs will be applicable when providing cognitive-behavioral coping skills training in a primary prevention fashion.

It appears as if these cognitive-behavioral programs lend themselves to experimental research efforts and that a number of clinically oriented researchers have studied their merits empirically, offering proof of their efficacy for treating various maladaptive syndromes. What remains to be seen is whether or not the same ideas are useful from a primary prevention perspective. There seems to be great prevention potential in these cognitive-behavioral tactics. Thus, we hope to whet the appetite of practitioners and researchers alike in the following suggested primary prevention ideas.

PROGRAMS FOR PREVENTING PASSIVE–AVOIDANT RESPONSE TO STRESS

Assertiveness Training

■ *Goals.* Similarities and differences exist between the goals of assertiveness (or assertion) training programs for primary prevention purposes and those of programs established for therapy. In this presentation, the focus is on primary prevention. Viewing assertiveness as situation-specific rather than being a general way of behaving, exponents view assertive behavior as a set of skills that can be learned (Galassi & Galassi, 1977).

The general goal of assertiveness training is to help recipients to achieve direct or open, honest, and appropriate expression of their affectionate or oppositional feelings, preferences, needs, and opinions (Alberti, 1977; Galassi & Galassi, 1977). Appropriate assertive expressions neither threaten nor punish others (Galassi & Galassi, 1977; Shelton, 1977). The underlying philosophical belief on which assertiveness training is founded is that people have a right to express themselves while also being free of anxiety so long as others are not injured in the process (Alberti, 1977). More specific goals are related to times when assertiveness is necessary for survival (e.g., to prevent being taken advantage of), is desirable (e.g., to approach others), or is good for one's mental health by enhancing self-esteem (e.g., preventing depressive moods or anxiety in interpersonal situations).

Galassi and Galassi (1977) suggest that there are different categories of important assertive behaviors that can be taught in order to achieve the goals cited above. Positive assertive behaviors include giving and receiving compliments; making requests; expressing liking, love, and affection; and initiating and maintaining conversations. Self-affirming assertive behaviors include expressing one's legitimate rights, refusing requests, and maintaining conversations. On the other hand, negative assertive behaviors include expressing justified annoyance, displeasure, and justified anger.

While increased assertiveness may lead to greater self-confidence, awareness, self-respect, and respect from other persons, recipients should not consider changing others to be a goal of assertiveness training (Wilk & Coplan, 1977). Indeed, if assertiveness training is to change or influence others, the social systems in which the assertiveness trainee resides must tolerate assertiveness and reinforce assertive behaviors (Schmidt & Patterson, 1979).

■ *Tactics.* In general, assertiveness trainers employ tactics through which adaptive verbal and nonverbal response repertoires are developed. Where nonadaptive response repertoires exist, trainers attempt to decondition/extinguish them. If the emphasis is on primary prevention, programs will employ adaptive tactics. Where counterconditioning tactics are used or prevail, the program emphasis is moving toward secondary or tertiary prevention. Again, we are concerned with primary prevention programs in this presentation.

The adaptive assertiveness training literature is quite extensive, and there are variations across the spectrum. Many or most of them employ several well-known cognitive-behavioral tactics either alone or in some combination. Combinations are employed more often than individual tactics. Social modeling, covert modeling, reinforcement, behavioral rehearsal, feedback, coaching, instructions, and homework are the commonly used behavioral tactics. Individual trainers will employ other tactics such as microtraining, transactional analysis, bibliotherapy, and systematic desensitization to suit themselves because of their own background or because of the unique needs of their trainees.

Publications that may serve as the foundation for a training model are: Adler (1977), Cotler and Guerra (1976), Galassi and Galassi (1977), and Lange and Jakubowski (1976). Some of the manuals cited above were perused to yield an overview of tactics and topics.

Most assertiveness training programs begin with some sort of assertion self-assessment. Following that, recognition of the differences among assertion, nonassertiveness, and aggression seems to be an important topic. Learning how to appraise situations, evaluating one's own behavior, deciding how to behave, learning assertive skills, and implementing the new skills in everyday situations are common training topics.

Several issues seem to loom on the assertiveness training horizon as important concerns for all who would partake in such programs. First, there is the selection and training of trainers. Shelton (1977), for example, warns of abuses due to trainer naïveté because of the popularity of assertiveness training. More specifically, Ralph (1982) explains that naive trainers may express their opinions to trainees about those circumstances in which they have a right to be assertive as if the opinions were facts or truths. Schmidt and Patterson (1979) cite fitting goals and techniques to trainee needs, evolving a structure from those needs, and embedding the training program in what is acceptable to the trainees' social system as important broad issues for all trainers to consider.

■ *Evaluation of Effects.* According to Heimberg, Montgomery, Madsen, and Heimberg (1977), research had not kept pace with the growing number of assertion training programs in the mid-1970s. From the reports they surveyed, it appeared as if the selection of behavioral training tactics (e.g., modeling, instructions) for popular assertiveness training programs (i.e., primary prevention) was based on successful experiments with nonassertive college students (i.e., secondary prevention) and psychiatric patients (i.e., tertiary prevention). Methodological problems were cited as having prevented appropriate validation of group assertiveness training programs. In a review of a little later vintage, additional aspects of popular training programs that lack experimental support were identified (Brown & Brown, 1979). Those aspects were the supposed benefits of cotherapists, of group versus individual training, of assertive trainers, and of same-sex, -race, or -age trainers and trainees; the value of training trainers; and the value of homework assignments and videotaped feedback during training.

Sifting through more recent studies of the effects of assertiveness training, several reports were identified as being akin to an assessment of the effects of a primary prevention program. Studies reported by Michelson and Wood (1980), Rotheram and Armstrong (1980), and Rotheram, Armstrong and Booraem (1982) indicated that group assertiveness training for elementary and high school students could have positive effects on teacher ratings, comportment, achievement, popularity with teachers, group cohesiveness, and measured levels of assertiveness. In addition, Rotheram (1982) found that direct modeling of assertive behaviors with fourth- and fifth-graders had its advantages and disadvantages, in that assertive leaders were effective in producing assertive behaviors but nonassertive leaders were more effective in enhancing problem solving and decision making behaviors.

Social Problem–Solving Training

■ *Goals.* Since the problem solving literature is replete with caveats and debates, it is difficult to present information about problem solving training straightforwardly. Among the caveats mentioned above are Horan's (1979) observation that there is not a universally accepted definition of a problem and Heppner's (1978) caution that the means by which people solve problems are largely unknown.

Even with this lack of foundation, proponents of problem solving approaches in counseling have established purposes and procedures. Yet there is debate among the proponents as to which approach has the better foundation. D'Zurilla and Goldfried (1971) believe that problem solving may be divided into definable stages, and stepped training can be derived from those stages (i.e., general orientation, problem definition and formulation, generating alternatives, decision making, and verification). Horan (1979) suggests that if individuals understand that problematic situations are common to everyone and that they can be coped with in an adaptive manner, then following a set of prescribed steps should lead to determination of adaptive alternatives and discovery of means to implement and assess them. The D'Zurilla and Goldfried (1971) model is founded on these assumptions. Given these assumptions, then, individuals who use the model and resolve their problems successfully may find that related anxieties are relieved.

On the other hand, Spivack, Platt, and Shure (1976) believe that problem solving skills should be taught as mediators to enhance adjustment, not as ends in themselves. Those in this Cognitive Theory of Successful Adjustment camp have based their position on studies of causal thinking in children, and they argue that the D'Zurilla and Goldfried (1971) plan is primarily based on impersonal research. Thus, whether or not their model works with persons remains to be seen (Spivack & Shure, 1974). The problem solving skills advocated by Spivack, Platt, and Shure (1976) are: sensitivity to interpersonal problems, ability to generate alternate solutions (alternative thinking), ability to generate specific means by which a goal can be achieved (means–ends thinking), capacity to anticipate possible consequences of actions (consequential thinking), and the ability to view a problem from the perspective of others involved in it (perspective taking). According to Kennedy (1982), means–ends thinking and perspective taking differentiate the Spivack and Shure model from that of D'Zurilla and Goldfried. Although aware of these differences, we will engage in an eclectic approach to the issue, striving to highlight the best of all positions and offering readers an opportunity to decide for themselves the relative merits of different problem solving training programs.

Extracting common goals for problem solving training led to the following conclusions. First, counselors are interested in helping persons to solve problems, particularly troublesome problems (Heppner, 1978). Second, introducing problem solving strategies through formal training programs, counselors may help trainees to reduce their trial-and-error behaviors and prevent trainees from resorting to maladaptive responses such as inaction and impulsivity (Horan, 1979).

■ *Tactics.* Our literature review led to identification of three social problem–solving programs that focused on children or adolescents as subjects and a derivative of the D'Zurilla and Goldfried (1971) model that was designed for a late adolescent clientele (collegiate undergraduates). Common tactics across many of the programs were instructions, social modeling, practice, homework, reinforcement, cognitive modeling, and forms of affective training peculiar to the perceived needs of the trainees (e.g., cognitive self-instruction, cognitive restructuring, empathy training, and imaginative exercises).

Galvin's (1983) Alternative Interactive Network (GAIN) consists of eight 60-minute training sessions for elementary school children. A five-step systematic problem solving sequence is taught in conjunction with an emphasis on creativity—generation of thoughts and responses that are unique to individual trainees.

Although originally designed for prevention and early treatment of emotional and behavioral problems, Spivack and Shure's (1974) Interpersonal Cognitive Problem Solving (ICPS) program has also been adapted for classrooms of preadolescent children and adolescents. The ICPS program involves 40 or more 20- to 30-minute lessons employing a wide variety of tactics to develop language and attention skills, to identify emotions and ways to influence emotions, to develop sensitivity to the interpersonal nature of problems, to learn to understand the perspectives of others, and to learn about the consequences of one's actions.

The Rochester Social Problem Solving Training Program (Weissberg & Gersten, 1982) presents 34 highly structured 20- to 30-minute lessons for second- to fourth-grade children in a school setting. This program represents an integration of the D'Zurilla and Goldfried (1971) and Spivack and Shure (1974) approaches to social problem–solving training.

The program designed for a collegiate clientele and based on the D'Zurilla and Goldfried (1971) model is reported by Dixon, Heppner, Peterson, and Ronning (1979). Dixon et al. (1979) developed a 7 1/2-hour program with a sequential lattice technique for helping trainees recycle their thinking within the five problem solving phases.

D'Zurilla and Goldfried (1971) offer a useful explanation of what may be the primary purpose of all social problem–solving programs from a learning theory perspective. In their view, operant conditioning takes place through the establishment of a decision making response chain. Each link or step serves as a cue for the next one and a conditioned reinforcer for the last one with the entire chain being reinforced by satisfactory problem resolution.

■ *Evaluation of Effects.* Reporting the effects of problem solving training is confounded by our current inability to clearly identify a long-term causal relationship between problem solving and mental health (Durlak, 1983). From a short-term perspective, there is evidence that problem solving skills can be taught effectively and that some benefits have accrued. For example, Shure and Spivack (1975) found that social problem–solving skills could be taught and they were related to a decrease in maladjustment ratings, Christiansen (1974) discovered that acquisition of problem solving skills helped adolescents who were experiencing interpersonal anxiety, Medonca and Siess (1976) learned that students experiencing vocational indecisiveness could be helped, and Richards and Perri (1978) ascertained that problem solving training enhanced the effects of subjects in a self-controlled study skills program.

Evidence that problem solving skills can be taught to children is provided by Galvin (1983) and Stone and Noce (1980). Working with children ages 7 through 10, Galvin (1983) found that they were able to generate quality definitions of and solutions to problems as well as formal strategies to execute their plans of action. Stone and Noce (1980) worked with first-grade children and discovered that their students were able to demonstrate significant acquisition of problem solving skills after participating in a training program consisting of adult demonstrations of strategies for generating solutions and strategies and from self-instruction via verbal and covert reading of prepared cue cards.

The efficacy of citing evidence that problem solving skills can be taught successfully might best be founded on Shure, Spivack, and Jaeger's (1971) conclusion that there is a strong relationship between social problem solving skills and various indexes of adjustment. Thus, it might be deduced that the enhancement of problem solving competence may lead to lower incidences of maladjustment.

If we accept the above proposition about the potential efficacy of problem solving training as tenable, the following cautions are offered to those who decide to implement preventive problem solving training programs. First, many children and adolescents may already be capable of making good decisions when recruited for such training programs. Thus, trainers need to be alert for potential ceiling effects where trainees demonstrate little or no gain in problem solving ability due to having possessed relatively high levels at the outset (Nezu & D'Zurilla, 1981). Second, Heppner, Hibel, Neal, Weinstein, and Rabinowicz (1982) point out that the nature of the problem and the individual may affect the problem solving process. Whereas training programs tend to treat problems and trainees unilaterally, Heppner et al. (1982) believe that an individual responds differently to various problems encountered and also responds differently from another person to the same problem. This conclusion presents a difficult challenge to would-be developers of training programs. Third, Stone (1980) concluded that there is a shortage of evidence supporting the existence of a relationship between acquisition of problem solving skills and making better decisions. This is basically a criterion problem. What is a better decision? With regard to this issue, Krumboltz, Scherba, Hamel, and Mitchell (1982) have tried to resolve it by suggesting that a good decision is one that yields consequences that are consistent with the values of the decision maker.

PROGRAMS FOR PREVENTING COGNITIVE–PALLIATIVE RESPONSES TO STRESS

Cognitive Restructuring Training

▪ *Goals.*   Several terms are found in the professional literature that refer to programs that have common cognitive restructuring goals and tactics. The most prevalent of these synonymous terms are cognitive self-instruction (Meichenbaum, 1977), systematic rational restructuring (Goldfried, Decenteceo, & Weinberg, 1974), rational–emotive therapy (Ellis, 1975), and stress inoculation (Meichenbaum & Turk, 1976). One central theme of these programs is the assumption that individuals may experience maladaptive emotions and exhibit corresponding maladaptive covert behaviors because of inappropriate, faulty, or self-defeating beliefs, attitudes, and expectations. These beliefs, attitudes, and expectations being viewed as mental cognitions, a corollary assumption is that faulty, self-defeating cognitions can be replaced by positive self-enhancing thoughts (Cormier & Cormier, 1985). Therefore, the goal of cognitive restructuring training is to prepare trainees to recognize their self-defeating thoughts when they occur and replace them with self-enhancing cognitions in order to cope better with stressful situations.

▪ *Tactics.*   Cognitive restructuring is founded on principles of problem definition, focused attention and response guidance, self-reinforcement, and self-evaluating coping skills with error-correcting options (Stone, 1980). As in other cognitive behavior modification programs, trainer instruction, modeling, and feedback are important ingredients in conjunction with trainee rehearsal and in vivo homework. A typical training program may be conducted as follows: The instructor explains the assumptions and procedures, self-defeating thoughts are identified, corresponding coping thoughts are identified, trainees are taught to stop self-defeating thoughts when they occur and replace them with coping thoughts, trainees are taught to reinforce themselves with positive self-statements, in vivo homework is assigned, and follow-up sessions are conducted. These steps may be supplemented in several ways. For instance, relaxation training is often used in conjunction with learning to make the transition from self-defeating to coping thoughts. In addition, trainees may be taught some direct action coping skills (e.g., collect information or identify escape routes) in conjunction with their acquisition of cognitive coping thoughts. Cormier and Cormier (1985) provide detailed information about the content of cognitive restructuring training from which preventive training programs may be developed.

■ *Evaluation of Effects.* Cormier and Cormier (1985) reported that cognitive restructuring has been a successful tactic in therapeutic settings where clients were helped who suffered from test anxiety, speech anxiety, social interpersonal anxiety, depression, pain-related stress, maladaptive anger, tension headaches, and avoidance behavior. In other studies, Kerns, Turk, and Holzman (1983) reported additional support for the therapeutic efficacy of cognitive restructuring as a treatment for chronic pain, and Dush, Hirt, and Schroeder (1983) found that treatment subjects in several controlled studies where covert self-statements were directly modified experienced considerable gains beyond those of no-treatment control subjects. Very little research on the effects of cognitive restructuring as a primary prevention tactic has been reported. One of the coauthors of this book has conducted two such studies, finding modest support for the tactic while also discovering several thorny problems (Baker & Butler, 1984; Baker, Thomas, & Munson, 1983). Chief among the problems facing researchers is the difficulty of identifying appropriate criteria for assessing outcomes of primary prevention research. Problems that trainers will likely encounter have to do with delivering the programs in mass or group settings.

Motivation and cognitive readiness are not constant across either adolescent populations or samples of those populations. Instead, they are characteristics that vary, presenting trainers with stiff selection and organizational challenges. Those who advocate preventive cognitive restructuring training programs view them as a source of coping skills in instances of work and occupational stress, academic stress, medical stress, and social/environmental stress (Jaremko, 1984).

Emotive Imagery Training

■ *Goals.* As is the case with cognitive restructuring, emotive imagery procedures are, in part, founded on the assumption that some maladaptive emotions and overt behaviors result from faulty cognitions. Thus, one goal of emotive imagery training is to teach trainees to block fearful or anxiety-provoking thoughts by focusing their cognitions on positive images because it is very difficult to think about both pleasant and negative things at the same time. Pain and tension are undesirable physical manifestations that

people encounter that also may be reduced by self-managed emitting of pleasant images. Therefore, a second goal of emotive imagery is to prepare trainees to cope with physical pain and tension through imagery.

This form of imagery is described as emotive because those who use it must learn to instruct themselves consciously and purposefully to generate covert imaginary scenes—act them out in their imaginations. Horan (1976) points out that technically the term in vivo emotive imagery is more accurate because the tactic is being used to control life's actual distressing situations rather than fantasized problems.

■ *Tactics.* Some people are not at all motivated to use imagery in this way and others, although highly motivated, find it difficult to picture vivid scenes in their imaginations (Kazdin, 1976). Thus, trainers will encounter the initial challenge of assessing the imagery capacity of their trainees. Cormier and Cormier (1985) state that several possible assessment techniques are available. One technique is via designed self-report questionnaires such as the Visual and Auditory Imagery sections of the Imaginal Process Inventory (Singer & Antrobus, 1972), the shortened form of the Betts Questionnaire Upon Mental Imagery (Sheehan, 1967), or the Imagery Survey Schedule (Cautela & Tondo, 1971). White, Sheehan, and Ashton (1977) have reviewed similar instruments that readers may be interested in.

Another technique is to develop trainer-generated practice scenes and ask prospective trainees to narrate the events in those scenes aloud in detail after the imagery exercise ends. During this observational assessment process, trainers can ask questions that help them to ascertain how vividly the scenes were imagined and how highly motivated the prospective trainees are (Cormier & Cormier, 1985). If one's capacity for imagery is less than vivid but the motivation is high, there are ways to teach more detailed imagery production, but doing so will add to the total amount of time devoted to a training program (Phillips, 1971),

Following an explanation of program content and purpose and an assessment of imagery potential, the next step is to teach the trainees to develop imagery scenes. Multiple scenes that promote calmness, tranquility, or enjoyment and that can be imagined in great sensory detail are recommended. Practice of the imagery scenes is the next step. Cormier and Cormier (1985) suggest that practice may be focused on development of increasing awareness of details and related sensations and/or on responding to simulated anxiety-provoking or painful situations. The final step in this training program is to apply it to real-life situations under appropriate self-management circumstances with planned follow-up sessions for evaluation and additional training when necessary. As is true with the other training programs in this chapter, trainer instructions and modeling, trainee rehearsal and trainer feedback are basic program ingredients.

■ *Evaluation of Effects.* We know of no reported instances of imagery-related primary prevention programs that have been assessed experimentally and reported in the professional literature. Cormier and Cormier (1985), Horan (1976), and Kerns, Turk, and Holzman (1983) cite several studies where emotive imagery was used successfully as a therapeutic agent or in an analogue study (e.g., school phobia, reducing discomfort, and relieving boredom or tension.)

PROGRAMS FOR PREVENTING OVERRELIANCE ON ACTIVE RESPONSES TO STRESS

Meditation Training

■ *Goals.* Development of a definition of meditation is complicated by the existence of many different meditation techniques. Shapiro (1982) attacked this problem by using mechanisms of achieving attention as the basis for developing a definition. He concluded that "meditation refers to a family of techniques which have in common a conscious attempt to focus attention in a nonanalytical way and an attempt not to dwell on discursive, ruminating thoughts" (p. 268). Explaining this definition further, Shapiro (1982) stressed that meditation is a process involving one's intention to focus his/her attention on an object or field or on whatever arises, does not depend on a religious framework for understanding, and is more dependent on consciousness or awareness of the process of thoughts than the content of those thoughts.

The general goal of meditation is calmly to limit one's thought and attention in order to become more calm, more aware, and more in control of oneself (Cormier & Cormier, 1985). Furthermore, meditation is viewed as a cognitive relaxation procedure that serves to counterbalance environmental effects of stress. According to Benson (1976), regular practice will have physiological effects such as decreased systolic and diastolic blood pressure, heart rate, respiratory rate, and oxygen consumption via stimulation of the brain's hypothalamus area.

■ *Tactics.* Cormier and Cormier (1985) provide a stepped meditation program that is drawn from several prominent sources. After learning the rationale on which meditation is founded, trainees receive assistance in selecting a mental device which they will repeat silently or in a low tone while meditating in order to focus on breathing and resist distracting thoughts. Single-syllable sounds or words are usually used. Next, the trainees are taught procedures for achieving body comfort during meditation, are taught how to achieve focused breathing and to use the mental device, and are instructed on how to maintain a passive attitude during meditation. A brief meditation exercise is then followed by trainer–trainee discussion of the experience, appropriate correctional behavior, and homework with trainer–trainee follow-up. The training program overview described above is brief and simplistic and does not provide important detailed information such as how to assist trainees whose attention wanders or how to assess the physiological effects of meditation exercises. Prospective trainers must know about these details and other nuances before embarking on meditation-related training programs.

■ *Evaluation of Effects.* While Smith (1975) reported evidence that meditation has therapeutic effects on client subjective or cognitive responses, Holmes (1984) concluded that there is no adequately researched evidence that meditation more effectively reduces somatic arousal than simply resting. On the other hand, while Murray (1982) agreed that methodological problems limit firm conclusions about the therapeutic effects of any form of meditation, he also stated that various meditation tactics may cause beneficial quiet and relaxation as well as temporary symptom relief—perhaps the most likely goal when using meditation as a primary prevention tactic.

Progressive Muscle Relaxation Training

■ *Goals.*   Progressive muscle relaxation is a tactic that focuses primarily on physical sensations. Introduced by Jacobson (1929) several decades ago, progressive muscle relaxation is a tactic whereby individuals learn to relax by becoming aware of the sensations of tensing and relaxing major muscle groups. Since relaxation is incompatible with tension, progressive muscle relaxation reduces tension and counteracts the effects of stress (Bernstein & Borkovec, 1973; Cormier & Cormier, 1985).

■ *Tactics.*   There are several issues and cautions that should be expressed before citing a model progressive muscle relaxation training program. One issue involves Jacobson's (1938, 1970) more or less purist view that muscle relaxation should be devoid of outside stimuli versus the position of those who have modified the technique by incorporating suggestions of sensations via verbal or tape-recorded instruction and suggestions reminiscent of hypnosis (e.g., Wolpe & Lazarus, 1966). Lehrer (1982) reported that this issue had not been resolved empirically. However, it should be noted that one advantage of the modified forms over the pure form is that they are shorter in duration.

A related issue is whether or not tape-recorded instructions and electromyogram (EMG) biofeedback make useful contributions to progressive muscle relaxation training. According to Lehrer (1982), live training appeared to be more effective although that conclusion, based on a review of related research, conflicted with observations based on his own clinical experiences. He reported that EMG biofeedback seems to render superficial training more effective, and Cormier and Cormier (1985) suggested that tape-recorded instructions may be used where homework assignments are given.

Bernstein and Borkovec (1973) caution that trainees should have medical clearance prior to engaging in progressive muscle relaxation training. Some potential sources of difficulty reside in lower back pain, headaches, and incompatibility with selected medications that trainees may be using (Cormier & Cormier, 1985).

As was the case in our presentation of a sample meditation program, this stepped overview of the progressive muscle relaxation technique is taken from Cormier and Cormier (1985). Following a verbal explanation of the program as involving progressively learned skills, trainers instruct trainees on the importance of wearing comfortable clothing and securing a comfortable environment. When these items are taken care of, the trainer models some of the training exercises, then instructs the trainees progressively through the steps in the program. Various combinations of muscle groups may be selected for a training program. For example, Bernstein and Borkovec (1973) have developed programs for sets of 4, 7, and 17 muscle groups. A trainer might use the following dialogue when instructing trainees to relax one of their fists:

> First think about your right arm, your right hand in particular. Clench your right fist. Clench it tightly and study the tension in the hand and in the forearm. Study those sensations of tension. (Pause.) Now let go. Just relax the right hand and let it rest on the arm of the chair (or floor). (Pause.) And note the difference between the tension and the relaxation. (Cormier & Cormier, 1985, p. 460)

Upon completion of relaxation training, the trainer summarizes and reviews the muscle groups in order to locate and dispel remaining tensions. This should be followed by trainer–trainee discussion of reactions, questions, and problems (e.g., cramps, intrusive thoughts, and falling asleep). The next step is to assign homework with provision for follow-up although some individual problems may have to be rectified before assigning homework.

■ *Evaluation of Effects.*   While citing several methodological issues noted in their review of 80 empirical studies of relaxation training research, Hillenberg and Collins (1982) tentatively concluded that it is an effective therapeutic intervention for a variety of problems. As was stated above with regard to meditation, progressive muscle relaxation may at least bring about general relaxation and temporary relief of physiological symptoms. This would seem to mirror the central goal for using progressive muscle relaxation training as a primary prevention tactic.

CASE STUDIES

Cleaning Up Our Thinking: A Cognitive Restructuring Training Unit

Scheduling the Program and Selecting Participants.   The unit[1] was presented to ninth-grade students assigned to two required guidance classes and to students in grades 10 through 12 who were enrolled in an elective psychology course. One guidance class was led by a school counselor and the other by one of the coauthors of this book while the psychology class was taught by a social studies teacher. Consequently, the program was presented to students who were assigned to regularly scheduled courses in the school curriculum.

First Session.   Pretests for evaluation purposes were accompanied by an introduction to the unit. The introduction consisted of verbal and printed explanations. Printed explanations were offered via a seven-page booklet designed by a coauthor of this book entitled "Cleaning Up Our Thinking: A Unit in Self-Improvement." In addition to explaining the scope and purpose of the program, materials and instructions for subsequent exercises were included. Thus, students were using the booklet for the duration of the program.

---

1. This program was designed by Stanley B. Baker and implemented by James N. Butler and Ronald N. Thomas.

Verbal explanations focused on the importance of controlling one's thinking in order to become aware of self-defeating thoughts and of the importance of self-improving thoughts. Examples of each were stated by the trainers. Examples were as follows: self-defeating thoughts: "What if so-and-so doesn't like me?", "I'll probably mess up this assignment." "I can never say the right things to strangers."; self-improving thoughts: "I'm just going to be myself when meeting this person," "Experiences such as this help me to improve myself," "I'll talk about something I enjoy." The first session concluded with an opportunity for trainees to ask questions and react. The responses were mixed, ranging from high interest through strong disinterest—challenges that face many classroom teachers when the students are assigned heterogeneously.

Second Session.   The trainers helped their students to take inventory of self-defeating thoughts that occur in their lives. In this session and throughout the training program, the trainers modeled the behaviors being requested of the trainees in order to assist them in their performance of acts that were quite possibly unfamiliar to them. While the trainers shared examples of their own self-defeating thoughts with the group verbally, the trainees wrote theirs on an inventory or log sheet, maintaining as much confidentiality as they desired.

The primary skill to be taught in this exercise was the process of translating passing thoughts or images into sentences. To accomplish this, the trainers first suggested several common cues or qualities associated with self-defeating thoughts such as "I'm afraid," "I won't do well," "If . . . happens, it will be awful," "I never . . . ," or "I always . . . ." Next, questions were presented to them such as "Do I make unreasonable demands of myself?", "Do I feel that others are approving or disapproving of my actions?", and "Do I often forget that this situation is only one part of my life?" Finally, it was suggested that the trainees try to recall things as if they were running movies in their heads, supplementing that with a demonstration of how the trainers translated their imagined events into verbal sentences depicting self-defeating thoughts.

Third Session.   Students were instructed to compile a listing of self-improving thoughts (or sentences) that could be used to counteract each of the self-defeating thoughts (or sentences) they had previously determined. Again, while the students were doing this exercise privately in their logs, the trainers were providing stimuli, suggestions, and demonstrations to the entire group.

The trainers opened with an explanation of the purpose behind this exercise: thinking negative thoughts creates negative feelings while positive thoughts counteract the negative ones. It is impossible to think negatively and positively at the same time. Thus, the induction of self-improving thoughts will help those who use them to manage negative situations and prevent themselves from becoming overwhelmed by them. Examples of self-improving thoughts were offered such as "Stay calm in anticipating this," "Do the best I can. I'm not going to worry about how people will react," "Take one step at a time," "Just think about what I want to do or say." The trainers then tried to help the trainees to understand subtle differences among situational self-improving statements (e.g., "It will be a challenge."), task-oriented self-improving statements (e.g., "What do I want to accomplish?"), and statements for coping with being overwhelmed ("Stay calm!"), and for positive reinforcement ("Nice going.").

Fourth Session.   The next step in the training program was to teach the trainees a procedure for shifting from self-defeating to self-improving thoughts when discovering themselves in the process of negative thinking. To do this, components of emotive imagery and progressive muscle relaxation training were incorporated. After trainer demonstrations of the process, the trainees were instructed to close their eyes and relax their bodies while seated at their desks/chairs. They were then requested to imagine themselves experiencing the most prevalent self-defeating thought on their log sheets. When the image of that experience was clear, and they recognized what was happening, they were instructed to stop or interfere with that line of thinking and purposely replace it with their corresponding self-improving thoughts. The exercise was repeated by using the remaining stimuli on their log sheets.

Fifth Session. Continued practicing of the procedure for replacing self-defeating thoughts with self-improving ones took place in this session, and a new dimension was added to the process. Rewarding self-statements were added to the program by teaching the trainees verbally to reinforce their successful attempts to replace self-defeating thoughts with self-improving ones. This was done by first offering them examples of rewarding self-statements such as "Hey, I handled that OK," "I didn't let my emotions get the best of me," and "I made some progress, and that feels good." The training concluded with an in vivo homework assignment in which the trainees were asked to keep over a week's time a log of events in which they identified themselves as experiencing self-defeating thoughts and purposely using the cognitive restructuring procedure in order to cope with the situation. This assignment met with a mixed response in that about half of the trainees did not submit evidence of having been able to transfer the training to real life during the one-week interim. A sixth session was conducted in order to collect the in vivo assignment materials, collect posttest data, and debrief the participants.

Evaluation. Where the cognitive restructuring program was matched against a high-demand traditional lecture and discussion group in the guidance classes, there were no differences favoring the treatment group (Baker, Thomas, & Munson, 1983). In the psychology class, there were effects on measures of attitudes toward the training program and state anxiety that favored the trainer-directed cognitive restructuring program over one in which the trainees received the instructional materials and were encouraged to teach themselves the program (Baker & Butler, 1984).

Teaching Social Problem-Solving Skills to Third-Grade Students

Scheduling the program and selecting participants. Five third-graders (three girls, two boys) were arbitrarily selected by the classroom teacher and a counseling intern[2] because three had exhibited frequent and repeated questioning, acting-out, and impulsive behaviors and two were models of appropriate behavior in the same categories. Thus, it was more or less a secondary prevention program. We include it in this book because of our feeling that it also has potential for primary prevention programming. The program was directed by the counseling intern over a period of 6 weeks using Russell's (1976) *Decision Making Book for Children* (*DMBC*).

First Session. After introducing the children to the purpose of the program, the trainer directed them to complete the first part of the *DMBC*, which consists of information about difficult and simple decisions everyone encounters and points

---

2. This program was designed and implemented by Patricia Day-Shomburg.

out that making decisions necessitates solving problems. This part of the *DMBC* program concludes with listening to an audiotape about "John's Problem" and attempting to distinguish between difficult and simple problems.

Second Session. An audiotape about "Chris's Problem" is used to point out that choices have to be made while solving problems and that the choice/decision is ultimately the responsibility of the person encountering the problem.

Third Session. Through listening to "Bill's Problem" on an audiotape, the children learned that problems often have more than one solution. They were also instructed to generate as many choices or alternatives as possible and to try to differentiate between good and poor choices.

Fourth Session. To facilitate efficient problem solving, the children were presented with a standard set of questions to be asked when evaluating alternative solutions to a problem: Who?, What?, Where?, When?, How?, and How much? They were then presented with an exercise requiring them to use the questions cited above.

Fifth Session. Focusing on personal values, this section of the *DMBC* was designed to enhance the skills needed to compare the personal values associated with each of the available choices. Using their own value system, the children again listened to "Bill's Problem" and assigned negative or positive weights to the choices Bill was considering.

Session Six. A simple decision making chart was introduced in order to help the children graphically plot the steps involved in the resolution of "John's Problem." They then used the same chart to work through the resolution of one of their own current problems. This was followed by the children completing a knowledge test and reacting to a simulated problem solving situation.

Evaluation. There was a significant increase in the number of alternatives generated by the children in the posttraining problem solving situation as compared with their pretraining alternatives-generating behaviors. Caution is necessary when generalizing the results of this evaluation because there was no comparative control group, and the simulated problem presented after the training had concluded was the same one presented before it began. On the knowledge test, all trainees were able to record the six decision making steps presented in the *DMBC*.

An Assertiveness Training Program for Middle School Students

Scheduling the Program and Selecting Participants. The program[3] was instituted during a 30-minute period of time set aside in the school schedule every Tuesday for faculty and staff to meet with students in order to discuss topics deemed relevant to adolescents. Five weekly sessions were held for five students who had volunteered to participate in the program.

First Session. Without explanation, the trainer introduced herself aggressively (e.g., unrealistic rules of deportment voiced harshly with threatening body movements) and then passively (e.g., meek, laissez-faire manner, almost apologetic). This was followed by a discussion of the contrasting feelings experienced by the trainees. The contrast was then completed by a leader demonstration of an appropriately assertive introduction. The session concluded with a discussion of trainee feelings

---

3. This program was designed and implemented by Sandra Hay Manos.

about the third introduction and an overview of the relationship between standing up for one's rights and respecting the rights of others. Homework took the form of recording examples of aggressive, passive, and assertive behaviors in their own lives in a log book.

Second Session. Each student was asked to introduce him/herself in an aggressive, assertive, or passive manner with the leader discerning the accuracy of their understanding of that particular mode. This was preceded by a sharing and discussing of the entries in their logs. Again, the leader was interested in discerning whether the trainees could accurately identify the three categories of behavior. They seemed to have a fairly good grasp of the differences. The group members then discussed their responses to a handout containing four unfinished questions. Each question was discussed in terms of whether it generated thoughts of aggressive, assertive, or passive behaviors. Homework consisted of the students observing and recording incidences of aggressive, assertive, and passive behaviors displayed by others and recording their feelings when witnessing those behaviors.

Third Session. After mutually sharing observations from their homework assignments, the trainees participated in a discussion of how their bodies act when they engage in aggressive, assertive, or passive behaviors. The discussion was enhanced by a handout containing ten ideas to keep in mind about assertive behavior (e.g., "Assertive behavior not only is concerned with *what* you say but *how* you say it."). Eye contact, tone of voice, voice quality, posture, facial expressions, and gestures were demonstrated by the trainer in support of the discussion. The session closed with a discussion of emotional blocks that keep people from being assertive and from experiencing positive feelings toward others. Homework consisted of practicing assertive behavior and sharing positive emotions with others.

Fourth Session. Discussion of the homework·assignment revealed that most trainees experienced difficulty expressing positive emotions to peers whom they did not know very well. However, when expressing positive emotions to others, they all received positive feedback. The group was then led through a discussion of the relationship between compromising and assertiveness. A point was made that assertiveness begets assertiveness and that assertively behaving persons must be prepared to accept assertiveness in others.

Fifth Session. The leader and the trainees reviewed the program content and discussed what had been covered. This was followed by discussion of what had been accomplished.

Evaluation. Assessment of this program was derived from comments made by the participants during the final session. All present stated that they enjoyed the activities, thought that they had benefited from the experience, and would recommend it to others. As is often the case in voluntary programs of this nature, activities associated with traditional schooling are least well received. Thus, homework assignments garnered the lowest ratings while simulated activities were more popular. Circumstances beyond her control forced the leader to conduct this program near the end of the school year. As a result, she was prevented from being able to gather observational evidence of the effects of participation on real behavior.

SUMMARY

Cognitive-behavioral tactics that have proved effective in psychotherapy treatments may also be used successfully in primary prevention programming. As a result, health and wellness may be enhanced across that segment of the population that receives cognitive-behavioral coping skills training. In part, it is analogous to medical inoculations. Those who successfully add the coping strategies to their behavioral repertoires should be better able to handle life's stressful situations and prevent undue wear and tear on their mental and physical well-being. In addition, trainees learn healthy ways to think and behave in general. Thus, their general state of mental health is enhanced.

Although cognitive-behavioral writers have advocated prevention, most of what is known about the effects of cognitive-behavioral strategies has been derived from clinical studies. Results of these studies and a limited number of prevention studies indicate that assertiveness, social problem–solving, cognitive restructuring, emotive imagery, meditation, and progressive muscle relaxation training have good potential as primary prevention tactics. Case studies were cited in which cognitive restructuring with corresponding muscle relaxation and emotive imagery training was used preventively with high school students, social problem–solving skills were taught to third-graders, and middle school students were given assertiveness training that included a cognitive restructuring component.

Currently, the value of cognitive-behavioral primary prevention strategies lies more in their promise than in their known products. Given the strength of evidence from empirical clinical studies, the potential value of primary prevention applications looks good.

PUBLISHED RESOURCES

Alberti, R. E., & Emmons, M. L. (1974). *Your perfect right.* San Luis Obispo, CA: Impact.

Apgar, K., & Callahan, B. N. (1980). *Four one-day workshops.* Boston: Resource Communications.

Becker, W. C. (1971). *Parents are teachers: A child management program.* Champaign, IL: Research Press.

Bry, A., & Bair, M. (1979). *Visualization: Directing the movies of your mind.* New York: Barnes & Noble.

Callahan, B. N. (1980). *Assertiveness training.* Boston: Resource Communications.

Carkhuff, R. R. (1973). *The art of problem solving.* Amherst, MA: Human Resource Development Press.

Carrington, P. (1978a). *Clinically standardized meditation (CSM): Instructor's manual.* Kendall Park, NJ: Pace Educational Systems.

Carrington, P. (1978b). *Clinically standardized meditation (CSM): Course workbook.* Kendall Park, NJ: Pace Educational Systems.

Cautela, J. R., & Groden, J. (1978). *Relaxation: A comprehensive manual for adults, children, and children with special needs.* Champaign, IL: Research Press.

Davis, G. A. (1973). *Psychology of problem solving: Theory and practice.* New York: Basic Books.

Herr, E. L., Horan, J. J., & Baker, S. B. (1973). Performance goals in vocational guidance and counseling: Clarifying the counseling mystique. *American Vocational Journal, 48,* 66–72.

Jack, G. B. (1981). *Assertive behavior training: A bibliography update.* San Luis Obispo, CA: Impact.

Jakubowski, P., & Lange, A. J. (1978). *The assertive option: Your rights and responsibilities.* Champaign, IL: Research Press.

Jakubowski-Spector, P. (1973). *An introduction to assertive training procedures for women.* Alexandria, VA: American Association for Counseling and Development.

Janis, I. L., & Mann, L. (1977). *Decision-making: A psychological analysis of conflict, choice, and commitment.* New York: Free Press.

Jarrell, H. R. (1985). *International meditation bibliography: 1950–1982.* Metuchen, NJ: Scarecrow Press.

Meichenbaum, D. H., & Jaremko, M. E. (Eds.). (1983). *Stress reduction and prevention.* New York: Plenum.

Palmer, P. (1977). *The mouse, the monster, and me: Assertiveness for young people.* San Luis Obispo, CA: Impact.

Rashbaum-Selig, M. (1976). Assertive training for young people. *School Counselor, 24,* 115–122.

Sank, L. I., & Shaffer, C. S. (1984). *A therapist's manual for cognitive behavior therapy.* New York: Plenum.

Sheikh, A. A. (Ed.). (1983). *Imagery: Current theory, research, and application.* New York: Wiley.

Shorr, J. E., Sobel-Whittington, G., Robin, P., & Connella, J. A. (Eds.). (1984). *Imagery: Vol. 3. Theoretical and clinical applications.* New York: Plenum.

Spring-Moore, D. M., & Jack, G. B. (1981). *Assertive behavior training: A cross-referenced annotated bibliography.* San Luis Obispo, CA: Impact.

Woolfolk, R. L., & Lehrer, P. M. (Eds.). (1984). *Principles and practices of stress management.* New York: Guilford Press.

REFERENCES

Adler, R. B. (1977). *Talking straight.* New York: Holt, Rinehart, & Winston.

Alberti, R. (1977). *Assertiveness: Innovations, applications, issues.* San Luis Obispo, CA: Impact.

Baker, S. B., & Butler, J. N. (1984). Effects of cognitive self-instruction training on adolescent attitudes, experiences, and state anxiety. *Journal of Primary Prevention, 5,* 10–14.

Baker, S. B., Thomas, R. N., & Munson, W. W. (1983). Effects of cognitive restructuring and structured group discussion as primary prevention strategies. *School Counselor, 31,* 26–33.

Benson, H. (1976). *The relaxation response.* New York: Avon.

Bernstein, D. A., & Borkovec, T. D. (1973). *Progressive relaxation training.* Champaign, IL: Research Press.

Brown, S. D., & Brown, L. W. (1979). Trends in assertion research and practice: A content analysis of the published literature. *Journal of Clinical Psychology, 36,* 265–269.

Cautela, J. R., & Tondo, T. R. (1971). *Imagery survey schedule.* Unpublished questionnaire, Boston College.

Christiansen, C. (1974). *Development and field testing of an interpersonal coping skills program.* Toronto: Ontario Institute for Studies in Education.

Cormier, W. H., & Cormier, L. S. (1985). *Interviewing strategies for helpers: Fundamental skills and cognitive-behavioral interventions.* Monterey, CA: Brooks/Cole.

Cotler, S. B., & Guerra, J. J. (1976). *Assertion training.* Champaign, IL: Research Press.

Dixon, D. N., Heppner, P. P., Peterson, C. H., & Ronning, R. R. (1979). Problem-solving workshop training. *Journal of Counseling Psychology, 26,* 133–139.

Durlak, J. A. (1983). Social problem-solving as a primary prevention strategy. In R. D. Felner, L. A. Jason, J. N. Moritsugu, & S. S. Farber (Eds.), *Preventive psychology: Theory, research, and practice* (pp. 31–48). New York: Pergamon.

Dush, D. M., Hirt, M. L., & Schroeder, H. (1983). Self-statement modification with adults: A meta-analysis. *Psychological Bulletin, 94,* 408–422.

D'Zurilla, T. J., & Goldfried, M. R. (1971). Problem solving and behavior modification. *Journal of Abnormal Psychology, 78,* 107–126.

Ellis, A. (1975). *Growth through reason.* North Hollywood, CA: Wilshire Book Co.

Eysenck, H. J. (1959). Learning theory and behaviour therapy. *Journal of Mental Science, 105,* 61–75.

Galassi, M. D. & Galassi, J. P. (1977). *Assert yourself! How to be your own person.* New York: Human Sciences Press.

Galvin, M. (1983). Making systematic problem solving work with children. *School Counselor, 31,* 130–136.

Goldfried, M. R., Decenteceo, E. T., & Weinberg, L. (1974). Systematic rational restructuring as a self-control technique. *Behavior Therapy, 5,* 247–254.

Heimberg, D. G., Montgomery, D., Madsen, C. H., & Heimberg, J. S. (1977). Assertiveness training: A review of the literature. *Behavior Therapy, 8,* 953–971.

Heppner, P. P. (1978). A review of the problem-solving literature and its relationship to the counseling process. *Journal of Counseling Psychology, 25,* 366–375.

Heppner, P. P., Hibel, J., Neal, G. W., Weinstein, C. L., & Rabinowicz, F. E. (1982). Personal problem solving: A descriptive study of individual differences. *Journal of Counseling Psychology, 29,* 580–590.

Hillenberg, J. B., & Collins, F. L. (1982). A procedural analysis and review of relaxation training research. *Behavior Research and Therapy, 20* (3), 251–260.

Holmes, D. S. (1984). Meditation and somatic arousal reduction: A review of the experimental evidence. *American Psychologist, 39,* 1–10.

Horan, J. J. (1976). Coping with inescapable discomfort through in vivo emotive imagery. In J. D. Krumboltz & C. E. Thoresen (Eds.), *Counseling methods* (pp. 316–320). New York: Holt, Rinehart, & Winston.

Horan, J. J. (1979). *Counseling for effective decision making.* North Scituate, MA: Duxbury Press.

Jacobson, E. (1929). *Progressive relaxation.* Chicago: University of Chicago Press.

Jacobson, E. (1938). *Progressive relaxation: A physiological and clinical investigation of muscular states and their significance in psychology and medical practice.* Chicago: University of Chicago Press.

Jacobson, E. (1970). *Modern treatment of tense patients.* Springfield, IL: C. C. Thomas.

Jaremko, M. E. (1984). Stress inoculation training: A generic approach for the prevention of stress-related disorders. *Personnel and Guidance Journal, 62,* 544–549.

Jason, L. A., & Bogat, G. A. (1983). Preventive behavioral interventions. In R. D. Felner, L. A. Jason, J. N. Moritsugu, & S. S. Farber (Eds.), *Preventive psychology: Theory, research, and practice* (pp. 128–143). New York: Pergamon.

Kazdin, A. E. (1976). Assessment of imagery during covert modeling of assertive behavior. *Journal of Behavior Therapy and Experimental Psychiatry, 7,* 213–219.

Kazdin, A. E. (1978). *History of behavior modification: Experimental foundations of contemporary research.* Baltimore: University Park Press.

Kennedy, R. E. (1982). Cognitive-behavioral approaches to the modification of aggressive behavior in children. *School Psychology Review, 11,* 47–55.

Kerns, R. D., Turk, D. C., & Holzman, A. D. (1983). Psychological treatment for chronic pain: A selective review. *Clinical Psychology Review, 3,* 15–26.

Krumboltz, J. D., Scherba, D. S., Hamel, D. A., & Mitchell, L. K. (1982). Effect of training in rational decision-making on the quality of simulated career decisions. *Journal of Counseling Psychology, 29,* 618–625.

Lange, A., & Jakubowski, P. (1976). *Responsible assertive behavior.* Champaign, IL: Research Press.

Lehrer, P. M. (1982). How to relax and how not to relax: A re-evaluation of the work of Edmund Jacobson: 1. *Behavior Research and Therapy, 20* (5), 417–428.

Medonca, J. D., & Siess, T. F. (1976). Counseling for indecisiveness: Problem-solving and anxiety-management training. *Journal of Counseling Psychology, 23,* 339–347.

Meichenbaum, D. (1977). *Cognitive-behavior modification: An integrative approach.* New York: Plenum.

Meichenbaum, D., & Turk, D. (1976). The cognitive-behavioral management of anxiety, anger, and pain. In P. O. Davidson (Ed.), *The behavioral management of anxiety, depression, and pain.* New York: Brunner/Mazel.

Michelson, L., & Wood R. (1980). A group assertive training program for elementary school children. *Child Behavior Therapy, 2,* 1–9.

Murray, J. B. (1982). What is meditation? Does it help? *Genetic Psychology Monograph, 106,* 85–115.

Nezu, A., & D'Zurilla, T. J. (1981). Effects of problem definition and formulation on decision-making in the social problem-solving process. *Behavior Therapy, 12,* 100–106.

Phillips, L. W. (1971). Training of sensory and imaginal responses in behavior therapy. In R. D. Rubin, H. Fensterheim, A. A. Lazarus, & C. M. Franks (Eds.), *Advances in behavior therapy* (pp. 111–122). New York: Academic Press.

Ralph, K. M. (1982). Asserting rights: A seductive option. *Personnel and Guidance Journal, 60,* 398–399.

Richards, C. S., & Perri, M. G. (1978). Do self-control treatments last? An evaluation of behavioral problem solving and faded counselor contact as treatment maintenance strategy. *Journal of Counseling Psychology, 25,* 376–383.

Rotheram, M. J. (1982). Variations in children's assertiveness due to assertion level. *Journal of Community Psychology, 10,* 228–236.

Rotheram, M. J., & Armstrong, M. (1980). Assertion training with high school students. *Adolescence, 15,* 267–276.

Rotheram, M. J., Armstrong, M., & Booraem, C. (1982). Assertiveness training in fourth and fifth grade children. *American Journal of Community Psychology, 10,* 567–582.

Russell, M. (1976). *The decision making book for children.* Waco, TX: Baylor College of Medicine.

Schmidt, J. P., & Patterson, T. E. (1979). Issues in the implementation of assertion training in applied settings. *Behavior Therapy and Psychiatry, 10,* 15–19.

Shapiro, D. H. (1982). Overview: Clinical and physiological comparison of meditation with other self-control strategies. *American Journal of Psychiatry, 139* (3), 267–274.

Sheehan, P. W. (1967). A shortened form of Betts' questionnaire upon mental imagery. *Journal of Clinical Psychology, 23,* 386–389.

Shelton, J. L. (1977). Assertive training: Consumer beware. *Personnel and Guidance Journal, 55,* 465–468.

Shure, M. B., & Spivack, G. (1975). *A preventive mental health program for young "inner city" children: The second (kindergarten) year.* Paper presented at the meeting of the American Psychological Association, Chicago.

Shure, M. B., Spivack, G., & Jaeger, M. (1971). Problem-solving thinking and adjustment among disadvantaged preschool children. *Child Development, 42,* 1791–1803.

Singer, J. L., & Antrobus, J. S. (1972). Daydreaming, imaginal processes, and personality: A normative study. In P. W. Sheehan (Ed.), *The function and nature of imagery* (pp. 175–202). New York: Academic Press.

Smith, J. C. (1975). Meditation as psychotherapy: A review of the literature. *Psychological Bulletin, 82,* 558–564.

Spivack, G., Platt, J. J., & Shure, M. B. (1976). *The problem-solving approach to adjustment.* San Francisco: Jossey–Bass.

Spivack, G., & Shure, M. B. (1974). *Social adjustment of young children.* San Francisco: Jossey–Bass.

Stensrud, R., & Stensrud, K. (1983). Coping skills training: A systematic approach to stress management counseling. *Personnel and Guidance Journal, 62,* 214–218.

Stone, G. L. (1980). *A cognitive-behavioral approach to counseling psychology: Implications for practice, research, and training.* New York: Praeger.

Stone, G. L., & Noce, A. (1980). Cognitive training for young children: Expanding the counselor's role. *Personnel and Guidance Journal, 58,* 416–420.

Weissberg, R. P., & Gersten, E. L. (1982). Considerations for developing effective school-based social problem-solving (SPS) training programs. *School Psychology Review, 11,* 56–63.

White, K., Sheehan, P. W., & Ashton, R. (1977). Imagery assessment: A survey of self-report measures. *Journal of Mental Imagery, 1,* 145–170.

Wilk, C. A., & Coplan, V. M. (1977). Assertive-training as a confidence-building technique. *Personnel and Guidance Journal, 55,* 460–464.

Wolpe, J., & Lazarus, A. A. (1966). *Behavior therapy techniques.* New York: Pergamon.

5

CAREER EDUCATION

ROLE IN PRIMARY PREVENTION

Numerous proponents of career education as an application of career development theory have emerged since the late 1950s, making the idea one of the most popular and written-about topics in the counseling literature. Unfortunately, career education sometimes was used as a label attached to programs and activities without theoretical underpinnings and goals. For our purposes, useful definitions have been offered by Herr (1969), who described *career education* as the unification of the entire system of education around a career development theme and by Hoyt (1977), who defined *career education* as helping individuals to utilize knowledge, skills, and attitudes that are necessary for making work meaningful, productive, and satisfying.

The career development concept represents attempts to explain effective vocational behavior from positions such as a trait-and-factor approach, decision theory, socioeconomic class structure, cognitive dissonance theory, personality theory, and self-concept theory. None has emerged dominant, and all combined represent evidence that human behavior is complex. A popular position that has evolved from all of this is that a developmental process is involved, complete with stage and tasks through which persons need to progress, gradually building on earlier task accomplishments. The process is lifelong, and persons differ in their readiness to plan and make decisions. Consequently, career development theory stages do offer suggestions for primary prevention tactics that may help large numbers of children and youth to progress successfully through current and future career development stages.

The goal of career education is achievement of the developmental tasks of career development theory as spelled out by those who have contributed to that body of knowledge (e.g., Ginzberg, Ginzberg, Axelrod, & Herma, 1951; Ginzberg, 1972; Super, 1953, 1957). Among these goals are identifying with a worker, acquiring basic habits of industry, acquiring an identity as a worker in the occupational structure, becoming a productive person, awareness of interests and values and their relation to occupational choices, crystallizing a vocational preference, specifying a vocational preference, implementing a vocational preference, stabilizing in a vocation, consolidating status, and advancing in a vocation. Although comprehensive, these goals are by no means all-encompassing; and because the concept is so massive, it has been suggested by Herr (1969) that the best way to achieve the goals of career education may be to unify entire systems of education around a career education theme.

Herr (1975) thinks that career education proponents hold views about educational reform that are similar to those held by proponents of psychological education. He states:

> Approaches to both career and to psychological education stress the importance to student development of self-understanding, planning, problem-solving and decision-making skills. Career education is likely to advocate casting these against possible educational and work alternatives while psychological education would likely cast them in terms of interpersonal relations or moral and ethical reasoning. (pp. 63–64)

Herr's quotation presents us with a suggestion for the role of career education in primary prevention. Career education programs are planned interventions that are in many ways similar to programs presented earlier in chapters about communication skills, psychological education, and behavioral approaches, but the content and goals are focused on career development themes. Attention is given to linking present learning to future educational and vocational options and to preparations for work, jobs, and careers. Proponents argue that such efforts are needed in order to make basic education more relevant and less abstract for many students.

BACKGROUND AND CURRENT STATUS

It appears as if two basic strategies for achieving career education goals have been used. One strategy is to attempt to infuse entire school systems with a career education curriculum while a second has been to develop individualized primary prevention programs with career education goals.

Among those communities opting to attempt the infusion approach are Hackensack, New Jersey; Jefferson County, Colorado, Los Angeles, California; Mesa, Arizona; Pontiac, Michigan; Tuscaloosa, Alabama; Monticello, Florida; Akron, Ohio; and Atlanta, Georgia (Bottoms, 1972; Hoyt, 1976;

Jesser, 1976). In all cases, countless hours of planning, consultation, curriculum development, materials production, and evaluation were devoted to explaining and selling the concept, training individuals to participate, acquiring agreements from strategic persons to provide needed support services, and delivering the products to the children and adolescents being served. As one program's brochure implied, all of these efforts are directed toward combining the academic world with the world of work at all levels from kindergarten through the university for all students. Furthermore, the goals of a complete program are to enhance an awareness of the world of work, broaden the orientation to occupations, provide in-depth exploration of career clusters, and prepare all students for careers by incorporating career education activities into all basic education subjects throughout the curriculum.

All of this is certainly a tall order requiring massive cooperative efforts from many people just to get started, let alone to succeed. Some state departments of education developed curriculum guides for career education planning that would be helpful to school systems trying to get started. Pennsylvania (Pennsylvania Department of Education, 1974) and Wisconsin (Wisconsin Department of Public Instruction, 1971) are examples. Most, if not all, of these massive systemic projects were supported by federal funds from such sources as Part D, Section 142(C) of the Vocational Education Act Amendment of 1968 and Sections 402 and 406 of the Educational Amendments of 1974 (PL 93-380). Changes in national priorities led to a "drying up" of these resources and a concurrent decline in systemic efforts to infuse career education in the 1980s.

Several writers have expressed their disappointment in the state of the art of evaluating effects of large scale career education projects (Bonnet, 1979; Herr, 1977; Terry & Kenneke, 1980). Apparently, the evaluations of first-generation career education projects raised more questions than were answered, leaving interested observers to conclude that neither their effectiveness nor their ineffectiveness can be clearly concluded. Evaluation reports often related difficulties attributable to implementation problems, political factionalism, cost-effectiveness, and attitudes. They also tended to lack specificity about program content, making generalization impossible. Perhaps the lessons learned will generate a second generation of large scale career education infusion projects having clearer goals and content and more sophisticated evaluation strategies.

Although attempts to unify educational systems around a career development theme were stifled by the loss of funding support, reports about individual prevention programs espousing career education goals continued to appear in the professional literature. Thus, there are programmatic ideas to be shared with the readers of this volume, suggesting tactics that may be employed preventively on a less than system-wide scale. However, our presentation should not be viewed as meaning that we disagree in principle with the idea of a more comprehensive approach. We do agree, but our strategy must be to offer suggestions that may be implemented on a smaller scale, yet have potential for incorporation into systemic programs. In the next section, we will report on several preventive career education programs that have been evaluated and reported in the professional literature. Whether or not they are direct or indirect primary prevention programs is difficult to determine. Perhaps it is best to assume that, where the programs were delivered by counselors, direct services were provided, whereas programs delivered by teachers were indirect in nature.

EVALUATED CAREER EDUCATION PROGRAMS

The Vocational Exploration Group

▪ *Goals.* Developed by Daane (1972), the Vocational Exploration Group (VEG) is designed to help participants learn about jobs, satisfactions to be derived from work, requisite skills and interests for different occupations, and a variety of job functions involved in different occupations (Berglund & Lundquist, 1975). As various structural topics are presented, participants are encouraged to think about their own attributes relative to the topics being covered.

▪ *Tactics.* VEG groups are led by professionals who direct the participants from topic to topic while encouraging them to share thoughts and feelings in an accepting, uncritical atmosphere. Programs reported in the literature have ranged in length from 2 1/2 to 5 hours (five weekly 1-hour sessions). The major activities include explaining what one would do with a million dollars, categorizing jobs according to function and training needed, naming jobs one likes and dislikes the most, choosing suitable jobs and evaluating them, discussing satisfactions to be derived from jobs, identifying alternative jobs, and elaborating on follow-up plans related to the group experience.

▪ *Evaluation of Effects.* Glaize and Myrick (1984) reported that VEG has been effective in changing perceptions and attitudes about careers across several studies they had reviewed. In addition, Yates, Johnson, and Johnson (1979) found that career maturity (attitude and knowledge) was enhanced through VEG participation. They reported later that the effects held 6 months after treatment (Johnson, Johnson, & Yates, 1981). The reports cited above involved students ranging in age from junior through senior high school.

Training Programs for Enhancing Rational Decision Making Skills

▪ *Goals.* Students of career choice and career development have noted that individuals will encounter circumstances that require them to make important career-related decisions over their life spans. They have also noted that many people never learn to make such decisions in a rational manner (Berglund, Quatrano, & Lundquist, 1975). Assuming that rationality is an important ingredient for career-related decisions, several stepped models have been suggested (e.g., Gelatt, 1962; Katz, 1963). The steps that these models include are not unlike the problem solving stages cited in chapter 4: problem definition, identification of alternatives, clarification of values, gathering and exploration of information, evaluation of alternatives, tentative planning, and follow-up. Related training programs are designed in order to teach rational decision making skills, which, in turn, are to lead to good career-related decisions.

■ *Tactics.* Several published training programs are available, and there have been reported effects of hybrid models. Published offerings include Gelatt, Varenhorst, and Carey (1972), Gelatt, Varenhorst, Carey, and Miller (1973), and Krumboltz and Hamel (1977). Samples of hybrid models are those reported by Berglund et al. (1975), Egner and Jackson (1978), Jepson, Dustin, and Miars (1982), and Johnson and Myrick (1972). The methods used resemble the tactics cited in the problem solving section of chapter 4. Lesson plans focus on teaching the skills and accompanying attitudes associated with rational decision making, which include adaption to thinking in a rational, stepped manner.

■ *Evaluation of Effects.* Reports on effects of these programs have been sparse because appropriate outcome criteria are difficult to determine. Thus, several researchers have turned to assessing process variables such as whether trainees were able to demonstrate knowledge of program content or whether they were able to use the decision making steps in a simulation. Modest, yet positive, evidence of program effects on these process variables can be summed up across studies reported by Berglund et al. (1975), Brenner and Gazda-Grace (1979), Egner and Jackson (1978), Jepson et al. (1982), Johnson and Myrick (1972), and Laskin and Palmo (1983). As stated in chapter 4, Krumboltz, Sherba, Hamel, and Mitchell (1982) suggested that an alternative response to the outcome dilemma is to look for effects on the quality of resultant decisions. The studies cited above included student trainees ranging from middle school– through high school–age levels.

Programs to Enhance Development of Career Attitudes

■ *Goals.* The group of programs to be cited in this section had in common an effort by the designers to present stimuli that systematically enhanced the career-related attitudes of recipients in a positive direction. Since the specific attitudes to be enhanced varied across programs, the remainder of this section is organized differently from those above. The material is organized according to age/grade levels, and each report is summarized, providing information about authors, program content, specific goals, audience, and effects.

■ *Elementary School Children.* Edington (1976) developed an interest center in which mannequins dressed for particular occupations, tools for their trade, and tape-recorded interviews from workers in the field were all in a small house-shaped location that could be visited by kindergarten children. Through this approach, he hoped to make the children more aware

of the world of work and the place of work in life. Although effective, this approach was not found to be as effective as field trips to work sites or classroom visits from live models.

A group of studies assessed the effects on vocational role preferences of integrating into kindergarten and preschool curricula materials based on nontraditional role concepts (Weeks & Porter, 1983; Weeks, Thornburg, & Little, 1977). Results of these studies indicate that this may be a promising age at which to begin the process of modifying occupational stereotypes, especially in women.

■ *Middle School Students.* Cramer, Wise, and Colburn (1977) developed an 11-times-50-minute unit, Women at Work, for eighth grade girls in order to expand their career perceptions while also not denigrating traditional career choices. Unit content included definitions and discussions of stereotypes, an introduction to differing work roles, work force data, and an investigation of sexual stereotyping in the media. Results of the program evaluation indicated that some young women were stimulated to explore nontraditional jobs while others were not, an evaluation the researchers viewed as promising.

In an attempt to learn whether Values Clarification techniques actually clarify values, Tinsley, Benton, and Rollins (1984) presented seventh- and eighth-grade students with five 50-minute group Values Clarification sessions following a required five-session career decision–making enhancement group. Several widely known Values Clarification exercises such as "Twenty Things I Like to Do" and the "Values Auction" were employed. Differing results led the researchers to conclude that seventh-graders may not be ready for such exercises while eighth-graders will become aware of the need to cope with their values but will not be able to crystallize them.

A role clarification workshop entitled Opening Career Options (OCO) was presented to seventh- and eighth-grade students by Wilson and Daniel (1981). In the five-session workshop, role clarification exercises based on the program by Cochran and Warren (1976) were blended with exercises on the appraisal of vocational roles and with structural thinking about career decision making. The goal was to determine whether sex role stereotypes were influenced and choices expanded. As in the Cramer et al. (1977) study, results of this evaluation revealed modest effects, indicating promise for the OCO program.

▪ *High School Students.* Amatea, Clark, and Cross (1984) assessed the effects of a 2-week classroom unit entitled "Lifestyles." Presented to upper-level high school students, the "Lifestyles" program was designed to increase awareness of one's values and preferences related to work, family, and marriage; help examine sources of those life role preferences; increase awareness of costs and benefits associated with a variety of life-styles, and help examine one's own way of choosing and planning a life-style. Didactic and experiential activities were blended. Limitations of the study and the complexity of the outcomes indicate caution in drawing conclusions about the usefulness of this approach, yet it does seem possible to use it to cause some adolescents to consider their career planning more consciously and deliberately.

Simulated job experience kits were used by Johnson (1971) to assess whether 9th-and 11th-grade girls would learn more about specific occupations and occupations in general. Kits simulating medical laboratory and x-ray technology careers contained illustrated booklets in a programmed instruction format with explanations, imagined exercises, and related problems to solve. They were used during a 50-minute social studies class. Results of the study supported earlier research that demonstrated that students do become interested in the specific occupations presented in the brief simulation. However, there was no evidence of this activity generalizing to increased interest in learning more about occupations in general.

A short-term career awareness program was designed for 10th grade girls by Woodcock and Herman (1978). The goal of this program was to improve trainee awareness of the important role careers play in life planning. Eight 65-minute sessions were conducted over a 4-week period with the content including an introduction to sex role stereotyping, information about women who work outside of the home, estimated projections of their future lives, and visits by working women who served as potential role models. The program had an effect on overall career awareness and on factual knowledge of the current occupational status of women.

Career Development Course/Units

■ *Goals.* The career education programs presented thus far in this chapter have essentially been brief programs or short-term curriculum units that were incorporated within existing courses or scheduled independently within the school curriculum. The two examples presented in this section are of courses designed around the career education theme. They are of a longer duration and have more varied and comprehensive content than the programs cited above. Both took place in secondary schools.

■ *Tactics and Evaluation of Effects.* Mackin and Hansen (1981) presented an 11-week elective course entitled "Career—Thinking About Your Future" to 11th- and 12th-grade students in an upper midwest inner-city high school. Their general goal was to enhance the participants' career maturity through a blend of units drawn from work by Tennyson, Hansen, Klaurens, and Antholz (1980). The course included self-awareness units (e.g., Interests, Values and Needs), career awareness units (e.g., Career Development, The Future), and a unit designed to teach decision making skills in which *Decision and Outcomes* (Gelatt et al., 1973) was employed as a resource. A variety of traditional and innovative teaching methods were used, and results of the course evaluation led to the researchers concluding that career maturity attitudes and skills in self-appraisal and goal selection were affected. In addition, students in the class considered themselves to be more self-aware and better able to decide and plan than was the case at the outset.

An 18-week career development course instituted into three secondary schools in a city in the deep south was reported by Smith (1981). The general purpose of the classes was expressed as providing opportunities for self- and career exploration. Unit titles listed in the report covered topics such as relating the valuing process to career education, integrating related data from standardized tests, learning about the decision making process, using career information to test reality, developing individualized career exploration plans, and acquiring basic employment seeking and work adjustment skills. Findings from the course assessment indicated that attitudes toward selected career development concepts were influenced positively and that students' knowledge and skills were enhanced in the areas of occupational information and employment seeking skills.

Programs for Presenting Career Information

▪ *Goals.*   An important component of the career development process is individual acquisition of useful information. This information helps us to achieve career and self-awareness and enhances the decision making process. The following programs report on tactics used to achieve that goal—acquisition of career-relevant information.

▪ *Tactics and Evaluation of Effects.*   Jepsen (1972) studied the effects of presenting videotaped field trips to high school students in several rural communities. The 20-minute videotape contained information about such occupational clusters as the paper industry, marine construction, office occupations, and petroleum retailing and were accompanied by readings and discussion during a 14-week unit of twice-weekly 40-minute classes. Students in a comparison group read published materials about the same clusters and held similar discussions. In both instances of studying about occupations while remaining in the classroom, changes in several aspects of occupational knowledge occurred. Moreover, students experiencing the videotaped presentations conveyed accurate images of the occupations they studied more frequently.

The Life Career Game (Boocock, 1967) was studied by Johnson and Euler (1972) as a means of communicating information about careers to 9th- and 10th-grade students. Life Career Game is a simulation providing profiles of different adolescents for whom teams of players must make a series of career-related decisions. Each decision has its consequences and related informational needs. Participants are able to become actively involved in trying to make successful decisions for their simulated adolescent. Compared with a group being taught by traditional classroom methods, the Life Career Game group learned less educational information and learned and retained an equal amount of occupational information, while retaining more occupational information.

Four career exploration approaches were compared by Wiggins and Moody (1981) on several dimensions, one of which was occupational information needs. The programs were conducted daily by classroom teachers for nine weeks. While details about most of the course content were not made available in the report, it was stated that they differed according to the use of the following instruments, procedures, and programs: One teacher used the *Career Survey* (Wiggins, 1974) and Holland's (1978) *Vocational Preference Inventory* for individualized career exploration; a second teacher employed Holland's (1974) *Self-Directed Search* in conjunction with procedures for self-exploration activities as presented in Holland's (1977) *Understanding Yourself and Your Career* booklet; the third teacher followed planned exercises based on parts of Crites's (1978) *Career Maturity Inventory* (e.g., "Knowing Yourself," "Choosing a Job"); labeled as the "traditional approach," the fourth teacher's program consisted of assigned readings and reports on job clusters, followed up with question-and-answer sessions and knowledge tests.

Although the exact effect of the different approaches on expressed occupational information needs could not be extracted from the overall analysis, it was concluded that all of the more innovative approaches were more effective than the traditional approach, leading us to suggest that reliance on traditional teaching approaches such as those described herein be avoided when presenting programs designed to enhance the acquisition of career information.

Job Seeking Skills Training

■ *Goals.* Viewing the employment interview as an interpersonal influence situation, Wild and Kerr (1984) taught persuasion skills to 10th- through 12th-grade students. Trainees were to learn how to enhance their expertise, attractiveness, and trustworthiness in the eyes of others. They would then become more confident in their ability to communicate during job interviews and, perhaps, increase their probability of being hired.

■ *Tactics and Evaluation of Effects.* Students were taught verbal and nonverbal behaviors associated with being attractive, expert, and trustworthy in the eyes of others and then practiced those behaviors in simulated training interviews through five 50-minute sessions. Among the skills selected for the instructional program were warm greetings and leaning forward in the chair while smiling (attractiveness), reacting to the interviewer and listening carefully (expertness), and speaking and looking directly toward the interviewer (trustworthiness). The design for this program was developed by Kerr, Claiborn, and Dixon (1982). Results of ratings by adult interviewers after brief simulated employment interviews following training designated those in the training program as appearing to be more persuasive than a comparison group.

Involving Parents in Career Education

■ *Goals.* Realizing that parents play a significant role in the development of their children, those who have designed parent-related programs seek to enhance the child's career development indirectly. One approach is to provide opportunities for parents to learn about occupational opportunities and resources, and about the process of career choice. A second approach is to invite parents to learn about and/or participate in the career planning process along with their children.

■ *Tactics and Evaluation of Effects.* Lea (1976) described a program representative of the first approach cited above. A Parents' Workshop on Vocational Choice was designed to give information on the nature of vocational choice to parents of high school sophomores and juniors. Specifically, the parents in attendance responded to Holland's (1978) *Vocational Preference Inventory (VPI)* on three answer sheets indicating their own preferences, how they thought their children had responded, and how they hoped their children had responded. The workshop leaders distributed the parents' and children's VPI profiles and accompanying explanatory materials, explained the system, and asked discussion-inducing questions in hopes of achieving increased interest and understanding leading to student–parent dialogues. Answers by respondents to a follow-up survey indicated that most had thought more about their child's career planning after the program than they had beforehand, all had talked to their children about career planning, a majority had been approached by their children to converse about career planning, and most indicated that their children had demonstrated increased interest in career planning.

A systematic 6-week-times-2-hour program reported by Amatea and Cross (1980) represents the parent involvement in the planning process approach listed above. GOING PLACES was designed for 9th- through 12th-grade students and their parents. Basic content components were: individual goal-setting with cooperative efforts to achieve goals; exploring individual interests, values, and competencies; learning a system for organizing and exploring the world of work; developing information-gathering skills; studying the present and brainstorming about the future job market; and setting immediate and long range goals. Anecdotal evaluation data revealed high levels of satisfaction with and appreciation for the program among a group of motivated and conflict-free adolescents and their parents.

A Summative Evaluation of Career Education Programs

Baker and Popowicz (1983) reported results of a metaanalysis integration of studies of prevention programs using career education strategies and, in so doing, provided empirical evidence that these programs yielded respectable effects. The metaanalysis technique used was to transform posttest data from treatment and control groups across 18 studies (118 comparisons) to a standardized statistic known as the Effect Size (ES). The average ES for the 18 studies was 0.50 indicating that a hypothetical person at the mean of the control group can be expected to improve 0.50 standard deviations above the mean on outcome measures after receiving the career education treatments sampled across the 18 studies subjected to the metaanalysis. Although this conclusion is subject to arguable assumptions about control group distributions and the uniformity of treatment effects, the results still indicate moderate effects that are sufficient to justify the statement that positive outcomes have resulted from individualized primary prevention programs with career education goals.

CASE STUDIES

Job Seeking Skills for High School Students

Scheduling the Program and Selecting Participants. Arrangements were made with the teacher of a senior English class for the counseling intern[1] to meet with the class one period per week for 7 weeks. There were 20 students enrolled, and

---

1. This program was designed and implemented by Rose Ann Tunall.

the class was classified as one for students of low academic ability. It seemed logical to conclude that they would soon be applying for jobs.

First Session. Introductions were accompanied by a pretest of content to be covered in the unit. Students then completed a self-evaluation on which they merely listed their perceived employment strengths and weaknesses in two separate columns. They then viewed filmstrips on self-concept and jobs, read a brief handout that challenged them to think about their self-image and what prospective employees look for in applicants, and discussed the material as a group. Initially, some students demonstrated little interest but perked up when offered the option of returning to regular English class content.

Second Session. All students received simulations of completed job application forms used by local employers. After leader-directed instructions and discussion about common and peculiar segments of the forms, each student then selected one and practiced completing it in class. Two more were selected for completion during the intervening week as a homework assignment to be evaluated and graded by their English teacher.

Third Session. Completed application forms were collected and related discussion followed. The leader then instructed the class about personal inventories and résumés, showing a filmstrip on preparing résumés. A discussion followed. Some students complained that the topic was repetitive of earlier classwork but agreed that they still needed assistance with résumé preparation. Arrangements were made with the English teacher to incorporate the completed résumés into the English course as a graded assignment.

Fourth Session. Forms for writing résumés were reviewed, sample completed résumés were distributed, and discussion of similarities and differences across the samples was generated by the leader. This was followed by a filmstrip on job interviewing. After the filmstrip, printed handouts reinforcing the major points of the filmstrip were distributed. Related discussion followed and was to continue into the next session. Students seemed eager to participate in a simulated job interview.

Fifth Session. Discussion related to the interviewing process handouts continued. Students were especially interested in a list of "Interview Hints," and meaningful student-generated discussion followed.

Sixth Session. The counseling intern and English teacher role-played two job interview simulations. The first interview depicted their version of an appropriate performance while the second highlighted poor technique grossly enough not to serve as a model but realistically enough to serve as a stimulus for identifying appropriate and inappropriate behaviors. The students critiqued each interview, and a lively discussion followed. The leader then explained the ground rules for conducting and evaluating simulated student interviews.

Seventh Session. The students conducted simulated job interviews in triads, switching roles (interviewer, applicant, and observer) until all roles had been played by each participant. Evaluative and instructive discussions took place within the triads after each simulation was completed. While this took place, the counseling intern and English teacher circulated around the room attempting to observe and assist each group. Some time was devoted to a class discussion of the overall impact of the unit at the end of the period.

Evaluation. Pre- to posttest results on a true–false knowledge test indicated that 82% of the examinees had improved their performance. Results of a posttest survey of attitudes toward the training program indicated that 94% of the respondents thought the program was worth their time and helpful. They also indicated that the applications and résumés were the most useful components, more media presentations were desired, and more time was needed for interviewing practice.

Career Awareness Programs for High School-Aged Young Women

Scheduling the Program and Selecting Participants. Two career awareness programs were designed.[2] Basic content and teaching techniques were the same for both programs. They differed in one way: information, activities, and media presentations about nontraditional careers were added to the experimental group's program. Since the nontraditional career awareness group contained all the ingredients of the traditional group, the former will be presented in this case study. Volunteers were recruited from study halls, and groups were established accordingly. Thus, the participants met voluntarily during study hall periods. They were a mix of young women in grades 10 through 12. The groups met for six 45-minute weekly sessions.

First Session. The leader opened with a didactic presentation in which the term *nontraditional careers* was defined, potential advantages in selecting nontraditional careers were highlighted, and negative effects of occupational sex stereotyping were inventoried. This session closed with a get-acquainted exercise in which the leader and group members sequentially took the first letter in their given names, selected an appropriately descriptive adjective beginning with the same letter, and presented it to the group. The exercise seemed to serve successfully as an icebreaker.

Second Session. This session opened with the group leader didactically presenting material about the necessity for many families to have two incomes, economic needs of single women and widows, satisfactions accrued from having an enjoyable occupation, and the enhanced salaries and prestige many women enjoy who are in nontraditional jobs. Group participation was elicited. A fantasy exercise followed in which the participants were asked to imagine a perfect day for themselves five years henceforward. The leaders encouraged them to imagine themselves in nontraditional careers, thinking about concurrent living conditions, responsibilities, educational requirements, possessions, and companions. The session closed with a filmstrip entitled *Choosing Your Career* (Guidance Associates, 1968) in which the importance of making good career-related decisions in high school was emphasized.

Third Session. A group discussion on the conflict between home and career that many women face opened this session. Group members volunteered feelings they held about the future. The leader then asked the group to brainstorm compromises or solutions to perceived problems, using their own ideas or referring to solutions their parents had achieved. In addition, they were encouraged to brainstorm solutions to overcoming barriers to a quest for a nontraditional career. This was followed by a group discussion of a list of myths compiled by the leader from statistics published by the Women's Bureau (e.g., "Married women take jobs away from men," "Women don't want responsibility on the job; they don't want promotions or job changes which add to their load.") The session ended with a story completion exercise. Group members were asked to respond to a vignette in which a young

---

2. This program was designed and implemented by Marie A. Cini.

woman was frustrated in her efforts to consider nontraditional careers by a sexist guidance counselor.

Fourth Session. Group members were given a list of activities from Holland's (1974) *Self-Directed Search* and encouraged to consider nontraditional careers while completing the exercise. In order to assist them in determining what they do well, group members were next asked to complete the "Functional/Transferrable Skills Inventory" from Bolles's (1980) *What Color is Your Parachute?* They were encouraged to check nontraditional skills they may possess. When finished, the group then viewed a film entitled, *Vocational Education for a Changing World* (Nova Productions, 1980). In the film, female high school students are seen exploring and choosing traditionally male trades. Consequently, the film served as a source of symbolic models for the young women in the group.

Fifth Session. Group members were first asked to complete a job Values Clarification exercise entitled "Relating Your Values to Work" (Scholz, Prince, & Miller, 1975). In the exercise, they were asked to think about their favorite activities during the previous year's time. While so doing, they were encouraged to list enjoyable activities that may seem nontraditional to others. Next, the leader distributed a worksheet containing a six-step rational decision making paradigm for their perusal (Identify the problem; obtain alternatives; consider all the alternatives; choose among all the alternatives; develop an action plan; and decide and follow up). The session closed with the group viewing the second part of a filmstrip entitled *Jobs and Gender* (Guidance Associates, 1973) in which men and women were engaged in nontraditional work. Again, symbolic models were presented.

Sixth Session. Because this was the last session, the leader sought to pull everything together. Participants were encouraged to use the information they had acquired and respond to the challenges presented to them.

Evaluation. Because the career awareness programs were involved in an experimental study, the traditional and nontraditional groups were compared with a control group on measures of attitudes toward occupational sex stereotypes and occupational goals. No differential effects occurred on these measures, but members of all groups increased the number of occupations they thought to be appropriate for both men and women. There was no formal effort to evaluate group member attitudes toward the content and method of their programs. Informal comments and observations led the program designer and leader to conclude that it was of too short a duration to have any differential impact on attitudes toward nontraditional careers among young women in a rural, semiisolated community where traditional values are strongly ingrained and seldom questioned. On the other hand, the program content may have been valuable relative to traditional variables that were not assessed (e.g., awareness of the need to make decisions, increased knowledge about the world of work).

A Career Awareness Program for Sixth-Graders

Scheduling the Program and Selecting Participants. The program[3] was presented to all 23 students enrolled in a sixth-grade class in a rural elementary school. Thirty-minute sessions were conducted 2 days per week for 10 weeks. Sixth-

---

3. This program was designed and implemented by Barbara A. Baeckert.

graders were selected as a target group because they were to enter the junior/senior high school the following year, and it was hoped that the program would enhance their sophistication about and readiness to use the career development opportunities they would encounter in high school. No systematic career education programming had preceded this one for the children attending the program.

First Session. In order to enhance group interrelations and to have the children begin exploring personal goals and characteristics, the leader opened the session by asking them to write their names in the middle of an index card. On the corners of the card, they were asked to list something they like to do, their favorite school subject, what they want to be, and one word that described them. In the following class discussion, the students were asked to share with the group a response they had written on any of the four corners on the index card. Each member was then asked to tell the group what was listed in the "What I Want to Be" corner. They were then subdivided into smaller groups with others in the class who stated similar career plans. When conversing in the subgroups, they were encouraged to share perceptions about careers. The session closed with everyone again meeting in one group to discuss resultant perceptions, observations, and questions. The activity seemed enjoyable, and some had misconceptions about careers that were clarified during the small group session.

Second Session: Why Work? Throughout this session, the class met as one large discussion group while the leader asked them to imagine themselves responding to suggested future events. In the first journey into the future they were to imagine themselves inheriting a considerable amount of money while, in the second, they were to be living in a society where robots performed all of the work. Following each imagined exercise, the leader directed thought-provoking discussion questions to the group, challenging the students to think about whether they would work and what they would do if not working. The leader and the class found the discussion interesting and exciting. Numerous ideas were generated. Interestingly, most students objected to not being able to work.

Third Session: I Can Be Anything. At the outset, all students were asked to complete five sentences on a sheet of paper, each beginning with "Because I am a boy (girl), I am good at . . . ." During the ensuing discussion, the leader attempted to focus group thinking by asking questions about jobs in terms of gender stereotypes. Next, the group was asked to complete five sentences beginning with "Because I am me, I am good at . . . ." Again, the writing exercise was followed by a group discussion. In the discussion, leader-directed questions focused group member attention on themselves (e.g., "Would your qualities be helpful in a career?", "How did it feel to say good things about yourself?"). After a slow start, the students willingly and intensely engaged in the discussion on gender stereotypes.

Fourth Session: It Takes All Types, 1. As in the second session, the students were asked to take an imaged journey into the future. In this case, the students engaged in an exercise on deciding which persons should be chosen to colonize a new planet. This was accompanied by a one-page handout listing 49 jobs and stating that there are actually 20,000 jobs from which to choose. The brainstorming technique was used by the entire group for the remainder of the meeting time in order to develop a hierarchy of important jobs for colonists to the new planet. In this group, all jobs were viewed as essential. It seemed as if the group enjoyed this exercise.

Fifth Session: It Takes All Types, 2.   Using the listing distributed in the fourth session, the group attempted to classify the 49 jobs according to five cluster categories listed on the blackboard by the leader: Arts, Industry, Commerce, Services, and Social Sciences. The leader acted as clarifyer and resource person. Students deemed the exercise as tough but fun. Due to confusion that was experienced by the students, the Services and Social Sciences categories were combined.

Sixth Session: Industry.   In order to involve the children briefly in occupational exploration, the leader assigned them to seven subgroups, each asked to acquire information about a specified occupation and report it back to the entire group. To accomplish this task during the session, each student was given a career card identifying an occupation and a "Popeye" comic from the King Comic Career Services containing information about the occupation assigned. They were also given specific questions to research (i.e., "What is _____'s job?", "What training is needed?", "Where does a person having your job work?") Although the students completed the task and seemed to learn something from it, they were also disgruntled, viewing it as too similar to regular school work.

Seventh Session: Commerce.   During the entire session, the group engaged in a simulation called the Network Game. Four teams were assigned: a shipping company, a bank, a store, and an advertising agency. Given a limited amount of capital, each team was to accomplish the same goal (get shirts from a manufacturer to a consumer at the lowest possible cost). In so doing, they were forced to make decisions that sometimes brought them in to direct competition with each other. At other times, they were forced to cooperate. This activity was received more enthusiastically than any previous one, with group members wanting to engage in the game again, switching roles.

Eighth Session: Services and Social Sciences.   As a group, the children were asked to brainstorm all the occupations they could think of that would be performed in a hospital, categorizing those occupations on the blackboard as unskilled, semi-skilled, semiprofessional, professional, or "high professional." In the accompanying discussion, the leader directed questions to the group about requisite training, comparative pay, and opportunities. The group seemed quite capable of assigning levels to various occupations. In the interim, the classroom teacher reported instances of some members engaging in self-initiated efforts to acquire career information.

Ninth Session: Arts.   In order to simulate activities at a television station, the students developed their own commercial, directed it, and acted in it. In so doing, they identified 13 related occupations. Due to the nature of this exercise, an additional 30-minute session was needed. Noticing that communications had broken down in the planning subgroups during the first session, the leader was forced to engage the entire group in discussion to solve problems and share feelings. This turned out to be an excellent object lesson for the group. The members worked through their problems independently of the group sessions, engaged successfully in the assigned task, and generally felt pleased about having responded to the challenge in a mature manner. In addition, the leader was able to generate an ad hoc discussion on being a responsible worker.

Tenth Session: Evaluation.   This session was devoted to answering questions on a leader-designed survey and discussing student responses as a group.

Evaluation.   Responses to the brief opinion survey and comments made during the last session caused the leader to conclude that the program as a whole was well accepted by the children. Simulation exercises were more popular than writing exercises. Self-reports indicated that some students thought they had experienced increased self-awareness while others felt they had expanded their knowledge about careers.

SUMMARY

Career education is founded on the principle that career development may be enhanced for those who are the recipients of such programming. The benefits of career education programming will not be available for everyone until curricula reflecting such goals are infused systematically across all grade levels. Until that time arrives, guidance professionals will have to settle for delivering or causing other professionals to deliver primary prevention programs that have a career education flavor.

Several potentially useful programs have been evaluated and reported in the professional literature. They include Daane's (1972) Vocational Exploration Group; several systems for teaching rational decision making skills; programs designed to effect career-related attitudes such as occupational stereotypes, awareness of one's values, and awareness of the role careers play in life planning; programs for presenting career-related information; methods for improving job seeking skills; and ideas for getting parents involved in their children's career development process.

The case studies presented above provide useful ideas for practitioners. Designed by students preparing to become professionals, implemented in the field, and tested, the case study programs suggest interesting methods for others to consider and point out that some children and adolescents are not easily motivated to use the information and ideas presented to them constructively. It appears as if preventive career education programming is appropriate at all grade levels as both a direct and indirect service. Many of the tactics presented in the career education literature resemble those also espoused in other primary prevention camps. The main difference, which identifies these programs with the career education description, is a linkage to career development theory and goals.

PUBLISHED RESOURCES

Amatea, E., & Cross, G. (1982). *Lifestyles: Program handbook for counselors.* Tallahassee, FL: Florida Department of Education.

Azrin, N. H., & Besalel, V. A. (1980). *Job club counselor's manual: A behavioral approach to vocational counseling.* Baltimore: University Park Press.

Bartsch, L., & Sandmeyer, L. (1979). *Skills in life career planning.* Monterey, CA: Brooks/Cole.

Bem, S. L., & Bem, D. J. (1973). *Training the woman to know her place: The social antecedents of women in the world of work.* Harrisburg, PA: Bureau of Instructional Support Services.

College Entrance Examination Board (1977). *Career skills assessment program.* Princeton, NJ: Author.

Drier, H. N., Jr. (1972). *K–12 guide for integrating career development into local curriculum*. Worthington, OH: C. H. Jones.

Evans, R. N. (1973). *Career education in the middle/junior high school*. Salt Lake City: Olympus.

Farmer, P. H. (1980). *A counseling workshop manual for women seeking nontraditional work*. Harrisburg, PA: Pennsylvania Department of Education.

Ferguson, J. (Ed.). (1974). *The career guidance class*. Camarillo, CA: Metcalf.

Jaques, J. W., & Schwartz, B. (1976). *Career education bibliography* (2nd ed.). Upper Montclair, NJ: National Multi-Media Center for Adult Education.

Kilby, J. E. (Ed.). (1980). *Career education and English: K–12*. Urbana, IL: National Council of Teachers of English.

Mangum, G. L., Becker, J. W., Coombs, G., & Marshall, P. (Eds.). (1975). *Career education in the academic classroom*. Salt Lake City: Olympus.

McClure, L. (1975). *Career education survival manual: A guidebook for career educators and their friends*. Salt Lake City: Olympus.

Miller, J. V. (1978a). *Career development needs of nine year olds: How to improve career development programs*. Washington, DC: National Vocational Guidance Association & Association for Measurement and Evaluation in Guidance.

Miller, J. V. (1978b). *Career development of seventeen year olds: How to improve career development programs*. Washington, DC: National Vocational Guidance Association & Association for Measurement and Evaluation in Guidance.

Raymond, C. D. (1980). *Career education infusion: A review of selected curriculum guides for the middle school*. Columbus, OH: National Center for Research in Vocational Education.

Talbot, W. (1972). *Utah model for career guidance: K–12*. Salt Lake City: Utah State Board of Education, Division of Special Service. (ERIC Document Reproduction Service No. ED 079 516)

Tiedeman, D. V., Schreiber, M., & Wessell, T. R., Jr. (1976). *Key resources in career education: An annotated guide*. DeKalb, IL: ERIC Clearinghouse in Career Education.

United States Department of Health, Education and Welfare, Office of Career Education. (1979). *Career education programs that work*. Washington, DC: Author.

Winefordner, D. (1977). *The career decision-making program*. Bloomington, IL: McKnight.

REFERENCES

Amatea, E. S., Clark, J. E., & Cross, E. G. (1984). Life-styles: Evaluating a life role planning program for high school students. *Vocational Guidance Quarterly, 32,* 249–259.

Amatea, E. S., & Cross, E. G. (1980). Going places: A career guidance program for high school students and their parents. *Vocational Guidance Quarterly, 28,* 274–282.

Baker, S. B., & Popowicz, C. L. (1983). Meta-analysis as a strategy for evaluating effects of career education interventions. *Vocational Guidance Quarterly, 31,* 178–186.

Barclay, L. (1972). The emergence of vocational expectations in preschool children. *Journal of Vocational Behavior, 4,* 1–14.

Berglund, B. W., & Lundquist, G. W. (1975). The vocational exploration group and minority youth: An experimental outcome study. *Journal of Vocational Behavior, 7,* 289–296.

Berglund, B. W., Quatrano, L. A., & Lundquist, G. W. (1975). Group social models and structured interaction in teaching decision making. *Vocational Guidance Quarterly, 24,* 28–36.

Bolles, R. N. (1980). *What color is your parachute?* Berkeley, CA: Ten Speed Press.

Bonnet, D. G. (1979). Career education evaluation: The state of the art. *Journal of Career Education, 5,* 230–249.

Boocock, S. (1967). The Life Career Game. *Personnel and Guidance Journal, 46,* 328–334.

Bottoms, G. (1972). *Career development education: Kindergarten through postsecondary and adult levels.* Atlanta: Georgia Department of Education.

Brenner, D., & Gazda-Grace, P. A. (1979). Career decision making in women as a function of sex composition of career-planning groups. *Measurement and Evaluation in Guidance, 12,* 8–13.

Cochran, D. J., & Warren, P. M. (1976). Career counseling for women: A workshop format. *School Counselor, 24,* 124–127.

Cramer, S. H., Wise, P. S., & Colburn, E. D. (1977). An evaluation of a treatment to expand the career perceptions of junior high school girls. *School Counselor, 25,* 124–129.

Crites, J. O. (1978). *Career maturity inventory.* Monterey, CA: McGraw–Hill.

Daane, C. J. (1972). *Vocational Exploration Group.* Tempe, AZ: Studies of Urban Man.

Edington, E. D. (1976). Evaluation of methods of using resource people in helping kindergarten students become aware of the world of work. *Journal of Vocational Behavior, 8,* 125–131.

Egner, J. R., & Jackson, D. J. (1978). Effectiveness of a counseling intervention program for teaching career decision-making skills. *Journal of Counseling Psychology, 25,* 45–51.

Gelatt, H. B. (1962). Decision making: A conceptual frame of reference for counseling. *Journal of Counseling Psychology, 9,* 240–245.

Gelatt, H. B., Varenhorst, B., & Carey, R. (1972). *Deciding.* New York: College Entrance Examination Board.

Gelatt, H. B., Varenhorst, B., Carey, R., & Miller, G. (1973). *Decisions and outcomes.* New York: College Entrance Examination Board.

Ginzberg, E. (1972). Toward a theory of occupational choice: A restatement. *Vocational Guidance Quarterly, 20,* 169–176.

Ginzberg, E., Ginsburg, S. W., Axelrod, S., & Herma, J. L. (1951). *Occupational choice: An approach to a general theory.* New York: Columbia University Press.

Glaize, D. L., & Myrick, R. D. (1984). Interpersonal groups or computers? A study of career maturity and career decidedness. *Vocational Guidance Quarterly, 32,* 168–176.

Guidance Associates (Producer). (1968). *Choosing your career* [Filmstrip]. Pleasantville, NY: Producer.

Guidance Associates (Producer). (1973). *Jobs and gender* [Filmstrip]. Pleasantville, NY: Producer.

Herr, E. L. (1969). *Unifying an entire system of education around a career development theme.* Paper read at the National Conference on Exemplary Projects and Programs of the 1968 Vocational Education Amendments, Atlanta, GA.

Herr, E. L. (1975). Career education: Some perspectives on validity and content. *Journal of Career Education, 2,* 57–70.

Herr, E. L. (1977). *Research and evaluation in career education: The state of the art.* Columbus, OH: ERIC Clearinghouse in Career Education.

Holland, J. L. (1974). *The self-directed search.* Palo Alto, CA: Consulting Psychologists Press.

Holland, J. L. (1977). *Understanding yourself and your career.* Palo Alto, CA: Consulting Psychologists Press.

Holland, J. L. (1978). *Vocational preference inventory.* Palo Alto, CA: Consulting Psychologists Press.

Hoyt, K. B. (1976). *Profiles of career education projects: Second year's program fiscal year funding.* Washington, DC: Office of Career Education.

Hoyt, K. B. (1977). *A primer for career education.* Washington, DC: Superintendent of Documents.

Jepsen, D. A. (1972). The impact of videotaped occupational field trips on occupational knowledge. *Vocational Guidance Quarterly, 21,* 54–62.

Jepsen, D. A., Dustin, R., & Miars, R. (1982). The effects of problem-solving training of adolescents' career exploration and career decision making. *Personnel and Guidance Journal, 61,* 149–153.

Jesser, D. L. (1976). *Career education: A priority of the chief state school officers.* Salt Lake City: Olympus.

Johnson, N., Johnson, J., & Yates, C. (1981). A 6-month follow-up on the effects of the Vocational Exploration Group on career maturity. *Journal of Counseling Psychology, 28,* 70–71.

Johnson, R. G. (1971). Job simulations to promote vocational interest. *Vocational Guidance Quarterly, 20,* 25–30.

Johnson, R. H., & Euler, D. E. (1972). Effect of the Life Career Game on learning and retention of educational-occupational information. *School Counselor, 19,* 155–159.

Johnson, R. H., & Myrick, R. D. (1972). MOLD: A new approach to career decision-making. *Vocational Guidance Quarterly, 21,* 48–53.

Katz, M. R. (1963). *Decisions and values.* New York: College Entrance Examination Board.

Kerr, B. A., Claiborn, C. D., & Dixon, D. N. (1982). Training counselors in persuasion. *Counselor Education and Supervision, 22,* 138–149.

Krumboltz, J. D., & Hamel, D. A. (1977). *Guide to career decision making skills.* New York: College Entrance Examination Board.

Krumboltz, J. D., Sherba, D. S., Hamel, D. A., & Mitchell, L. K. (1982). Effect of training in rational decision making on the quality of simulated career decisions. *Journal of Counseling Psychology, 29,* 618–625.

Laskin, S. B., & Palmo, A. J. (1983). The effect of decisions and outcomes on the career maturity of high school students. *Journal of Vocational Behavior, 23,* 22–34.

Lea, H. D. (1976). A personalized parents' workshop on career choice. *Vocational Guidance Quarterly, 24,* 373–375.

Mackin, R. K., & Hansen, L. S. (1981). A theory-based career development course: A plant in the garden. *School Counselor, 28,* 325–334.

Nova Productions (Producer). (1980). *Vocational education for a changing world* [Film]. Harrisburg, PA: Department of Education.

Pennsylvania Department of Education. (1974). *Pennsylvania career development guide.* Harrisburg, PA: Author.

Scholz, N. T., Prince, J. S., & Miller, G. P. (1975). *How to decide: A guide for women.* New York: College Entrance Examination Board.

Smith, C. W. (1981). Cognitive and affective benefits of a career development course. *Journal of Career Education, 8,* 57–66.

Super, D. E. (1953). A theory of vocational development. *American Psychologist, 8,* 185–190.

Super, D. E. (1957). *Psychology of careers.* New York: Harper.

Tennyson, W. W., Hansen, L. S., Klaurens, M. K., & Antholz, M. B. (1980). *Educating for career development* (rev. ed.). Arlington, VA: National Vocational Guidance Association.

Terry, A. E., & Kenneke, L. J. (1980). A model for evaluation of career education in education personnel programs. *Journal of Career Education, 6,* 225–239.

Tinsley, H. E. A., Benton, G. L., & Rollins, J. A. (1984). The effects of values clarification exercises on the value structure of junior high school students. *Vocational Guidance Quarterly, 32,* 160–167.

Weeks, M. D., & Porter, E. P. (1983). A second look at the impact of nontraditional vocational role models and curriculum on the vocational role preferences of kindergarten children. *Journal of Vocational Behavior, 23,* 64–71.

Weeks, M. O., Thornburg, K. R., & Little, L. (1977). The impact of exposure to nontraditional vocational role models on the vocational role preferences of five-year-old children. *Journal of Vocational Behavior, 10,* 139–145.

Wiggins, J. D. (1974). *The career survey.* Washington, DC: National Vocational Guidance Association.

Wiggins, J. D., & Moody, A. (1981). A field-based comparison of four career-exploration approaches. *Vocational Guidance Quarterly, 30,* 15–20.

Wild, B. K., & Kerr, B. A. (1984). Training adolescent job-seekers in persuasion skills. *Vocational Guidance Quarterly, 33,* 63–69.

Wilson, J., & Daniel, R. (1981). The effects of a career-options workshop on social and vocational stereotypes. *Vocational Guidance Quarterly, 29,* 341–349.

Wisconsin Department of Public Instruction. (1971). *Guide to integration of career development into curriculum—Grades K–12.* Madison, WI: Author.

Woodcock, P. R., & Herman, A. (1978). Fostering career awareness in tenth-grade girls. *School Counselor, 25,* 256–264.

Yates, C., Johnson, N., & Johnson, J. (1979). Effects of the use of the Vocational Exploration Group on career maturity. *Journal of Counseling Psychology, 26,* 368–370.

6

DEVELOPING COMPETENCE IN YOUNG CHILDREN

T he general concept of competence appears to have first been articulated by Robert White (1959). Since that time it has become the focus
of a great deal of research and discussion, mainly among developmental psychologists. There seems to be general agreement that competence
is a learned characteristic (White, 1959; Bandura, 1977) and that parents play
the most crucial role in its development (Baumrind, 1971; White, 1975a).
There is also a strong suggestion that the earliest months and years of life are
the most crucial in its development. Studies of populations where efforts to
promote competence were begun with children at the age of three or four
almost routinely indicate that although outcomes are positive they are modest
and do not continue throughout a child's school history (Bronfenbrenner,
1975; Cicirelli, 1969; Gray 1983). These findings coupled with those of White
(1975b) suggest that the age of three or four, for most children, may be too
late to initiate such efforts and that it is necessary to begin much earlier.

Another factor clouds the interpretations that can be made of the studies
cited above. This is the fact that the primary, although not the only, focus of
these efforts was the child, not the parents. While some attempts were made
to provide parents with information, changing parent behavior in relation to
their children in order to facilitate the development of competence was not
the basic thrust. From a primary-preventive point of view, it would appear
most appropriate to attempt to change parental behavior in relation to the
child rather than attempting to provide, for relatively brief periods each
week, a stimulating environment for the child. Such an approach would not
only result in a parent being effective with a given child over a long period

of time but has the potential to generalize to other children subsequently born to the same parents.

Efforts to develop competence in children, if they are to be most effective, focus on the following three groups: (a) The parents of infants still in the first few months of life, (b) Parents-to-be, and (c) General populations where there is a reasonable expectation that, at some future date, a high proportion may become parents, specifically high school students.

The argument can immediately be made that the first two of these populations are not and have never been considered appropriate clients for schools. If, however, primary prevention is "beginning at the beginning" as White (1980) has suggested and if the schools are interested in ultimately receiving children who are as competent as it is possible for them to be then these two populations become an appropriate focus for the professional activities of school personnel. That it is possible cannot be doubted. The Brookline Early Education Project (Pierson, Walker, and Tivnan, 1984) was a project focusing on infants and their parents and was carried out through the structure of the school system for over a decade. Such an undertaking constitutes a considerable departure from normal school practices. The potential for improving the subsequent school performance of children and reducing learning and behavior problems would appear to make the effort worthwhile (Pierson, et al., 1984).

BARRIERS TO THE PROVISION OF SERVICES AIMED AT DEVELOPING COMPETENCE

There are two major barriers to the delivery of such services. One has already been indicated above: the reluctance of schools to undertake provision of services to parents who are not ordinarily considered to be their clients. The other potential barrier is embedded in the economic situation of some families.

It has been suggested (Carey, 1974) that a sense of powerlessness develops in family situations where basic needs for food, clothing, and shelter are either unmet or perpetually in doubt of being met. Carey is doubtful that cognitive competence can be developed in such settings. Her views are supported by Keniston's report (1977) on the needs of the U.S. family. A dissent is entered by Seeman (1983), whose research indicated that "durable qualities" related to competence were found in spite of differences in socioeconomic status. Nevertheless, from a Maslovian point of view, it seems reasonable to suggest that where "basic needs" are unmet, programs aiming at the development of competence will be less effective then they might otherwise be. No one, including the present authors, has suggested that competence-building programs be withheld from any population on the basis of their economic status, only that expectations for success may be less in such situations.

DEFINITIONS OF COMPETENCE

As might easily be anticipated, the definition of a term as broad as *competence* is not precise. At the same time, there is considerable commonality among different definitions and it is possible to arrive at a central core of agreement. White (1959), whose original formulation appears to have initiated the subsequent interest in the topic, defined *competence* as "an organism's capacity to interact effectively with its environment" (p. 297). He elaborated on this definition by indicating that interacting effectively with the environment entailed the exercise of behaviors that led to a feeling of effectiveness and a sense of gratification. He asserted that there was a motivation to become competent, and differentiated it from a drive state.

Connolly and Bruner (1974) felt that competence implied *action*, the ability to change the environment as well as to adapt to it. They differentiated between *knowing how* and *knowing that*. Competence, in their view, is not merely possessing information but being able to use it to change one's personal environment. The concept was viewed in bipolar terms by Baumrind (1971) who saw two dimensions to competence. These two dimensions were (a) responsible behavior versus socially disruptive behavior and (b) active behavior versus passive behavior.

Others have used the term *social competence* rather than *competence* alone. In spite of this distinction, such definitions do not appear to vary greatly from definitions of simple *competence*. A list of 29 social competencies has been presented by Anderson and Messick (1974) but their list clearly includes both ability and knowledge dimensions as well as social skills and attitudes. A definition of social competence that sounds quite close to White's (1959) definition of competence has been proposed by Waters and Sroufe (1983). To them, "the competent individual is one who is able to make use of environmental and personal resources to achieve a good developmental outcome" (p. 81).

Still others have referred to *cognitive competence* in contrast to simple *competence* or *social competence*. The early thrust of Headstart programs was on raising IQ, an approach that came to be recognized as too narrow in scope (Zigler & Seitz, 1980; Zigler & Trickett, 1978). There are, according to Carey (1974), three fundamental components of cognitive competence. These include (a) basic linguistic capacities, (b) general ability in acquiring new skills, and (c) personality factors such as sense of efficacy, goal setting and seeking, and the ability to delay gratification. While the first two are clearly cognitive competencies, others might define the third component as a personality variable rather than a cognitive variable.

The main point derived from a study of these various definitions is that whether authors speak of *competence* or *social competence* or *cognitive competence*, there appears to be some common core of agreement. Almost any definition of *competence*, regardless of the modifiers used in front of the term, includes a personal–social component relating to a child's ability to interact with others and a cognitive component that relates either to the possession of, or the ability to acquire, new skills. Intelligence, as such, is not considered a critical variable.

A serious dissent to usual definitions of *competence* has been voiced by Ogbu (1981). He raised the question of whether our generally accepted idea of competence and its development was not culture-bound and value-loaded. He further denied the relevance to urban, black children of our basic assumptions about the development of competence. It is difficult to refute the assertions in his essay since there appears to have been no research specifically aimed at this issue. On the other hand, Seeman (1983) asserts that socioeconomic and ethnic status were not factors in the appearance of effective behavior in children he studied. A similar finding was reported by Pierson and his colleagues (1984).

CHARACTERISTICS OF COMPETENT CHILDREN

Consideration of the characteristics of competent children will provide a clearer understanding of what competence is. A number of authors have proposed lists of competencies (Anderson & Messick, 1974; Baird, 1983). The clearest and most solidly based list of such characteristics is that proposed by White (1975b). His list, which is a description of the competent six-year-old, includes the following:

1. the ability to get and maintain the attention of adults in socially acceptable ways
2. the ability to use adults as resources when a task is clearly too difficult
3. the ability to express both affection and hostility to adults
4. the ability to lead and follow peers
5. the ability to express both affection and hostility to peers
6. the ability to exhibit interpersonal competition
7. the ability to praise oneself and/or show pride in one's accomplishments
8. the ability to involve oneself in adult role-playing behaviors or otherwise to express a desire to grow up
9. linquistic competence, represented by grammatical capacity, vocabulary, articulation, and extensive use of expressed language
10. intellectual competence, including
    a. the ability to sense dissidence or know discrepances
    b. the ability to anticipate consequences
    c. the ability to deal with abstractions
    d. the ability to take the point of view of another person
    e. the ability to make interesting associations
11. executive ability, including
    a. the ability to plan and carry out multistep activities
    b. the ability to use resources effectively
12. the ability to attend to two things simultaneously or in rapid alternation

These criteria have been developed on the basis of extensive research that is now into its second decade. It should be noted that intelligence, or IQ, per se, is not a basic consideration. In line with the thinking of nearly everyone who has written on the topic of competence, the basic emphasis is on learned skills and behaviors. The basic question that needs to be considered next is how and under what conditions competence is learned.

HOW COMPETENCE IS LEARNED

All research on the development of competence begins with the assumption that competence is learned. White (1959) and Bandura (1977) specifically state that this is so. Others seem to take it as given. If competence is learned, then the question of how it is learned will be determined in part by when it is learned and from whom it is learned.

The Period During Which Competence Develops

There appears to be general agreement that competence begins to develop in early infancy and continues to develop at least through the elementary school years. Specific programs of interpersonal skill development have been shown to produce results from the age of 4 through the elementary school years (Shure, 1980; Shure & Spivack, 1978; Shure & Spivack, 1979). The emphasis in early childhood education programs already cited (Bronfenbrenner, 1975; Gray, Ramsey, & Klaus, 1982) has been on preschool children 3 or 4 years of age. Relatively few authors have investigated or written about competence in infancy, although there are exceptions (Ainsworth & Bell, 1974; Beckwith, 1971; Stone, Smith, & Murphy, 1973; Wenar, 1964; White, 1975a, 1975b, 1979, 1980).

The work most relevant to the question of when competence is learned is that conducted by Burton White and cited above. His extensive research indicated that competence is clearly identifiable at the age of 3 and he concluded that by that time patterns of future achievement or underachievement are often visible (White, Kaban, Attanucci, & Shapiro, 1978). White has further targeted the developmental period from approximately 8 to 24 months as the most critical in the development of competence (White, 1975b). While it is reasonable to conclude that various kinds of competence can and do continue to develop throughout the childhood years, White's work suggests that the critical period in the development of competence occurs prior to the time that most efforts are undertaken. This idea casts a new light on the modest results obtained by the various preschool programs and points up a new role for schools interested in ensuring that children arrive at their door ready to make maximum use of the school's resources.

White's work also infers new responsibilities for schools in relation to parents. While many schools and preschool programs do provide parent programs, the school that provides programs for the parents of infants,

parents-to-be, or potential parents is rare indeed. Yet that is the need suggested by White's work. White pulls no punches on this score. He states categorically, "Children who enter the first grade significantly behind their peers are not likely to ever catch up" (1980, p. 339).

Who Can Promote Development of Competence Most Effectively?

If the period from birth to three years is the most critical in the development of competence it is clear that the basic responsibility falls to the parents. More specifically, it is likely to fall on the mother or, in increasing numbers of cases, on a primary caregiver outside of the home. In any event, there is likely to be little argument among professionals about the qualifications of parents or child care facilities to accomplish the necessary tasks. Parenting was referred to as the last great preserve of the amateur by Toffler (1970). White (1980) has been more specific. Speaking of parents, he stated, "They are not prepared for the job, and are not knowledgeable; indeed, there is a lot of misinformation around" (p. 340). He also points out that the early developmental period is a period of high stress and that in most cases mothers usually face the child rearing task essentially alone (White, 1980).

An important general statement was made on the issue of parental teaching by Hess and Shipman (1965). Based on their study of 160 4-year-old black children, they concluded that parental teaching can be for better or for worse. This is an important idea because there appears to be a general assumption, even among experts, that although parental teaching may not be effective it cannot be literally for the worse. Somewhat more specifically, Hess and Shipman indicate that poor teaching occurs in cognitive environments where behavior is controlled by status roles rather than by attention to the individual characteristics of a specific situation and where behavior is not mediated by verbal cues.

How the Development of Competence is Facilitated or Retarded

Having established that the basic development of competence takes place beginning in infancy (particularly in the period from 8 to 24 months) and having further established that parents (particularly mothers) or primary care givers are likely to be most responsible for facilitating the development of competence, we are in a position to attempt to answer the question of how the development of competence can be facilitated most effectively. Although there is an abundance of research on competence, relatively few of those who have conducted such research have spoken directly to the issue of how competence is developed. Some, particularly those involved in large scale child care–type programs, appear to have assumed that we know how to help children toward maximum competence. This assumption has not been confirmed by the results obtained. On the other hand, of those researchers who have conducted smaller scale investigations of competence, relatively few have used their research as a basis for defining the characteristics of environments leading to the optimum development of competence.

In a study of patterns of parental authority, Baumrind (1971) suggests four characteristics of parents whose behavior leads to the development of competence in children. These include the following: (a) They are intellectually stimulating, (b) they are "tension producing," (c) they are firm, and (d) they demand mature behaviors, including high levels of self-control and independent action.

Baumrind further comments that the most demanding parents are also the warmest (most supportive) parents. This observation is important because it indicates that parents who assist children to become competent not only make demands but provide the emotional support that gives the child the self-confidence necessary to attempt to meet the demands.

From a negative point of view, the classic studies of René Spitz (1945) are highly relevant. His studies of the impact of institutionalization on the development of infants in their first year of life suggest those conditions that actually are capable of reversing development, so that children who begin life with normal or better levels of development actually decline in that respect during their first year of life. Even children from very poor homes as well as illegimate children cared for by their own mothers in the nursery of a penal institution showed dramatically better levels of development than did children in an orphanage who, although cared for in every respect physically, were essentially raised in what he referred to as "solitary confinement." These children had no toys, a visual radius restricted to the ceiling over their cot, a radius of locomotion circumscribed by the size of the cot, and only a minimum of personal interaction with their mothers or the nurses. The result of this, as measured by a developmental scale, was a dramatic and tragic plunge in developmental quotient from the first 4 months of life to the last 4 months of the first year of life. Spitz concluded that early deprivation has a permanent effect on development. In his opinion the most serious aspect of deprivation is the lack of competence stimulation from any person who could act in the capacity of a parent surrogate. His work provides a basis for being certain that an inappropriate environment can have a strong and probably lasting, negative, effect on a child. These conclusions are confirmed in a more positive sense by Beckwith (1971), who found that both verbal and physical contact with the mother, plus the freedom to explore, resulted in higher scores on an infant development scale.

The effects of isolation from peers during childhood were studied by Asher, Oden and Gottman (1977). They concluded that such isolates were more likely to have problems at higher age levels including higher school drop-out rates, a higher incidence of juvenile delinquency, and more mental health problems as adults. It appears that social (or environmental) isolation at any time from infancy through the preschool years will have a negative effect on development, although the earlier the isolation occurs, the more serious its effects are likely to be.

One of the most common aspects of a number of definitions of competence is the infant's or child's belief that his or her behavior can result in modifying or controlling the environment. A number of studies demonstrating this aspect of competence have been conducted. Bruner (1973) concluded that a form of mutual expectation was established very early between an infant and a parent when the parent responded to the child's initiative. This appears to lead the infant to expect a response following its own initiating behavior. Over the course of time this leads the child to expect to be able to obtain an adult response. A similarly rigorous study by Lewis and Goldberg (1969) led them to conclude that there was a positive relationship between mothers' responses to their infants and the children's cognitive development. Failure to obtain a response appears likely to reduce the child's exploration of the environment, a primary requisite for the subsequent development of competence.

Both the human and inanimate aspects of the environment were found to be significant determinants of development by Yarrow, Rubenstein, Pederson, and Jankowski (1973). In particular they stress the importance of the variety of inanimate objects available to the infant. The availability of a wide selection of such objects had a positive effect on almost every aspect of infant development.

■ *The Results of Burton White's Work.* Reference has already been made to some of the research of Burton White. Since his findings are supported by a variety of other studies already cited and are central to basic notions of primary prevention, they will be further summarized here. White asserts that the first 3 years of life are the most critical in all of child development. Even more definitively, he states, "To begin to look at a child's educational development when he is two years of age is already much too late" (1975a, p. 4). He states further, "The informal education that families provide for their children *makes more of an impact on a child's total educational development than the formal educational system*" (1975a, p. 4). Unfortunately, as has already been pointed out, most preschool programs do not begin until the age of 3 and the period from birth to 3 years is a time long before most schools provide services for children, except for those who are developmentally disabled.

According to White, there are four key development processes that must be encouraged during the first 3 years of life (White, 1975a). The first of these is *language*. During this period and especially during the period from 7 to 8 months on, children develop facility with language. A second important area of development is *social skills and attachment*. This development takes place from birth, but the period from about 7 to 24 months of age is particularly crucial. White (1975a) takes a dim view of the possibilities of changing basic social attitudes after the age of 2. The third developmental process that it is important to consider is *curiosity*. By the age of 8 months nearly every child is intensely curious and, when encouraged, continues to be so throughout the first 3 years. The fourth important area is the development of *problem solving skills*. In Piaget's terms, this would be the development of instrumental learning, which takes place largely during the first 2 years of life.

White reflects a belief throughout his writings that a mother may be in the best position to provide the teaching necessary to the development of full competence. On the other hand, he recognizes that this is not always a possibility in a world where over half of mothers are employed and recognizes that fathers and others may sometimes be the primary care givers. He has summarized, however, what things primary care givers do that lead to the development of competent children (White & Watts, 1973). These behaviors include the following:

1. They talk a great deal to the child.
2. They provide the child access to many objects and diverse situations.
3. They make the child feel that what they do is interesting.
4. They lead the child to believe that he or she can expect help and encouragement most, but not all, of the time.
5. They demonstrate and explain things to the child, mostly at the childs request.
6. They prohibit certain activities consistently and firmly, particulary those where there is some danger involved to the child.
7. They can say no without the fear of losing the child's love.
8. They make imaginative and interesting associations and suggestions to the child.
9. They skillfully strengthen a child's motivation to learn.

10. They give the child a task orientation, the idea that it is desirable to do things well and completely.
11. They make a child feel secure.
12. They are capable of taking the child's perspective; they listen well.
13. They do not spend all of their time with their children; rather, they make many relatively short responses to the child throughout the day; at other times they are engaged in their own pursuits.
14. They provide a physical environment full of manipulable objects, which challenges the child's curiosity; many of these are not toys in the usual sense but (depending on age level) could be empty boxes, pans, or other interesting and available materials.
15. They provide exposure to interesting things to look at, including magazines, books, and television.
16. They have high energy levels.

Primary care givers face three barriers in their attempt to help their children to develop (White, 1980). The first of these is ignorance. Not only do they lack knowledge but, in many cases, they have picked up a great deal of misinformation. A second problem is that of stress. The curiosity of an 8-month-old child, coupled with her increasing mobility, can make the typical home a dangerous place. The child has a tendency to put every movable object into its mouth. A little later, about 16 to 18 months, children begin to test their ability to control their environment. If there is more than one child during this period stress on the primary care giver will be more than doubled in attempting to manage both children. A third major source of stress is lack of assistance for the primary care giver. As White says starkly, "Mothers usually face this job alone" (1980, p. 341). Of course, this need not be the case and part of any training program should be to teach *both* parents to assume significant responsibility in child rearing.

In summary, White (1975a) notes three basic functions performed by effective primary care givers. These include the following:

1. Designing the living area: Effective care givers designed a living area in such a way that the child was protected from the dangers of the home and, conversely, the home was protected from the child. Of prime importance was the provision to the child of maximum access to the living quarters. In the process of making the home safe for the child, effective care givers did not limit the child's physical exporation of the environment.
2. Consulting: They responded promptly, although usually briefly, to the child's overture. They were alert to the infant's purpose of the moment and used language at or slightly above the child's level of comprehension to provide what was needed. They might provide an additional association or idea but they did not prolong the consultation longer than the *infant* wanted.
3. Authority: Although competent care givers made maximum use of love, encouragement, and praise, they were firm and set clear limits

regardless of the child's age. If such limits required a change in behavior on the child's part they had techniques available for bringing about such change. Typically, from 8 to 13 months, distraction was the favored method. From 13 to 18 months distraction was attempted, and if it did not work the child was physically removed from the situation. During the period from 18 to 24 months, distraction and physical removal were also used but verbal restrictions were added as a form of enforcing limits where necessary.

AN INSTRUCTIONAL PROGRAM TO ENHANCE THE DEVELOPMENT OF COMPETENCE IN INFANTS

The following program outline is intended for use either with parents-to-be, the parents of infants in the first several months of life or with high school students. Congruent with the evidence thus far presented, the emphasis is on the period from birth to about 3 years of age. It must be recognized, in line with the observations of Carey (1974), Keniston (1977), and White (1980) that the provision of an educational program to parents whose basic physical needs are either not being met or are continually in doubt of being met, is likely to be ineffective unless the program is also accompanied by other forms of assistance, including a range of social services or referral to social agencies that can assist in overcoming the lack of basic needs. This problem has been considered by Goodyear and Rubovits (1982), who utilized Maslow's need hierarchy to develop a parent education model for low-income parents.

Locating Parents-to-Be and New Parents

We fully recognize the difficulty that will be faced by most school districts in attempting to provide educational programs for parents-to-be and for the parents of newborn infants. At the same time, it must eventually be recognized that the modest gains reflected by Headstart are unlikely to be improved upon until genuine programs for infants and their parents are initiated. The argument in favor of such efforts seems overwhelming: We are unlikely ever to be dealing with fully functioning children in the school setting until such efforts are made.

The school-based practitioner may not have extensive relationships in the community through which to make contact with appropriate groups but there are a variety of ways through which such contact can be made. Many communities have organizations interested in prenatal and neonatal care. Two examples of such organizations are La Maze and La Leche. These groups are interested in certain aspects of birth and postnatal care but, typically, not in the aspects discussed here. A tactful approach to the director of such a group, offering the services of school personnel free of charge to those of their members who care to volunteer, might be very positively received.

Another resource can be found in local hospitals. Many hospitals now provide courses on infant care to expectant parents. Again, typically, they do not cover the concerns addressed in this chapter and might be happy to add such a dimension to their training program. Local physicians, especially obstetricians, can provide another source of information on new parents. There are, undoubtedly, other specific resources in any given community that could be added to this list. If the foregoing resources are tried without adequate results, it is always possible to utilize birth records (which in some communities are reported in the paper) to obtain the names and addresses of new parents who can then be sent a carefully worded letter offering them the school's services.

Programs for High School Students

In addition to new parents and parents-to-be, there is another category of persons whom schools might legimately, and with minimum effort, serve. These are high school students, most of whom are likely ultimately to have children of their own. It is certainly possible, either through the medium of existing courses, or through setting up special courses, to teach these individuals some of the basics that will help them to provide a setting in which their children can develop to their fullest during the critical period from birth to 3 years.

The location of a relevant population in the school is not so difficult as deciding where to build in such a component and, even more difficult, getting the necessary permission to do so. Home economics courses may provide an appropriate location for a unit on enhancing competence in infants but often have the drawback of including female students only. To the greatest extent possible male students should also be included in the program. Some schools have a guidance course that might make an appropriate place for introduction of a infant development unit; others have a free or homeroom period that could be used for the same purpose. Schools differ so greatly that specific advice on this score is extremely difficult to give. It is likely to take a certain amount of persuasion, assertiveness, creativity, and tact to introduce such a unit, especially in these days of emphasis on "basics." The point should be made in all negotiations for the inclusion of this unit that it will ultimately result in (among other things) helping children to enter school at a higher level of competence and readiness than would otherwise be the case.

Some General Considerations

If the focus of the unit is to be on parents (or parents-to-be), then the initial problem will be that of obtaining parent participation. Several general approaches to this problem have already been discussed. Each potential participant should receive a letter giving the place, date, times, number, and length of meetings and the availability of child care during meetings. *Both* parents should be encouraged to attend. Stress that the intent of the meetings is to help parents give their baby the best possible start in life. Provide a specific means by which parents can indicate their interest, such as return postcards. Be sure to obtain their phone numbers.

Call all interested parents 3 or 4 days ahead of the first scheduled meeting to remind them of the first session. Experience suggests that roughly half of those who indicate initial interest will actually attend the first meeting, although this can vary widely. The ratio of those who actually attend the first meeting to those who have indicated interest can be considerably improved by providing baby sitting services at the meeting site for parents who have children.

Experience suggests that in dealing with parents it is wise to avoid the role of "expert." If the trainer is associated with a college or university it also seems wise not to emphasize that connection either (Goodyear & Rubovits, 1982). Some parents do not like the feeling that they might be told what to do.

For those participants who are parents it is a good idea to include homework assignments that they can carry out between meetings and discuss at subsequent meetings. This will add a deeper level of involvement to the process and also provide actual practice.

Regardless of whether the participants are already parents or not, there are some general considerations that should be noted. The trainer should expect most concern to be with child management problems, discipline, and spoiling the child. Such concerns should be dealt with completely and openly. Participants should be involved as actively as possible in the instructional process. Some ways to do this are through regular solicitation of their opinions, drawing on their own experience, the use of small groups, and getting participants to model specific behaviors. It is a good idea, if at all possible, to have a baby of the age under discussion available for observation for a part of each meeting; this is especially important for those participants who have not yet had children of there own.

Each meeting should begin with a summary of what was discussed the last time and an overview of what will be considered in the present meeting. Each meeting should be summarized at its end and a short, simple quiz given to reinforce learning. The results of such a quiz will also reveal the extent to which parents are understanding what is being taught.

It will be very helpful to have a copy of *The First Three Years of Life* (White, 1975a) available for each participant. If this is not possible it is a good idea to have dittoed summaries of important material available. The total outline of the course presented here is designed to cover each of the seven phases covered by White in his book, with one meeting devoted to each phase.

The First Meeting

Provide a brief summary of the purposes of the instruction to be provided. If it is a group where the participants do not know each other have them introduce themselves and tell something about themselves that will help others to remember them. After the participants have introduced themselves, introduce yourself at greater length, giving something of your background but making sure not to intimidate the participants with a show of expertise. Give a brief overview of the structure and purposes of the course, stressing the importance of sharing experience with one another. If there are males in the group, stress the importance of fathers in the child rearing process. The general material to be covered in the first session is that which White (1975a) calls Phase 1, covering the period from birth to 6 weeks.

1. Give the parents a brief true–false quiz covering the first 3 years of life. Discuss the answers briefly with them. Use the results to determine their general level of information at that time.
2. Briefly discuss the importance of the first 3 years of life in the child's subsequent behavior and achievement.
3. Discuss the basic characteristics of the Phase 1 (birth-to-6-weeks) infant as outlined by White (1975a, pp. 15–31).
4. Discuss the recommended child rearing practices during this phase.
5. Discuss the child rearing practices not recommended during this phase.
6. Observe a Phase 1 infant.
7. Provide time for questions and discussion of either the material you have presented or of the observation of the infant.
8. Summarize the important points to be remembered about Phase 1.
9. Give a brief quiz covering the important material presented in this meeting.
10. Make homework assignments requiring further observation of an infant in Phase 1. Provide guidelines detailing what behaviors should be expected or looked for.
11. Close with a reminder of the next meeting.

The Second Meeting

(Subsequent meetings will follow a format similar to this one. Meetings will differ primarily in the phase of infant development being covered.) This meeting will cover the Phase 2 infant, the period from 6 weeks to 3½ months.

1. Review the homework assignment, answer questions, and encourage discussion about the observations.
2. Briefly summarize the salient features of Phase 1.
3. Provide a brief overview of the purposes of this session.
4. Cover the important aspects of Phase 2 (the period from 6 weeks to 3½ months) as outlined by White (1975a, pp. 33–58). Be sure to include not only the major features of this period but also the recommended and not recommended child rearing practices. Encourage maximum parent participation and discussion.
5. Observe a Phase 2 infant.
6. Provide time for discussion and questions generated by the observation.

7. Summarize the major points you want parents to remember.
8. Give a short quiz on the important points to be remembered about the Phase 2 infant.
9. Give as a homework assignment observation of a Phase 2 infant, with special instructions on what to look for.
10. Close with a reminder of the next meeting. If parents who were present at the first meeting have failed to attend the second meeting call them on the phone within the next few days to encourage their attendance at subsequent meetings.

The Third Meeting

The basic format for meetings 3 through 7 is the same as the second meeting. As the only difference is the material to be covered, it is unnecessary to repeat, in detail, the plan of each meeting. During this meeting the material to be covered involves the Phase 3 infant (the period from 3½ to 5½ months) as described by White (1975a pp. 59–75).

The Fourth Meeting

The basic material to be covered in this session concerns the Phase 4 infant, which includes the period from 5½ to 8 months (White, 1975a, pp. 77–102).

The Fifth Meeting

The *special* importance of the period from 8 to 36 months should be emphasized at this and subsequent meetings. Perhaps it would be useful to quote White's statement that, *"Relatively few families, perhaps no more than ten percent, manage to get their children through the eight-to-thirty-six month age period as well educated and developed as they can and should be"* (1975a, p. 103). The specific topic for this meeting is the Phase 5 infant, covering the period from 8 to 14 months of age (White, 1975a, pp. 103–150). Meetings 5, 6, and 7 may be somewhat longer than previous meetings not only because of the increased significance of this period but also because there is more material to cover.

The Sixth Meeting

The material to be covered in this meeting includes the period from 14 to 24 months of age, labeled Phase 6 by White (1975a, pp. 151–189).

The Seventh Meeting

The final meeting covers Phase 7, the period from 24 to 36 months of age (White, 1975a, pp. 191–213).

If this instructional unit has been carried out with high school students it will end at this point. If it has been carried out with a group of parents or parents-to-be, it is sometimes a good idea to have a "reunion" sometime after the last meeting. In the case of parents-to-be the reunion should probably come several months after the birth of the infants. Since the mothers-to-be will not all be at the same stage of pregnancy this could be 6 or 7 months later. In the case of those who are already parents such a reunion might be held 6 or 8 weeks after the final meeting. Such a reunion can serve at least two purposes. First it may help reinforce parents' understanding of appropriate child rearing procedures by providing an opportunity for them to discuss with each other their experience with their infants. Second, it can provide the instructor with insight and information on the effectiveness of the program and on what might be done to improve its effectiveness in the future.

SUMMARY

The idea of competence as a characteristic amenable to environmental influences is relatively new. It encompasses intellectual and personal skills as well as the ability to foresee and plan. Research suggests that the basis of competence is formed during the early years, more specifically in the period from 8 to 24 months. During this period, the primary care giver can behave either in ways that promote or in ways that retard the development of subsequent competence. A number of specific behaviors have been identified that characterize those primary care givers who do the most effective job of developing competence in children. Most primary care givers are not only unequipped to assist maximally in the development of competence, but possess misinformation as well.

Effective primary care givers perform three basic functions: they make it possible for the child to explore his or her environment safely; they respond promptly, though briefly, to the child's overtures; and they set firm, clear limits. The provision of instruction to new parents has been found to be an effective way to increase the development of competence in children. Offering such programs to parents-to-be as well as to high school–age students may also have positive impacts on the development of competence in children. Plans for, and an outline of, such a teaching program are presented.

REFERENCES

Ainsworth, M. D. S., & Bell, S. M. (1974). Mother–infant interaction and the development of competence. In K. Connolly & J. S. Bruner (Eds.), *The growth of competence.* New York: Academic Press.

Anderson, S., & Messick, S. (1974). Social competence in young children. *Developmental Psychology, 10,* 282–293.

Asher, S. R., Oden, S. L., & Gottman, J. M. (1977). Children's friendships in school settings. In L. G. Katz (Ed.), *Current topics in early childhood education* (Vol. 1). Norwood, NJ: Ablex.

Baird, L. L. (1983). *Attempts at defining interpersonal competencies* (Report No. ETS-RR-83-15). Princeton, NJ: Educational Testing Service. (ERIC Document Reproduction Service No. ED 237 519)

Bandura, A. (1977). Self-efficacy: Toward a unifying theory of behavioral change. *Psychological Review, 84,* 191–215.

Baumrind, D. (1971). Current patterns of parental authority. *Developmental Psychology Monographs, 4* (1), Pt. 2.

Beckwith, L. (1971). Relationships between attributes of mothers and their infants' IQ scores. *Child Development, 42,* 1083–1097.

Bronfenbrenner, U. (1975). Is early intervention effective? In M. Guttentag & E. L. Struening (Eds.), *Handbook of evaluation research* (Vol. 2, pp. 519–601). Beverly Hills: Sage.

Bruner, J. S. (1973). Volition, skill, and tools. In L. J. Stone, H. T. Smith, & L. B. Murphy (Eds.), *The competent infant.* New York: Basic Books.

Carey, S. (1974). Cognitive competence. In J. K. Connolly & J. S. Bruner (Eds.), *The growth of competence.* London: Academic Press.

Cicirelli, V. G. (1969). *The impact of Head Start: An evaluation of the effects of Head Start on children's cognitive and affective development.* Washington, DC: National Bureau of Standards, Institute for Applied Technology.

Connolly, K. J., & Bruner, J. S. (1974). Competence: Its nature and nurture. In K. J. Connolly & J. S. Bruner (Eds.), *The growth of competence.* London: Academic Press.

Goodyear, R. K., & Rubovits, J. J. (1982). Parent education: A model for low income parents. *Personnel Guidance Journal, 60,* 409–412.

Gray, S. W. (1983). Enduring effects of early intervention: Perspectives and perplexities. *Peabody Journal of Education, 60* (3), 70–84.

Gray, S. W., Ramsey, B. K., & Klaus, R. A. (1982). *From 3 to 20: The early training project.* Baltimore: University Park Press.

Hess, R. D., & Shipman, V. (1965). Early experience and socialization of cognitive modes in children. *Child Development, 36,* 869–886.

Keniston, K. (1977). *All our children.* New York: Harcourt, Brace, Jovanovich.

Lewis, M., & Goldberg, S. (1969). Perceptual cognitive development in infancy: A generalized expectancy model as a function of the mother–infant interaction. *Merrill–Palmer Quarterly, 15,* 81–100.

Ogbu, J. U. (1981). Origins of human competence: A cultural–ecological perspective. *Child Development, 52,* 413–429.

Pierson, D. E., Walker, D. K., & Tivnan, T. (1984). A school-based program from infancy to kindergarten for children and their parents. *Personnel and Guidance Journal, 62,* 448–455.

Seeman, J. (1983). Personality integration in children and adults: Some developmental continuities. *Peabody Journal of Education, 60* (3), 29–44.

Shure, M. B. (1980). Real life problem solving for parents and children: An approach to social competence. In D. P. Rathjen & J. P. Foreyt (Eds.), *Social competence.* New York: Pergamon.

Shure, M. B., & Spivack, G. (1978). *Problem solving techniques in child rearing.* San Francisco: Jossey–Bass.

Shure, M. B., & Spivack, G. (1979). Interpersonal cognitive problem solving and primary prevention: Programming for preschool and kindergarten children. *Journal of Clinical Child Psychology, 8,* 89–94.

Spitz, R. A. (1945). Hospitalism: An inquiry into the genesis of psychiatric conditions in early childhood. *Psychoanalytic Study of the Child, 1,* 53–74.

Stone, L. J., Smith, H. T., & Murphy, L. B. (1973). The competent infant—Research and commentary. New York: Basic Books.

Toffler, A. (1970). *Future shock.* New York: Random House.

Waters, E., & Sroufe, L. A. (1983). Social competence as a developmental construct. *Developmental Review, 3,* 79–97.

Wenar, C. (1964). Competence at one. *Merrill–Palmer Quarterly, 10,* 329–342.

White, B. L. (1975a). *The first three years of life.* Englewood Cliffs, NJ: Prentice–Hall.

White, B. L. (1975b). Critical influences in the origins of competence. *Merrill–Palmer Quarterly, 21,* 243–266.

White, B. L. (1979). *The origins of human competence: The final report of the Harvard Preschool Project.* Lexington, MA: Heath.

White, B. L. (1980). Primary prevention: Beginning at the beginning. *Personnel and Guidance Journal, 58,* 338–343.

White, B. L., Kaban, B., Attanucci, J., & Shapiro, B. (1978). *Experience and environment: Major influences on the development of the young child* (Vol. 2). Englewood Cliffs, NJ: Prentice–Hall.

White, B. L., & Watts, J. C. (1973). *Experience and environment.* Englewood Cliffs, NJ: Prentice–Hall.

White, R. W. (1959). Motivation reconsidered: The concept of competence. *Psychological Review, 66,* 297–333.

Yarrow, L. J., Rubenstein, J. L., Pedersen, F. A., & Jankowski, J. J. (1973). Dimensions of early stimulation and their differential effects on infant development. In L. J. Stone, H. T. Smith, & L. B. Murphy (Eds.), *The competent infant.* New York: Basic Books.

Zigler, E., & Seitz, U. (1980). Early childhood intervention programs: A reanalysis. *School Psychology Review, 9,* 354–368.

Zigler, E., & Trickett, P. K. (1978). IQ, social competence, and evaluation of early childhood intervention programs. *American Psychologist, 33,* 789–798.

7

ORGANIZATIONAL AND STRUCTURAL ASPECTS OF THE LEARNING ENVIRONMENT

The material included in the preceding chapters has addressed itself fundamentally to various important modes of human interaction between children and adults. There are, however, other determinants of children's learning and behavior in school. These include the physical environment and the manner in which learning is organized and encouraged including the use of classroom reward structures, ability grouping, and open versus self-contained classrooms. In some of these areas, research has much to tell us; in others there is little that is available. In still others, the research information is contradictory and few reliable conclusions can be drawn. There is, however, little argument that all of these variables do have an impact on children's learning.

Perhaps many guidance specialists may react that these are not areas in which they have expertise. On the other hand, two things are clear. The first is that there is a relationship between primary prevention and most of these variables. The second is that examination of who might reasonably be expected to have the most expertise in these areas suggests that they are more relevant to guidance professionals than to others involved in the educative process. There can, of course, be disagreement about this, but since the aim of this book is to present a wide range of primary preventive strategies, the organizational and structural features of the classroom and the school will be discussed.

The material presented here will take a broad view of the issue. The best available evidence in relevant areas—not always convincing—will be presented from the point of view of whether or not it has implications for preventing learning or behavior problems in school children. Only those variables will be considered over which individual teachers and individual schools may reasonably be expected to exert some control. For example, school size, although it has been demonstrated to affect student social participation (Morgan & Alwin, 1980) as well as other student behaviors (Baird, 1969), is not within the power of teachers or building administrators to change on their own initiative, hence it will not be considered here. The same is true for certain aspects of the physical environment of the school and its setting.

As Hunt (1975) points out, a major problem exists in the fact that different individuals do not necessarily respond similarly to similar environments. At the applied level, this principle has been recognized, at least implicitly, in the requirements of PL 94-142 which mandate an individualized educational plan for each child who is determined to be eligible for special education services. Regular education, on the other hand, continues to provide a given type of learning environment to groups (classes) of students with little recognition that different children might learn more effectively in different environments. Most of the studies on which the material in this chapter is based have been conducted with this (experimental) assumption undergirding them. We are unable, given our present knowledge, to do other than generalize from this type of data. This is both a reality and a deficit that the reader will want to bear in mind. It may well be (and very probably will be) that, in the future, true behavior–person–environment interactions (Hunt, 1975) can be considered. Both Hunt (1971) and Glaser (1972) have made proposals that we attempt to "characterize the forms of educational environment likely to be most appropriate for different persons" (Hunt, 1975, pp. 212–213), but at present the kind of information required to do so effectively is not available.

Beyond the lack of research data that would permit genuine behavior–person–environment matchups is a corresponding lack of inclination to do so at the applied level. School personnel do not seem willing to extend the individualized educational plan idea to all children and, indeed, this seems quite understandable. Given typical class sizes, such an approach does not appear currently feasible. The experimental approach taken by most of the research to be reported here therefore matches what is practiced in most schools. While there may be, and undoubtedly are, more individualized ways to approach both research and practice, these approaches lie in the future and we must deal with the present.

The wide variety of environmental manipulations that have been tried in the schools suggests the strength of the belief that learning and behavior are directly affected by such variables. The physical structure of the school, the specific features of the classroom environment, the number of children or teachers in learning groups, and the aesthetic characteristics of the learning situation are all matters of obvious concern to educators. The *evidence* in many of these areas is, however, not always strong. The lack of evidence is easy to understand and resides in the difficulty of conducting in vivo research and in the complexity of the variables to be considered. This lack of evidence does not prevent the existence of strong *opinions*, however. In this chapter, only those topics will be included on which there is, at least, a minimum of research on which to base informed practice.

INCENTIVES FOR LEARNING

The treatment of this subject as briefly as is necessary in this volume may be considered by some to be ill-advised. The research literature that bears on this topic is considered to be a speciality in itself. On the other hand, the practical issues surrounding this topic are encountered daily by guidance specialists. These practical considerations range from individual students who are unmotivated to teachers whose classrooms are routinely out of control, making learning almost impossible for the children in their classes. The issues of incentives or reward structures often lies at the bottom of such problems.

Experience suggests that most teachers appear to subscribe to the dictum that learning is its own reward or, even more narrowly, that it is a child's duty to learn and that this duty should provide all necessary motivation. These prevailing points of view appear to work, at least minimally, among middle-class children whose parents may support such attitudes and who have been imbued with the idea that education is a good thing in and of itself, (although this opinion fails to take into account the profound boredom, restlessness, and failure to achieve at optimum levels that exists in most middle-class schools). These assumptions appear to have worked considerably less well in schools with less than middle-level socioeconomic status. In these schools there is typically much more active resistance, including truancy, aggressive behavior, and dropping out of the educational system at the earliest possible moment.

The typical reactions of educators to both passive and active resistance to learning range from attempts to shame students ("What will your parents think?") to threats ("You're not going to graduate if you keep this up.") to punishment (suspension or expulsion). The research evidence for the effectiveness of such approaches is unimpressive. This is due to the fact that they tend uniformly to hold the child exclusively responsible when, in many cases, the greater problem lies in the classroom or in the home.

Many teachers resist the idea of establishing specific incentives or rewards for learning. What they fail to recognize is that a reward structure exists whether it is formalized or not. Given this situation, it is necessary to differentiate between an informal and a formal reward structure. Either of these approaches may be effective (or ineffective) depending upon the potency of the individual delivering the reward and the nature of the reward itself. A formal reward structure may include the use of grades (good or bad), prizes, stars, or points among many other possible rewards. There is usually a reasonably well described way in which such rewards may be earned.

There is always an informal reward structure although there may not always be a formal reward structure. The informal reward structure may include praise or blame, a smile or a frown, encouragement or criticism, or other spontaneous teacher reactions to students. The most prevalent case appears to be the use of the informal structure with little attempt to create a more formal reward structure. At an even more specific level, it appears that the main type of incentive used is aversive rather than positive.

Teachers often express the belief that formal reward structures are unnecessary since children should want to learn. With many this appears to be an essentially moral position rather than a carefully reasoned educational position. Unfortunately for children, it seems generally true that almost any systematic reward structure has produced better performance than the absence of a systematic reward structure (e.g., Hamblin, Hathaway, & Wodarski, 1971). If this is true, then it suggests that guidance specialists should intervene actively in an appropriate manner to assist teachers to establish more formal and effective reward structures in their classrooms.

Types of Reward Structures

There is more than one way to categorize the hierarchy of reward structures. The one used here reflects that used by Michaels (1977). A similar structure is also used by Slavin (1977). The four major types of structures include the following:

1. Individual competition: Rewards are earned by individuals according to relative performance. The achievement of the reward by individual A forecloses individual B from receiving a like reward.
2. Group competition: Rewards are differentially earned by groups according to relative performance. The achievement of a given reward by group A means that group B cannot win a like reward.
3. Individual reward contingencies: The performance of individuals is compared with an established standard to determine each individual's reward. The fact that a given individual achieves a reward does not foreclose another individual's opportunity to achieve a reward.
4. Group reward contingencies: The performance of a group is compared with an established standard to determine achievement of a reward by a group. The attainment of a reward by a given group does not foreclose the opportunity of another group to win a like reward.

To these four categories must be added, of course, the category of *no formal reward structure* with the caveat that classrooms without reward structures do not exist, even when a formal reward structure has not been articulated. The basic consideration is the question of what reward structures are most effective under what conditions. Johnson and Johnson (1974) indicate that "cooperative, competitive, and individualistic goal structures are all appropriate and effective under different conditions, that educators should use all three goal structures depending upon the specific instructional objectives, and that students should be taught the basic skills necessary to function in all three types of situations" (p. 213). These same authors point out a fact that is often ignored. "Each type of goal structure has an implicit value foundation that is taught subtly, as an unconscious curriculum, to the student who interacts within it" (p. 213). Further, each type of reward structure may result in learning outcomes that are more positive for some, but less positive for others. In addition to individual learning outcomes, there are also individual personal/social outcomes that appear to stem from each type of reward structure, and these outcomes differ from one structure to another. It appears that no single structure can have both the most positive learning outcomes and the most positive personal/social outcomes. Therefore, in the best of all possible worlds, reward structures would be carefully selected and implemented to achieve different kinds of learning and personal/social goals.

■ *Reward Structures Based on Individual Competition.* This approach is the one that appears to be implemented most frequently in classroom situations. Even in those situations where there is no formally announced reward system, individual competition tends to receive emphasis. It has been pointed out (Johnson & Johnson, 1974) that even when students are placed in a situation where reward structures are unannounced, they will tend to "place the traditional, competitive structure upon themselves" (p. 216).

There appears to be widespread belief that individual competition is required in the schools in order to teach students to survive in our society, and, as a matter of fact, individual competition has been judged by some reviewers of the literature (Michaels, 1977) to be consistently superior in strengthening the independent academic performance of students. While this global statement may be correct, there are some caveats that must go with it. The first of these has to do with the relationship between academic ability and grades. As Slavin (1977) points out, many students cannot make acceptable grades, regardless of effort, while, in Slavin's words, "other students can hardly avoid getting these grades" (p. 638). Achievement motivation theory suggests that individuals make an assessment of the difficulty of a given task and of their own ability level. An individual of low academic ability, therefore, is not likely to strive to achieve once they have experienced the interaction of their capacity to achieve with the difficulty of getting good grades. A second caveat lies in the nature of most of the studies that have been done in order to demonstrate the effectiveness of individual competition. In the main, these studies have been experimental and have involved the use of tasks that did not extend over long periods of time. It seems reasonably clear that prolonged exposure to a task that appears impossible is not only likely to decrease attempts to achieve but may also bring about the development of other undesirable school behaviors. Still a third caveat in relation to a competitive mode has to do with broader impacts on children's behavior. The review by Johnson and Johnson (1974) resulted in their making their following summary of the impact of competition on the behavior of students:

There is evidence that (1) most students perceive school as being competitive . . . (2) American children are more competitive than are children from other countries . . . (3) American children become more competitive the longer they are in school or the older they become . . . (4) Anglo-American children are more competitive than are other American children, such as Mexican-American and Afro-American . . . and (5) urban children are more competitive than are rural children. (p. 212)

Nelson and Kagan (1972) raised the possibility that competition in certain kinds of situations may actually interfere with children's ability to work in more cooperative kinds of situations. These are all serious considerations that should be taken into account when competition is used as a reward structure and become even more serious considerations when competition is used as the *only* reward structure. There is no abundant evidence to suggest that competitive reward structures will result in generally higher achievement than cooperative reward structures. We live in a world in which the problems to be solved are increasingly complex and require cooperation among individuals for their solution. The individual competitive model may be good for limited numbers of high-ability students in the sense of increasing their achievement and strengthening their self-confidence, but in learning to enjoy and value individual competition, they may not learn how to cooperate in the solution of problems.

Unfortunately the children most likely to be most highly motivated by the individual competitive reward structure are the very children whose abilities will be required to solve scientific, technical, and social problems in a cooperative manner in the future. Low-ability children will learn early that they do not have the ability to compete successfully in the academic game and that even when they try they are essentially "punished" with low grades. They are likely to stop competing for grades, will not develop self-confidence, will not develop cooperative behavior and are likely to develop generally negative attitudes toward school that may have serious consequences for them, for the school, and ultimately for the larger society.

There are perhaps two reasons why individual competition remains the predominant reward structure in schools. The first is that it reflects a major value of our society. We are taught from an early age that life is a matter of the survival of the fittest, that life is a jungle, and a matter of everyone for him- or herself. These are values that may be understandable and workable in a frontier society but are much less understandable and workable in a highly technological and more crowded society where cooperation is more likely to result in survival than is competition. It is also clear that it is a value that is not about to disappear.

The second reason that individual competition is probably more widely used than other reward systems is that it is by far the easiest for the teacher to organize and manage. The other reward systems to be discussed all require, although in varying degrees, more organization and planning. These are tasks that teachers are already required to carry out to a high degree in their daily work. Additional responsibilities in these areas are unlikely to be received positively by teachers unless there is also a reward for the teacher.

■ *Reward Structures Based on Group Competition.* The use of group competition is probably the second most widely used type of reward structure. As with individual competition, there are winners and losers. Team games of various types probably best exemplify this general type of reward structure in the school setting. Much of what is true about individual competition also appears to be true about group competition. At the same time, it has been reported (Julian & Perry, 1967) that individual competition is a more effective reward structure than group competition in improving the academic performance of students. A similar finding was reported by Scott and Cherrington (1974).

An important difference between individual and group competition exists in the interpersonal domian. While Julian and Perry (1967) found individual competition to be more effective than group competition as a reward structure, they also found that group competition had more positive effects on several interpersonal dimensions. Similar findings have been reported by Julian, Bishop, and Fiedler (1966) and Fiedler (1967). They reported that group competition had a positive impact on self-esteem, lack of anxiety, and rating of self as responsible and capable. It appears that group competition, though perhaps less effective than individual competition in stimulating individual achievment behaviors, is more effective than individual competition in the production of positive interpersonal behaviors.

While group competition may result in some of the same undesirable outcomes as individual competition (e.g., groups of low potential giving up, negative feelings toward school and self, etc.) it is possible, at least, to arrange the situation so that groups are better balanced in terms of their potential for whatever activity is to be undertaken. Few physical education teachers are likely to deliberately create intramural teams where the athletic talent is all consigned to one team. They are well aware of the negative effects of such an arrangement. The same principles apply within the classroom. If the task to be undertaken by various groups in a competitive situation is academic, then means must be found to spread the academic talent, both high and low, among the various groups that will be competing. In this way, some of the negative results of individual competition may be avoided and some of the positive results of group cooperation may be realized.

■ *Reward Structures Based on Individual Contingencies.* Within this type of reward structure, each individual's performance is compared with an established standard to determine who will receive a reward. The fact that one individual receives a reward does not bar another from receiving a similar reward, as is the case in individual competition. Such structures are not uncommon in the educational setting. An example would be the assigning of grades based on a fixed standard, e.g., from 90 to 100 is an A, from 85 to 90 is a B, from 80 to 85 is a C, and so on. A less common system is one in which each individual's ability level determines what fixed standard he or she must meet in order to achieve given rewards. This latter approach exemplifies highly individualized educational programs and is little used with children in regular education.

Unfortunately, there are relatively few studies that compare structures utilizing individual contingencies with either individual or group competition–based reward structures. This is an interesting finding in light of the almost continual emphasis placed by various educational writers on "individualizing education." There are, in fact, so few appropriate studies of such reward structures that there is little, based on research, that can be said about the application of this approach. Two studies (Clifford, 1971; Scott and Cherrington, 1974) report that individual competition was more effective than individual reward contingencies in strengthening students' performances on two different kinds of tasks. Unfortunately, these tasks were not relevant to typical classroom learning tasks. The Scott and Cherrington study also reported that group competition and individual reward contingencies were equally effective. On the other hand, it must be noted that the apparent success of programmed learning material and mastery programs, both examples of individual reward contingencies, suggests that this approach has promise for certain kinds of learning tasks.

▪ *Reward Structures Based on Group Contingencies.* While there have been a number of studies of the use of group contingencies, there seem, unfortunately, to have been relatively few comparing group contingencies with other approaches. Further, these studies that have been done do not appear to resolve the issue (e.g., Hamblin, Hathaway, & Wodarski, 1971; Herman & Tramontana, 1971; Wodarski, Hamblin, Buckholdt, & Ferritor, 1973). According to Slavin (1977) no studies comparing cooperative and competitive structures in the classroom existed as of 1977.

The cooperative group approach has probably received more attention than any other in the last several years. A general conclusion appears to be that a group contingency approach produced the most positive personal and interpersonal results. These results include greater interpersonal attraction among group members, more group cohesiveness, more helpfulness, more positive emotional states, and more supportive statements. There is evidence that in interracial settings there are positive effects on interracial friendships, positive interracial attitudes, interracial cooperation, and reduction in interracial conflict. These findings are summarized by Slavin (1977) who says, "In other words, abundant evidence exists to portray the cooperative setting as one characterized by a positive, mutually supportive group climate" (p. 645). A more recent and more rigorous review has been reported by Johnson, Maruyama, Johnson, Nelson, and Skon (1981). Using the technique of meta-analysis they studied the achievement outcomes of 122 studies of cooperative, competitive and individualistic goal structures. Their results indicate that straightforward group cooperation is considerably more effective in producing achievement outcomes than either competitive or individualistic approaches. Even cooperation with intergroup competition was more effective than either interpersonal competition or individualistic techniques.

They reported that the more "superiority of cooperation increases the more subjects are required to produce a group product" (p. 56).

A specific type of cooperative group structure that has received considerable attention is the Jigsaw approach (Aronson, Blaney, Stephan, Sikes, & Snapp, 1978). The technique structures group work in such a way that group members are required to cooperate with one another in order to complete a given task. Fundamentally, the approach provides students with practice in cooperating with each other at specified times during the school day. Typical research studies report using from 2 to 4 hours a week of class time. Advocates of Jigsaw report positive effects on student achievement (Lucker, Rosenfield, Sikes, & Aronson, 1976) as well as on personal and attitudinal variables (Blaney, Stephan, Rosenfield, Aronson, & Sikes, 1977). More recently, some possible limitations in the method have been pointed out by Moskowitz, Malvin, Schaeffer, and Schaps (1983) who implemented a study of Jigsaw in a real-life setting. They found that only 7 of a group of 15 teachers expressed interest in learning more about the approach, in spite of a 200-dollar payment and academic credit, and that of those who did go through the training, only three used the method in an "exemplary" manner. Very few of the predicted affective outcomes were found, even in the exemplary settings.

This finding is undoubtedly not restricted to this particular method. It is probably true of *any* approach that requires the teacher (a) to invest time in mastering some relatively complex new behavior, and (b) to set aside a specific time during the school day for its accomplishment. At the same time, the superiority of group-cooperative approaches both for achievement and attitudinal outcomes suggests that effort invested in helping teachers to use group-cooperative approaches would be time well-spent.

Implications of Current Knowledge on Reward Structure

The presence of a formal reward structure, regardless of its nature, will be more effective in producing desired performance outcomes than is the case in situations that have no formalized reward structure. It appears also to be the opinion of knowledgeable researchers that lack of any announced reward structure is characteristic of most classrooms. A first step that a guidance specialist might want to take, then, would be to assist teachers to establish more formal reward structures in their classrooms. In order to do this, it is clear that teachers would need to understand that the extra planning required to do this would be likely to result in a payoff, either in the form of increased student learning or increased ease of student management.

The choice of reward structures may depend upon specific goals. If the goal is to increase performance over the short term, then individual competition might be chosen. This approach has the additional benefit of being the easiest to organize and administer. Over the long run, however, it should be remembered that individual competition is likely to result in a loss of motivation among students who, by virtue of ability, cannot compete on a reasonably equal basis. The net result could be both an ever-widening gap between those highest and lowest in ability and (possibly) an increase in discipline problems as those whose motivation diminishes seek other outlets for their interests and energies. It would thus appear that individual competition might best be applied to short-term learning or performance situations and where there is a certain homogeneity of ability.

The use of individual contingencies is probably the second easiest type of reward structure to initiate and administer. It has the advantage that more than one person can achieve the highest level of reward and also that no one need fail by virtue of the structure of the reward system used. On the other hand, the heterogeneity of ability found in most classrooms is likely to make for winners and losers in most situations. For example, if a test grade of 90% is required to achieve an A, and a grade of less than 70% results in an F, then, in the practical situation, differences in ability will result in winners (those who receive As) and losers (those who receive Fs). A way around the situation is to establish individual reward contingencies based on each child's ability or current level of achievement in a given area. While this permits each child to be a winner, in the true sense of the word, it introduces an organizational problem of considerable magnitude. In addition, it raises a value question of even greater proportions. While the idea of individualizing education with respect to exceptional children appears to have gained some acceptance, this acceptance has not, apparently, generalized to the broad student population. In the main, teachers seem to favor the idea that there is a fixed standard which all must meet. At the same time, there may be teachers willing to accept this idea with the understanding that overall results are likely to be better than they would be if either individual competition or individual reward contingencies based on fixed standards were used.

The use of any group reward structure, as opposed to any individual reward structure, is likely to require greater effort on the part of the teacher. Such a choice will also be mediated to a considerable extent by the teacher's values and goals. The teacher interested in personal and interpersonal outcomes, as opposed to academic outcomes only, may be the teacher most interested in a group approach. The group competition idea is likely to be more acceptable to most teachers than cooperative group approaches. Some of the problems with group competition can be minimized through attempts to balance ability levels among groups. Physical education teachers handle this problem by permitting children to choose up sides for participation in team games. The result is competition which is more enthusiastic and fair than it might be if some arbitrary means were used to form teams (groups). As with individual competition, unfair group competition, over a long period of time is likely to result in loss of motivation in low-performing groups that cannot compete on a reasonably equal basis with other groups. In the best situation, then, group competition, like individual competition, will be used in events or exercises of relatively limited duration.

The use of group contingencies emphasizing cooperation within the group is undoubtedly the most difficult type of reward structure to institute and maintain but the benefits of such an approach are several. First, there is a heightened level of performance, although apparently not the same level as that engendered by individual competition. Second, there are personal and interpersonal benefits, which some teachers may see as being equal in importance to, or even more important than, achievement. Such an approach might be particularly helpful in a class or situation where students are not getting along with each other or where there are even more specific problems such as interracial conflict.

The old cliche applies here, guidance specialists will need to begin where the teachers are. One teacher may be willing to consider the initiation of a fairly complex reward structure with multiple benefits where another teacher may be willing only to consider the most rudimentary kind of reward structure and, to face reality squarely, it may not be possible to interest some teachers in any kind of reward structure. Perhaps the provision of a general in-service dealing with particular kinds of reward structures and their benefits might be a first step, followed by individual contacts with those teachers who express interest in making some kind of shift in their classroom reward structures. Continued, brief, regular meetings of teachers who want to make change, under the leadership of a guidance specialist, may serve to provide a supportive situation in which teachers who are tentative will be encouraged to attempt at least small steps, while teachers who may be fully committed to more complex approaches can provide feedback on what works, what doesn't work, and general outcomes. A few teachers may even be ready to try the application of different reward structures to different specific situations in the classroom, depending both on their goals and the nature of the task to be rewarded.

As has been suggested previously, it is likely that teacher values may be a major stumbling block in the institution of a specific reward structure. To deal with this, guidance specialists may need to exercise their own counseling skills in order to help in the exploration of personal values and the clarification of attitudes. A recital of research outcomes on reward structures is unlikely, in and of itself, to be convincing to teachers whose values currently place them against the use of rewards other than grades.

GROUPING STRATEGIES

A particular grouping of children exists in classrooms whether there is a rationale for it or not. Experience suggests that the most common grouping structure is heterogeneous grade level grouping. It appears to be almost random in nature, although in specific situations particular children or particular teachers may be taken into account in the placement of an individual child. Other grouping strategies have been tested and tried, however, generally with the idea of improving academic performance, but sometimes with the idea of contributing to personal development or interpersonal skills.

The general idea that placing certain children with each other (and not with other children) to achieve learning or personal goals is hardly new. Perhaps the most generalized example of the use of procedures of grouping is seen in the homogeneous placement of various groups of exceptional children in the period from 1945 to about 1975. The assumption was that exceptional children (the retarded, those with sensory deficits and, occasionally, the gifted) would be able to profit more from their educational experience if they were placed in a learning situation with other children who had similar learning needs. Since the advent of PL 94-142, of course, all of that has changed and the new assumption is that exceptional children will profit most from integrated or mainstreamed classes.

Grouping, like many other kinds of educational strategy, seems to wax and wane in popularity. Currently most kinds of homogeneous groupings are in political, social, and, therefore, educational disfavor. Requirements for the maximum integration of special education children into regular education classrooms is now the law of the land; tracking, a process of assigning children to specific kinds of academic programs (college preparatory, vocational, etc.) has been challenged successfully in the courts. The emphasis on nongraded classes, another form of grouping, which was present in the early 60s (Goodlad & Anderson, 1963) also appears to have diminished considerably. At the same time, given the basic purposes of this volume, it is appropriate to examine the pros and cons of various grouping strategies from a more dispassionate point of view than sometimes marks the trendiness of educational methods.

Possible Grouping Strategies

The concept of grouping has both a *vertical* and *horizontal* dimension. The vertical dimension refers to an age/grade time line and indicates whether or not children are placed in a particular school grade, in a multigraded or a nongraded setting. Of these vertical options, the graded school is by far the most common. Neither the multigraded nor the nongraded option have attracted significant support in this country.

The horizontal aspect of grouping refers to the relative homogeneity/heterogeneity of a particular group of children, regardless of whether they are vertically grouped in graded, multigraded, or nongraded situations. Criteria that have been used or suggested for homogeneous grouping include academic aptitude, achievement, personal/social maturity, sex, learning styles (modalities), and retention in grade. This latter criterion is not generally conceptualized as related to grouping, but as that appears to be its basic intent, it will be treated within this section. Putting the vertical and horizontal options together, provides an idea of the possible number of grouping options. The most common combination of vertical and horizontal options is the hetereogeneously grouped, graded classroom. Whether this is the best approach has been seriously questioned by both theorists and researchers. As was true of the topic of classroom reward structures, there is a tremendous amount of research available, not all of which is consistent. The quality of this research differs considerably from one study to another, as do some of the specific variables upon which research has been conducted. We will review the most important strategies and what appear to be some of the best studies and draw some generalizations about the effectiveness of different kinds of grouping, especially as they impact pupil achievement and personal and social development.

Horizontal Grouping Strategies and Their Effects

While a number of types of homogeneous grouping are possible, only a few have had enough research to warrant discussion, and even in some of these areas the fundamental criterion is often undifferentiated. For example, the term "ability grouping" may be used to designate grouping based on academic aptitude, academic achievement as measured by tests, or academic achievement as measured by grades. In fact, having said this, we have covered the major forms of homogeneous grouping that have been the subject of substantial research. While grouping on the basis of maturity or development has often been recommended and occasionally implemented, there has been little research bearing on grouping done in this way. The same can be said for the idea of grouping on the basis of learning styles or modality perferences. Grouping on the basis of sex was common at one time, but now appears to be restricted to some private schools and there has never been any substantive research on the effects of this type of grouping. It should be noted that in most studies of homogeneous grouping the heterogeneous approach is regarded as a control rather than as a treatment. There is a certain irony in this since this most common of approaches is as much a treatment as any other.

■ *Ability Grouping.* Ability grouping, as used in this context, refers to the placement of students in class-sized groups through the use of intelligence, scholastic aptitude, or achievement criteria. Specifically excluded are grouping procedures used by individual teachers *within* a given class; research suggests that this approach may have different effects than grouping by class. The concept and use of ability grouping in the schools of this country is not new. It is reported by Kulik and Kulik (1982) that the first steps toward ability grouping were initiated in St. Louis in 1867, followed by a fully developed ability grouping scheme called the Concentric Plan in Santa Barbara at the turn of the century. Between that time and the early 1970s a number of different ability grouping schemes were tried. Since the early 1970s, however, there has been an obvious diminution, both in the use of ability grouping and in the studies reported in the literature. This shift has probably been due both to the resurgence of interest in individualized instruction and to the challenges raised by opponents of ability grouping in the courts (Kirp, 1974).

Ability grouping has been assumed by its proponents to have a variety of positive effects including improved achievement, improved motivation resulting in better attitudes toward school, improved attendance, improved self-concepts, and better interpersonal relations. The detractors of ability grouping have assumed that it has not only failed to achieve these goals, but that it also has resulted in greater social, economic, and ethnic discrimination with the net effect of creating first and second class students, both in the minds of educators and in the minds of the students themselves. Certainly it is possible to find support for both of these views from among the dozens of available studies. It has been pointed out (Goldberg, Passow, & Justman, 1966) that a high proportion of these studies contain serious methodological flaws. If, however, studies are regarded from the point of view of their overall research quality, a picture emerges that is different from those painted by both proponents and opponents.

In a review of the literature conducted by Esposito (1973) four general findings are reported. These include the following:

1. Ability grouping demonstrated no consistent value in helping students to achieve more academically.
2. The effects of ability grouping on affective development are unfavorable.
3. Ability grouping results in the separation of students along social, economic, and ethnic lines.
4. Where there are improvements in scholastic performance, they appear to be related more to changes in teaching methods and materials than to the grouping strategy used.

In a more recent and more rigorously designed review confined to the secondary level, Kulik and Kulik (1982) came to mildly different conclusions. They found differences in grouped classes that were all positive and suggested that there was no evidence that homogeneous grouping is harmful. On the other hand, the differences they found were so slight that they call into question the worthwhileness of grouping when other considerations are taken into account. More specifically they found the following:

1. With respect to achievement outcomes students in grouped classes outperformed ungrouped students only slightly (approximately 1/10 of a standard deviation). High-ability students did perform better than they would have in heterogeneous classes while students in classes for the academically deficient showed no difference in performance from what would have been expected in a mixed ability class. It might be noted that highly similar findings were reported by Esposito (1973), but not included in his general summary.
2. Effects of grouping on self-concept are described as "trival" (p. 424).
3. When students were homogeneously grouped in subject matter–oriented classes (mathematics or English composition), grouping had a significant, positive effect on student attitudes toward the subject being taught.

4. Homogeneous grouping had no statistically significant effect on student attitudes toward school in general.

Considering the very different frames of reference and techniques of analysis used, these two reviews lead to surprisingly similar general conclusions. While Esposito (1973) suggests that there are no positive outcomes of homogeneous grouping and infers that there may be negative ones, Kulik and Kulik (1982) in their summary suggest that while there are no negative effects of homogeneous grouping the positive effects are so small, even when statistically significant, that the overall impact of homogeneous grouping on achievement, attitudes, and self-concept is negligible. Thus, neither of these excellent summaries provides support for the technique of ability grouping.

It should be noted, however, that several issues remain unresolved. For example, does ability grouping *within* a class differ in its effects from full-time ability grouping schemes? Certainly primary grade teachers in the typical graded classroom have used this approach for many years. A study by Venezsky and Winfield (1979) found that schools highly successful in teaching reading used this type of within-class grouping. Further research exploration of this approach seems warranted.

Another question is raised by a study reported by Beckerman and Good (1981). They deliberately *balanced* classes in terms of ability so that equal numbers of high-, middle-, and low-ability students were included in the composition of each classroom. They found that both high- and low-ability students achieved more in mathematics in such classrooms. It should be noted that there is a distinct difference between the approach used by Beckerman and Good and the usual heterogeneous classroom where students are either grouped on some random basis or where there are attempts to place students on the basis of predicted teacher–student interactions. This actually constitutes a third type of ability grouping which has received almost no attention.

A third issue is reflected in the fact that the present preference for classroom heterogeneity of ability bumps squarely into another current ideal, namely the emphasis on what is called individualized instruction. It has been reported by Evertson, Sanford, and Emmer (1981) that high heterogeneity of ability in junior high school English classes limited teacher adaptation of instruction to the academic and affective needs of individual students. Even on a commonsense basis it would appear that given current class sizes, the ideal of individualized instruction is likely to be frustrated by the heterogeneity of ability.

A fourth important issue related to ability grouping is to be found in the question of whether homogeneous grouping may have positive effects on one group, but negative effects on another. For example, both Esposito (1973) and Kulik and Kulik (1982) reported that a number of studies of homogeneous grouping do suggest that the achievement of high-ability students is enhanced by such grouping even though that of middle- and low-ability students is not. Another study (Wolk & Solomon, 1975) reported that students assigned to lower tracks were less satisfied with their placement and became more so over time while higher-track students became more satisfied with their placement over time. A similar assertion has been made by Kelly (1975). These studies point up a genuine dilemma, namely that any type of grouping strategy may have positive effects for one group and less positive or even negative ones for another. This opens the grouping issue to questions of values as well as of research. If one group of students profits from a particular grouping structure, but another does not, which takes precedence?

Given the present state of our knowledge of the effects of ability grouping what can counselors or psychologists recommend to their administrative and teaching colleagues when ability grouping issues arise? The following seem reasonable:

1. Since the achievement gains claimed for ability grouping are neither great nor equally spread across ability levels, it appears questionable whether ability grouping is worth the time and trouble involved or worth the negative feelings it will inevitably engender in minority, ethnic, and lower socioeconomic status groups.

2. Although information is minimal at this point, it appears appropriate to suggest the possibility of using class groups balanced for ability as opposed to the less systematic "heterogeneous" method. Even Esposito (1973) who is firmly against generalized grouping strategies suggests utilizing "flexibility in the use of the educational environment so that individuals or small groups of children have a greater opportunity to engage in activities more closely related to individual strengths and needs" (p. 173).

Since the effects of class-sized homogeneous ability grouping on attitudes and self-concepts are either negligible or negative, attempts to bring about growth or improvement in these variables are probably best accomplished through changes in the structural and dynamic properties of the environment (Barker, 1968). Ability grouping cannot be viewed as an easy vehicle to the improvement of achievement or personal development of students. The teacher is the main determinant of the overall classroom environment, therefore it would seem appropriate to continue attempts to improve teacher skills (as suggested elsewhere in this volume) and to assist teachers to provide specific programs with specific purposes. For example, if improved interpersonal skills levels among students are a goal, then, in addition to providing a general environment in which these skills can flourish, there should be a specific program to teach such skills, such as that proposed by Shure and Spivack (1979). In sum, it appears that the effort required to achieve homogeneous ability grouping and the anger and frustration likely to be engendered by it are not balanced either by its effects on academic achievement or on personal or social variables. Other means, more difficult of accomplishment, seem necessary in order to improve the general level of academic achievement and personal–social growth.

▪ *Retention as a Form of Ability Grouping.* The retention of students is not ordinarily considered a form of grouping and yet the net result of such a practice is to keep together students of like ability, like achievement, or similar maturity levels. Since the alleged purpose of retention is to help the student to develop optimally and since candidates for retention are often members of an at-risk population, the topic is appropriate for inclusion within the primary prevention context. Retention is an issue in most schools and both counselors and school psychologists are annually called upon to provide judgments about the retention of specific children.

For purposes of this discussion, grade retention is defined as "the practice of requiring a student who has been in a given grade level for a full school year to remain at that level for a subsequent school year" (Jackson, 1975). U.S. Census Bureau data indicate that the use of retention declined sharply beginning in the decade from 1950 to 1960 and continued to decline from 1960 to 1970 (Rose, Medway, Cantrell, and Marus, 1983). In spite of this decline in its use, substantial numbers of children are retained. In the 13 states that reported retention data for the period from 1978 to 1980, retention included from 4% to over 8% of the student population (Rose, et al., 1983). With the current widespread trend of adopting grade level educational objectives, it seems very likely that retention is likely to become much more extensively used than it currently is. For example, in the fall of 1981, after the Atlanta schools had adopted such objectives, 18% of first-graders were not promoted to the second grade (Rose, et al., 1983). It is unfortunate that there is likely to be such a wide scale return to the practice of retention in the absence of an examination of the research for or against the practice.

As anyone knows who has been involved with the issue of retention, it is an emotionally charged issue. Both professional and lay persons tend to have strong feelings for or against it. A majority of what appears in the educational literature is in the domain of personal opinion rather than research. Unfortunately, the research itself tends to confuse the issue. However, as Jackson (1975) points out, this confusion tends to result from the use of inadequate research designs as much as from anything else. Jackson's review resulted in the location of only three studies of retention that employed an adequate research design, and one of these by Klene & Branson in 1929 is over 50-years-old. A review of the research on retention conducted between 1975 and the present indicates that no additional studies meeting Jackson's criteria of adequacy have been reported in the meantime. The main problem in existing research designs is that children whom it has been decided to retain have not been randomly assigned to a retention and a nonretention group, resulting in unknown and probably considerable bias in the samples studied. Thus the basic unanswered question remains: Would retained children have been equally or even more successful if they had not been retained at all?

Results of the three adequately designed studies that were located by Jackson (Cook, 1941; Farley, 1936; and Klene & Branson, 1929) indicated either that there was no difference between retained and promoted groups, or that students in the promoted groups showed greater academic progress. Given the small size of the groups in some of these studies, as well as the limited grade levels considered, it is not possible to draw firm conclusions from them. Instead, it is only possible to draw a general conclusion. Jackson phrases it in this manner: *"Thus, those educators who retain pupils in a grade do so without valid research evidence to indicate that such treatment will provide greater benefits to students with academic or adjustment difficulties than will promotion to the next grade."* Others who have reviewed the total literature have reached highly similar conclusions (Bocks, 1977; Lehr, 1982; Lindelow, 1982; Reiter, 1973). It should be taken as a given that in spite of all of the discussion and feeling it engenders, retention has not proved to be an effective type of intervention. Put in other words, it can be said that there is no firm evidence to demonstrate that retention is of benefit to the child who is retained.

The lack of evidence notwithstanding, it is reasonable to assume that retention considerations will occur annually in most schools. Given this situation, how can the counselor or school psychologist involved in such decisions behave most constructively? The broadest step that could be taken would be to begin to help administrators and teachers understand that while the idea of retention is appealing at a commonsense level, there is no factual basis demonstrating its effectiveness. Such efforts may take the form of specific in-service training or simply of taking opportunities to discuss the issue with individuals or groups in more casual settings. Since most experienced educators are likely to point to a specific child who was "helped" by retention, it can be pointed out that while growth may have occurred, it is not possible to know whether more growth would have occurred had that particular child been promoted rather than retained.

Another tack to take would be the attempt to separate value issues from the more objective question of whether promotion or retention would most benefit the given child. It is not unusual for teachers to talk in terms of whether a specific child "deserves" to be promoted. The implication is that they have not worked as hard as they should have or that their behavior has, in some other way, made them "undeserving" of promotion. At a more positive level, teachers, either individually or collectively, should be encouraged to identify specific and objective criteria to be considered in dealing with retention questions. The primary criterion should probably be academic achievement and that, rather than depending only on teacher judgment, should be determined by more objective means, such as achievement test results. If necessary, such tests should be given precisely for the purpose of providing such information. It appears that in many cases teachers' judgments of children's achievement are clouded by their behavior. There is often an apparent assumption that if the child is a behavioral problem in class, he or she is, ipso facto, low in achievement. While this is often true, it is also often not true.

The concept of "maturity" is often invoked in retention considerations. Judgments about maturity, like judgments about achievement, are often related to problem classroom behavior rather than to a more objectively defined determination of maturity. It seems reasonable that maturity should *not* be a factor considered in retention unless it has already been objectively demonstrated that a child's achievement is far below grade level. It is suggested by Lindelow (1982) that a child's rate of progress (achievement) in the year before retention should be less than half the normal rate before retention is seriously considered.

There sometimes appears to be a punitive aspect to some retention decisions. It is unlikely that such a contention could ever be objectively demonstrated, but such a judgment seems, in some cases, to be reasonable. The school will do best by the student when it focuses on specific criteria, particularly achievement, and when these criteria are objectively, not subjectively, determined.

On balance, the major responsibility of the counselor or school psychologist involved in retention decisions appears to be to attempt to promote among the faculty a factual knowledge of the uncertain state of our information on effects of retention, with the aim of reducing the overall number of retentions. In specific cases of possible retention, the appropriate role would be to insist upon the use of objectively obtained information, with major emphasis on achievement rather than personal or behavioral variables.

■ *Other Forms of Horizontal Grouping.* We have suggested that horizontal grouping may take a number of forms. While this may be true, the literature suggests that in actual practice horizontal grouping as a specific and separate way to place children in clusters for the purpose of helping them to learn more effectively is not only a declining practice but, with respect to grouping other than ability grouping, almost a dead practice. There are no reports in the recent literature of attempts to group class or school-sized groups on the basis of maturity unless kindergarten screening programs (discussed in chapter 6) are taken as a special case of placement by maturity. There are studies of placement on the basis of sociometric status. These studies, however, are ordinarily carried out with small groups of sociometrically selected students to determine the effectiveness of small working groups (e.g., Stam & Stam, 1977). Studies of grouping by sex, by learning modality preferences, and other specific horizontal grouping strategies are not reported in the literature. If the number of reports on horizontal grouping by class-sized units can be taken as an index of the extent to which such practices are used, then it is correct to say that, with the possible exception of ability grouping, the use of this strategy has declined to a point where it is not a major factor in education at this time.

Vertical Grouping Strategies and Their Effects

The concept of vertical grouping, as we have suggested, would appear to be relatively straightforward. Unfortunately, as the idea is treated in the educational and psychological literature, it is anything but. The location of well-designed studies reflecting pure vertical grouping considerations has proven all but impossible. Most reviews of the literature appear to include biased samples of the studies available or to reflect studies where such a multiplicity of definitions has been used that comparison among them is not possible. The general categories include "open end, continuous pupil progress, ungraded, learner centered, flexible primary unit, flexigrade, primary block, primary continuum, achievement levels, individualized programs, individualized progress, appropriate placement, innovative or experimental schools, and individualized instruction" (Pavan, 1973, p. 335). In addition, other commonly used names are *family grouping* (the apparently favored British designation), *multiage grouping*, the *ungraded school, open education, open schools,* and *open classrooms.* This complex picture is further confused by the fact that identical terms are used in very different ways by different authors and researchers. The concept of vertical grouping is plagued by lack of agreed-upon definitions.

If the number of journal articles on this general topic be taken as an index of level of interest in it, then it appears that interest peaked in the mid-60s or early 70s, and has declined, in the United States, since that time. Using the same index it appears that interest in what the British tend to call "family grouping" has remained high there until the present, although a large share of what is published there is opinion, rather than research, and tends to appear in the pages of the Education Supplement of the London Times.

In its simplest form, the ungraded class is one in which children of differing ages may be found. According to Goodlad and Anderson (1963), a common ungraded organizational structure is one that includes children on two different grade levels although each such group is likely to include some who are older and some who are younger than is typical for a particular group. Grouping may be based "on age, random selection, social relationships, or similar factors" (p. 70). In addition, children may shift to another class at almost any time during the year; there is no set time for promotion to occur. Within each class there can be subgrouping on the basis of ability, achievement, interest, work and study habits, or other such variables. In such a case, the situation contains elements of both vertical and horizontal grouping strategies.

Another problem in evaluating the research in this area is the obvious partisanship of those who conduct or report it. One such supporter refers to the "indignities of the graded school that cry out for resolution" (McLoughlin, 1970, p. 95). Another supporter entitles her review of the research literature, "Good News: Research on the Non-Graded Elementary School" (Pavan, 1973). This is not an approach that gives confidence to the consumers of such information.

The research in this area ordinarily concerns itself with both cognitive and personal–social outcomes. Cognitive outcomes are usually assessed through the use of standardized achievement tests; personal–social outcomes are studied through the use of a highly varied array of measures reflecting such variables as anxiety, self-concept, attitude towards school, adjustment, social acceptance, and others. Three summaries of the research in this area have been reported. The first was done by Pavan (1973). This review included 16 studies which were reported between 1968 and 1971. Twelve of the 16 studies used standardized achievement tests that resulted in 19 actual comparisons. Of these, one favored graded schools, 11 favored nongraded schools, while 7 showed no significant difference between graded and nongraded schools. Thirteen of the 16 studies used what the reviewer called a "mental health" measure. These results were highly varied, generally favoring nongraded over graded situations, or reporting no significant difference. These outcomes must be viewed with some caution. The wide variation in achievement measures, in mental health measures, and in the approaches used in the 16 studies included served to cloud the issue somewhat. Further, some of the studies included in Pavan's review are not so much reports on vertical grouping as they are on open classrooms, a concept that differs from that of vertical grouping.

A more recent review has been reported by Ford (1978). This review concerned itself only with the domain of affective development. The author concludes that "multiage grouping appears to offer some advantages in affective growth" (p. 158). The author reports that children in ungraded (or multiage) settings have a better attitude toward school, more positive self-concepts, higher self-esteem, higher aspirations, greater feelings of success, and more positive perceptions of parental approval. The research reviewed failed to verify that children in multiage groups had lower anxiety, displayed more self-direction, or had better social adjustment. A third, although considerably briefer, review of research on the achievement outcomes of the nongraded approach (Martin & Pavan, 1976) concluded, "In all cases where students were matched for IQ the nongraded achievement scores were significantly higher" (p. 312). These reviewers also concluded that the nongraded approach fosters positive attitudes toward school.

One of the assumptions of the advocates of the nongraded approach is that it encourages socialization among all participants. A study by Ahlbrand and Doyle (1976) utilized a sociometric approach to determine the extent to which sociometric status was enhanced by cross-age grouping. They concluded that only the older group benefitted in leadership and popularity ratings, although not in scholarship ratings. Another assumed benefit of cross-age grouping is the encouragement of social interaction across age groups. A study by Day and Hunt (1975) indicates that while a significant number of interactions occurred between children of the same age, social interaction across age groups was significantly less than would be expected. The results of these two studies suggest that unless specific steps are taken to encourage socialization across age levels such interaction may not occur

and, further, that the social advantage in ungraded situations apparently accrues to the older students in that situation.

The most recent study comparing ungraded to graded classrooms (in the United States) appears to have been reported by Milburn (1981). The manner in which the study is reported makes it difficult to determine whether or not sound research procedures were utilized. On the other hand, the attractiveness of the study is that it includes two schools studied over a 5-year period. Since some research indicates that exposure to the ungraded situation has a cumulative effect (Papay, Costello, Hedl, and Spielberger, 1975) the outcomes of Milburn's study are of particular interest. Milburn reports few significant differences in basic skills achievement, but better attitudes toward school among the ungraded groups.

The generally reported outcomes of ungraded grouping strategies indicate that they may have a positive effect on attitudinal variables. These include attitude toward school and self-concept. Advantages are also reported for this approach in fostering academic achievement. There are two reasons for viewing these claimed outcomes cautiously, however. These include the disparity that exists among varying definitions used in studies of ungraded education outcomes and a similar disparity among reported results.

Current Status of Horizontal and Vertical Grouping Strategies

The most salient characteristic of both of these general methods of grouping is that they appear to be presently in decline. Perhaps the legal challenges that some of them have encountered, the social disapproval of minority groups as well as the uncertainty of outcome have contributed to the reduction of interest in these approaches. Further, as noted by both Goodlad and Anderson (1963) and Wilt (1971) any grouping strategy is merely a structural change. By itself, such a change is not likely to be potent enough to produce a significant positive change in either student achievement or student attitude. To attain maximum benefits such structural changes must be accompanied by changes in teaching methods and in the curriculum itself.

While there has been a reduction of interest in horizontal and vertical grouping strategies considered separately there has been an increase of interest in a melding of these approaches. This approach, which combines features of both horizontal and vertical grouping strategies, is known most frequently as open education. If the number of articles dealing with open education are an index of its current popularity, then it is popular indeed. While interest in specific methods of horizontal and vertical grouping have clearly diminished in recent years, interest in open education has increased. Since open education represents, in part, a structural approach to the delivery of educational services and since it is an apparent outgrowth of the horizontal and vertical grouping movements it will be considered next.

OPEN EDUCATION

As interest in horizontal and vertical grouping strategies has declined, the interest in open education has accelerated. The concept appears to be as much a philosophy as an organizational structure, but the implementation of the philosophy results in identifiable structural components. The basic ideas appear to derive from progressive education in this country and certainly resemble in most ways the philosophy and approach of the British infant schools. The earliest research reports date from the early 40s (e.g., Baker, 1941) and were heavily influenced by research coming from Columbia University and Bank Street School, through the 40s and 50s (Minuchin, Biber, Shapiro, and Zimiles, 1969). There was an apparent decline in interest through the early 60s, but in the middle of that decade reports of the methods used in the British infant schools apparently triggered a resurgence of interest in the open education approach in this country. Since then, dozens of articles dealing with this topic have appeared in American educational and psychological journals.

Like so many other expressions of educational methods, the term *open education* suffers seriously from a lack of specificity. A number of other descriptors are often used as the equivalent of open education. These include, at least, the terms *open classrooms* and *open schools*. While what is presently denoted *open education* certainly derives substantially from progressive education, it also appears to owe something to those who, in the late 60s, supported the ungraded classroom concept. Some authors who write about the ungraded classroom appear to use that term interchangeably with the term *open education* (Pavan, 1973).

Quite apart from the specific terminology used to denote open education is the problem of how it is defined. To some, particularly earlier, writers, *open education* literally meant a large open space with few walls where many children were dealt with by several different teachers. This type of limited definition is seldom encountered now, however, and while it may be a part of the total definition of *open education* in the minds of some authors it is clearly not the most important part. Fortunately, there has been a series of outstanding reviews of open education, each one of which has been progressively more complex and more sophisticated than the previous one. These reviewers have attempted, on the basis of reported studies, to define the common elements in open education (Giaconia & Hedges, 1982; Horwitz, 1979; Marshall, 1981; Peterson, 1979; Traub, Weiss, Fisher, & Musella, 1972; Walberg & Thomas, 1972). For present purposes, the most recent and most sophisticated of these reviews will be used to provide a definition for open education. Table 1 (Giaconia & Hedges, 1982, pp. 593–594) details the seven features that most distinctively characterize open education. These defining characteristics can be summarized as follows:

1. Instruction is student-centered; the child participates in choosing methods, materials, and the pace of learning. (The extent to which the child chooses the *topic* of learning remains unclear).
2. Evaluation is used to guide instruction and is not used to assess children's performance in relation to other children. Grading, in the traditional sense, is unlikely to be used.
3. The environment is enriched in the sense that a great variety of materials are available for the student to use. The purpose of these materials is to motivate the student to learn.
4. Instruction is individualized so that each student may progress at his/her own speed. Instruction is mainly individual or in small groups and learners proceed according to their own rates and learning styles.
5. Ungraded grouping, as opposed to grade level grouping, is used. Children may move from one ungraded situation to another with relative fluidity.

6. Classrooms are characterized by open spaces and a lack of physical structuring. Traditional seating arrangements are taboo and learning centers may be utilized.
7. More than one teacher is used in the planning and conduct of instruction for the same students.

It should be noted that not all learning situations that are called "open education" are characterized by all of these features. Indeed, some situations described as exemplifying open education may reflect none of the necessary components, an issue noted by Marshall (1981) and dealt with more generally by Charters and Jones (1973). The general problem of implementation of different component features of open education has been pinpointed by Marshall as an explanation for some of the differences reported among research studies of open education.

Outcomes of Open Education.

A summary of open education conducted over a period of over 40 years suggests that this approach probably has an important positive impact on social, personal and attitudinal variables such as cooperation, attitude toward school, curiosity, independence, creativity, self-concept, and locus of control. It should be pointed out that although the comparison of open with traditional education appears to indicate a definitely more positive outcome with open education, in many cases the major finding is one of no significant difference between open and traditional education.

When achievement differences between open and traditional education are examined, normally with reference to reading, mathematics, and language, the most general finding is either one of no significant difference between the two approaches or a slight difference favoring traditional education. When more fine-grained analyses are conducted, some additional interesting information is brought to light. Such an analysis is reported by Giaconia and Hedges (1982). Using a total of 153 studies, including 90 doctoral dissertations, they conducted a metaanalysis of the results. Outcomes for student adjustment, attitude towards school, attitude toward teacher, and curiosity favored the open education groups by about ⅕ of a standard deviation. Differences were near zero for student locus of control, self-concept, and anxiety. The student characteristics of cooperativeness, creativity, and independence also favored open education and Effect Sizes (ESs) were between ¼ and ⅓ of a standard deviation. Differences for achievement variables (language, mathematics, and reading) were approximately zero indicating that neither open nor traditional education had an advantage. The direction of the differences, however, favored traditional education. In general terms, these findings tend to confirm what others had previously reported: open education has a positive effect on a variety of noncognitive measures, and approximately zero effect on achievement measures.

Table 7-1
Descriptions of the Features of Open Education on Which Larger Effect and Smaller Effect Studies Were Compared

Feature: Role of Child in Learning
  Definition: Child is active in guiding her own learning; child actively chooses materials, methods, and pace of learning; role of teacher as resource person; less teacher-centered instruction and more student-centered instruction.
  Indicators and descriptive statement:
    voluntary action on the part of the child
    active agent in his own learning process
    self-motivated learning
    student initiates activities
    active participant rather than recipient to commands
    trust in the student's ability to choose his own learning experiences
    child-centered environment
    child's freedom and responsibility for his learning and development
    democratic learning atmosphere
    student sets rate of learning
    high degree of child contributions to the learning environment
    teacher as resource person
    teacher is authoritative not authoritarian

Feature: Diagnostic Evaluation
  Definition: Purpose of evaluation is to guide instruction; little or no use of conventional tests, but extensive use of work samples, observation, and written histories, of the student.
  Indicators and descriptive statements:
    charting of progress toward specific individual goals
    evaluation used to facilitate and guide learning
    child's performance not compared to that of other children
    teacher's record-keeping combines constant jotting in class and thoughtful writing about each child
    less standardized concept of student progress
    nongraded approach to evaluate student's performance

Feature: Materials to Manipulate
  Definition: Presence of diverse set of materials to stimulate student exploration and learning.
  Indicators and descriptive statements:
    sensory materials
    exploration and discovery-oriented materials
    use of natural materials
    rich material environment
    alternative modalities for learning
    diversity of materials
    abundance of instructional aids
    tactile confrontation with manipulative materials
    real world materials

Feature: Individualized Instruction
  Definition: Instruction based on the individual needs and abilities of each student; individualization of rate of, methods, and materials for learning; small group as opposed to large group instruction.
  Indicators and descriptive statements:
    individualized instruction
    individualized approach
    individualized work
    environment responsive to individual learner needs
    individualizing the curriculum
    individualized goal setting
    learning in accord with their own rate and style
    small group or individual instruction

Table 7-1 (*cont.*)

Feature: Multiage Grouping of Students
　Definition: Grouping students for instruction in which grade labels are not applied; two or more grades may be housed in the same area.
　Indicators and descriptive statements:
　　family grouping
　　nongrade school
　　heterogeneous age grouping
　　children from different grades work together in same classroom
　　ungraded classrooms
　　vertical grouping
　　continuous progress education

Feature: Open Space
　Definition: Physical environment of the classroom involving flexible use of space and furnishings.
　Indicators and descriptive statements:
　　open area classroom
　　open space architecture
　　flexible school architecture
　　open instructional area
　　activity centers
　　fluid space
　　decentralized classroom
　　pod facility school
　　open plant facility
　　no interior walls or movable walls
　　school without walls
　　flexible seating arrangements
　　physically unstructured

Feature: Team Teaching
　Definition: The sharing in planning and conducting instruction offered to the same group of students by two or more teachers; use of parents as teaching aides.
　Indicators and descriptive statements:
　　team teaching organization
　　team teaching units
　　teachers work together in teams with a team leader
　　large spaces with two or more teachers

Note. Identifying Features of Open Education by R. M. Giaconia and L. V. Hedges, 1982, *Review of Educational Research, 52*, pp. 579–602. Copyright 1982 by The American Educational Research Association. Reprinted by permission.

They then carried their analysis one step further, dividing the 153 studies into thirds on the basis of ESs. Studies with larger ESs (the top ⅓) were identified, as were those with smaller ESs (the lower ⅓.) They then used the seven defining features of open education reflected in table 7-1 to compare the number of features implemented in studies with larger and smaller ESs. An interesting difference occurred: for the nonachievement variables (self-concept, creativity, and favorable attitude toward school) the more effective programs included a larger number of the seven basic features than less effective programs. For achievement outcomes, the less effective programs included more of the seven basic features than the more effective programs. Of particular interest was the finding that the last three features shown in table 7-1 (open space, multiage grouping, and team teaching), all of which are regularly associated with open education, failed to differentiate between more and less effective open education programs for both achievement and nonachievement outcomes.

Results of this study indicate that open education programs can produce improved self-concepts, higher creativity, and more positive attitudes toward school. Those programs that produce these effects to the greatest extent are typically characterized by special freedom for the child to guide his or her own learning; the use of evaluation for guiding instruction, not for making comparisons among students; the presence of a wide variety of stimulating materials; and the use of instructional approaches based on individual differences. These results tend to echo many previously reported findings to the effect that no combination of open education program features is effective in producing higher academic achievement than traditional classrooms. It should be emphasized that there is no basis for saying that achievement is lower in open education classrooms, only that it is not higher than in regular classroom.

Forty years of research in open education appears to suggest, with some reason for confidence, that this approach is more effective than the traditional classroom approach in producing higher levels of student functioning on certain personality and attitudinal variables including self-concept, creativity, favorable attitude toward school, and possibly other variables. Open education does not produce higher levels of academic achievement, as measured by standardized tests, but neither does it seem to diminish student achievement.

Open education is a poorly defined concept in spite of its over forty years of existence, but when its component parts are defined as reflected in table 7-1 it appears that freedom for the child to direct his or her own learning, the use of evaluation to guide instruction, the presence of materials to manipulate, and individualized approaches to instruction are its most important features. Considerably less important are multiage grouping, team teaching, and the presence of open space. These latter three variables do not seem to contribute to either academic or personal growth. Those called upon to provide advice on open versus traditional classrooms can be reasonably confident in emphasizing these findings. At the same time, a caveat must be added. Just as open education has been ill-defined, so has traditional education. It may be that study of the special features of traditional education programs might reveal more specific and more useful information with respect to which of its features contribute to the effectiveness of traditional education.

THE PHYSICAL ENVIRONMENT

Our assumptions about the impact of the physical environment on learning have changed considerably since James A. Garfield said, "Give me a log hut, with only a simple bench, Mark Hopkins on one end and I on the other, and you may have all the buildings, apparatus and libraries without him."[1] The vastly increased complexity of science and technology that has occurred since Garfield made his famous pronouncement emphasizing the importance of the teacher in the educational process now mandates the availability and the use of equipment undreamed of when he spoke. At the same time, the word *assumption,* used in our opening phrase is not inappropriate. Periodic reviews of the literature on the importance of the physical environment in learning (e.g., Drew, 1971; Kevan & Howes, 1980; Randhawa & Fu, 1973; and Weinstein, 1979) serve to emphasize the primitive state of our knowledge with respect to the ways in which different aspects of physical environment interact with children's learning. Architectural and artistic opinion appear to have a great deal more to do with the way that school buildings are built than does hard information on the interaction between children's learning and the physical environment. It could hardly be otherwise since the amount and quality of the research in this area is not only limited but also relatively new.

The problem is complicated by the fact that different children apparently prefer different kinds of environments. For example, Pizzo (1981) conducted a study with sixth-graders in which their preferences for noise level in the classroom was determined. Those who expressed a preference for a quiet environment manifested better reading comprehension in that kind of environment than they did in a noisy environment while those who preferred some background noise achieved higher reading comprehension scores when there was talking in the background. A similar study conducted by Krimsky (1982) with respect to the preferred level of lighting reported essentially similar results. In addition to the issue of children's preferences there is some evidence that some children, regardless of their preferences, learn better in a special physical environment. A series of older studies of brain-damaged children, for example, Strauss and Lehtinen (1947) and Cruse (1961) among others, suggested that these children would learn best in an environment free of distracting influences such as colorful bulletin boards and the hustle and bustle of the regular classroom and should perhaps be provided with individual learning booths or carrels painted a flat gray. These suggestions flew in the face of the conventional assumptions that classrooms should be cheerful, highly decorated, and stimulating places. In most situations it is not possible to match children's preference for an environment with the environment that they prefer and most research reports only on the general effects of specific aspects of the physical environment on the learning of all children.

A number of aspects of the physical environment have been studied but not all are directly relevant to the purpose of this book. For example, there have been studies of the effect of urban–rural environments on learning. Since there is little that can be done about the fact that particular children are located in urban or rural areas, such research is not included in this

---

1. Address to Williams College alumni, New York, Dec. 28, 1871.

section. The aspects of the learning environment on which there has been enough research to make some practical contribution include classroom design, seating position, density and crowding, noise, windows, lighting, and temperature.

Classroom Design

An environmental variable that has always been of great interest is that of color. It is generally assumed that a profusion of bright colors will help to create an environment in which learning is encouraged. As noted above, however, there have been studies that suggest that certain children do not learn well in the stereotypic situation, and studies of color suggest that indeed different colors do have different effects. Studies by Birren (1965) and by Srivastava and Peel (1968) suggest that locomotion and other physical reactions are faster under conditions of red lighting and slower under green lighting. Goldstein (1942) reported that judgments of time, length, and weight were influenced by lighting color and reported results congruent with those of Birren. It was reported by Harmon (1944) that mental and visual task performance was enhanced by the presence of "soft" and "deep" colors in the environment. In summarizing his review of the literature Drew (1971) suggests:

> Activities in different areas within a classroom might be facilitated with different coloration depending upon the instructional program. Space in which more active instruction (and learning responses) are [sic] conducted could perhaps be more workable if colored in light reds. Areas where more passive participation is desired may function better if colored in dark blues or greens. (pp. 457–458)

Considerably fewer research studies of the effect of color on human learning have appeared in the literature since 1970 than appeared before that time. At present there is little that can be added to Drew's summary statement above.

Another area related to classroom design that has received a little research attention is the "ugly"–"beautiful" concept. There is, of course, no commonly agreed upon or objective definition as to what constitutes *ugly* or *beautiful*. For this reason, comparison among studies is extremely difficult and conclusions must be arrived at very tentatively. Few studies done on this concept have been conducted in schools. In an experimental study, Kasmar, Griffin, and Mauritzen (1968) assessed patients' moods and their ratings of a psychiatrist in a "beautiful" and an "ugly" room. There were no differences in patient ratings in either of these environments although patients did rate the environments themselves as being significantly different. In another study designed to assess the effects of beautiful and ugly surroundings, Mintz (1956) studied the reactions of psychological examiners to prolonged testing in beautiful and ugly rooms. Outcomes suggested that those working in the ugly environment completed their testing in a shorter time, felt more fatigue, discomfort, and monotony than did examiners in the contrasting environment who expressed feelings of enjoyment, comfort, pleasure and energy. A study conducted in the school setting by Santrock (1976) discovered that first- and second-graders worked longer at a task in a happy setting than in a sad or neutral one. The happy room was decorated with happy pictures; the sad room was decorated with sad pictures and the neutral room with neutral pictures.

The effect of design on achievement was studied by Winnett, Battersby, and Edwards (1975). These authors concluded that the architectural changes themselves had no impact on either achievement or behavior although the use of individual instruction and group contingencies did. The architectural changes in this study were quite minor, so these results must be accepted tentatively. In a study at the college level, Horowitz and Otto (1973) examined the scholastic achievement of students in the traditional classroom with those in a specially designed classroom containing a complex lighting system, a great deal of color, movable walls and comfortable seats. Grades throughout the semester indicated no achievement differences between the two groups although attendance was better in the experimental room and there was more class participation as well as a higher number of visits to the office of the instructor.

In general, studies of the effect of environments differing in their aesthetic appeal failed to support the existence of achievement differences. They do suggest that exposure to aesthetically appealing surroundings may create more positive attitudes and, perhaps, more active learning behaviors in students. Most of the studies reported have been of relatively short duration. It is possible that long-term exposure to more aesthetically attractive surroundings might lead to improved performance. If such factors as task persistence, stress, and attendance can be favorably influenced, as suggested by some of these studies, then it seems reasonable to assume that over time achievement will also be favorably influenced.

Both Weinstein (1977) and Evans and Lovell (1979) have demonstrated that the manipulation of internal design characteristics of classrooms can bring about certain specific changes in the behaviors of students. For example, Weinstein demonstrated that second- and third-graders in an open classroom could be influenced to change their travel pattern, their range of behaviors and the frequency of certain categories of behavior, such as the manipulation of materials. Working in an open plan alternative high school, Evans and Lovell were able to reduce classroom interruptions and improve the quality of the dialogue between teacher and students by the use of sound-absorbent partitions added for the purpose of redirecting traffic away from class areas and to define class boundaries.

Studies of furniture arrangement suggest that differences in attentiveness to a task, teacher perception of students, amount of classroom noise, and student–teacher interaction are all influenced by furniture arrangement, suggesting that classroom management problems might be amenable to change through the use of different arrangements of student's desks or tables, the use of barriers such as bookcases, and the placement of the teacher's desk. Those who consult with teachers ordinarily begin with the teacher behavior. A simpler first approach might be to consider the physical arrangement of the classroom furniture.

Seating Position

Experienced teachers routinely use seating position to discourage social interaction, ensure attention, or to provide for children with visual difficulties. Most studies of seating position deal with social interaction variables and most of the conclusions tend to verify the generally accepted wisdom, cheaters tend to sit together, seating at small tables encourages social interaction, seating in rows discourages social interaction, and so forth. When students are permitted to exercise their own choice of seats, those who sit near the front of the room tend to to place a positive value on learning while those who sit in the back of the room or near windows tend to have negative attitudes toward learning. As might be expected, students who prefer to sit near friends have a high need for affiliation (Walberg, 1969).

One investigator (Rist, 1970) found that socioeconomic criteria were unconsciously utilized when teachers make seating assignments. Children with middle-class attitudes and behaviors were placed nearest the teacher and received most of the instruction and attention. Children whose family backgrounds, language patterns, and appearance differed from those of the teacher's ideal student were assigned to tables further away from the teacher, received less attention, and were characterized as slow learners.

In another study of the effect of seating on teacher behavior Zifferblatt (1972) observed that the attention span of children in two third-grade classrooms with similar curricula, activities, and teacher styles was markedly different. He concluded that this difference was due to the way the rooms were arranged. In the room with longer attention span, desks were arranged so that any two or three children could work together and were placed out of the central traffic flow, thus providing greater privacy. The teacher's desk was in a corner which made it necessary for her to leave her desk and to move around the room to direct activities. Furniture, such as bookcases, was used to define areas for specific activities. The room with short attention span had large numbers of desks, as many as 12, clustered together and the teacher's desk was centrally located so that she could manage activities without leaving it. Barriers were not used to designate areas for specific activities.

There can be little doubt that seat location is a variable that influences the amount of interaction between teacher and student. Studies by Adams (1969) and Adams and Biddle (1970) found that this interaction was located mainly in the front–center part of the classroom and in a line directly up the center of the room. They characterized this area as the "action zone." This finding was striking enough that other investigators replicated it and verified these results (Koneya, 1976; Wulf, 1976). A study by Schwebel and Cherlin (1972) suggests that it is the students' physical location in the classroom which results in this outcome. These investigators found that even when seats were assigned on a random basis, students in the action zone spent a greater amount of time on task and less time on unassigned activity than those outside of the zone. Further, when seats were changed teachers' ratings of students' attentiveness and likeability also changed to favor those in the action zone.

Since it seems reasonably clear that subjective judgments on the part of teachers have an effect on what student is placed where and since it seems reasonably clear that the student who is front and center will have more teacher attention and more interaction with the teacher than other students, it would seem appropriate, other things being equal, for teachers to assign children randomly to seats and to routinely change the seating pattern so that all children had an equal opportunity to be in the action zone. These comments apply most clearly to classrooms in which traditional seating patterns are used and are somewhat less applicable in open classrooms although the general principles suggested here would apply with respect to any seating arrangement. It also seems reasonable to suggest that teachers need to direct activities while moving around the room, rather than attempting to do so from a central location.

Classroom Density

An issue addressed by architects and administrators in planning classrooms and in assigning students to them is that of density. Unfortunately, there is very little classroom-based research available to provide guidelines. Most studies of crowding tend to be of the experimental rather than the in vivo variety. On the basis of their research, Heller, Groff, and Solomon (1977) concluded that crowding or density is not a problem when the task to be completed does not require physical interaction among subjects. Similarly, it was concluded by Winer, Elkin, Loewy, and Weldon (1977) that density was not a problem in cooperatively structured classroom tasks. A similar conclusion was reached by Drew (1971) and Weinstein (1979) following their reviews of the current literature on this topic.

A variation of the crowding study was conducted by Shapiro (1975) at a preschool. He concluded that noninvolved behavior was most frequent in those classrooms where the space was less than 30 sq/ft per pupil and least frequent in classrooms where the space was between 30 and 50 sq/ft per pupil. But he also found that noninvolvement was high when there was more than 50 sq/ft per pupil, suggesting the possibility that there may be an optimum amount of space per child in a typical classroom. It seems reasonably clear that pupil density would need to be extreme (perhaps less than 30 sq/ft per pupil) before the kinds of tasks normally performed in a classroom would be affected.

Noise

Classroom noise has been a factor used by some administrators to determine whether a teacher was good or bad. Many teachers also feel that a classroom as near silent as possible is indicative of good teaching. Those who have embraced the open classroom idea have changed their thinking about the relationship of noise to learning, but there is still a solid phalanx of educators who equate a quiet classroom with an effective classroom. As was true of most of the other areas relating to the physical environment of the school, good studies conducted in the school setting are rare. There are, however, some studies that are suggestive.

There are at least two kinds of noise and they must be considered in separate categories. The first is what might be called normal classroom noise, or school noises such as talking, the sound of the band practicing in the gym, or the teacher next door showing a film. In most cases these are nonintrusive noises although they can, at times, reach intrusive intensities. The other kind of noise relates mainly to urban schools situated near major traffic arteries, rail lines, or under the flight patterns of large airports. In many instances this type of noise is not merely intrusive but is also highly variable so that there may be relative quiet for some periods of time with very sudden and high levels of noise at others. There is little research dealing with either of these kinds of noise.

Studies by Slater (1968) and Weinstein and Weinstein (1979) came to essentially similar conclusions. In the first study, children in seventh grade were exposed to three different levels of noise from quiet to extremely noisy. Under these conditions they took a standardized reading test. Results indicated that the noise did not either help or harm their performance on the test. In the second study the experimenters used two different levels of noise and under these conditions compared the reading performance of fourth-graders. They found no difference in performance.

At least three studies of the effect of external noise on children's school performance have been conducted. These include a study of the effect of freeway traffic (Kyzar, 1977), aircraft noise (Crook & Langdon, 1974), and train noise (Bronzaft & McCarthy, 1975). Only the study of train noise examined the impact of noise on achievement and it was found to be negative. All three studies, however, reported on the impact of these noises on teaching time and in all three cases teaching time was seriously reduced due to the periods of high noise intensity. It might be assumed that children who experience a significant loss of teaching time would, over time, not fare as well in achievement as students not exposed to such handicaps. However, subsequent studies by Cohen, Krantz, Evans, and Stokols (1979) and Cohen (1980) indicated that children in schools located under the flight pattern of the Los Angeles International Airport performed as well on math and reading achievement tests as did children from quiet schools. They did find, however, that children from the noisy schools were more distractible, less persistent on a puzzle task, and had significantly higher blood pressure. These findings are of great importance and suggest that continued exposure to noise may have both affective and health impacts on children.

There is little that the typical school personnel worker can do about a school that is already situated near a railroad or an airport. Current findings, however, argue persuasively that every possible step should be taken to avoid the location of schools in such places in the future. Research suggests that achievement, health, and affective states may all be negatively affected, over time, by exposure to such situations. If one side of a school building is more noisy than another, perhaps classes could be rotated from noisy to less noisy classrooms on a daily or weekly basis since it is continued exposure that appears to cause problems. Although teachers have not been the subject of this type of research, it seems reasonable to conclude that they too, over time, would suffer negative effects on their mental and physical health in such settings so that they might also benefit from some kind of relief from continued exposure.

In most schools, of course, the main issue remains the level of noise in the classroom, whether it is generated within the classroom or from the other sources of noise which exist in all schools. The research is sparse but it suggests that our traditional concerns about too much such noise are not well-founded. Most children function adequately under moderate levels of in-school noise. The silent classroom does not appear to be a requirement for effective learning.

The Windowless Classroom

During the decade of the 60s one of the most highly debated issues in school architecture was the idea of the windowless classroom and during that period a number of schools of this design were constructed. A certain press for the continued construction of such schools remains but whether it is due to a belief that children learn better in such circumstances or to the fact that windowless schools significantly reduce a major source of school vandalism is somewhat uncertain. The heat generated by discussions of windowless classrooms is not matched by the 'light shed by research. Relatively few studies, especially long-term studies, have been conducted.

A study using a projective approach was conducted by Karmel (1965) and compared students being taught in windowless classrooms with those attending regular classrooms. He had the high school students in his study draw pictures of schools. Those in the windowless classrooms drew schools with significantly more windows than students in the schools which had windows. Further analysis led him to conclude that there were more unhappy children in the windowless classrooms than in the classrooms with windows. Given the state of the art of analyzing drawings the latter conclusion must be taken as a starting point in research rather than as a final conclusion. Another study conducted at about the same time (Demos, 1965) but over a much longer period found no differences in school health records or personality test results from fifth-grade students in windowless classrooms. A study conducted in a windowless elementary school by Larson (1965) asked elementary teachers to compare their students' achievement with their ability levels. Results of this subjective assessment indicated no differences due to the absence of windows. A review of the literature on windowless environments by Collins (1975) led to the conclusion that exposure to a windowless environment has little impact on students although Collins also suggested caution in adopting windowless designs.

Available research results suggest that windowless environments have little impact on student achievement. At this point it seems reasonable to say that there is no compelling evidence suggesting that windowless classrooms have either negative or positive effects on children's learning, health, or personality.

Lighting

An issue of general concern, but of even more particular importance in windowless classrooms, is lighting. Most studies have dealt with the intensity of light required to do various kinds of work with some agreement that 50 to 100 footcandles are required for most indoor kinds of work. It is pointed out by Wurtman (1975) that this is less than 10% of the light to be found outdoors in the shade of a tree on a sunny day. He concludes that generally accepted standards of lighting are based more on economic and technological considerations than on knowledge of biological needs. Until better studies are done, the 50 to 100 footcandle standard is likely to be used. Certainly, there is reason for concern if levels of lighting in school rooms are less than this.

In addition to the intensity of light there has been scrutiny of the effects of fluorescent lighting. One study (Mayron, Ott, Nations, & Mayron, 1974) indicated that children taught in special fluorescent lighting conditions designed to simulate natural sunlight showed a decrease in hyperactivity compared to children taught in rooms with standard fluorescent lighting.

While it is clear that minimum amounts of light, probably in the 50 to 100 footcandle range, are required in classrooms, information on the precise amount of light which is best for school children doing different types of work is not available. It seems possible that fluorescent light, due to its wavelength characteristics, may have unknown effects on learning, behavior, or psychological variables, but this has not clearly been demonstrated in school settings. Until further research data are available, the best that can be done is to ensure minimum lighting levels, either through use of artificial light or through regulation of window blinds. Completely unstudied is the question of what might constitute too much light such as might come through windows from direct sunlight and be reflected off white pages.

Classroom Temperature

Studies of the effect of temperature on classroom performance are few. A significant decline in academic performance due to higher temperatures was found in a study of two groups of eight- and nine-year olds by Holmberg and Wyon (1969). The three temperature levels used by these investigators were 20°, 27°, and 30° C (68°, 81°, and 86° F, respectively). Unfortunately, they do not mention the conditions of relative humidity, a variable which clearly affects the subjective perception of temperature. These results at least suggest that extremes of temperature may affect academic performance.

It is pointed out by Kevan and Howes (1980) that cultural differences probably have an effect on temperature levels which are best suited to school work. British children, for example, are used to lower temperatures than U.S. children and tend to wear heavier clothing. Kevan and Howes suggest that acclimatization occurs and that the British children function better at lower temperatures than would be true for U.S. children. The same authors suggest that increased heat reduces willingness to work rather than the capacity to work. If this is true, then teachers as well as students are likely to be affected. A study of teacher preferences for temperature (Pepler, 1971a) indicated that 21° C (70° F) was the preferred temperature. Teachers who worked in climate-controlled (air-conditioned) classrooms had less tolerance for temperature variations than those who did not. A similar study of students (Pepler, 1971b) reported similar findings for students: the performance of those in climate-controlled schools was affected negatively by relatively small temperature changes (1.0 to 1.5° C) while the performance of students in non-climate-controlled schools was not affected until much larger shifts occurred (4.5 to 5.5° C).

There is a possibility that temperature may have different effects on different individuals. Evidence is cited by Kevan and Howes (1980) indicating that less able students are more seriously affected by heat stress than are more able students. They also cite research that concludes that children working at the limit of their ability may be more affected by heat than those who are not.

The available evidence suggests that the classroom performance of most children is likely to be affected when temperature (and humidity) are within relatively broad normal limits. A temperature around 70° F seems generally preferred, although it is probably because this is the approximate temperature to which U.S. citizens (until recently) have acclimatized. It will be interesting to see if preferences change as lower indoor temperatures become more the norm. It is possible that ability level in relation to task demands is also a factor in deteriorating performance; distraction may come first to those working near the limits of their ability.

SUMMARY

There are a number of organizational and structural aspects of the child environment which contribute to positive or negative outcomes. One of these important variables is the system of incentive or rewards used by the teacher. While individual competition appears to be the most widely used single approach, research suggests that the use of group contingencies, particularly where this approach is coupled with cooperative endeavor within the group, is about as effective as individual competition in promoting achievement, that it promotes achievement across a wider spectrum of ability levels, and that it also promotes a certain positive social behavior, which individual competition does not.

Various kinds of grouping strategies, both horizontal and vertical, have been studied over a considerable number of years. At the present time, these strategies are neither the subject of extensive research nor do they appear to be widely utilized in practice. Studies of homogeneous grouping have generally found no meaningful impact on achievement, with the exception of high-ability students, but some positive social and personal gains have been reported. It is the general conclusion that results of ability grouping do not justify the time and effort involved in organizing it.

The decline in interest in various forms of grouping appears to have occurred, in part, due to the newer interest in open education. Open education makes use of various kinds of grouping, particularly nongraded grouping, and, in addition, introduces new elements, both structural and philosophical. A review of the better studies of open education indicates that it has its greatest impact on social, personal, and attitudinal variables. Achievement differences between open and traditional education are generally not significant.

It may be that President Garfield's assertion that a student on one end of a bench and a good teacher on the other as the most fundamental requirement for education is not too far from the truth. In concluding his review of the literature on the effects of the physical environment on learning, Drew (1971) stated, "It might be the case that the influences we are dealing with are so fragile as to be inconsequential in the real world" (p. 460). In a similar vein, Moos, Harris, and Schonborn (1969) concluded that only 10% of the total variance of psychiatric patient and staff reactions could be accounted for by the environmental effect of a room. Somewhat more specifically, Weinstein (1979) in concluding her excellent review of the literature stated, "It would seem that the physical environment of the conventional classroom has little impact on achievement" (p. 598).

There is also evidence to suggest that other aspects of the environment set the stage for the development of attitudes and behaviors as well as interpersonal interactions that can either help or hinder learning. Such important characteristics as the amount of interaction between student and teacher, general feelings of positiveness or negativeness, student–student interaction, student traffic patterns within a room, and degree of teacher control of the class, are among those affected. Most of the studies available have been short-term in nature. If some of the findings reported persist over time, it seems inevitable that, in good environmental settings, achievement may be increased.

All of this suggests that those who provide consultant help to teachers should attend to environmental variables, particularly those directly under the teacher's control. These would certainly include arrangement of desks and furniture, control of lighting, provision of learning areas where both social interaction and private study can take place, and the general aesthetic qualities of the room. It does not seem too much to say that the contribution of environmental conditions to problems in classrooms should be ascertained before complex changes in teacher behavior are considered. Teachers usually want simple solutions to classroom problems. It is not often that such solutions are available, but a consideration of environmental factors may, in some cases, provide just such straightforward solutions.

REFERENCES

Adams, R. S. (1969). Location as a feature of instructional interaction. *Merrill–Palmer Quarterly, 15*, 309–322.

Adams, R. S., & Biddle, B. J. (1970). *Realities of teaching: Explorations with video tape.* New York: Holt, Rinehart, & Winston.

Ahlbrand, W. P., & Doyle, W. J. (1976). Classroom grouping and sociometric status. *Elementary School Journal, 76*, 493–499.

Aronson, E., Blaney, N., Stephan, C., Sikes, J., & Snapp, M. (1978). *The jigsaw classroom.* Beverly Hills, CA: Sage.

Baird, L. L. (1969). Big school, small school. *Journal of Educational Psychology, 60*, 253–260.

Baker, G. D. (1941). *New methods vs. old in American education: An analysis and summary of recent comparative studies.* New York: Teacher's College, Columbia University.

Barker, R. G. (1968). *Ecological psychology: Concepts and methods for studying the environment of human behavior.* Stanford, CA: Stanford University Press.

Beckerman, T. M., & Good, T. L. (1981). The classroom ratio of high- and low-aptitude students and its effect on achievement. *American Educational Research Journal, 18*, 317–328.

Birren, R. (1965). *Color psychology and color therapy.* New York: University Books.

Blaney, N., Stephan, C., Rosenfield, D., Aronson, E., & Sikes, J. (1977). Interdependence in the classroom: A field study. *Journal of Educational Psychology, 69*, 121–128.

Bocks, W. M. (1977). Non-promotion: A year to grow? *Educational Leadership, 34*, 379–383.

Bronzaft, A. L., & McCarthy, D. P. (1975). The effect of elevated train noise on reading ability. *Environment and Behavior, 7*, 517–529.

Charters, W. W., & Jones, J. E. (1973). On the risk of appraising non-events in program evaluation. *Educational Researcher, 2*, 5–7.

Clifford, M. M. (1971). Motivational effects of competition and goal-setting in reward and nonreward conditions. *Journal of Experimental Education, 393*, 11–16.

Cohen, S. (1980). Physiological, motivational, and cognitive effects of aircraft noise on children: Moving from the laboratory to the field. *American Psychologist, 35*, 231–243.

Cohen, S., Krantz, D., Evans, G. W., & Stokels, D. (1979). Community noise and children: Cognitive, motivational, and physiological effects. In J. Tobias (Ed.), *Proceedings of the third international congress on noise as a public health problem.* Washington, DC: American Speech and Hearing Association.

Collins, B. L. (1975). *Windows and people: A literature survey. Psychological reaction to environments with and without windows.* National Bureau of Standards Building Science Series, No. 70. Washington, DC.: Government Printing Office.

Cook, W. (1941). Some effects of the maintenance of high standards of promotion. *Elementary School Journal, 41,* 430–437.

Crook, M. A., & Langdon, F. J. (1974). The effects of aircraft noise in schools around London Airport. *Journal of Sound and Vibration, 34,* 221–232.

Cruse, D. P. (1961). Effects of distraction upon the performance of brain-injured and familial retarded children. *American Journal of Mental Deficiency, 66,* 86–92.

Day B., & Hunt, G. H. (1975). Multiage classrooms: An analysis of verbal communication. *Elementary School Journal, 75,* 458–464.

Demos, G. D. (1965). Controlled physical classroom environments and their effects upon school children (windowless classroom study). Riverside County, CA: Palm Springs School District.

Drew, C. J. (1971). Research on the psychological–behavioral effects of the physical environment. *Review of Educational Research, 41,* 447–465.

Esposito, D. (1973). Homogeneous and heterogeneous ability grouping: Principal findings and implications for evaluating and designing more effective educational environments. *Review of Educational Research, 43,* 163–179.

Evans, G. W., & Lovell, B. (1979). Design modification in an open school plan. *Journal of Educational Psychology, 71,* 41–49.

Evertson, C. M., Sanford, J. P., & Emmer, E. T. (1981). Effects of class heterogeneity in junior high school. *American Educational Research Journal, 18,* 219–232.

Farley, E. S. (1936). Regarding repeaters—Sad effects of failure upon the child. *Nation's Schools, 18,* 37–39.

Fiedler, F. E. (1967). Effect of intergroup competition on group member adjustment. *Personnel Psychology, 20,* 30–44.

Ford, B. E. (1978). Multiage grouping in the elementary school and children's affective development: A review of recent research. *Elementary School Journal, 78,* 149–159.

Giaconia, R. M., & Hedges, L. V. (1982). Identifying features of open education. *Review of Educational Research, 52,* 579–602.

Glaser, R. (1972). Individuals and learning: The new aptitudes. *Educational Researcher, 1,* 5–12.

Goldberg, M. L., Passow, A. H., & Justman, J. (1966). *The effects of ability grouping.* New York: Teacher's College Press, Columbia University.

Goldstein, K. (1942). Some experimental observations concerning the influence of color on the function of the organism. *Occupational Therapy and Rehabilitation, 21,* 147–151.

Goodlad, J., & Anderson, R. (1963). *The nongraded elementary school* (Rev. ed.). New York: Harcourt, Brace, and World.

Hamblin, R. L., Hathaway, C., & Wodarski, J. S. (1971). Group contingencies, peer tutoring, and accelerating academic achievement. In E. Ramp & W. Hopkins (Eds.), *A new direction for education: Behavior analysis.* (pp. 41–53). Lawrence, KS: University of Kansas.

Harmon, D. B. (1944). Lighting and the eye. *Illuminating Engineering, 39,* 481–500.

Heller, J. F., Groff, B. D., & Solomon, S. H. (1977). Toward an understanding of crowding: The role of physical interaction. *Journal of Personality and Social Psychology, 35,* 183–190.

Herman, S. H., & Tramontana, J. (1971). Instructions and group versus individual reinforcement in modifying disruptive group behavior. *Journal of Applied Behav-*

ior Analysis, 4, 41–53.

Holmberg, I., & Wyon, D. (1969). The dependence of performance in school on classroom temperature. *Educational and Psychological Interactions, 31,* 1–20 (School of Education, Malmo, Sweden).

Horowitz, P., & Otto, D. (1973). *The teaching effectiveness of an alternative teaching facility.* Alberta, Canada: University of Alberta. (ERIC Document Reproduction Service No. ED 083 242

Horwitz, R. A. (1979). Psychological effects of the "open classroom." *Review of Educational Research, 49,* 71–86.

Hunt, D. E. (1971). *Matching models in education: The coordination of teaching methods with student characteristics.* Toronto: Ontario Institute for Studies in Education.

Hunt, D. E. (1975). Person–environment interaction: A challenge found wanting before it was tried. *Review of Educational Research, 45,* 209–230.

Jackson, G. B. (1975). The research evidence on the effects of grade retention. *Review of Educational Research, 45,* 613–635.

Johnson, D. W., & Johnson, R. T. (1974). Instructional goal structure: Cooperative, competitive, or individualistic. *Review of Educational Research, 44,* 213–240.

Johnson, D. W., Maruyama, G., Johnson, R., Nelson, D., & Skon, L. (1981). Effects of cooperative, competitive, and individualistic goal structures on achievement: A meta-analysis. *Psychological Bulletin, 89,* 47–62.

Julian, J. W., Bishop, D. W., & Fiedler, F. E. (1966). Quasi-therapeutic effects of intergroup competition. *Journal of Personality and Social Psychology, 3,* 321–327.

Julian, J. W., & Perry, F. A. (1967). Cooperation contrasted with intra-group and inter-group competition. *Sociometry, 30,* 79–90.

Karmel, L. J. (1965). Effects of windowless classroom environment on high school students. *Perceptual Motor Skills, 20,* 277–278.

Kasmar, J. V., Griffin, W. V., & Mauritzen, J. H. (1968). The effect of environmental surroundings on outpatients' mood and perception of psychiatrists. *Journal of Consulting and Clinical Psychology, 32,* 223–226.

Kelly, D. H. (1975). Tracking and its impact on self-esteem: A neglected dimension. *Education, 96,* 2–9.

Kevan, S. M., & Howes, J. D. 1980. Climatic conditions in classrooms. *Education Review* (British), *32,* 281–292.

Kirp, D. L. (1974). Student classification, public policy, and the courts. *Harvard Educational Review, 44,* 7–52.

Klene, V., & Branson, E. (1929) [Unknown title]. *Education Research Bulletin of the Los Angeles City Schools,* [unknown issue]. Reported in *Elementary School Journal, 29,* 564–566.

Koneya, M. (1976). Location and interaction in row and column seating arrangements. *Environment and Behavior, 8,* 265.

Krimsky, J. S. (1982). A comparative study of the effects of matching and mismatching fourth grade students with their learning style preferences for the environmental element of light and their subsequent reading speed and accuracy scores (Doctoral dissertation, St. John's University). *Dissertation Abstracts International, 43* (1), 66A.

Kulik, C., & Kulik, J. A. (1982). Effects of ability grouping on secondary school students: A meta-analysis of evaluation findings. *American Educational Research Journal, 19,* 415–428.

Kyzar, B. L. (1977). Noise pollution and schools: How much is too much? *CEFP Journal, 4,* 10–11.

Larson, C. T. (1965). *The effect of windowless classrooms on elementary school children.* Ann Arbor, MI: University of Michigan.

Lehr, F. (1982). Grade repetition vs. social promotion. *Reading Teacher, 36,* 234–237.

Lindelow, J. (1982). Synthesis of research on grade retention and social promotion. *Educational Leadership, 39,* 471–473.

Lucker, G., Rosenfield, D., Sikes, J., & Aronson, E. (1976). Performance in the independent classroom: A field study. *American Educational Research Journal, 13,* 115–123.

Marshall, H. H. (1981). Open classrooms: Has the term outlived its usefulness? *Review of Educational Research, 51,* 181–192.

Martin, L. S., & Pavan, B. M. (1976). Current research on open space, non-grading, vertical grouping, and team teaching. *Phi Delta Kappan, 57,* 310–315.

Mayron, L. W., Ott, J., Nations, R., & Mayron, E. L. (1974). Light radiation and academic behavior: Initial studies on the effects of full spectrum lighting and radiation shielding on behavior and academic performance of school children. *Academic Therapy, 10,* 33–47.

McLoughlin, W. P. (1970). Continuous pupil progress in the nongraded school: Hope or hoax? *Elementary School Journal, 71,* 90–96.

Michaels, J. W. (1977). Classroom reward structures and academic performance. *Review of Educational Research, 47,* 87–98.

Milburn, D. (1981). A study of multi-age or family-grouped classrooms. *Phi Delta Kappan, 62,* 513–514.

Mintz, N. L. (1956). Effects of esthetic surroundings: II. Prolonged and repeated experience in a "beautiful" and "ugly" room. *Journal of Psychology, 41,* 459–466.

Minuchin, P., Biber, B., Shapiro, E., & Zimiles, H. (1969). *The psychological impact of school experience: A comparative study of nine-year-old children in contrasting schools.* New York: Basic Books.

Moos, R. H., Harris, R., & Schonborn, K. (1969). Psychiatric patients and staff reaction to their physical environment. *Journal of Clinical Psychology, 25,* 322–324.

Morgan, D. L., & Alwin, D. G. (1980). When less is more: School size and student social participation. *School Psychology Quarterly, 43,* 241–252.

Moskowitz, J. M., Malvin, J. H., Schaeffer, G. A., & Schaps, E. (1983). Evaluation of a cooperative learning strategy. *American Educational Research Journal, 20,* 687–696.

Nelson, L. L., & Kagan, S. (1972, September). Competition: The star-spangled scramble. *Psychology Today,* pp. 53–56, 90–91.

Papay, J. P., Costello, R. J. Hedl, J. J., & Spielberger, C. D. (1975). Effects of trait anxiety and state anxiety on the performance of elementary school children in traditional and individualized multi-age classrooms. *Journal of Educational Psychology, 67,* 840–846.

Pavan, B. M. (1973). Good news: Research on the nongraded elementary school. *Elementary School Journal, 73,* 333–342.

Pepler, R. D. (1971a). The thermal comfort of teachers in climate controlled and non–climate controlled schools. *American Society of Heating, Refrigerating, and Air-Conditioning Engineers Transactions, 77.*

Pepler, R. D. (1971b). Variations in student's test performances and in classroom temperatures in climate controlled schools. *American Society of Heating, Refrigerating, and Air-Conditioning Engineers Transactions, 77.*

Peterson, P. L. (1979). Direct instruction reconsidered. In P. L. Peterson & H. L. Walberg (Eds.), *Research on teaching.* (pp. 57–69) California: McCutchan.

Pizzo, J. S. (1981). An investigation of the relationship between selected acoustic environments and sound, an element of learning style, as they effect sixth grade students' reading achievement and attitudes (Doctoral dissertation, St. John's University). *Dissertation Abstracts International, 42* (6), 2475A

Randhawa, B. S., & Fu, L. L. W. (1973). Assessment and effect of some classroom environment variables. *Review of Educational Research, 43,* 303–321.

Reiter, R. G. (1973). *The promotion/retention dilemma: What research tells us* (Report No. 7416). Philadelphia, PA: Philadelphia School District Office of Research and Evaluation (ERIC Document Reproduction Service No. ED 099 412)

Rist, R. (1970). Student social class and teacher expectations: The self-fulfilling prophecy in ghetto education. *Harvard Educational Review, 40,* 411–451.

Rose, J. S., Medway, F. J. Cantrell, V. L, & Marus, S. H. (1983). A fresh look at the retention–promotion controversy. *Journal of School Psychology, 21,* 201–211.

Santrock, J. W. (1976). Affect and facilitative self-control: Influence of ecological setting, cognition and social agent. *Journal of Educational Psychology, 68,* 529–535.

Schwebel, A. I., & Cherlin, D. L. (1972). Physical and social distancing in teacher–pupil relationships. *Journal of Educational Psychology, 63,* 543–550.

Scott, W. E., Jr., & Cherrington, D. J. (1974). Effects of competitive and individualistic reinforcement contingencies. *Journal of Personality and Social Psychology, 30,* 748–758.

Shapiro, S. (1975). Preschool ecology: A study of three environmental variables. *Reading Improvement, 12,* 236–241.

Shure, M. B., & Spivack, G. (1979). Interpersonal cognitive problem solving and primary prevention: Programming for pre-school and kindergarten children. *Journal of Clinical Child Psychology, 8,* 89–94.

Slater, B. (1968). Effects of noise on pupil performance. *Journal of Educational Psychology, 59,* 239–243.

Slavin, R. E. (1977). Classroom reward structure: An analytical and practical review. *Review of Educational Research, 47,* 633–650.

Srivastava, R. K., & Peel, T. S. (1968). *Human movement as a function of color stimulation.* Topeka, KS: The Environmental Research Foundation.

Stam, P. J., and Stam, J. C. (1977). The effect of sociometric grouping on task performance in the classroom. *Education, 98,* 246–252.

Strauss, A. A., & Lehtinen, L. E. (1947). *Psychopathology and education of the brain injured child.* New York: Grune & Stratton.

Traub, R. E., Weiss, J., Fisher, C. W., & Musella, D. (1972). Closure and openness: Describing and quantifying open education. *Interchange, 3,* 69–84.

Venezsky, R. L., & Winfield L. F. (1979). *Schools that succeed beyond expectations in teaching reading* (Report for Grant NIE-G-78-0027). Newark: University of Delaware.

Walberg, H. (1969). Physical and psychological distance in the classroom. *School Review, 77,* 64–70.

Walberg, H. J., & Thomas, S. C. (1972). Open education: An operational definition and validation in Great Britain and the United States. *American Educational Research Journal, 9,* 197–208.

Weinstein, C. S. (1977). Modifying student behavior in an open classroom through changes in the physical design. *American Educational Research Journal, 14,* 249–262.

Weinstein, C. S. (1979). The physical environment of the school. *Review of Educational Research, 49,* 577–610.

Weinstein, C. S., & Weinstein, N. D. (1979). Noise and reading performance in an open space school. *Journal of Educational Research, 72,* 210–213.

Wilt, H. J. (1971). A comparison of student attitudes toward school, academic achievement, internal structures, and procedures: The nongraded school versus the graded school (Doctoral dissertation, University of Missouri). *Dissertation Abstracts International, 31,* 5105A.

Winer, J. I., Elkin, D. J., Loewy, J. H., & Weldon, D. E. (1977). *Factors affecting perception of and responses to crowded classroom environments.* Paper presented at the annual convention of the American Psychological Association, San Francisco, CA. (ERIC Document Reproduction Service No. ED 151 634)

Winnett, R. A., Battersby, C. D., & Edwards, S. M. (1975). The effects of architectural change, individualized instruction, and group contingencies on the academic performance and social behavior of sixth graders. *Journal of School Psychology, 13,* 28–40.

Wodarski, J. S., Hamblin, R. L., Buckholdt, D., & Ferritor, D. (1973). Individual consequences versus different shared consequences contingent on the performance of low achieving group members. *Journal of Applied Social Psychology, 3,* 276–290.

Wolk, S., & Solomon, R. (1975). Affective response to ability group experience in high school. *Journal of Social Psychology, 95,* 289–290.

Wulf, K. (1976). *Relationship of assigned classroom seating area to achievement variables.* Paper presented at the annual meeting of the American Educational Research Association, San Francisco, CA.

Wurtman, R. J. (1975). The effects of light on the human body. *Scientific American, 233,* 69–77.

Zifferblatt, S. M. (1972). Architecture and human behavior: Toward increased understanding of a functional relationship. *Educational Technology, 12,* 54–57.

8

ASSESSMENT AND PRIMARY PREVENTION

Some experts in primary prevention may take exception to the inclusion of a chapter on assessment in a book on primary prevention and, indeed, some definitions of primary prevention would preclude the incorporation of such material. The definition used in this book, however, includes consideration of individuals and groups considered to be at risk of developing problems and it is the identification of these persons that makes the use of assessment relevant to primary prevention.

WHAT IT MEANS TO BE AT RISK

To be at risk means that a particular child or group of children presently faces a situation that holds potential for disrupting, delaying, or otherwise interfering with normal learning or development. This negative potential may be inherent in the family situation, the school setting, or the broader social structure in which the child lives. It may also be inherent in the child him-/ herself due to such factors as delayed development, lack of learning skills, or lack of social skills. Children faced with a particularly ineffective teacher may be at risk; children living in families with ineffective parents may be at risk; children entering school whose development is delayed in critical areas may be at risk; children living in a community environment not conducive to development may be at risk; and children who are undergoing, or have recently undergone, specific traumatic events such as death, divorce, or abuse may be at risk.

A POTENTIAL PROBLEM IN USING ASSESSMENT IN PRIMARY PREVENTION

The line between children who may be at risk and those who may already have problems as a result of exposure to some of the kinds of situations suggested above is not always clear. It seems inevitable that in any efforts to identify children at risk some who already have problems will be identified. The possibility of moving from primary-preventive to secondary preventive service delivery efforts is very real. Moreover, given the predilection of school guidance specialists for dealing with those who already have problems, the temptation to use assessment results to locate and treat children with preexisting problems will be substantial. The focus must remain on the before-the-fact quality of primary-preventive efforts in order for assessment techniques to be used properly within this framework.

THE NATURE AND FOCUS OF ASSESSMENT IN PRIMARY PREVENTION

The term *assessment* is used in a different manner here than is usually the case in schools, and more traditional uses of assessment have no place in primary-preventive considerations. The types of techniques used to identify individuals or groups at risk of developing problems may include the use of screening instruments, demographic criteria (e.g., shifts in attendance, grades, or test scores), the use of criteria to identify ineffectively functioning adults, the use of observation, anecdotal material, or specific types of instruments (e.g., sociometry) to locate children lacking in certain kinds of skills. There may also be attempts to identify general aspects of childrens' learning environments that may lead to problems through the use of scales designed specifically for such purposes (e.g., scales reflecting student or teacher perceptions of the learning environment). The types and purposes of assessment used in a primary-preventive context are far removed from the more ordinary attempts to utilize assessment for the diagnosis, treatment, or placement of individual children who already manifest problems.

There are three basic purposes for assessment in primary prevention. These include the identification of (a) specific children at risk, (b) ineffective adults (parents/teachers), and (c) nonfacilitative environments. Table 8-1 highlights each of these three purposes and suggests some of the indexes that may suggest the need for the initiation of preventive efforts.

There are three basic techniques used to achieve the purposes of assessment in primary prevention. These include the use of formal assessment devices, the use of school records, and the use of informal, or anecdotal, information. Two of these three approaches are unobtrusive and do not require the use of new procedures or formal assessment devices. The basic methods of assessment used in primary prevention are outlined in table 8-2

Table 8-1
Major Purposes of Assessment in Primary Prevention

Identification of Specific Children at Risk	Identification of Ineffective Adults (Parents/Teachers)	Identification of Nonfacilitative Environments
Lack of . . .	*Lack of . . .*	*Rate of . . .*
Development	Behavior management	School failure
Social skills	skills	Drop-out
Learning skills	Group management	Truancy
Self-management skills	skills	Absence
Positive self-perceptions	Disciplinary skills	Vandalism/delinquency
Specific life events el	Communication skills	Drug use
Death	Communication skills	Teacher perceptions of school
Divorce	Stress management	Child perceptions of school
Abuse/neglect	skills	
Serious illness/accident	*Knowledge deficits . . .*	
General lack of a support	Child development	
network	Child rearing	

under the headings that denote the basic purposes of assessment. This table also includes some indication of the specific types of assessment or criteria that may be used under each of the major headings.

THE RELATIVE IMPORTANCE OF ASSESSMENT IN PRIMARY–PREVENTIVE SCHOOL PROGRAMS

Given the limited resources of most schools, it is often necessary to make choices among a wide variety of relevant activities. In settings where a fully developed program of primary prevention is under way the implementation of assessment procedures, particularly those aimed at identifying ineffective adults and nonfacilitative environments, may be a lower priority than conduct of the ongoing primary-preventive program. This is due to the fact that in full-scale, ongoing programs, efforts to reach all adults and to deal with the total environment are likely to be in progress. One of the major purposes of assessment in primary prevention is to help in defining areas where initial efforts are likely to be most effective. Once the program is under way and a direction has been established, assessment efforts may be less important.

It should be pointed out that one type of assessment does remain of singular importance regardless of the state of development of the total primary-preventive program. This is the assessment that aims to identify specific children at risk. Since there are important events in some children's lives that may impede their normal development and school progress, efforts to identify such children should be continuous.

The basic role of the guidance specialist in relation to assessment and primary prevention will be as a consultant to administrators and teachers. There are three major facets of this role. The first is to provide information

Table 8-2

Identifying Specific Children at Risk	Identifying Ineffective Adults (Parents/Teachers)	Identifying Nonfacilitative Environments
Formal Assessment	Formal Assessment	Formal Assessment
Kindergarten screening Sociometry Self-concept scales Observation	Flanders Interaction Analysis Carkhuff communication scales	Child perceptions of school Teacher perceptions of school
Informal/Anecdotal	Informal/Anecdotal	
Teacher or parent report	Signs of stress General consensus re teachers' effectiveness and frequent class management problems General consensus re parents whose prior children have had problems	
Use of Records	Use of Records	Use of Records
Declining attendance Declining achievement Increasing problem behavior Discrepancies between ability and achievement	Excessive absence *Excessive referrals for . . .* behavior problems discipline problems special education consideration retention	*Rate of . . .* School failure Drop-out Truancy Vandalism Delinquency Drug use

and advice on how assessment can be used in a primary-preventive context. This will require careful explanation, since the main experience of most education professionals with assessment is its use in the identification and diagnosis of existing problems, not in the prevention of future ones. A second aspect of the consultant's role involves the provision of information on how to do it, with whom to do it, and when to do it. The third segment of the consultant role involves the provision of help in using the results constructively and in a manner consistent with primary-preventive goals.

A final disclaimer is necessary before launching into the substance of this chapter. Many of the areas to be mentioned here, such as the determination of preschool readiness, sociometry, and the use of environmental assessment procedures, are separate areas of expertise in their own right. The purpose of including them in this chapter is to point up their utility in the identification of schoolchildren at risk and to show how they can be used in a primary prevention–oriented school program. While examples of specific approaches will be used, the interested reader may want to turn to additional resources in order to amplify knowledge in a given area.

IDENTIFICATION OF SPECIFIC CHILDREN AT RISK

While this is the aspect of assessment that is of continuing concern in any program of primary prevention, it is also the aspect that holds the greatest risk for moving from primary prevention into secondary prevention in an almost unaware fashion. It is only when this type of assessment is clearly before the fact that its use is appropriate in the primary-preventive context. In order to be before the fact, information resulting from assessment must be obtained prior to anyone noticing, referring, or otherwise identifying a specific child as having a learning or behavior problem. This is an extremely fine line to draw and it will not be possible, in all cases, to be sure which side some children are on. The important thing is to make the attempt to locate such children so that appropriate steps can be taken prior to the development of problem behavior. It should be recognized that in the process of attempting to identify such children, other children who already have problems will also be identified. Provisions for dealing with such children, whether through remedial activities or referral, should be a part of the total program plan.

Identification of Children at Risk Using Formal Assessment Procedures

Only two general types of formal assessment procedures will be included. The first is the use of assessment to determine school readiness. The other is the use of sociometry to determine children's social status. The use of formal observation techniques might be included but this approach is most often used where a referral has already been made by a teacher concerned about a child's behavior, moving the main uses of observation of children out of the primary prevention category. For this reason formal observation of children is not included here, even though, at times, it could serve the purposes of primary prevention.

■ *Determining School Readiness.* The assessment of a very broadly defined variable known as school readiness has a long place in school practices. The earliest use of information derived from such assessment was fundamentally of a primary-preventive nature, but since the advent of PL 94-142, such results have focused more on the purposes of special education, that is, the identification of children with preexisting problems (Glazzard, 1977; Lichtenstein, 1982; Vance, Kitson, & Singer, 1983). The basic concern here, of course, is the use of school readiness tactics in the service of primary-preventive aims.

There are some relatively serious and unresolved problems in the determination of school readiness. One of these problems is the number of different kinds of variables that have been used to attempt to predict school readiness. A listing of some of the more common variables includes (a) cognitive ability (b) readiness (c) social development (d) emotional maturity or adjustment (e) visual discrimination (f) visual reception (g) visual motor development (h) language development (i) health status (j) learning styles and (k) demographic factors (e.g., educational level of the mother or father, socioeconomic status, ethnic status, language status)

Definitions of the above terms do not always coincide. There is some agreement on the definition and measurement of *cognitive ability* and *readiness* as reflected in correlations between instruments being used to assess these variables. There is much less agreement with respect to the definition of other variables as reflected in the types of instruments used to assess them. One result of this situation is that it is necessary to compare the predictive abilities of specific instruments rather than being able to rely on the use of the terminology reflected in the above list.

A second problem is that many, perhaps most, of the available instruments fail to meet minimal psychometric standards. This situation is succinctly expressed by Lichtenstein (1982) who states, "Screening instruments have been particularly remiss in failing to meet basic standards for educational and psychological tests" (p. 70). The use of inadequate screening instruments is, quite properly, viewed as an ethical problem by Wendt (1978). Related to the general issue of psychometric inadequacy is the fact that one screening instrument is often validated against another instrument rather than against a criterion that would provide predictive validity (e.g., Begin, 1983; Lindeman, Goodstein, Sachs, & Young, 1984; Naglieri & Harrison, 1982). Another common and, by itself, unsatisfactory method used to validate screening instruments is to correlate them with teacher ratings (e.g., Flook & Velicer, 1977; Tokar & Holthouse, 1977).

While many studies report significant correlations between a given readiness test or variable and an outcome criterion, the fact is that no single instrument appears to account for enough of the total variance to make it a useful predictor for individuals. With this in mind, Schmidt and Perino (1985) warn, "Prudent use of individual children's test results is cautioned" (p. 150). For example, an author may conclude, on the basis of research, that an instrument with the correlation of .67 between the instrument and another criterion is "moderately valid" (Lindeman, Goodstein, Sachs, & Young, 1984). In purely technical psychometric terms this conclusion is warranted but in terms of the utility of the results of the instrument for predicting the behavior of a given individual the result is less than adequate. It is important to keep in mind the distinction between statistical significance and educational meaningfulness.

Related to the psychometric properties of a given instrument, but seldom discussed, is the issue of false negatives and false positives. In this instance, false negatives would be represented by those children identified by a screening instrument or program as being at risk who turn out not to be at risk, while false positives would be those children not identified as being at risk who turn out indeed to have been at risk. A study conducted by Gallerani, O'Regan, and Reinherz (1982) raised this issue when 52% of the children identified in their study turned out to be false negatives. No studies reporting false positives were found. The potential for considerable damage exists in any program that incorrectly identifies a high proportion of children as being at risk who, in fact, are not.

There is clear evidence that the predictive value of school readiness assessment devices varies with the socioeconomic status and language background of children who are being assessed. In a study assessing children across schools of varying socioeconomic levels, Abrahamson and Bell (1979) found the predictive value of a comprehensive school readiness battery was best in a school that was high socioeconomically. In another study attempting to predict scores on the Metropolitan Readiness Test (Nurss & McGauvran, 1976) socioeconomic status was found to be the best predictor of scores on this test. In another comprehensive study of school readiness (Gandura, Keogh, & Yoshioka-Maxwell, 1980) it was found that relatively good predictions could be made of the achievement of Anglo-American children in first grade and somewhat less accurate predictions for English-speaking Mexican-American children in the first grade, but that the battery was nonpredictive for Spanish-speaking Mexican-American children in first grade even though the tests were not language- or culture-specific.

Even in the absence of clear socioeconomic or language variables the predictive validity of screening instruments varies from school to school (Caskey & Larson, 1983; Tsushima, Onorato, Okumura, & Sue, 1983). Results of these studies suggest the absolute necessity of developing local norms, not only for a given district but for a given school as well.

- *Developing a Program of Readiness Screening.* Given the somewhat confusing situation described above, it is necessary to raise a question of whether or not the implementation of such programs is worth the time, money, and effort. The answer to the question must be equivocal. In the form that such programs appear to be carried out in most places, the answer would probably be no. Many such programs seem to depend on single instruments with dubious psychometric properties, local norms are seldom developed, and local validity studies almost never carried out. Finally, and surprisingly, it appears that after school readiness information is collected, little or no effort is made to use it in the on-going program of the school for either preventive or remedial purposes. On the other hand, the evidence suggests that there are readiness screening instruments with appropriate psychometric standards, that it is possible to put together a multicriteria screening program, that it is eminently possible to develop local norms and to study the utility of obtained outcomes and that it is, of course, possible to utilize sound results in preventive ways.

The following questions will need to be answered in the planning, implementation and use of a preschool readiness screening program:

1. What is the purpose of the program?
2. What instruments or procedures are to be selected for accomplishing these ends?
3. How specifically, will the results be used? Will it be suggested to the parents of low-scoring children that they withhold their children from school for a year or a half-year? Will the kindergarten teachers receiving the children be appraised, in detail, of the results of the screening process? Will kindergarten teachers receive assistance in utilizing the results of the screening inventory? If so, who will provide the assistance? How frequently will assistance be provided? What will the nature of the assistance be provided? What will the nature of the assistance be—consultation, provision of curricular materials, provision of skill training in deficit areas, or other?
4. What steps will be taken to avoid labeling children who do not have a problem but are only considered to be at risk? Failure to pay attention to this problem may result in having such children thought of as learning disabled by kindergarten teachers, possibly before they even see the child.
5. Who is responsible for developing local norms and for assessing the local predictive validity of the battery?
6. Will there be an annual review of the screening process to determine whether or not the time, money, and effort required are justifiable?
7. What provision will be made to determine whether children determined to be at risk were incorrectly singled out?

If attention is paid to the questions cited above, it is likely that an effective, useful, primary-preventive screening program can be developed. The time and effort involved in accomplishing these tasks will need to be balanced against the ways in which they might be used in other primary-preventive efforts.

■ *An Adequate Preschool Readiness Screening Program.* A complete kindergarten screening program has been outlined by Lorion, Work, and Hightower (1984). This program includes a screening component as well as the use component. It provides information about "cognitive, motoric and psychosocial status, academic readiness and emotional maturity" (p. 481). In addition, parents are asked to provide information about their child's medical and developmental history, family background, disciplinary techniques, and adjustment.

Parents are recruited and trained to conduct the screening. During screening, the child proceeds through four stations staffed by these trained parents. At the first station the child's height and weight are obtained and it is explained to him/her that he/she will participate in a number of games and answer a number of questions. At the second station an assessment is made of gross motor development, coordination, balance, and ability to imitate motor movements. At the third station tests involve receptive and expressive vocabulary, short-term visual and auditory memory, and conceptual and numerical reasoning. At the final station, tests assess counting ability, eye–hand coordination, fine motor coordination, laterality, directionality, and body awareness.

Using information obtained from parents, a computer profile is generated reflecting the outcomes for each child. Profiles allow for the comparison of each child with his/her classmates in a particular school.

During the first month of school a guidance specialist (school psychologist or educational diagnostician) meets periodically with teachers to discuss the implications of the profile for each child. An attempt is made to determine strategies and instructional approaches which will meet the child's cognitive and social needs. Decisions are made on the basis of genuine discussion; every attempt is made to avoid mere summarization of the results of the screening material. In addition, potential topics for future parent–teacher meetings are identified on the basis of information that has been provided by the parent, and consideration is given to how best to obtain parent cooperation and involvement.

Lorion and his colleagues (1984) report that school personnel believe that this program has contributed significantly to the individualization of instruction. Consultation among professionals is reported to enable the teacher to respond quickly to cognitive, perceptual, emotional, and behavioral needs.

This is not, by any means, the only possible preschool screening program; many other variations on a similar theme are possible. It is, however, a sound example of a thorough real-life program. Although it is not mentioned by Lorion, et al., considerable time in planning, training parents, developing a computer profile, and consulting with teachers is involved.

The Use of Sociometry in Primary-Preventive Programs.

The technique of sociometry ranks among the older psychometric devices. The term was first used by J. L. Moreno in 1916 and the first sociometric analysis was presented at a convention by Moreno in 1933 (Evans, 1962). Moreno's classic work, *Who Shall Survive? A New Approach to the Problem of Human Interrelations*, first appeared in 1934. The general purpose of any sociometric measure is to give an objective picture of relationships existing between members of any group of people who know each other well enough to have feelings about individual group members. The technique has been used in business and industry as well as in education, in the half-century that has followed publication of Moreno's original work.

The psychometric properties of sociometric technique have been reasonably well established (Asher & Renshaw, 1981; Foster & Ritchey, 1979). Sociometry has the distinct advantage of being a direct measure of a particular child's level of social acceptance or rejection. Depending somewhat upon the specific technique used, it is possible to identify children who are isolates and children who are actively rejected by others (Peretti, Lane, & Floyd, 1981). Use of the technique has been found to be a more valid measure of children's level of acceptance or rejection in a group than teacher judgments (Gronlund, 1959; Tolor, Carpetti, & Lane, 1967).

A large number of studies have been reported that indicate that poor sociometric status leads to a variety of negative consequences. Thus, a child who is an isolate or who is rejected by peers may be considered to be at risk. It is reported that 5 to 10% of elementary school children are named as a friend by no one in their class (Asher & Renshaw, 1981). They indicate that this is due to personal characteristics such as appearance or ethnicity; to situational factors such as the lack of opportunity for participation; or to lack of social skills. They summarize a number of studies indicating the success of social skill training as defined by improved sociometric status.

Poor sociometric status has been linked with a number of specific subsequent negative behaviors. One researcher states, "Lack of social competency in earlier grades is directly related to dropping out of school" (Barclay, 1984, p. 477). A similar finding of a relationship between social incompetence and subsequent school drop-out was reported by Ullmann (1957). Low sociometric status has also been linked with subsequent underachievement in school (McCandless, 1967) and with subsequent delinquent behavior (Roff, Sells, & Golden, 1972). It was reported by Connally and Doyle (1981) that lack of peer acceptance has been identified among elementary school children as a reliable predictor of later psychosocial maladjustment, a finding supported by De Apodaca and Cowen (1982).

It seems clear that a child with poor sociometric status is at risk of developing a variety of maladaptive behaviors. The assessment of sociometric status is therefore highly relevant to primary prevention.

In spite of a 50-year history of writing and research in the area of sociometric measurement, relatively little has been said about its use (Gade, 1977). Fortunately, the purpose of sociometry in primary prevention is relatively clear: the identification of children who are at risk for the development of inadequate behaviors stemming from the fact that they are either social isolates or are actively rejected by their peers. The primary purpose of identification is to assist them to improve their sociometric status either through the provision of social skill training or by changing the social milieu in which they work in school to one more conducive to the development of positive social behaviors. Evidence for the success of social skill training is reasonably clear (Mannarino, Christy, Durlak, & Magnussen, 1982; Spivack & Shure, 1974). Evidence for the improvement of social behaviors through changing a child's social milieu is lacking.

The most widely used approach in sociometry is the technique of peer nomination. It is, like other sociometric techniques, best used in a group situation where children know each other reasonably well. A typical self-contained classroom is an excellent setting in which to use it. The usual approach is to ask each child in the class to name three children whom they would like to be with in a specific kind of activity. It is desirable to include several different types of activities in the questionnaire. Some fairly typical sociometric items would include the following: (a) "Name three children whom you would like to work with on a class project," (b) "Name three children whom you would like to have on your team at recess," (c) "Name three children whom you would like to invite to a party," (d) "Name three children whom you would like to sit with in school," and (e) "Name three children whom you would like to play with after school."

There is nothing fixed about these activities. The idea is to use different activities so that a variety of different kinds of social situations are covered providing an opportunity for the selection of as many children as possible.

Items in the above form will result in the identification of children who are selected by many other children for a number of different activities ("stars") and, more important for our purposes, the identification of children who are selected rarely or not at all for any activity (isolates).

The item form provided above will identify a mixed group of children, some of whom are isolates, but others of whom may be actively rejected (rejectees) by children. If it appears desirable to differentiate these two groups an additional type of item can be included in the sociometric instrument. The items may cover the same situations indicated above but are worded differently. Such an item would read, "Name three children whom you would *not* like to play with after school," and so forth. The result of analyzing these items would provide information on children who are actively disliked or rejected by their peers.

Scoring the results of sociometric tests can be extremely complex (Evans, 1962; Gronlund, 1959), but for the purpose of identifying isolates or rejectees, such complex techniques are not necessary. All that is required is that the teacher, or whoever is scoring the instrument, make note of children who are picked few times or not at all when the positive form of the item is used, and who are picked the most number of times when the negative form of the item is used. There are no firm guidelines for the number of choices or lack of choices necessary to define an isolate or a rejectee. It seems reasonably clear that the child who receives no choices when the positive form of the item is used can safely be considered to be an isolate (or a rejectee). Those few children who receive the most choices when the negative form of the item is used are certainly going to be the most rejected in the particular group surveyed.

Children identified as isolates or rejectees are the prime candidates for social skills training (see chapter 4). Consideration may also be given to rearranging groups within the classroom so that children of low sociometric status can be placed with some children of higher sociometric status in order to provide the former with role models for social behavior. As Evans (1962) says, "To group together a number of isolates is to court disaster" (p. 54).

In summary, it appears that sociometry offers a simple, psychometrically sound, quick and direct measure of a child's social status in the peer group. Low sociometric status is indicative of a variety of subsequent maladaptive behaviors. For these reasons it is an extremely useful tool in a primary-preventive program.

Identifying Children at Risk Through Informal Methods

A considerably less objective form of assessment is represented by the attempts of education professionals to identify children at risk through observation of their behavior or the use of anecdotal material obtained either from the child or from adults who know the child. In spite of their lack of objectivity such efforts represent an important part of a total plan to identify children at risk.

At one time there was considerable emphasis placed on the inclusion of anecdotal material in cumulative records so that a particular child's successive teachers would be provided with information presumably helpful in dealing with a particular child. Such records, properly done, could provide an additional and important resource in the identification of children at risk. Changes in behavior, particularly negative changes in achievement, classroom or playground behavior, mood or interpersonal style could reveal the existence of a negative process that might suggest that a child is at risk.

In recent years, however, the anecdotal aspect of cumulative records has all but disappeared. This is due, in part, to the misuse of such records by some teachers; rather than objectively describing children's behaviors that were worthy of note, some teachers included highly personalized comments and labels. With the new emphasis on parent rights and, in particular, due to the passage of the Family Educational Rights and Privacy Act, the inclusion of anecdotal material in cumulative records has all but ceased. This does not mean that information about children is no longer available to teachers, only that it is no longer used in formal ways. Within the social system of a school, particularly the elementary school, there is considerable awareness of what is going on in children's lives, both in and out of school. Effective utilization of such information can be important in the identification of children at risk. Observations of child behavior and the reports of teachers, parents, children, and others can all help in leading to this goal.

Some kinds of events, not at all uncommon in schools, will, by their very nature, have the potential for placing children exposed to them at risk for a variety of kinds of negative consequences. The specific impact of such stressful events on a given child will be determined by two factors. The first is the child's perception of the impact or demands of the situation. The second determinant will be the child's personal assessment of his or her resources for dealing with the situation (Jaremko, 1984). Since each child and each situation is different it is not possible to make gross generalizations about the impact of such stressful events as family disruption, a death in the family, or exposure to abuse or neglect. Nevertheless, information about these types of events in children's lives should be noted, disseminated and constructively utilized in dealing with that child. Some teachers are prone to ignore such events but since children will be affected by them, both in the short and the long run, they must be considered in dealing with a child who has been exposed to them if it is our intention to provide an effective learning situation for a child in spite of traumatic outside events over which neither we nor the child have any control.

■ *Children at Risk as a Result of Abuse.* Child abuse has been recognized relatively recently as a huge problem both in terms of the number of children affected and in terms of both the short- and long-run effects it has on the lives of those who are abused. All states require that suspected child abuse be reported and, likewise, all states provide immunity from prosecution for those who report child abuse in good faith (Camblin & Prout, 1983). In spite of this, it is suspected that a high proportion of child abuse goes unreported and precise figures on the extent of child abuse are not available. It is estimated that a million or more children annually are subjected to abuse in the United States (Kline, Cole, & Fox, 1981). Although it has been asserted (Gill, 1970) that teachers are "the most important link in the preventive and protective chain" (p. 329), the fact is that only 15% of all abuse reports originate in schools (Camblin & Prout, 1983)!

At a more specific level, a national survey of the involvement of school psychologists with child abuse indicated that 71% of the psychologists employed by school districts have had some experience with child abuse but only 34% were involved in a reporting role. A miniscule 2.9% reported involvement in the primary prevention of child abuse (O'Block, Billimoria, & Behan, 1981). The relatively small magnitude of these figures is surprising since professional educators, more than any other group, are likely to be exposed on a regular basis to the warning signals of abuse given by children and their parents (Richey, 1980). It seems probable that there is still a reluctance among school personnel to report suspicions of such problems and that they probably tend to report only the most blatant cases of abuse (Camblin & Prout, 1983).

The amount of research in this area is relatively low compared to the total amount written. This applies to the presumed indicators of child abuse as well as to the short- and long-term consequences. There does appear to be little doubt that there is "a clear and convincing connection between child abuse and neglect and educational problems" (Kline, Cole, & Fox, 1981, p. 66). There is also abundant clinical evidence to suggest that abused children may suffer long-term emotional damage and may themselves become abusing parents. For all of these reasons the early identification of children at risk because of exposure to abuse is important in a primary-preventive program.

The most basic primary-preventive approach for this problem is represented by attempts to deal with it in the long run. The provision of family life education to young persons in secondary schools, the use of affective education curricula and the provision of information on appropriate child rearing practices are three such techniques (Richey, 1980). The major primary-preventive technique in the short run is to develop an awareness of the problem among *all* school employees and to disseminate information on the signs of child abuse. Such lists, like much of our other current information on child abuse, appear to have been derived on the basis of experience rather than on the basis of research.

Many persons have written on the indicators of child abuse both with respect to the abuser and the abused. Since it is unlikely that school personnel will be in a position to know potential abusers well enough to use such information and also because such information is often couched in clinical terms useless to school personnel (e.g., Weinberg, 1955), the emphasis here will be on potential indicators of abuse in the abused child. Another caveat is in order. No single sign (apart from obvious evidence of physical abuse) is indicative of child abuse. When several indicators are present in the same child, however, the possibility of abuse should not be ignored. A number of authors have provided lists of indicators of child abuse (e.g., Kline, et al., 1981; Miller & Miller, 1979; Wilson, Thomas, & Schuette, 1983; Roscoe, Peterson, & Shaner, 1983). Fortunately, there is overlap among the various lists, in spite of the fact that research validation of such indicators does not appear to have been conducted. Since there is some agreement that signs of physical abuse and sexual abuse may differ, this distinction will be made here. Ten signs of physical abuse are listed by Miller and Miller (1979). The physically abused child

1. seems unduly afraid of adults and parents
2. repeatedly has unexplained cuts, bruises, burns, etc.
3. exhibits abnormal behavior such as extremely aggressive and destructive or extremely passive and withdrawn behavior
4. exhibits sudden changes in behavior and achievement, especially in the adolescent population.
5. is habitually truant
6. often arrives at school without lunch or adequate clothing for the weather
7. consistently wears long sleeves, long dresses, or turtlenecks and refuses to disrobe for physical education
8. uses language demonstrating knowledge of sexual activities inappropriate for age and development
9. repeatedly prefers to stay after school rather than going home
10. has parents who show no interest in school-related activities nor in performance of the child.

Signs of sexual abuse will apply overwhelmingly, but not exclusively, to female children. A list of the possible indicators of sexual abuse is provided by Kline, et al. (1981). While it overlaps somewhat with the list provided above, it is different enough that it merits inclusion here. These signs include:

1. unwillingness to participate in physical activities
2. indirect comments to a trusted teacher such as, "I'd like to live with you," "I'm going to find a foster home to live in," or similar statements
3. regression, the appearance of infantile behaviors, or withdrawal in fantasy
4. aggression and/or delinquency
5. running away

6. poor peer relationships due to guilt or serious emotional problems
7. seductive behaviors with peers and adults
8. drug use to help deal with guilt and anxiety.

The role of the guidance specialist in relation to abuse in a primary prevention program is to assist as many members of the staff as possible to be alert to the magnitude of the problem, to know what some of the indicators of the problem are, and to inform appropriate personnel at the first suspicion, even before a report to legal authorities seems appropriate. Subsequent to being alerted, the guidance specialist will want to take steps to validate or invalidate the suspicions and, if validated, to make certain that required legal reports are made and, equally important, to begin to provide appropriate services to the at-risk child.

■ *Children at Risk Due to Family Disruption.*   The magnitude of family disruption due to divorce and the consequences of divorce such as single parent families and the formation of stepfamilies is so generally recognized that the presentation of figures documenting the size of the problem seems unnecessary. Until quite recently, however, the focus of behavior specialists on the problem of divorce has been primarily on the divorcing couple. The effects of divorce on children have been largely ignored. While it is clear that the personalities of all involved, the situation leading up to a divorce and the degree of resolution achieved by all parties in the divorce will all affect the extent to which children experience problems, it seems now generally assumed that nearly all children involved in such situations will experience some negative effects. For some, these effects may be transitory; for others, they may be long-lasting indeed. Oehmen (1985) suggests that, for children, divorce leads to a form of grief like that which accompanies the death of a parent. He further suggests that children go through the same grief process as that described by Kubler-Ross (1974). The first phase is one of denial, a refusal to believe that divorce could happen. This is followed by a "why me?" phase in which the child feels unfairly singled out for this event. This, in turn, is followed by anger, which is partially generalized but may also be directed at the divorcing parents. This phase, in turn, is followed by guilt, during which the child tends unrealistically to assume responsibility for the occurrence of divorce, and, finally, by a healthy resolution of the event, understanding of their role in it, and an acceptance of the reality of the divorce.

It is further suggested by Oehmen (1985) that steps must be taken to provide help or else there is "likelihood that the child will remain overwhelmed by unspoken negative feelings" (p. 316).

The impact of family disruption on children in school is generally considered to be a significant one and there is evidence that suggests that this is the case. Some of the general effects of family disruption have been suggested by Bundy and Gumaer (1984). These include (a) a reduced level of self-esteem fostered by feelings of guilt, anger, hostility, helplessness, and inadequacy; (b) a diminished sense of belonging, not only in the family group but in the social group as well; and (c) a severe loss of security.

It seems inevitable that such consequences will affect the child in more specific ways in school, and research evidence suggests that this is so. A study of 8,000 elementary and secondary school children (Brown, 1980) in one-parent families found differences between them and children from unbroken homes indicating lower school achievement, more tardiness, more absenteeism, more truancy, more suspensions from school, more expulsions from school, and more drop-out from school among the one-parent group. It seems reasonably clear that negative changes in the family structure do have negative school consequences (as well as negative personal consequences) for children caught in such a position. Therefore, it is reasonable to assume that children experiencing family problems, whether they are predivorce problems, divorce problems, single parent family problems or stepfamily problems, are at risk. For this reason such problems are a matter of concern in primary-preventive programs.

Knowledge of family problems among teachers and other school personnel appears to be widespread, although there have apparently been no surveys attempting to assess the amount or accuracy of such knowledge among school personnel. One authority (Wallerstein & Bundy, 1984) has asserted not only that teachers know about most divorces and pending divorces, but that about half of the cases of divorce come out during "show-and-tell" time in elementary schools. Since such knowledge is widely available it should be relatively easy to establish a formal, early warning system channeling such information to a guidance professional. All members of the staff, including clerical, custodial and transportation workers, could be alerted to provide such information. This does not mean it would be accepted at face value and that intervention would be attempted on the basis of unvalidated information, but having such information would make it possible to check further to determine whether such problems existed. While there would be great sensitivity on the part of some parents, others, perhaps most, would be pleased to have the school take steps to provide supportive help to their children. Certainly, they should be informed that there are generally negative school effects in such situations and at least given the opportunity to deny the provision of services to their children.

 ▪ *Children at Risk Due to Death in the Family.* The subject of death is one that has received wide attention in recent years. The work of Kubler-Ross (1974) is perhaps the most widely known. There has been emphasis on "death education" but very little attention has been paid to childhood bereavement (Balk, 1983). There is evidence that unresolved childhood grief may have both short-term and long-term negative effects (Beck, Seti, & Tuthill, 1963).

Research summarizing the relationship between chronological age and different conceptions of death indicates that such conceptions are different at different age levels (Matter & Matter, 1982). Therefore, death may have a different impact on a child depending upon the child's age. Further, the impact of such a loss may depend upon the extent to which individuals are prepared to anticipate and deal with the stress brought on by such life crises (Danish, Smyer, & Nowak, 1980) as well as on their level of psychological development (Nagy, 1959). It appears that children in loss situations are at risk and that it would be appropriate for guidance professionals to provide services to them (Ryerson, 1977). Failure to do so may result in confusion, depression, guilt, loss of motivation, and lower grades (Balk, 1983). In the longer run, serious adult depression may result from unresolved childhood bereavement (Beck, Seti, & Tuthill, 1963).

The extent to which a particular child may be affected by a particular death is not entirely predictable from the nature of the relationship existing between the child and the person who has died. While it would normally be assumed that a death among members of the immediate family would have the greatest impact, there is also a serious impact when the person who dies is one with whom the child has a strong personal identification, such as a friend, a person of the same age and sex, or a member of a school class (Getson & Benshoff, 1977).

According to Jones (1977), some of the specific kinds of emotional reactions may include anger, loneliness, depression, guilt, shock, and hopelessness. Behaviors may include inability to concentrate, social withdrawal,

asserted by Forman and O'Malley (1984) that school stress constitutes a large portion of the total stress in the lives of students. They define two main stressors in school: (a) achievement stress, including test anxiety, resulting from fear of not doing well and resulting in poor performance on ability and achievement measures including teacher-made tests and (b) social stress resulting from teacher or peer rejection, hostility, avoidance, lack of acceptance, and lack of cooperativeness among teachers or peers.

The identification of children suffering undue stress will be quite subjective. Some of the possible indicators of stress include the following:

1. abuse (including neglect), family disruption, impending or recent death in the family, and lack of support networks
2. low sociometric ratings
3. prolonged illness
4. negative self-reports of the "I'm no good for anything" variety
5. unemployment or other economic problems in the family
6. otherwise unexplainable changes in behavior, including increased absence or tardiness, decreased achievement, or increase in behavior problems
7. suggestions of negative feelings in art work, including negative self-perception and suggestions of family or social problems

While not all of these signs may be indicative of an overstressed child there is a chance that they may, in combination with other indexes, reflect the attitudes and behaviors of a child at risk due to stress. As with the other subjective identification problems, further verification is necessary before steps are taken to deal with the situation.

Brief Summary of Informal Identification Methods

The emphasis in this section has been on the informal identification of children who may be at risk due either to specific events occurring in their lives or to certain kinds of general situations. The primary ingredients for success in such an endeavor are a predetermination to look for such children, the establishment of the means whereby identification procedures can be accomplished, and the existence of procedures for verifying suspicions once they have been raised. The means by which these steps are accomplished may differ from one place to another, but the basic requirement is awareness that many children are at risk due to situations in their lives over which they have little or no control. Help provided to these children at the earliest possible discovery of such conditions may prevent the development of more serious and long-lasting problems.

Identifying Children at Risk Through the Use of Records

Schools have gone through two stages with respect to the maintenance and use of student records in approximately the last 30 years and are now in the midst of a third phase. In the first phase cumulative records, including the anecdotal records mentioned previously, were considered an important part of the school program. The keeping of these records was formerly considered an important part of the responsibility of the school counselor (Traxler, 1957). Such records ordinarily contained a variety of personal and identifying information and, in addition, included ability and achievement test scores, grades, samples of the child's work and teacher comments. The second phase in the life of cumulative records began, quite clearly, with the passage of the Buckley Amendment of the Family Educational Rights and Privacy Act. This legislation gave parents essentially unrestricted access to all records kept on their child. Teacher comments and other informal records became, almost overnight, a thing of the past. It should be said that counselor responsibility for such records was diminishing before the advent of the Buckley Amendment. There had also been, prior to that time, an apparently growing disenchantment with anecdotal records and some of the inappropriate uses to which they were sometimes put.

The third phase in school records is upon us although it has by no means fully developed at this time. Computers provide the capacity to store and retrieve data with great efficiency. They also make it possible to utilize combinations of data which would have been unthinkable in the past due to the amount of labor involved in the process. At the moment, computers appear to be used in schools mainly for business functions and, somewhat, for attendance accounting; they have yet to be utilized to their fullest capacity in helping students, but that potential is clearly there and will be discussed subsequently.

School records have been used for a variety of purposes but, so far as has been possible to determine, not in any systematic way for identifying children who may be at risk. Nearly all schools routinely keep records that could be used for this purpose. These records include information on attendance, achievement as reflected by both grades and test scores, behavior as reflected in referrals for disciplinary reasons and suspension from school. Using only these data, it is possible to identify children at risk who might not otherwise be spotted until problems had progressed to the point where primary prevention was no longer possible and remedial measures might be necessary.

■ *School Attendance and Children at Risk.* There has recently been considerable research on the relationship of attendance to school achievement. In general, the findings tend to support the idea that absence from school results in lowered achievement (Easton & Engelhard, 1982; Monk & Ibrahim, 1984; Wiley & Harnischfeger, 1974). The dynamics of this phenomenon have not been fully explored. According to some (Wiley & Harnischfeger, 1984) it is likely to be due simply to lost instructional time. This is consistent with Carroll's (1963) model of school learning. Others, however, are less sure and believe that the relationship between absence and achievement may be more complicated. Regardless of the dynamics, it seems true that lowered attendance does result in lowered achievement both as measured by grades and by standardized test scores.

From the point of view of primary prevention, a change in the *pattern* of a child's attendance at school may signal a child at risk. Such absence may stem from illness or personal, social, or family problems, which, in turn, are likely to affect school performance. Schools are generally concerned about prolonged absences, but seldom investigate changes in attendance patterns unless they are of long duration. Since such changes are indicative of a child at risk, they will be of interest to the professional interested in primary prevention.

■ *School Achievement and Children at Risk.* A decline in achievement, like a decline in attendance, may indicate a child at risk. Such a decline may be seen on a more long-term basis in achievement test scores from one year to the next or, on a short-term basis, between school grades from one marking period to the next. In cases where such shifts are general, that is, across several subject matter areas, there should at least be the suspicion that something is going on in a child's life that may place him or her at risk. Investigation of declines in achievement is called for in situations where primary prevention is a focus.

■ *School Behavior and Children at Risk.* As with attendance and achievement, children tend to develop patterns of behavior that are recognized by school personnel as normal for a particular child. When there is a negative deviation from such a pattern, it may indicate that the child is experiencing additional stress with a potential for creating more serious problems. Such changes may be noted by an individual teacher or, in situations where such records are kept, may be seen in increased number of referrals outside the classroom for disciplinary reasons or in an increased number of suspensions.

■ *A Computer-Based Approach to the Use of Records.* The knowledgeable professional will recognize that attempting to discern changes in the achievement, attendance, and behavior patterns of individual children is a task that, if required of the classroom teacher, might be almost impossible to accomplish successfully. Further, a change in more than one of these behaviors is likely to be more indicative of a child at risk than a shift in only one of them. This further complicates the problem for any individual teacher. Computers are ideally suited for use in this kind of situation and it seems inevitable that schools will, in the near future, utilize computers not only for the management of business operations but also more broadly as part of a general management information system.

It appears true that at present few school systems have fully developed and fully functioning computer-based management information systems, but the potential is present. The development of a student file for a school district's computer-based management information system would allow education personnel to develop programs that would enable a periodic identification of children manifesting negative shifts in attendance, achievement, and behavior. Standards for the development of such files already exist (National Center for Educational Statistics, 1974).

Such a statement does oversimplify the problem, since such a program would need to be designed to meet the needs of a specific school situation (Ein-Dor & Segev, 1978), but this is far from an impossible task. Most school districts routinely keep information on attendance, student grades, and student achievement test scores. Such information may be kept by different people and may not even be physically in the same place. Some schools also keep records of various types of disciplinary referrals or disciplinary actions, while others do not. Due to the relatively low incidence of behavior referrals, keeping such records is likely to entail only a trivial increment in workload.

An additional task likely to accompany the development of a computer-based method of identifying children at risk is the fact that initially it will be necessary to select arbitrary, although common sense, criteria as indicative of children at risk while local normative data are developed that will permit more reliable and valid identification of children truly at risk.

The use of a computer-based system for the identification of children potentially at risk has advantages that may offset the initial work involved in its development. First, it can make the regular and routine identification of such children possible with a minimum of cost and work, once the system is in place. Such identification could occur on a monthly basis. Second, by utilizing combinations of data, such a system will permit, over time, the development of an identification program with a reliability and validity far beyond that which could be accomplished by requiring individual teachers to make such distinctions. The utility of such a system in a program of primary prevention has apparently yet to be tried, but the feasibility of doing it is not in doubt.

One caveat is necessary in relation to the use of such an approach to data collection and management. The use of such systems has raised new problems in connection with confidentiality and other ethical issues. Computers make confidential data more easily accessible and schools must take the most serious precautions to limit access to such data to fully qualified personnel who have both a legal and ethical right to it (Walker & Larabee, 1985).

IDENTIFICATION OF INEFFECTIVE ADULTS

Of all the topics to be discussed in this book, this one is perhaps the most sensitive. Public education has a way of holding the child accountable for almost anything that is less than adequate in his or her achievement or behavior repertoire. This almost universal tendency on the part of adults to blame the victim (Ryan, 1971) has made it difficult to deal effectively with adults whose inadequate behavior may be impinging on large numbers of school children. There are some encouraging signs that this tendency may be in the process of shifting. Public concern about teacher tenure may well reflect an increasing conviction that without effective teachers there cannot be effective learners. Likewise, legislative insistence that teachers be competent in the subject matter that they teach and the recent acquiescence of the National Education Association to requiring new teachers to take and pass achievement tests are encouraging signs of a shift away from the tendency to hold the child fully responsible for inadequate achievement or behavior.

There has, as yet, been little unified public attention directed at the responsibility of parents. It seems generally agreed that the parental role is a significant one in determining children's school performance, but parents have yet to be held accountable in the ways that teachers are starting to be held accountable. This may be slower in coming and considerably more difficult to accomplish, but it is unlikely that parental responsibility will be ignored indefinitely.

In spite of some of the shifts that appear to be in the making, the identification of adults whose behavior may not be conducive to children's learning and development remains an extremely sensitive issue. At the same time, a book on primary prevention cannot ignore this issue.

Identification of Ineffective Adults Through Formal Assessment

Our knowledge of what constitutes effective teaching has advanced considerably over what it was in 1960 when Ryans, following a large and thorough study, was unable to identify the characteristics or behaviors that made for an effective teacher. Several more or less formal means of identifying effective and ineffective teachers are available and will be discussed.

The situation is different with respect to parents. While there are many kinds of sound advice that can be given to parents about effective child rearing practices, these have not been synthesized into systems that permit the identification of effective and ineffective parents through formal means. It is also unlikely that widespread cooperation would be obtained from parents in such an assessment program. For these reasons the emphasis here will be on teachers.

■ *Identifying Ineffective Teachers.* The risks of identifying ineffective teachers have already been mentioned. There is possibility of a loss of teacher support, vitally necessary in any primary-preventive program, if the guidance specialist decides to undertake some form of evaluation of teacher effectiveness. It is imperative that such a role be clearly separated from the administrative role of teacher evaluation, both in the minds of the teachers and administrators. Such an approach must be seen by all as facilitative rather than evaluative. Teachers must see the guidance specialist as being on their side and not as a part of management. This means that no information collected in this process can, under any circumstances, be transmitted to administrators. This may be difficult for some administrators to accept but unless this understanding is reached, *no* attempts to evaluate teacher effectiveness should be made.

Three formal structures for assessing teacher effectiveness will be discussed below, but regardless of which is used the guidance specialist involved cannot adopt a confrontational role and expect to be effective. One means of downplaying the confrontion inherent in such a situation is to use the interpersonal process recall technique discussed in chapter 2 (Kagan, 1983) in discussing teacher effectiveness. It should also be noted that it is the most adequate teachers who may first be interested in such a process and that the poorest teachers may never participate in it. At the same time, if the better teachers are interested and active, a considerable amount of social approval will exist in the school, making it easier for less secure teachers eventually to participate in the process.

Three specific techniques for identifying effective or ineffective teacher behavior will be presented here. The use of all three of these techniques assumes that teachers are not always aware of how they are behaving and that their behavior may not be congruent with their intentions (Hunter, 1977). It is therefore possible that analysis of a teacher's behavior may bring to light characteristics of which the teacher is unaware.

The characteristics of classrooms with more positive learning environments include more positive social climates, more classroom participation, and stronger teacher perceptions of links between learning and classroom mental health conditions (Schmuck, 1966). All three of the systems described here attempt, in different ways, to get at the extent to which conditions creating positive environments are present or absent in the behavior of a given teacher.

The oldest, most thoroughly researched, and probably the most widely used system for analyzing teacher behavior is Flanders Interaction Analysis (Flanders, 1970). This system is based on analysis of verbal interaction between a teacher and his or her pupils. It has the advantage of being highly objective. If tape recordings are made of the interactions to be analyzed, then teachers can be directly and privately involved in the analysis of their own classroom interactions rather than requiring the use of an on-site outside rater.

The basic task of the rater is to categorize the verbalizations of teachers and students. There are three broad categories, which include *teacher talk*, *student talk* and a category that includes periods of time in which there is silence, board work or pandemonium called *no talk/all talk*.

Teacher talk is broken down into two general subcategories: *indirect* and *direct* teacher talk, and each of these two categories is, in turn, broken down into a series of subcategories as is *student talk*. The total number of subcategories to be categorized by a rater is 10. The major categories and their accompanying subcategories are presented in table 8-3.

The first step is to obtain a sample of teacher–student interaction. As suggested above, tape-recording provides a sound method of doing this since it is possible to stop the tape in order to rate more accurately and it makes it possible also for teachers to become involved in rating their own interactions with the added benefit of privacy. For any individual teacher it is best to obtain samples of different types of classroom activity since the nature of teacher–student interactions is likely to differ from one type of activity to another; show and tell is unlikely to involve the same types of verbal

Table 8-3
Summary of Categories for Interaction Analysis

Teacher Talk	**Indirect**	1. **Accepts feeling:** Accepts and clarifies the feelings of the students in a nonthreatening manner (feelings may be positive or negative) predicting and recalling feelings are included. 2. **Praises or encourages:** Praises or encourages student action or behavior; jokes that release tension, not at student's expense, and nodding head or saying "uh-huh?" or "go on" are included. 3. **Accepts or uses student ideas:** Clarifying, building, or developing ideas or suggestions by the student; (as teacher brings more of his own ideas into play, shift to category 5). 4. **Asks questions:** Asking a question about content or procedures with the intent that a student answer.
	Direct	5. **Explaining or informing:** Giving facts or opinions about content or procedures; expressing his owns idea; asking rhetorical questions. 6. **Gives direction:** Directions, commands, or orders with which a student is expected to comply by action. 7. **Scolding/reprimanding or defending authority:** Comments intended to change student behavior from nonacceptable pattern; bawling someone out; stating why the teacher is doing what he is doing; extreme self-reference.
Student Talk		8. **Expected or predictable response:** Talk by students in response to teacher. Teacher initiates the contact or solicits student statement. 9. **Initiated response:** Talk by students, which they initiate (if "calling on" student is only to indicate who may talk next, observer must decide whether student wanted to talk; if he did, use this category).
No Talk/ All Talk		10. **No talk/all talk:** silence, confusion, pauses, short periods of silence, laughter, board work, pandemonium where observer cannot tell who is talking or cannot understand communication.

Note. There is no scale implied by the number. Each number is classificatory; it designates a particular kind of event. To write the numbers down during observation is to enumerate—not to judge a position on a scale.

From *Teacher Influence, Pupil Attitudes, and Achievement.* (Cooperative Research Project No. 397), By N. A. Flanders, 1960, Washington, DC: U.S. Office of Education, Department of Health, Education, and Welfare.

interactions as a lesson in long division. While it is anticipated that there will be consistency in the manner in which a given teacher interacts with students, it is appropriate to obtain a sample of teacher behaviors across different types of teaching activities. It is generally best to record an entire activity (e.g., a 20-minute arithmetic lesson) and then to select a smaller time sample from the longer segment for analysis.

There are three general types of information to be secured through the analysis. The first is a breakdown of the number of times each of the 10 different categories occurs. The second type of information is a ratio between teacher talk and student talk. The third general category of information is obtained from a matrix that makes it possible to study quantitatively the dynamics of the interactions that take place. Analyses of classroom interaction ranging from the relatively simple to the highly complex are possible using these three types of information. An extremely practical manual for this purpose has been prepared by Kryspin and Feldhusen (1974). Generally speaking, high proportions of indirect teacher talk and of student talk are considered more positive in the production of a sound classroom environment. High proportions of direct teacher talk, particularly in category 7 (scolding/reprimanding or defending authority) are considered more negative as is a high number of responses in category 10 (no talk/all talk). In summarizing a series of six of his own research projects using interaction analysis, Flanders (1970) states:

> When classroom interaction patterns indicate that pupils have opportunities to express their ideas, and when these ideas are incorporated into the learning activities, then the pupils seem to learn more and to develop more positive attitudes toward the teacher and the learning activities. (p. 401)

A second general method of analyzing teacher effectiveness is provided by what has come to be called communication skills. As noted in chapter 2, the general idea for these skills came from Rogers (1957) and was translated into a series of rating scales by Carkhuff and Berenson (1967). Four basic skills were originally proposed. These included empathy, respect, genuineness, and concreteness. Subsequently (Carkhuff, 1969), these four basic skills were expanded to include confrontation and immediacy. Since these basic skills were originally intended for application in counseling situations, as contrasted to teaching situations, not all of them have equal relevance in both. The extensive research of Aspy and Roebuck (1977) made use only of the empathy, respect, and genuineness scales. In spite of this limited use they were able to demonstrate higher achievement in children when high levels of each of these conditions were present.

Each of the core dimensions postulated by Carkhuff can be rated on a 5-point scale. The scales are arranged so that the minimum rating of 3.0 is required in order for minimally facilitative levels of that particular core dimension to be present. Thus, in diagnosing teacher behavior with the use of these scales, teachers scoring below 3.0 could be identified as not providing conditions for effective learning. As with the Flanders system, taped samples of teacher interaction with students can be used for analysis and teachers can be taught to rate their own interactions. This system does have the advantage of being simpler to learn than interaction analysis and also has the appearance, to teachers, of greater face validity than interaction analysis.

A third structure that may be used for the analysis of teacher effectiveness is provided by the principles of behavior modification. Unfortunately, there are no tested and readily available formats for utilizing this approach in assessment fashion. This is somewhat surprising in view of the very broad influence that the behavioral approach has had on education in recent years. As Krasner (1976) has pointed out, such developments as programmed learning, computer-assisted instruction, the concept of behavioral objectives, behavior modification in classroom, token economies, competency-based education, the concept of accountability, and microteaching all grow from basic behavioral principles.

It is possible to view the environment of any classroom from the perspective of behavioral principles and to assess the extent to which a teacher creates positively reinforcing conditions within that environment, while reducing to a minimum those conditions that interfere with effective student learning and behavior. It is not our purpose to get into the complicated world of behavioral psychology but rather to present a simple technique that will permit a behavioral analysis of a given classroom.

Since the intent is to provide a practical and workable means of assessing a classroom environment, behaviorally some simplification (there are those who would say oversimplification) is necessary. The following assumptions undergird the behavior observation approach that will be presented:

1. Although positive reinforcement, negative reinforcement, and punishment may all be effective in controlling behavior, the type of reinforcement that can be delivered *most effectively* in a typical classroom situation by a typical teacher is positive reinforcement.

2. Most teachers do not have the opportunity to deliver negative reinforcement effectively in the classroom setting because the timing of such reinforcement is so critical. In addition, many teachers have a tendency to continue the delivery of aversive stimuli after the child has undertaken a desired behavior (e.g., returning to his seat). This has the unfortunate effect of associating an aversive stimulus with a positive behavior. At this point, the teacher's behavior has ceased to be negative reinforcement and has become merely punishment.

3. It is nearly impossible to meet the necessary conditions for the delivery of effective punishment in the classroom setting. These conditions and some of their outcomes include all of the following:
   a. A set of well-defined rules must exist.
   b. Any infraction of the rules must immediately cause the teacher to invoke an aversive consequence.
   c. Aversive consequences must be routinely and impartially enforced.
   d. Punishment tends to work mainly when the aversive stimulus is present, therefore its effects are not maintained.
   e. Punishment may create serious side effects in the child, such as continuing anger and hostility toward the teacher, which may impede future learning and reduce the potency of the teacher as a positive reinforcer in the future. The use of aversive responses is attractive to teachers both because it is easier to deliver, provides some emotional relief, and because its effects may be immediately obvious. A child peremptorily ordered to return to his seat is likely to do so, but his habit of being out of his seat is likely to be unaffected, especially if returning to the seat is accompanied by a continuing harangue.

Table 8-4
Relationship of Stimulus Quality to Reinforcement Condition

Stimulus Quality	Reinforcement Condition Resulting	
	Reinforcement Presented	Reinforcement Withdrawn
Pleasurable	Positive reinforcement (increases behavior)	Punishment (decreases behavior)
Aversive	Punishment (decreases behavior)	Negative reinforcement (increases behavior)

4. It is possible to identify positive and aversive stimuli in uniform fashion for most children; therefore it is legitimate to categorize certain broad types of events as positive or aversive.

A general paradigm that undergirds this approach is presented in Table 8-4.

Basic questions that need to be answered in assessing the effectiveness of teachers from a behavioral perspective include the following:

(a) What types of reinforcers are used? (b) With what frequency are different types of reinforcers used? (c) Are reinforcers routinely and systematically used? Which ones? and (d) Are similar reinforcers used with all students, or are some students the recipients of positive reinforcement, others of negative reinforcement, and still others the recipients of punishment for similar kinds of behavior?

The number of different kinds of possible teacher responses to children are presented in Table 8-5. Four basic types of response are included. These are: (a) positive, immediate teacher responses to student behavior, (b) positive, delayed teacher responses to student behavior, (c) aversive, immediate teacher responses to student behavior, and (d) negative, delayed teacher responses to student behavior.

Within each of these categories a series of common types of teacher reaction is presented. An immediate response is one that follows a student response with little or no time lag. A delayed response is one that occurs (or fails to occur) after some significant lapse of time. It is possible to use the kinds of information called for in table 8-5 as an outline for observing teacher behavior from a behavioral perspective.

The Identification of Ineffective Adults Through Informal Means

The topic of identifying ineffective adults through informal means has apparently not been covered in professional literature. It is included here because, as every experienced educator will know, there is often knowledge within a given school of who is and who is not an effective teacher. Such faculty lounge diagnoses must be treated with due caution since they may spring from specific philosophical biases about teaching or child management rather than from an assessment of a specific teacher's effectiveness.

Table 8-5
Behavior Observation Outline

Positive, Immediate, Teacher Responses
to Student Behavior

Social Responses
  Verbal: positive and encouraging comments
  Facial: smiles
  Physical: touches or pats gently
Tangible Responses
  Uses tokens, chips, stars, play money systematically
  Uses M & Ms, raisins, cereal systematically

Positive, Delayed, Teacher Responses
to Student Behavior

Social Responses
  Verbal: positive or encouraging comments on papers
Tangible Responses
  Stars, smileys, stickers on student work
  Outside activities: movies, zoo, trips, etc.
  Popcorn parties or other class or group rewards

Aversive, Immediate, Teacher Responses
to Student Behavior

Social Responses
  Verbal: negative comment, sarcasm, scolding, peremptory commands
  Facial: frowns, scowls, rolls eyes, shrugs shoulders, grimaces
  Physical: shakes finger, waves arms
Tangible Responses
  Shoves, pushes, or hits

Aversive, Delayed, Teacher Responses
to Student Behavior

Social Responses
  Verbal: no comments on papers
  Negative comments on papers, including frown faces, red checks, etc.

General Observations

1. Students have well established rules and expectations (Yes, No).
2. There are well understood and expected consequences for appropriate behavior (Yes, No).
3. There are well understood and expected consequences for inappropriate behavior (Yes, No).
4. Positive consequences are routinely and systematically employed (Yes, No).
5. Negative consequences are routinely and systematically employed (Yes, No).
6. Ratio of positive to negative reinforcers.

On the other hand, there often seems to be some validity to informal, largely covert, group consensus on who is an ineffective teacher.

Such teachers are often characterized by persistent class management problems. The idea of persistence is important here because every teacher seems, occasionally, to be faced with a difficult-to-manage class. Ineffective teachers also tend to make more out-of-class disciplinary referrals to administrators rather than dealing with their own problems in an effective way. There also are likely to be more referrals for special education consideration as well as more referrals to available specialists such as reading teachers, counselors, or school psychologists. These teachers tend to have manifested their inadequate behavior from a time early in their employment history but, at that point in their career, were excused on the grounds that experience would improve their effectiveness.

Another class of signs that may be diagnostic of teacher ineffectiveness is included under the general heading of stress. Such stress may be present in a teacher who is generally ineffective or may become manifest in a teacher who, after a term of service, begins to experience the burnout phenomenon. The symptoms in either case are likely to be similar. Such symptoms include absence to the point of using sick leave days as they are accumulated, vague chronic health problems involving stomach-, back-, or headache, depression, lack of energy, and a low tolerance for the normal frustrations of the classroom.

The informal identification of inadequate parents is likely to be less reliable and valid than the informal identification of ineffective teachers. Perhaps the best single criterion is what might be called a family history of children who have been school problems. Even here, caution must be used since school problems from an apparent lack of ability may be different from those stemming from inappropriate behavior, lack of attending skills, or general lack of interest. It is also tempting to blame families for most of the problems of children when such causes may be as much the responsibility of the school as of the parents—another example of blaming the victim. There also appears to be a tendency to judge the effectiveness of parents on the basis of their employment status or their alleged moral behavior. In any event, the identification of parents who place their children at risk in school due to the ineffectiveness of their own behavior is likely to be difficult and, in the long run, without any purpose. A primary prevention program broad in scope is more likely to be effective than an attempt to identify problem parents.

THE IDENTIFICATION OF INEFFECTIVE ENVIRONMENTS

It is a common experience to hear school personnel who spend time in different school settings state that different schools and different classes "feel" different. There is also a general belief that some schools and some teachers create and maintain learning environments that are effective in promoting the personal and educational growth of students while other environments may inhibit such growth. These are two sides of the same coin and there is an extensive body of literature bearing on this issue.

The available evidence suggests that this general area is extremely complex. Even the global dimensions of the concept of school environment have not been agreed upon (Moos, 1974; Tagiuri, 1968). On the other hand, there is agreement on some aspects of the issue. First, there is apparently no doubt that different schools do have unique environments (Kalis, 1980; Owens,

1970; Sinclair, 1970). Second, there seems to be agreement that school climate has an effect on important student outcomes of a wide variety (Barker, 1963; Brookover, Schweitzer, Schneider, Beady, Flood, & Wisenbaker, 1978; Bailey, 1979; Cox, 1978; Duke & Perry, 1978; Vyskocil & Goens, 1978). Beyond these reasonably well established findings is the assumption that understanding of school climate can be utilized to have a positive influence on student outcomes. Current efforts are focused at the classroom and school levels since research at the district level has suggested that it is too broad and diverse to result in useful generalizations (Bidwell & Karsarda, 1975).

Historically, the analysis of learning environments in a global sense apparently began with the work of Pace and Stern (1958) at the college level. This was followed by the attempt of Halpin and Croft (1963) to relate teacher morale to characteristics of the administrative structure of the school. Subsequently there have been a wide variety of instruments developed for identifying the salient characteristics of both school and classroom environments at the elementary and secondary school levels. A comprehensive and scholarly review of the literature by Anderson (1982) reports over 200 references and there appears to have been little reduction in output since that time.

Given the current state of knowledge, it is not appropriate to recommend the use of environment scales for precise diagnosis of a classroom or school environment. It has been suggested by one expert (Moos, 1979a) that the best use of such scales is as a basis for discussion among administration and faculty. He says that a good environment study serves the same purpose at the school level that the use of a personality assessment does at the individual level. Results will provide an indication of current types of functioning as well as an objective basis for suggesting directions for needed change. The kind of information derived from such a study is considerably "safer" than that obtained about individual teachers. It also provides a basis for group discussion and action rather than being limited to an individual teacher. At the same time, such information will be somewhat less precise and somewhat less directly related to the functioning of students. In a complete primary-preventive program, both individual analysis and school level analysis are desirable approaches.

A number of instruments are available for the purpose of analyzing various aspects of classroom and school environments, but only a few meet minimal standards of psychometric adequacy. Brief descriptions of some of the more adequate and widely used instruments follow.

1. The Classroom Environment Scale (CES) was originally developed by Trickett and Moos (1973) and is probably the most widely researched and used single instrument of its type. It focuses on the psychosocial environment of classrooms at the secondary school level and takes into account teacher behavior, teacher–student interaction and student–student interaction. It consists of 90 items divided into 12 scales that were derived through factor analysis. It is probably the

most psychometrically sound (Moos, 1979a) of the available instruments and has probably been more widely used than any of the others (Moos, 1979b). It is one of the few such scales that is published commercially (Moos & Trickett, 1974).

2. The Learning Environment Inventory (LEI) (Anderson, 1973) was originally developed as a measure of the general social environment of individual classrooms (Anderson and Walberg, 1974). It consists of 15 subscales, developed through factor analysis, of seven items per scale. Likert-type scales are used and results are machine scorable. The LEI is intended for use in classrooms at the secondary level. A form of this inventory called the My Class Inventory (MCI) has been derived from the LEI for use with elementary school children. The MCI consists of five nine-item scales in a simple agree–disagree format. Another derivative of the LEI is the My School Inventory. This is identical to the MCI except that the response set has been changed from the classroom level to the school level (Ellett & Walberg, 1979).

3. The Quality of School Life Scale (QSL) was developed by Epstein and McPartland (1976) to obtain a general measure of student reaction to school. It is short (27 items) and consists of three scales: general satisfaction with school; commitment to school work; and attitudes towards teachers. Psychometric qualities of the instrument are sound and include evidence for concurrent and discriminative validity. The QSL was designed for use with students in grades 4 through 12; it is commercially published.

4. The School Survey (Coughlan, 1970) differs from the three instruments discussed above in that it is a measure exclusively for use with teachers. It was designed originally as a measure of teacher morale and covers significant elements of the teacher's work environment. It consists of 13 subscales grouped into four general areas, namely, administration, working relationships, school effectiveness, and career fulfillment. It includes a total of 74 items. Some research suggests that it does distinguish between high- and low-achieving elementary schools (Coughlan & Cooke, 1974). It has not been as widely used as the other three instruments but does have relatively sound psychometric qualities.

SUMMARY

The role of assessment in primary prevention is extremely limited. Its three basic purposes are to identify children at risk, to identify ineffective adults in children's environments and to identify learning environments that are not effective. There are a number of formal assessment devices available for the purpose of identifying specific children at risk. In addition, there are less formal approaches that can be used for this purpose. A potential method of identifying children at risk is through the use of records, particularly where this approach is linked to computer-based student files reflecting such data as attendance patterns, achievement patterns, ability–achievement discrepancies, and indexes of behavioral problems.

The identification of ineffective adults is an especially sensitive area and should be approached in the most cautious manner. There are several formal means available for assessing teacher effectiveness. The formal assessment of parent effectiveness is unlikely to be a possibility. There are specific informal indexes of adult ineffectiveness, including signs of stress, continual class management problems and excessive numbers of referrals and, for parents, a history of prior children who have had problems. The use of records to identify ineffective teacher behavior is a possibility, but is likely to be superfluous given normally existing informal channels of communication.

Another general type of assessment in primary prevention is the identification of ineffective environments. This is probably the safer way to identify ineffectiveness in schools since it does not focus on individuals but, rather, on the context or setting. Use of such instruments also provides a basis for discussion and cooperation, as opposed to confrontation.

In any attempt to involve adults either in individual assessment or an assessment of the effectiveness of a general environment it will be necessary for the guidance specialist to distance him or herself from administrative uses of assessment. Whether the assessment is of individual performance or classroom environment, the participating teacher must be absolutely guaranteed confidentiality unless he or she chooses to waive such a right. Failure to observe this caution in even one instance may thoroughly damage the effectiveness of the guidance professional in a particular setting.

REFERENCES

Abrahamson, D. S., & Bell, A. E. (1979). Assessment of the school readiness section of the early detection inventory: Preschool prediction across situational factors. *Journal of School Psychology, 17,* 162–171.

Anderson, C. S. (1982). The search for school climate: A review of the research. *Review of Educational Research, 52,* 368–420.

Anderson, G. J. (1973). *The assessment of learning environments: A manual for the Learning Environment Inventory and My Class Inventory.* Halifax, Nova Scotia: Atlantic Institute of Education.

Anderson, G. J., & Walberg, H. J. (1974). Learning environments. In H. J. Walberg (Ed.), *Evaluating educational performances.* Berkeley, CA: McCutchan.

Asher, S. R., & Renshaw, P. D. (1981). Children without friends: Social knowledge and social skill training. In S. R. Asher, & J. M. Gottman (Eds.), *The development of children's friendships (pp. 273–296).* New York: Cambridge University Press.

Aspy, D. N., & Roebuck, F. N. (1977). *Kids don't learn from people they don't like.* Amherst, MA: Human Resource Development Press.

Bailey, M. (1979). The art of positive principalship. *Momentum, 10,* 46–47.

Balk, D. (1983). How teenagers cope with sibling death: Some implications for school counselors. *School Counselor, 31,* 150–158.

Barclay, J. R. (1984). Primary prevention and assessment. *Personnel and Guidance Journal, 62,* 475–478.

Barker, R. G. (1963). On the nature of the environment. *Journal of Social Issues, 19* (4), 17–38.

Barquest, K. A., & Martin, H. K. (1984). Use of lay home visitors: A primary prevention strategy for families with a newborn. *Personnel and Guidance Journal, 62,* 558–560.

Beck, A. T., Seti, B. B., & Tuthill, R. W. (1963). Childhood bereavement and adult depression. *Archives of General Psychiatry, 9,* 295–302.

Begin, G. (1983). Convergent validity of four instruments for teachers assessing social competence of kindergarten children. *Perceptual and Motor Skills, 57,* 1007–1012.

Bidwell, C. E., & Karsarda, J. D. (1975) School district organization and student achievement. *American Sociological Review, 40,* 55–70.

Brookover, W. B., Schweitzer, J. H., Schneider, J. M., Beady C. H., Flood, P. K., & Wisenbaker, J. M. (1978). Elementary school social climate and school achievement. *American Educational Research Journal, 15,* 301–318.

Brown, B. (1980, September). The school needs of children from one-parent families. *Education Digest,* pp. 1–5.

Bundy, M. L., & Gumaer, J. (Eds.). (1984). Guest editorial: Families in transition. *Elementary School Guidance and Counseling, 19,* 4–8.

Camblin, L. D., & Prout, H. T. (1983). School counselors and the reporting of child abuse: A survey of state laws and practices. *School Counselor, 30,* 358–367.

Cannon, W. B. (1942). "Voodoo" death. *American Anthropologist, 44,* 169–181.

Caplan, G. (1974). *Support systems and community mental health: Lectures on concept development.* New York: Behavioral Publications.

Carkhuff, R. R. (1969). *Helping and human relations* (Vol. 1). New York: Holt, Rinehart, & Winston.

Carkhuff, R. R., & Berenson, B. G. (1967). *Beyond counseling and therapy.* New York: Holt, Rinehart, & Winston.

Carroll, J. B. (1963). A model of school learning. *Teachers College Record, 64,* 723–733.

Caskey, W. E., & Larson, G. L. (1983). Relationship between selected kindergarten predictors and first and fourth grade achievement test scores. *Perceptual and Motor Skills, 56,* 815–822.

Connally, J., & Doyle, A. B. (1981). Assessment of social competence in pre-schoolers: Teachers versus peers. *Developmental Psychology, 17,* 454–462.

Coughlan, R. J. (1970). Dimensions of teacher morale. *American Educational Research Journal, 7,* 221–235.

Coughlan, R. J., & Cooke, R. (1974). Work attitudes. In H. J. Walberg (Ed.), *Evaluating educational performance.* Berkeley, CA: McCutchan.

Cox, W. B. (1978). Crime and punishment on campus: An inner city case. *Adolescence, 13,* 339–348.

Danish, S. J., Smyer, M. A., & Nowak, C. A. (1980). Developmental intervention: Enhancing life event processes. In P. B. Baltes & O. G. Brim, Jr. (Eds.), *Life-Span development and behavior* (Vol. 3, pp. 340–366). New York: Academic Press.

De Apodaca, R. F., & Cowen, E. L. (1982). Comparative study of the self-esteem, sociometric status, and insight of referred and nonreferred school children. *Psychology in the Schools, 19,* 395–401.

Duke, D. L., & Perry, C. (1978). Can alternative schools succeed where Benjamin Spock, Spiro Agnew, and B. F. Skinner have failed? *Adolescence, 13,* 375–392.

Easton, J. Q., & Engelhard, J., Jr. (1982). Longitudinal record of elementary school absence and its relationship to reading achievement. *Journal of Educational Research, 75,* 269–274.

Ein-Dor, P., & Segev, E. (1978). Strategic planning for management information systems. *Management Science, 24,* 1631–1642.

Ellett, C. D., & Walberg, H. J. (1979). Principals' competency, environment, and outcomes. In H. J. Walberg (Ed.), *Educational environments and effects (pp. 140–164).* Berkeley, CA: McCutchan.

Epstein, J. L., & McPartland, J. M. (1976). The concept and measurement of the quality of school life. *American Educational Research Journal, 13,* 15–30.

Evans, K. M. (1962). *Sociometry and education.* London: Routledge and Kegan Paul.

Flanders, N. A. (1960). *Teacher influence, pupil attitudes, and achievement* (Cooperative Research Project No. 397). Washington, DC: U.S. Department of Health, Education and Welfare, Office of Education.

Flanders, N. A. (1970). *Analyzing teaching behavior.* Reading, MA: Addison–Wesley.

Flook, W. M., & Velicer, W. F. (1977). School readiness and teachers' ratings: A validation study. *Psychology in the Schools, 14,* 140–146.

Fondacaro, M. R., Heller, K., & Reilly, M. J. (1984). Development of friendship networks as a prevention strategy in a university megadorm. *Personnel and Guidance Journal, 62,* 520–523.

Forman, S. G., & O'Malley, P. L. (1984). School stress and anxiety interventions. *School Psychology Review, 13,* 162–170.

Foster, S. L., & Ritchey, W. L. (1979). Issues in the assessment of social competence in children. *Journal of Applied Behavior Analysis, 12,* 625–638.

Gade, E. M. (1977). Innovative uses of sociometry in elementry school counseling. *Elementary School Guidance and Counseling, 12,* 133–137.

Gallerani, D., O'Regan, M., & Reinherz, H. (1982). Prekindergarten screening: How well does it predict readiness for first grade? *Psychology in the Schools, 19,* 175–182.

Gandura, P., Keogh, B. K., & Yoshioka-Maxwell, B. (1980). Predicting academic performance of Anglo- and Mexican-American kindergarten children. *Psychology in the Schools, 17,* 174–177.

Getson, R. F., & Benshoff, D. L. (1977). Four experiences of death and how to prepare to meet them. *School Counselor, 24,* 310–314.

Gill, D. G. (1970). *Violence against children: Physical abuse in the United States.* Cambridge, MA: Harvard University Press.

Glazzard, M. (1977). The effectiveness of three kindergarten predictors for first grade achievement. *Journal of Learning Disabilities, 10,* 95–99.

Gronlund, N. E. (1959). *Sociometry in the classroom.* New York: Harper & Brothers.

Halpin, A. W., & Croft, D. B. (1963). *The organizational climate of school.* Chicago: University of Chicago Press.

Hunter, C. (1977). An interpersonal relations and group process approach to affective education for young children. *Journal of School Psychology, 15,* 141–151.

Jacobson, T. (1984). Keeping track with computers: Student attendance accounting. *Thrust, 14* (3), 33–36.

Jaremko, M. E. (1984). Stress innoculation training: A generic approach for the prevention of stress related disorders. *Personnel and Guidance Journal, 62,* 544–550.

Kagan, N. (1983). Interpersonal process recall: Basic methods and recent research. In D. Larson (Ed.), *Teaching psychological skills: Models for giving psychology away* (pp. 229–244). Monterey, CA: Brooks/Cole.

Kalis, M. C. (1980). Teaching experience: Its effect on school climate, teacher morale. *NASSP Bulletin, 64,* 89–102.

Kline, D. F., Cole, P., & Fox, P. (1981). Child abuse and neglect: The school psychologist's role. *School Psychology Review, 10,* 65–71.

Krasner, L. (1976). The classroom as a planned environment. *Educational Researcher,* 5 (1), 9–14.

Kryspin, W. J., & Feldhusen, J. F. (1974). *Analyzing verbal classroom interaction.* Minneapolis: Burgess.

Kubler-Ross, E. (1974). *Questions and answers on death and dying.* New York: Macmillan.

Lazarus, R. S. (1980). The stress and coping paradigm. In C. Eisdorfer, D. Cohen, A. Kleinman, & P. Maxim (Eds.), *Theoretical bases for psychopathology* (pp. 44–82). New York: Spectrum.

Lichtenstein, R. (1982). New instrument, old problem for early identification. *Exceptional Children, 49,* 70–72.

Lindeman, D. P., Goodstein, H. A., Sachs, A., & Young, C. C. (1984). An evaluation of the Yellow Brick Road Test through a full prediction–performance comparison matrix. *Journal of School Psychology, 22,* 111–117.

Lorion, R. P., Work, W. C., & Hightower, A. D. (1984). A school-based multilevel preventive intervention: Issues in program development and evaluation. *Personnel and Guidance Journal, 62,* 479–484.

Mannarino, A. P., Christy, M., Durlak, J. A., & Magnussen, M. G. (1982). Evaluation of social competence training in the schools. *Journal of School Psychology, 20,* 11–19.

Matter, D. E., & Matter, R. M. (1982). Developmental sequences in children's understanding of death with implications for counselors. *Elementary School Guidance and Counseling, 17,* 112–118.

McCandless, B. R. (1967). *Children: Behavior and development.* New York: Holt, Rinehart, & Winston.

Miller, K. A., & Miller, E. K. (1979). Child abuse and neglect: A framework for identification. *School Counselor, 26,* 284–287.

Monat, A., & Lazarus, R. S. (1977). *Stress and coping: An anthology.* New York: Columbia University Press

Monk, D. H., & Ibrahim, M. A. (1984). Patterns of absence and school achievement. *American Educational Research Journal, 21,* 295–310.

Moos, R. H. (1974). Systems for the assessment and classification of human environments: An overview. In R. H. Moos & P. M. Insel (Eds.), *Issues in social ecology.* Palo Alto, CA: National Press Books.

Moos, R. H. (1979a). *Evaluating educational environments.* San Francisco: Jossey–Bass.

Moos, R. H. (1979b). Educational climates. In H. J. Walberg (Ed.), *Educational environments and effects* (pp. 79–100). Berkeley, CA: McCutchan.

Moos, R. H., & Trickett, E. J. (1974). *Classroom Environment Scale manual.* Palo Alto, CA: Consulting Psychologists Press.

Moreno, J. L. (1934). *Who shall survive? A new approach to the problem of human interrelations.* Washington, DC: Nervous and Mental Disease Publishing.

Naglieri, J., & Harrison, P. L. (1982). McCarthy Scales, McCarthy Screening Test, and Kaufman's McCarthy short form correlations with the Peabody Individual Achievement Test. *Psychology in the Schools, 19,* 149–155.

Nagy, M. (1959). The child's view of death. In H. Feifel (Ed.), *The meaning of death* (pp. 79–98). New York: McGraw–Hill.

National Center for Education Statistics (1974). *Student/pupil accounting: Standard terminology and guide for managing student data in elementary and secondary schools, community/junior colleges, and adult education.* Washington, DC: U.S. Department of Health, Education and Welfare.

Nurss, J. R., & McGauvran, M. E. (1976). *Metropolitan Readiness Tests, level II, teachers manual.* New York: Harcourt, Brace, Jovanovich.

O'Block, F. R., Billimoria, A., & Behan, M. (1981). National survey of the involvement of school psychologists with child abuse. *School Psychology Review, 10,* 62–64.

Oehmen, S. (1985). Divorce and grief: counseling the child. *Elementary School Guidance and Counseling, 19,* 314–317.

Owens, R. G. (1970). *Organizational behavior in schools.* Englewood Cliffs, N. J.: Prentice–Hall.

Pace, C. R., & Stern, G. G. (1958). An approach to the measurement of psychological characteristics of college environments. *Journal of Educational Psychology, 49,* 269–277.

Peretti, P. O., Lane, L., & Floyd, E. (1981). Perceived personality impressions of the sociometric isolate by elementary school classmates. *Education, 101,* 359–365.

Phillips, B. (1979). *School stress and anxiety.* New York: Human Sciences Press.

Richey, D. D. (1980). Educators and the primary prevention of child abuse. *Education Forum, 44,* 329–337.

Roff, M., Sells, S. B., & Golden, M. M. (1972). *Social adjustment and personality development in children.* Minneapolis: University of Minnesota Press.

Rogers, C. R. (1957). The necessary and sufficient conditions of therapeutic personality change. *Journal of Consulting Psychology, 21,* 95–103.

Roscoe, B., Peterson, K. L., & Shaner, J. M. (1983). Guidelines to assist educators in identifying children of neglect. *Education, 103,* 395–398.

Ryan, W. (1971). *Blaming the victim.* New York: Random House.

Ryans, D. G. (1960). *Characteristics of teachers, their description, comparison, and appraisal: A research study.* Washington, DC: American Council on Education.

Ryerson, M. (1977). Death education and counseling for children. *Elementary School Guidance and Counseling, 11,* 165–174.

Schmidt, M. G. (1980). *Personal networks: Assessment, care, and repair.* Paper presented at the 26th annual meeting of the Western Gerontological Society, Anaheim, CA.

Schmidt, S., & Perino, J. (1985). Kindergarten screening results as predictors of academic achievement, potential, and placement in second grade. *Psychology in the Schools, 22,* 146–151.

Schmuck, R. (1966). Some aspects of classroom social climates. *Psychology in the Schools, 3,* 59–65.

Selye, H. (1956). *The stress of life.* New York: McGraw–Hill.

Sinclair, R. L. (1970). Elementary school educational environments: Toward schools that are responsive to students. *National Elementary Principal, 49,* 53–58.

Spivack, G., & Shure, M. B. (1974). *Social adjustment of young children.* San Francisco: Jossey–Bass.

Tagiuri, R. (1968). The concept of organizational climate. In R. Tagiuri & G. H. Litwin (Eds.), *Organizational climate: Exploration of a concept* (pp. 11–32). Boston: Harvard University, Graduate School of Business Administration.

Tokar, E. B., & Holthouse, N. D. (1977). Validity of the subtests of the 1976 edition of the Metropolitan Readiness Tests. *Educational and Psychological Measurement, 37,* 1099–1101.

Tolor, A., Carpetti, W. L., & Lane, P. A. (1967). Teacher's attitudes toward children's behavior revisited. *Journal of Educational Psychology, 58,* 175–180.

Traxler, A. E. (1957). *Techniques of guidance.* New York: Harper & Brothers.

Trickett, E. J., & Moos, R. H. (1973). The social environment of junior high and high school classrooms. *Journal of Educational Psychology, 65,* 93–101.

Tsushima, W. T., Onorato, V. A., Okumura, F. T., & Sue, D. (1983). The predictive validity of the STAR: A need for local validation. *Educational and Psychological Measurement, 43,* 663–665.

Ullmann, C. A. (1957). Teachers, peers, and tests as predictors of adjustment. *Journal of Educational Psychology, 48,* 257–267.

Vance, B., Kitson, D. L., & Singer, M. (1983). Comparison of the Peabody Picture Vocabulary Test–Revised and the McCarthy Screening Test. *Psychology in the Schools, 20,* 21–24.

Vyskocil, J. R., & Goens, G. A. (1978). Collective bargaining and supervision: A matter of climate. *Educational Leadership, 37,* 175–177.

Walker, M. M., & Larabee, M. J. (1985). Ethics and school records. *Elementary School Guidance and Counseling, 19,* 210–216.

Wallerstein, J. S., & Bundy, M. L. (1984). Helping children of disrupted families: An interview with Judith S. Wallerstein. *Elementary School Guidance and Counseling, 19,* 19–29.

Waters, E. B., & Goodman, J. (1981). I get by with a little help from my friends: The importance of support systems. *Vocational Guidance Quarterly, 29,* 362–369.

Weinberg, S. (1955). *Incest behavior.* New York: Citation Press.

Wendt, R. N. (1978). Kindergarten entrance assessment: Is it worth the effort? *Psychology in the Schools, 15,* 56–62.

Wiley, D., & Harnischfeger, A. (1974). Explosion of a myth: Quantity of schooling and exposure to instruction, major educational vehicles. *Educational Researcher, 3*(4), 7–12.

Wilson, J., Thomas, D., & Schuette, L. (1983). The silent screams: recognizing abused children. *Education, 104,* 100–103.

THE INITIATION AND IMPLEMENTATION OF PRIMARY PREVENTION

C hange is inevitable. Change or, more properly, the results of change can be seen in every aspect of our daily lives. The explosion of knowledge has led to the development of technologies that affect everyone. Concurrent with these changes have been changes in social and personal values, and the schools, like every other social institution, have been deeply affected.

In the main, schools tend to follow rather than to lead the change process. For example, one of the major changes that has occurred in schools has been the introduction of the idea of a "free appropriate public education" for all children. This broadened concern for all children was introduced, sustained and brought to fruition not by educators but fundamentally by the parents of exceptional children. Another example may be seen in our entry into what is sometimes called the computer age. It seems clear to most knowledgeable observers that the computer revolution will ultimately have tremendous effects on schools and, yet, schools in general do not appear to be taking an active role in utilizing, expanding, and determining the appropriate use of computers in an instructional setting.

These situations appear to illustrate the typical way in which change occurs in education. Perhaps this is the result of a specific philosophy that asserts that public education should follow and not lead in the implementation of social and technological change. A much more likely explanation, however, is that it is simply easier to wait for things to happen than to attempt to assist schools deliberately to change course. There is no doubt that planned change requires energy and skill, that it is difficult, that it involves personal and professional risk taking, and that it is not certain of success.

Viewed from a different perspective, however, the argument can be made that planned change is a professional obligation of educators, that professionals are in the best position to know what directions should be taken in their fields and that self-direction is one of the hallmarks of a profession. This point of view literally requires educators to take those actions that will bring about the types of activities and services of maximum benefit to schoolchildren. It is obviously a minority view.

Guidance specialists who are interested in the introduction of primary-preventive components into their activities will be attempting to bring about change since these activities do not exist presently in most school settings. In the usual case, primary-preventive approaches will need to be introduced in on-going programs. The personnel in these programs are already fully occupied and other groups already established have perceptions of what guidance professionals do based on what they have already experienced. People tend to be comfortable with what exists even though it may not be accomplishing very much and those who rock the boat may not be especially welcome.

At least, the dilemma is clear. *Change is going to occur, but change will be resisted.* It is professionally appropriate for guidance specialists to undertake planned change, but it will be difficult and possibly unpopular. If guidance professionals wait for change to be imposed they may not like what results, any more than they like significant aspects of their current responsibilities. Taking into account the obvious vulnerability of the guidance professions the ultimate change that could occur is a reduction in the number of guidance personnel employed by school districts. In spite of difficulties and possible unpopularity, it appears wise for guidance specialists to undertake change in their goals and professional activities.

The focus here is on the introduction of primary-preventive components to existing programs. It is assumed that those attempting to make such change have appropriate skills and knowledge of primary prevention. Inducing change, however, is a process that has broad application and is not limited to primary prevention. What follows, therefore, has implications for any kind of planned change.

THE CHANGE PROCESS

Inducing change in schools appears to be a task of a considerably different magnitude than inducing change in other types of organizations, for example, a business. Most businesses are in competition with other similar enterprises, and a business that does not succeed in this competition is likely to disappear from the scene. Public schools, on the other hand, are monopolies. Different schools may experience varying degrees of success and there may be considerable dissatisfaction, but the school itself will continue. Another difference, not unrelated to the first, which makes change more difficult in schools than in other settings is that the goals of schools are typically more complex, vague, and difficult to assess. A business, for example, must have a goal of making enough money to stay afloat or, even better, of making a profit. In order to do this, it must produce a product or a service of sufficient attractiveness and quality at a price people are willing to pay. Businesses that fail to pay attention to these objectives, or that are unable to attain them, are unlikely to survive.

Schools, due to their monopolistic nature and to the captive nature of their clientele, are not required to sharpen their goals or to provide an attractive product. Whereas a business undergoes a stringent form of evaluation when it issues a profit and loss statement, schools are not subject to such an objective scrutiny of their performance. Some may feel that this view does not take into account the accreditation process that many schools undergo. Such processes appear related more to art than to science (House, 1978) and almost never examine the extent to which a school achieves its objectives and, in fact, typically don't even look to see if there are objectives.

The school, then, is a unique institution, and its uniqueness must be examined in order to understand how deliberate change can be implemented successfully. Baldridge, Curtis, Ecker, and Riley (1978) postulate six conditions in schools that have a direct relationship to the process of change. These conditions include the following:[1]

1. Inactivity prevails. This point has already been made. Relatively few school personnel see a need for change and even fewer are committed to bringing such change about. School personnel typically expect to do tomorrow whatever they did today. True, curriculum committees may examine new texts, but this often is due to the fact that the old ones are worn out and not to any desire to institute fundamental curricular revision. Even in those cases where the change to be made is only in a text, there is, experience suggests, often heavy resistance.
2. Participation in school affairs is fluid. Interest tends to be in specific issues that affect day-to-day functioning rather than in broad issues that affect the school and its personnel as a whole. The result is that individuals tend to focus on narrow concerns of immediate interest, to maintain an interest in these issues until they are resolved (most often until they are buried) and not to participate in, or have an interest in participating in, broader, deeper, more important issues.
3. Fragmented interest groups exist. Administrators, teachers, and guidance personnel often appear to view themselves as having differentiated concerns. While this a long-standing situation, it appears to have been exacerbated by collective bargaining. This we–they feeling often results in available time and energy being spent on the resolution of differences rather than on determination of common goals and purposes leading to improved education for children. The situation with

---

1. The headings are Baldridge's. The descriptive paragraphs are elaborations of his postulates.

guidance specialists is even more complicated since, while they may be viewed as a group by teachers and administrators, in actuality school counselors, school psychologists, and school social workers consider themselves to be independent entities. They often appear to disagree with each other on questions of turf as well as other issues. The concept of a unified pupil personnel services organization, as Penny (1969) told us, died aborning.

4. Conflict is normal. This is a fact of life that school personnel and guidance professionals in particular find almost impossible to accept. There is a general notion that stable, competent, well-meaning professionals shouldn't need to disagree with each other. When such conflict arises, as it inevitably must, there is a tendency to deny its existence by ignoring it.

5. Authority is limited. Management in schools is from the top down. School boards determine policy. Superintendents and their staff determine the implementation of that policy. While day-to-day management may be left to principals, they are limited in the scope of their authority by board policy and the superintendent's interpretation of that policy. Teachers have long recognized their lack of authority, one result of which has been the growth of teacher unions and collective bargaining. The very existence of contracts specifying working conditions and hours of work constitutes a new limit on administrative authority. Guidance personnel may be at the very bottom of this authority hierarchy. They are vested with no power of authority whatsoever, and their small numbers fail to give them political clout. This problem is heightened in some places by their apparent failure to identify themselves as a separate profession within the school. This failure is manifest in those situations where guidance specialists have opted to join teacher bargaining groups rather than to form their own.

6. External interest groups are important. There can be no mistaking the impact of outside groups on school functioning. School board members, who establish policy for the school as a whole, are elected by the general public. Many of them run on platforms reflecting the interests of relatively narrow constituent groups. The most popular of these relate to money and the use of money in schools. The recall of school board members has become a popular hobby in some U.S. communities reflecting both the heightened awareness of schools and the desire of the public to influence schools. In the local community, parent groups with specific, and often narrow, interests often influence what happens. Demands for alternative schools of one type or another are being implemented as a result of parental pressures. The entire special education movement has as its basic support base the parents of handicapped children. Other even narrower interests exist in specific communities.

At the political level, state and federal legislative bodies have had a profound effect on schools and what they do. Generally these bodies are reacting to some form of dissatisfaction with school functioning.

They may mandate statewide tests for students to assess educational outcomes. They determine criteria employed to certify or license school personnel, and they determine, at bottom, monies available for the conduct of public education.

If these assumptions are correct, they certainly have implications for the change process. At first look, they might appear to be disheartening, but for the guidance specialist interested in creating change, there are also some very positive indications. If inactivity is the normal state of affairs, if participation in matters affecting school programs is fluid, and if interest groups tend to coalesce around narrow issues as opposed to programmatic issues, the situation is made to order for any group of people willing to be active, willing to maintain participation, and willing to focus on issues pertaining to professional services and student outcomes. If conflict is normal, then such change agent groups must accept it as such, difficult as they may be, and anticipate opposition both within and outside of their ranks as they attempt to implement change. The fact that authority is limited suggests that efforts must be made to capture the support of a variety of groups within the school in order to bring change about. The importance of external interest groups cannot be ignored. The groups whose support will be sought will depend mainly on the level at which change is to be effected. If it is at the school level, then a significant external constituent group will be the parents of children in particular schools. If change is sought at a district level, then both parent and public support as well as board support will be important. If change is sought on a broader level, then obviously the support of appropriate legislative and licensing bodies may be needed.

The Guidance Specialist as Change Agent

The idea that a guidance specialist could, or should, function as a change agent within the school system is not new. In 1972, Baker and Cramer specifically suggested that school counselors should function in this kind of role. Others (Ciavarella & Doolittle, 1970; Cook, 1973; Rousseve, 1968; and Shaw, 1973) have at least intimated the desirability of such a role. In 1974, a specific model for the creation of change was proposed (Lewis & Lewis). The idea of the guidance specialist as change agent supports the philosophical positions of Ryan (1971) and Rappaport, Davidson, Wilson, and Mitchell (1975), with respect to viewing the institution, rather than the clients of the institution, as being in need of change.

More recently Shaw (1977) has suggested some fairly specific strategies that might be used to bring about changes in guidance programs. It does not appear, however, that the majority of guidance specialists have taken to heart suggestions that a change agent role is appropriate. The emphasis is still on changing the student to fit the institution rather than making changes that might be desirable in the structure, goals, and functions of the institution itself. Guidance specialists appear, like other educational role groups, to respond basically to demands from outside the profession rather than attempting to influence what they do from inside.

Certain differences exist among counselors, psychologists, and social workers in the school setting. Some of these differences have implications for the implementation of change. One salient difference is the organizational context within which each of these specialists tends to work. Counselors usually (not, by any means, always) tend to find themselves working at the secondary level with one or more counselor colleagues. Psychologists and social workers tend to work at the elementary level. In addition, these latter two professions tend to work individually rather than as members of a staff of two or more professionals at the same school.

These differences have some significance for how change can be effected. Psychologists and social workers may be able, as individual entrepreneurs, to effect changes in their own professional behaviors without the concurrence of other school psychologists or social workers. Counselors, on the other hand, will need to work more cooperatively with one another in order to achieve agreed upon changes.

The elementary/secondary difference in the locus of their professional activities also has implications for change. The generally recognized differences in interests and attitudes of elementary and secondary teachers will have a bearing on any change process. Elementary teachers are generally recognized as having a broader interest in the development of the whole child while secondary teachers tend to be considerably more subject matter–oriented. Working with teachers at different levels has implications for what they are likely to support and how that support can be achieved.

Conditions Necessary for Planned Change.

It is obvious that change is undertaken when (and only when) there is recognition of a felt need for change. Such a perceived need may originate within the school, or school system; most of the time, it does not. Change typically occurs when legislative bodies decide to change the requirements for a teaching certificate, change high school graduation requirements, or to provide a free, appropriate public education to all. It would be well to note carefully that the phrase used as the precursor of change was "felt need for change." Such felt needs are not always based on objectively verifiable facts, and sometimes when they are the proposed solutions are essentially untried and therefore unproven.

Our present concern, however, is not with change at a legislative level, but rather with change at a school level. What has been said about felt need for change applies at all levels. At the school level, needs for change appear to be most frequently discussed in the faculty lounge and seldom go beyond that point since they are more in the nature of complaints than reflections on a generalized need for change. The higher in the administrative hierarchy recognition of need for change occurs, the more likely it is to be pursued; within the individual school the role of the principal appears crucial (Aspy

& Roebuck, 1977; Shaw & Rector, 1968). While there is no guarantee that administrative support would lead to success (Atwood, 1964) such support appears to be a crucial ingredient in the implementation of change.

Another variable that seems important in the implementation of change is the development of what one author (Orlich, 1979) has referred to as a "critical mass" of advocates. It is not necessary that this group comprise over 50% of a given population. It is probably more important that such a support group be comprised of individuals who have the respect of others and who are willing to undertake the work involved in bringing change about. The main work involved will be the development of a plan. A major difference between a complaint on one hand and a perceived need for change on the other is that complainers simply register a protest typically reflecting a personal opinion about something they are against. The individual who wishes to create change will suggest solutions to the problem. These solutions are best embodied in a plan that has the support of a critical mass of individuals and which basically describes what will be done rather than what will not be done. The group presenting such a plan will also suggest how to deal with the inevitable resistance to any programmatic change.

It is generally assumed that change will entail increased expenditures. If this is the case, a proposed change may be foredoomed. We have heard a lot about "throwing money at a problem" and it appears to be true that this does not always result in a better or lasting situation. It appears not only wise but also possible to bring about significant change without the need for increased expenditures in every case. This suggests seeking new and less expensive ways to accomplish ongoing activities so that new (primary preventive) functions can be introduced at no additional cost.

Those who have had experience with soft money projects are often able to speak personally of the difficulty of maintaining change: when the money goes, so do the project activities (Berman & McLaughlin, 1978). If soft money is used to initiate a project, it is clear that the project management must seek ways to build it into the system in such a way that the school will either absorb the cost or in such a way that project functions can be accomplished by existing staff.

Another important strategy for insuring maintenance is to assign specific responsibility for evaluating the change on a systematic basis and to require regularly the provision of a written evaluation report to appropriate persons (e.g., principal, superintendent, and governing board). Such reports should include an evaluation of the extent to which program objectives are being met as well as a specific assessment of the extent to which the policy is and is not being implemented. Such reports hold the potential for becoming pro forma unless continuous efforts are made to make sure that they are data-based.

Methods of Creating Change

The typical approach of guidance specialists to almost any issue, including the issue of change, is what might generally be called a *human relations* approach. This approach has been compared by Baldridge (1972) with what he characterizes as the *political systems* approach. His work will be extensively cited in this section since it seems so appropriate to the question under discussion. He points out that while there is no single human relations approach, there is a thread of consistency that runs through various human relations approaches. These concerns include, "protecting personal values, solving problems of interpersonal relationships, reducing tensions between groups, and developing better methods of resolving conflicts" (p.5). The basic assumption of this approach is that contented cows give more milk, although little substantiation is provided for this point of view.

The human relations approach is, as one might expect, the typical approach of those in the guidance professions. They are concerned with feelings, attitudes, and conflict. There is a basic belief that everyone must agree to everything before any change can be initiated. According to Baldridge, "the prime values held by adherents of the approach seem to be psychological success, the reduction of conflict, the integration of the needs of individuals with the needs of the organization, and an emphasis on human values rather than organizational ones" (p. 6). There appears to be an assumption that what is good for every individual is good for the organization and its effectiveness. The basic techniques of this approach include the use of various kinds of group dynamics such as T-groups, growth groups, counseling procedures, group therapy, and information feedback.

The contrasting approach is characterized by Baldridge (1972) as the *political systems* approach. It differs substantially from the human relations approach. It assumes that conflict is natural between different interest groups and power blocks. It recognizes that in any organization, "small groups of political elites govern most of the major decisions" (p. 8). This latter fact of life has been recognized by Bennis (1966) who suggested that the power structure seldom resembles the formal organizational chart. In the political systems approach, decisions are assumed to be "negotiated compromises" and it is recognized that external interest groups greatly influence the organization.

The political systems approach looks at change from the point of view of values and long-range goals. Further, although Baldridge is not explicit on this point, the organization is viewed by political systems strategists as a *system*. A *system* can be simply defined as a structure that functions as a whole by virtue of the interdependence of its parts (Rapaport, 1968). A political systems approach recognizes this interdependence and takes it into account when change is sought.

■ *A Comparison of the Two Approaches.* The difference between these two approaches is substantial. It can safely be assumed that most guidance specialists are more attracted to the human relations approach than to the political systems approach. The real question, however, is not the attractiveness of these two approaches, but rather the question of which is more effective in the production of change. The human relations approach with its emphasis on feelings and on complete agreement among all parties seems unlikely to produce change in the school setting. Further, note that this approach largely ignores organizational goals. Put in another way, *the human relations approach largely ignores the client population by ignoring the issue of goals.* The population for whom the system presumably exists is not a major concern in the human relations approach since goals are not a major concern.

Some time ago, one of the authors was involved in a study of exemplary guidance programs. An extremely friendly interview was under way with the large counseling staff of a high school that had been nominated as having an outstanding guidance program. As a climax to a rather free interchange that had continued for nearly two hours, the interviewer asked the group, "What is the best thing about your guidance program?" A wide variety of answers, of course, would have been possible. They might have talked about the quality of their individual counseling, the success of some group counseling conducted with severely underachieving students, or a multitude of other services and outcomes. Instead, the initial response was, "The best thing about this program is the people I work with." This set the stage for a 10-minute discussion of how marvelous this group was, and what a pleasure it was to work with them. Not *one* counselor made a comment about the quality of their services or the effectiveness of their outcomes.

It sometimes appears that personal comfort in the professional setting is the most important consideration for guidance specialists. To the extent that this is true, the human relations approach will dominate any attempts at change. To the extent that goals are ignored, conflict may be avoided. Change is unlikely to come about. The political systems approach provides a point of view that will focus on the needs of client populations rather than the needs of guidance staff, and that holds a greater potential for creating change, once there has been a recognition of a need for change.

Implementing Change

A considerable body of literature attests to the fact that change is more likely to be successfully implemented in some situations than in others. What follows is a distillation of those conditions that appear to be relevant to the school situation specifically and, even more specifically, relevant to the type of change in guidance programs that we are discussing. It cannot be denied that there is a certain degree of subjectivity both in the existing body of literature and in the conditions specified here. At the same time, though existing benchmarks are somewhat vague, it appears more appropriate to use them than to ignore them. The first seven headings below are taken from Orlich (1979) while the remaining five are taken from Stolz (1981).

1. *The size of the project is unrelated to its success.* This tends to fit well with the type of change discussed here. Ordinarily, the units involved are small, sometimes consisting of a single person, and often the organizational unit will be an individual school. To the extent that this benchmark is an adequate predictor of successful implementation of change, it bodes well for success.

2. *Innovations which rely heavily on technology tend to be short-lived.* In the main, changes necessary to introduce primary-preventive services do not introduce technological changes requiring new hardware.

3. *The implementation of an innovation is directly related to immediate administrator support.* This suggests clearly that if change is to be brought about in an individual school that it is the principal who is crucial. If change is to be brought about at higher level then the responsible administrator at that level will ideally serve as a source of support. Such support cannot be taken for granted. It must be sought.

4. *There is a need for a critical mass of advocates before an innovation can be implemented.* This has been discussed previously. It should be reiterated that the critical mass is not necessarily a matter of size, but of power.

5. *Directives are seldom effective in stimulating the adoption or implementation of innovations.* Analysis of the program development model should make it clear why this approach cannot work. A much deeper involvement of all parties is required.

6. *Cosmopolitan sources of information tend to increase the probability of diffusion and adoption of innovations.* This condition reinforces two points already made. First, inputs must be sought from a number of different individuals and groups, and second, relevant data bearing on the program and the proposed changes to the program must be collected.

7. *The production of educational innovations and their concommitant acceptance is a political process.* This constitutes an independent reiteration of Baldridge's (1972) point of view. It is an approach that the majority of guidance specialists are unfamiliar with and that many are likely to find offensive. At the same time, it appears there can be little argument about the validity of this position. If change is to be made, politics is part of the process.

8. *The technology [should meet] the continuing mission of the adopting agency.* The word *change* can appropriately be substituted for the word *technology* in this quotation.

9. *The option [should be] proposed by policy makers, rather than by researchers who developed the technology.* Even though the work of planning change should be done by guidance specialists at the grass roots, at the point at which the change is proposed it is most effectively done by someone working at the administrative level.

10. *The intervention [should be] tailored to local conditions.* Planning and implementation of the program development model must begin at the local level. Canned programs, or programs successful elsewhere, will not necessarily be successful in all locations.

11. *Those who will have to implement the program [should be] involved in the preliminary research and in asking for the adoption.* The involve-

ment of grass roots personnel, from the beginning, is necessary to the ultimate adoption of change.

12. *A key person, trained, enthusiastic, and with significant social skills, [should persist] through political infighting to protect the program from going under.* This suggests that change in guidance programs may be initiated by a single individual, and that there is a single individual who will have much to do with the ultimate implementation of proposed changes. Again the reference to politics emphasizes the importance of these kinds of skills.

The Role of Policy in Change

Most guidance personnel will be familiar either with attempts at change that never got off the ground, or with other attempts at change that were extremely short-lived. Experience of this sort has sensitized many to be wary of any suggested or proposed change. They may have already spent time and effort that has resulted in nothing, and are reluctant to do so at further length. One explanation for the failure of innovations in guidance programs to maintain a long life is the informality with which they are introduced. Agreement may be reached among a relatively small segment of the guidance staff that certain new steps should be taken. This is often done without recourse to the use of a program development model, and constitutes a change in function but not in anything else. To further complicate this situation, such change is often not communicated broadly and, more importantly, does not have the status of a change in *policy*. It is important regardless of the level at which change is introduced, (i.e., the school level or the district level) that there be broad and formal recognition that the change has been made and that it is official. At the district level this implies that such change should be a board-adopted policy. At the school level it suggests that it should constitute a written agreement, publicly agreed to by the principal, and disseminated to all members of the school staff and to appropriate administrative officers at higher administrative levels. If change is not treated in this way, then, fundamentally, there is no official commitment to it and it is easier to drift back to whatever was done before or on to the next fad.

The Impact of Administrative Structure on Professional Behavior

The guidance program is basically a subsystem of the larger school system and is dependent in a variety of ways on various aspects of that larger system. At the same time, it can be treated, for purposes of discussion, as a system within itself. The structure of that system can act to either enhance or vitiate the efforts of guidance personnel. Unfortunately, the latter is more often the case than the former. This relationship has been discussed by Aplin (1978) who relates a number of behavioral symptoms to specific structural problems. Table 9-1, taken directly from Aplin's article, specifies these relationships. Note that a majority of the structural problems appearing in Aplin's table are characteristic of guidance programs and guidance personnel. As a matter of fact, there is probably not one of these structural problems that does not characterize guidance specialists in some places. The behavioral results of particular structural problems appear in the second column of this table. And, again, there will be a distinct feeling of familiarity among experienced guidance workers. Many of these behaviors do indeed seem characteristic of various guidance organizations.

The implication of Aplin's approach is basically supportive of the political systems approach: change in the structure of the system will result in a change in behavior. While these views may be difficult for guidance personnel to accept, they appear to reflect a reality that cannot be avoided if change is to come about.

The Role of Data in the Change Process

Most attempts to initiate change in schools appear to come from the heart rather than the head. Perhaps this is one reason they don't succeed. If a change is to be made, there should be some evidence of the need for that change, and that evidence should be as objective as possible. It is difficult to generalize about what kinds of data could be useful. This will depend on the situation. Such information may range from data on how guidance specialists spend their time, the feelings of various groups about guidance services, relevant objective data on student behavior, achievement, or aspirations, to the number of student absences, dropouts, or failures. The point is that in each situation there exists information that if appropriately collected and used will be more impressive than opinion on the desirability of change.

Professional opinions and experience can be brought to bear more effectively when they speak to data than they can in the absence of such information. Time and energy may be required to collect relevant data, but the results are likely to justify the effort. Attempts to introduce change in the absence of data are not as likely to be successful. One cannot help but remark on the difference between education and business in this regard. While many school systems have computers that could be used as management information systems,[2] they are, for the most part, used for storing records, paying bills, and other low-level functions. Business, on the other hand, uses computers for such low-level functions but in addition stores, retrieves, and processes data for purposes of making important management decisions.

The Importance of Power Bases

An issue that is rarely confronted squarely by guidance specialists is the need to establish and use power bases. Perhaps this is due to their (naive)

---

2. "A management information system is a system for collecting, sorting, retrieving, and processing information that is used, or desired, by one or more managers in the performance of their duties" (Ein-dor & Segev, 1978, p. 16).

Table 9-1
Structural Problems and Their Major or Most Likely Related Behavioral Manifestations

Structural Problems	Behavioral Manifestation/Symptom
1. Excessively differentiated and autonomous units/departments	1. Intergroup rivalry and conflict Communication barriers Self- or organizationally imposed isolation of units "We–they" attitude and comments Absence of cooperative efforts
2. Tightly structured operating guidelines and policies	2. Apathy–boredom Low levels of commitment Frustration–hostility Lowered self-image Subversion attempts
3. Inflexible and overly monitored externally imposed control systems	3. Low risk-taking behaviors Tension–stress High job dissatisfaction Supervisor–subordinate conflict Employee complaints/grievances
4. Reward systems not linking results/performance to compensation/promotion or penalty	4. Low rates of productivity Lack of commitment to work High job dissatisfaction Excessive need for supervision-direction
5. Lack of specific organizational goals and/or employee knowledge of goals	5. Constant effort to define "mission" Frequent shifting of priorities on projects Disagreement/conflicts over strategies Reluctance of employees to set goals Many false starts with MBO
6. Narrow career paths and bureaucratic rules on promotion and advancement	6. Personal conflicts over career goals Stress-related illnesses Personal feelings of being underutilized Loss of high-potential employees
7. Ambiguous role/job descriptions or poorly designed/implemented appraisal programs	7. On-job tension and stress Low rates of productivity Supervisory–subordinate conflict Subordinates seeking recognition and reinforcement Complaints of management uncertainty
8. Narrowly designed jobs requiring limited range of employee skills/talents	8. Lack of initiative Necessity of imposing tight controls Apathy–boredom Efforts to beat the system

Note. From "Structural Change vs. Behavioral Change" by J. C. Aplin, 1978, *Personnel and Guidance Journal, 56,* pp. 407–411. Copyright 1978 by American Association for Counseling and Development. Reprinted by permission.

belief that they are in the business of helping others and that they will be recognized and rewarded for their good intentions. If this is the case, it does not appear to have worked very well thus far. It is possible that there may also be a confusion between the concept of power bases and public relations

(PR). Unfortunately, the PR concept smacks more of Madison Avenue and advertising hype than it does of solid professional accomplishment. There is apparently a belief in some quarters that guidance specialists are simply not being recognized for the solid contributions that they make to education. Use of the PR approach is not likely to do much more than increase whatever cynicism may already be felt about the role of guidance in education.

If Baldridge (1972) is correct about the importance of the interaction of a system with its environment, and if the idea of requiring a "critical mass of advocates" (Orlich, 1979) is likewise accurate, then it appears that guidance specialists who wish to bring about real change in what they do must effectively seek the support of persons outside of their professional groups. For purposes of this discussion, a power base is considered to be a group of people—not necessarily tightly organized—who are able, when they choose, to have an effect on the policy or direction of the school. Such individuals need not have administrative power; they may often be individuals whose opinions are listened to and respected by their colleagues. Such a group becomes a critical mass at the point when it can actually influence a specific action or policy.

The development of such a group is possibly more difficult for guidance specialists than for any other professional group within the school. They do not possess the authority role of administrators, nor do they have the power of organized teacher groups due to lack of numbers. As Cook (1973) has pointed out, the counselor does not have any legitimate power base stemming from an authority role. Faced with the need to develop a power base in order to implement change and the fact that guidance specialists have neither the authority of administration nor the power of numbers, how can effective power bases be built? Unfortunately, there is not a body of research to fall back on with respect to this question. Guidance specialists have paid little or no attention to the development of real political power. There are, however, some steps that can be taken that appear to make sense and that will lead to the development of effective power bases. Perhaps a first step is to study specific situations in which change is to be made in order to determine the *real* power structure. In most places, any correspondence between publicly announced administrative structure and an actual decision making process is usually quite limited (Cook, 1973). The basic questions to be answered include a determination of the process by which decisions are usually made in a particular setting as well as the identification of individuals whose opinions are either sought or, whether sought or not, have an impact, positive or negative, on final decisions. Such mundane questions as who eats lunch together, who sits together at faculty meetings, who is listened to at faculty meetings, and what unofficial processes take place outside formal decision making channels are the kinds of questions that need to be asked. Most experienced educators recognize the existence of such an informal network of power. This network needs to be identified and people in the network need to be lobbied and their help enlisted when change is to be proposed.

Additional Steps Toward Effectiveness

Beyond such political efforts, however, guidance specialists must make other efforts in their own behalf. These efforts are fundamentally in the professional, as opposed to the political, domain. If a system is, as we have defined it, a structure that functions as a whole by virtue of the interdependence of its parts and if guidance is a subsystem of the total system, and if, further, the major (school) system might continue to function as a whole even with the subtraction of the guidance subsystem, then it can be said that the guidance subsystem is not a genuine part of the whole. While it cannot be asserted that the whole could function adequately with the subtraction of the guidance subsystem, it nevertheless appears to be a deepseated *belief* among certain power groups that guidance may not be required for the system to function adequately. No amount of PR is likely to overcome this belief. We must look for deeper causes and suggest remedies.

There appear to be two interrelated variables that may add to the belief that the guidance subsystem is unnecessary to the effective functioning of the main system. First, it is a generally accepted fact that services provided by guidance specialists are almost invisible. Counselors spend much of their time in their offices behind closed doors counseling individual students; psychologists spend much time behind closed doors testing students; school social workers are not only out of sight in the school, they are often not in the school at all. It is to overcome this lack of visibility that PR approaches are generally suggested. What seems true, however, is that simply telling people about what is done is unlikely to bring about a ground swell of support from other groups. What seems necessary is that guidance specialists change what they do. For example, the provision of relevant and effective in-services to teachers or relevant and effective programs to groups of parents would result in considerably heightened visibility, and it is this general type of approach, rather than advertising what currently is done, that is likely to result in an improvement in the power bases of guidance specialists.

Closely related to the problem of visibility is the issue of perceived effectiveness. The word *perceived* is important in this context. It is possible for guidance specialists to be highly effective, but if others are either not aware of this (as they might not be when the number dealt with is small) or if they do not value the changes that take place, then perceived effectiveness may be low. Perceived effectiveness is also related to the kinds of populations that receive most of the services of guidance specialists. In general, these populations tend to be small and, in addition, they often tend to be populations where the hope for success is not high. Given these two strikes, the chances for being perceived as effective is considerably diminished. To overcome these problems, it seems clear that services must be offered to a broader spectrum of the population, that some services should be provided directly to adult groups such as teachers and parents, that services provided should be viewed as relevant by the recipients and that some services should be provided to groups where the hope of change is high. These are strong arguments for primary-preventive services.

Closely related to the issues of visibility and perceived effectiveness is the idea of tangibility of services. One of the authors was talking in the hall of a large high school with an experienced counselor at class break. A teacher came by and thanked the counselor for sending to her a copy of the achievement test scores of all the children in one of her classes. She then added, "That's the first thing a counselor has ever done for me," and walked on. It was not intended as a slight, rather as a compliment, but the counselor was, understandably, speechless. The list of test scores, however, was tangible. Other services that the counselor might have provided were perhaps not only invisible but intangible as well. Guidance specialists need to think in terms of how they can provide useful, visible, and tangible services to individuals and groups who comprise potential power bases.

It is the nature and type of our professional contributions that, most fundamentally, render us suspect and leave us powerless. It therefore appears that these must change. This places guidance professionals in the middle of a paradox. Power bases are necessary to induce change. Power bases are built, in part at least, on the provision of services that may not presently be offered and that require change in order to make them available. The solution to the dilemma is to begin the development of power bases through the political process, introducing changes in services that lead to higher visibility and greater perceived effectiveness, which should, in turn, strengthen power bases. A highly interlocking process, to be sure.

THE PROGRAM DEVELOPMENT APPROACH

Much of what has been said to this point can be integrated into and synthesized with what is often called a program development approach. In attempting to introduce new functions, in this case primary-preventive ones, one has the choice of simply attempting to add some functions and subtract others, or of looking at the whole guidance program and attempting to shape it in such a way that the new (primary-preventive) functions will have a long-term rather than a short-term place and in such a way that the fit of the new functions with the total program can be understood by all. The program development approach is presented here because it is systematic, because relevant parts of it can be used, and because it addresses the role of primary prevention in the *total* guidance program.

A Definition of a Program

A program consists of four interrelated components. These are (a) a rationale, (b) a set of goals and objectives, (c) a description of the functions that will lead to the accomplishment of the goals and objectives, and (d) a description of the evaluation strategies to be used to determine whether goals and objectives have been accomplished (Shaw, 1977).

■ *The Rationale.* The first step in program development is to resolve certain value considerations. This is an easy step to bypass and, in fact, this is what most often happens. Values are often considered euphemistic or irrelevant, but in fact it is failure to consider basic value issues that leads to the growth of unrelated (and perhaps irrelevant) constellations of guidance services rather than integrated programs.

The most basic value question is, who are guidance services for? Viewing all of the guidance professions broadly, it appears that the bulk of such services are being provided to the relatively small segment of the population which has the greatest need. This is not wrong. However, there is still a relatively meaningless philosophical adherence to the concept that guidance services are (or ought to be) for all children. Until a specific, concrete, public decision is made to that effect, it is certain that most available services will go to relatively few children. If the decision is made that guidance services *are* for all children, then it becomes clear that ways must be sought to provide primary, secondary, and tertiary services. In other words, means must be sought to provide a *balanced* guidance program.

A second value consideration, which may seem obvious, has to do with the effectiveness of guidance services. While schools have theoretically entered the age of accountability, guidance services have lagged considerably in this regard. Analyses of cost effectiveness or cost benefits would be extremely difficult to carry out and possibly embarrassing if they were. The situation suggests that there has not been a philosophical commitment to effectiveness and that such a commitment is necessary.

If the decision is made that guidance services should *effectively* reach *all* children, then two consequences must follow. One is that there now exists a reason for the inclusion of *primary-preventive* services since it is through these services that the largest number of children can be reached effectively. A second consequence is that guidance staff are fundamentally committed at that point to following through on the rest of the program development model, since it is through this means that interrelated objectives, services, and subsequent evaluation can be established.

Relevant local circumstances as well as appropriate data can be used to buttress arguments for the proposed program. The main point is that the rationale should clearly and concisely state the commitment and direction of the proposed program and provide the most potent arguments available for the directions selected. Its purpose is not only to give direction to the guidance program but also to provide convincing arguments to those whose approval may be necessary.

■ *Goals and Objectives.* Following development of the rationale (and *only* following its development) it is possible to proceed with the development of the goals and objectives of the proposed program. The term *goals* is most often used to signify a broad outcome while the term *objectives* usually refers to a more restricted anticipated outcome. The most important thing about both of these items is that they describe the behaviors that *children* are expected to show following the activities of guidance professionals. This is not to say that the behaviors of teachers or parents, following provision of indirect services by guidance professionals, are not important—they are. This, however, is an *intermediate* step, and it is important to determine whether what teachers and parents have learned is being utilized and, if it is, whether it is having the anticipated effect on children's behavior.

It is important to state objectives in specific and behavioral terms. Failure to do so at this point is likely to make evaluation of outcomes (determination of effectiveness) either ineffective or too costly. There are some criteria that can be used to judge the adequacy of objectives. These include the following:

1. Objectives should be stated in clear and unequivocal terms. The use of ordinary professional jargon, while perhaps alright for interpersonal communication among guidance professionals, is inappropriate when dealing with objectives. Such terms as self-understanding, wise decision making, or adjustment need to be translated to agreed-upon behaviors.
2. Objectives for guidance services should be related to the generally accepted purposes of public education. A major problem experienced by guidance specialists results from the inability of other significant groups to comprehend how our efforts are related to the generally understood purposes of education. Objectives should be stated in such a way that individuals from these groups will readily understand our involvement in the general educational process and, further, understand that our intent is to support and complement their efforts.
3. Objectives should be capable of accomplishment. We should not present an impossible wish list of all possible objectives. If we do so, it is most likely that our evaluation will indicate failure to achieve any of them.
4. Objectives should imply unique and professional services. It is important to note that objectives never describe functions. At the same time, objectives should clearly suggest that the functions necessary to achieve them are unique to the guidance professions and that they require a different and professional level of training to carry out; guidance specialists too often appear to become involved in irrelevant, subprofessional or quasiadministrative activities.

■ *Functions.* A function describes a professional activity of a guidance specialist. There is considerable confusion, at times, between functions and objectives. Counseling, assessment, and home visits are all functions. To cast them into a different form, such as "to provide counseling," does not convert them into objectives. Any statement that describes an *activity* conducted by a guidance specialist refers to a function.

The normal procedure in developing programs or in considering program changes is to ask, "What should we do?" The program development model suggests this is not the appropriate place to begin but is the third, rather than the first, step in the process. Professionals tend to begin with functions because it is the easiest place to begin; it requires less thought than beginning elsewhere. At the same time, it is also probably the most self-defeating place to begin. It is unlikely that there will be any agreement on the question "What should we do?" The variety of functions is too great to permit of such a solution. Further, the tendency would be to attempt to provide such a smorgasbord of functions that none of them would be effective and, in the last analysis, effectiveness would be impossible to measure since anticipated outcomes had not been described.

To repeat: Functions cannot logically be considered until values and objectives have been established. Functions must reflect objectives and must, in the eye of the ordinary beholder, be clearly related to objectives.

In the present case, we are assuming that there will be three kinds of functions: (a) functions leading to the delivery of primary-preventive services, (b) functions leading to the delivery of remedial services (secondary prevention), and (c) functions leading to the delivery of therapeutic services (tertiary prevention).

▪ *Evaluation.* Evaluation refers, most importantly, to the determination of whether or not *objectives* have been achieved. Most evaluations do not do this. Rather they tend to be determinations of the amount and types of services offered. If programs do not have objectives, this evaluation of functions is essentially all that can be done. It must be stressed that evaluations dealing only with functions are completely unable to address the issue of *effectiveness*. Thus, the criterion of accountability is essentially unmet. *The fact that most guidance programs are in this position is probably one of the greatest factors contributing to continuing questions about the need for guidance services in schools.*

Evaluation must be treated as a process, not (as is usually the case) as an event. The evaluation process must be structured in such a way that minimum amounts of time and money are required. To the greatest extent possible, the acquisition and analysis of evaluation data should be a subprofessional responsibility, under professional oversight.

Most evaluations of guidance services also depend heavily on soft data. *Soft data* are represented by opinions of any kind from any population. The reason that soft data are so frequently used is that in the absence of objectives there is very little that can be done except to turn to people's opinions. The opinions of teachers, administrators, parents, and others are obviously important but opinions do not reflect effectiveness and it is effectiveness that is of prime concern. *Hard data* are reflected by such criteria as test scores, attendance, tardiness, number and cost of incidents of vandalism, and other verifiable criteria.

Soft data do play a part in program evaluation, but in a secondary rather than a primary role. The positive opinion of certain groups is essential to our continued effectiveness. If significant numbers of teachers, administrators, parents, and others consider us as essentially unnecessary or ineffective, our longevity in the school system is likely to be short. Therefore, the opinions of groups such as these need to be sought. Other kinds of data, although countable, do not constitute evidence of effectiveness, but they, too, are of some significance. For example, information on the time utilization of guidance specialists. This latter type of information may strike some as a bit superfluous and unnecessary, but the interesting thing is that guidance staffs are often unable to describe in concrete terms how they spend their time and, on occasion, are even mistaken about the basic thrust of their efforts. On one occasion, one of the authors was consulting with a group of elementary school counselors who intended to provide primary-preventive services. An analysis indicated that they had failed to meet their primary-preventive objectives. Fortunately, each of the 10 counselors involved had been required to keep systematic track of their time utilization on a daily basis. Analysis of this data indicated that they had drifted into a mode of service provision (in this case assessment) that was fundamentally unrelated to their most important objectives. Possession of this information permitted a correction to be made where, without it, everyone would have been guessing as to the reasons for failure to meet objectives, and a reasonable solution would have been impossible.

There is nothing complicated about the program development model. This is not to say that implementation of it may not be difficult. It goes against the "natural" tendencies of guidance specialists *not* to begin with the consideration of functions. Further, dealing with the issues of values and objectives will be time-consuming and school personnel often appear to consider time spent in planning to be wasted. Perhaps this is so because so much time is spent in planning that ultimately bears no fruit. Use of a program development model and of other approaches suggested in this chapter will help to ensure that professional time spent in program planning will not be wasted. Program development can be conceptualized as a system, with feedback from evaluation to the objectives phase providing data on which to base potential program change.

> In collecting and utilizing evaluation information we close the circle that began with the formulation of objectives. Appropriate evaluation plans can only occur after values, objectives, and functions have been established. The main purposes of program evaluation are to provide information that will describe the extent to which program objectives have been achieved and which will assist in restructuring the program, should that prove necessary. (Shaw, 1977, p. 341)

The Individual as a "Program"

The discussion in this chapter has, up to this point at least, inferred that when program changes are discussed, we are talking about a group of guidance specialists. In the best of all possible worlds this would indeed be the case, and it is likely to be the case when it is secondary school counseling that is under consideration. On the other hand, school psychologists, school social workers, and elementary school counselors often function as individuals rather than as groups. Their assignments are to specific individual schools and they may be the only person representing their particular profession at a particular school. It would be easy, therefore, to assume that what has been said about the implementation of primary prevention, about the program development model, and about the conditions necessary for implementing change is not relevant. This is not the case. It is perfectly appropriate to consider the individual guidance specialist in such a situation as a program. The basic rules that apply to program change with respect to staffs of professionals apply equally to individuals who want to change their programs. The same political factors are at work and the same needs for proceeding carefully, for planning, and for visibility are applicable. In some ways, change under these conditions is easier; in some ways it is more difficult. It is easier because negotiations among fellow guidance specialists will not be necessary. The individual may decide (within limits) what he or she wants to do, and the major negotiations will be between the individual who constitutes the "program" and the power figures in each school. It may be more difficult from the point of view that if a psychologist or social worker has multiple schools for which they are responsible, a common situation, then there may need to be as many different negotiations as there are schools.

PUTTING IT ALL TOGETHER

With the preceding background it is possible to put together a step-by-step approach to the introduction of primary-preventive approaches. In one sense, what follows constitutes a commonsense approach but one that is based on the best available research and opinion about the introduction and implementation of change. Not all steps will be required in all phases and these suggestions should be modified to fit specific situations. Some may feel there is such a readiness for the introduction to primary prevention that the first step is simply to get it going. If so, well and good, but such places are likely to be rare. If changes to be introduced are minor then the entire program which follows would be very much of an overkill. If however, the changes to be introduced are substantial, then the steps that follow, perhaps in modified form, are likely to be necessary.

It has already been recognized that many school psychologists and school social workers work independently, rather than as members of a coordinated staff. Such professionals may feel that what is proposed here is too elaborate a view of their autonomous work situation. If there is less formality and more freedom in these situations, then such a perception may be accurate. On the other hand, it is probably true that even though the "program" may consist of a single individual the steps suggested here are nearly all necessary. It is true, of course, that the professional who works individually does not need to arbitrate changes with fellow professionals. To this extent, the task of the individual is simpler than that of professionals who constitute a staff and who must agree with each other, as well as get agreement from those outside of their profession.

Step One

The obvious first step is that the decision must be made to introduce primary prevention as a legitimate part of the professional services of a particular staff or guidance specialist. This may be the decision of an individual who already perceives the need or it may be that of a group of individuals. In any event, it is clear that some individual or group must begin with an advocacy position on the introduction of such services.

Step Two

Once the decision has been made that primary-preventive services should be introduced, it is necessary to create a perceived need on the part of other persons who bear a relationship to guidance services, either as recipients, as supervisors, or as interested bystanders. This approach may smack of Madison Avenue to some, which is completely understandable. Nevertheless, there must be a heightened awareness that significant kinds of guidance services are not currently being offered and, as a result, the program is less effective than it otherwise could be. There are, basically, two phases to the development of a perceived need in others. The first is educational. Informal discussions with teachers, administrators, parent groups or others whose support would be helpful must take place. These discussions may be in the faculty lounge, over lunch, in the hallway, or wherever ordinary contacts between guidance specialists and others in the school take place. If interest is expressed by several teachers, it might be suggested to the principal that a short segment of a faculty meeting be devoted to an explanation of primary prevention and a description of some of the kinds of services that would be provided. Similarly, informal discussions with parent leaders as well as more formal presentations to organized parent groups provide other important ways of increasing the awareness of constituent groups of the need for primary-preventive services.

The second phase of developing a perceived need is the use of data. In most cases this means that appropriate data must be collected. Such data might reflect the way in which guidance specialists currently spend their time, including information on the professionalism and uniqueness of present services. The data might also reflect information on the number of children effectively reached and on perceptions of current services held by teachers, parents, and administrators. The uses of such data would be to demonstrate that a significant type of service was missing, that current services reached relatively few children effectively, and that some guidance specialists are currently required to spend a considerable proportion of their time in the provision of subprofessional services. The basic intent is, of course, to demonstrate that the introduction of primary-preventive services would help to remedy these situations.

Step Three

This step involves seeking support from specific individuals or groups for the idea of examining the possibility of providing primary-preventive services. This phase of the process will be going on at the same time as the

attempt to develop a perceived need for primary-preventive services. Its major purpose is to begin to develop the critical mass of advocates (Orlich, 1979) needed to gain ultimate acceptance of the introduction of primary-preventive services. Guidance specialists will, at this juncture, identify and begin to use existing power bases in the school.

It is important to seek and win administrator support. One study (Shaw & Rector 1968) of schools where teacher group discussions were going to be held with voluntary teacher participants on matters of professional concern to teachers suggested that there was a difference between active and passive administrative support. The participation of teachers was significantly higher in schools where administrators backed the project with such words as "I think this is a good idea and hope you will participate," than in schools where administrators merely introduced the idea by such statements as, "Here is someone to tell you about a new program." If a brief presentation is to be made to a school staff and if the principal is known to be supportive, then the principal should actually be coached about the importance of his or her public support and how to deliver it.

Step Four

As steps one through three are in the process of being successfully accomplished it is appropriate to begin to put together a specific group of individuals who are willing to serve as a planning group. In the best of all possible worlds the appropriate administrator (e.g., principal of the school, director of guidance, or superintendent of schools) will (a) give official endorsement to the group, (b) call the group together for the first meeting, (c) ask the group to produce a written plan to be ready at a specific time, and (d) guarantee that the final document will be fully considered by appropriate groups, for example, administrative council, governing board, and so forth.

Since this is a task-oriented group, its size and composition are important. If the plan to be developed is for a relatively small single school, the development group should be smaller (about three people) than if the plan were for a larger school (requiring about five people). If the plan is to be developed for a district, the issue of *representation* becomes important. Groups whose approval will ultimately be needed should all be included, in such a case; at a minimum, teachers, administrators, and guidance specialists should be included. Serious thought will need to be given to the possibility of also including parent representatives. Generally speaking, it is unwise to expand a working group beyond about seven individuals. A larger group than that makes for less personal involvement, less feeling of obligation to participate and, more importantly, less of a need to produce a product, and therefore risks the outcome of the entire enterprise.

The selection of specific individuals to comprise the working group is extremely important. The individuals with the greatest vested interest in the positive outcomes of this group's work should exercise influence to ensure that persons selected for this committee are those who are supportive of the introduction of primary-preventive functions. This view will perhaps shock a number of people, but if the goal is to introduce change and the use of primary-preventive services into the guidance program, steps to ensure accomplishment of that goal should be taken.

Step Five

Following formation of the working group, the next task is to organize the group, set its task, and proceed to the accomplishment of this task. The chair of the group should be a guidance person firmly in favor of introducing primary-preventive services. The task of the group is to develop a program using the outline of the program development model, including a rationale, statements of objectives, descriptions of functions, and an evaluation plan. It will be necessary for the chair to insist that steps be taken in sequential order.

The plan will also need to include a consideration of other issues. For example, if it is necessary or desirable to cease providing certain functions presently offered the plan will need to address itself specifically to these issues and, if the functions are deemed necessary to the operation of the school (e.g., scheduling students into classes), then the plan must propose alternative solutions (e.g., computer-assisted scheduling or arena-type registration). In addition, the plan must include a description of how new proposed functions will be phased in and how current functions will (if necessary) be phased out. Generally speaking, it is wise to phase high visibility functions in first so that others can literally see a new program in operation. Functions with lower visibility can be phased in at a later date.

Step Six

It is necessary to ensure that other groups with a legitimate interest in, and potential control over, changes in the guidance program are kept abreast of developments as they occur. For this purpose, the committee should make certain that copies of progress reports are periodically given to members of such groups. These groups certainly include other guidance specialists, teachers, and administrators. In some situations they may include parents or at least the members of organized parent groups.

At the time the committee completes its task, it is important to make a public presentation of the work of the committee to interested and affected groups. Again, these will include other guidance specialists, administrators, teachers, and possibly parents. Presentations should be made in such a way as to invite comment, criticism, and suggestions for change. Whether or not such suggestions are adopted will be for the committee to decide, but there should be opportunity for input from persons outside the working group itself.

When the final report is ready, it should be presented to the appropriate person (e.g., the principal) or group (e.g., a school board). The intent is to ensure a *formal* adoption of the document as *policy* so that the program has both official recognition and the means for ensuring its being carried out. It should be emphasized that the program must be a *mandate*. Individual guidance specialists (e.g., members of a counseling staff) do not have the option of going along or not going along with the program.

Step Seven

Formal adoption of the program does not ensure that it will be enacted, or if enacted that it will have a long life. Additional steps will be necessary. The first of these is built into the program proposal. This is the evaluation component. The process of evaluation should be initiated immediately. A focus on program outcomes will help to make certain that those who implement the program focus on the activities necessary to assure its success. A written annual evaluation report should be required and submitted to appropriate administrators. Such a report will help to reinforce the idea that there are expected outcomes and that services are focusing on the achievement of those outcomes.

The second necessary ingredient to ensure program implementation and longevity is the presence of an enthusiastic and committed supporter of the program who is in a position to ensure appropriate outcomes. In the case of a one-person program, it is obvious who this will need to be. In the case of programs involving several individuals it will, in the best circumstances, be a person with some administrative responsibilities such as a head counselor, director of guidance, director of pupil personnel services, or someone with a similar position.

A Brief Concluding Word

What is proposed here is neither simple nor easy. Variations from place to place make it impossible to insist that these seven steps be followed in detail or in some precise order. They do, however, contain the basic ingredients necessary to bring about and to ensure change. And while they are in some degree of a commonsense variety, they also reflect substantially what we know about the introduction and maintenance of change. Knowledge of the change process, commitment to change, and, in this instance, commitment to the idea of primary prevention are probably the most vital ingredients in this process. They are the basic building blocks on which the introduction and maintenance of primary-preventive processes into the school setting will depend.

REFERENCES

Aplin, J. C. (1978). Structural change vs. behavioral change. *Personnel and Guidance Journal, 56,* 407–411.

Aspy, D. N., & Roebuck, F. M. (1977). *Kids don't learn from people they don't like.* Amherst, MA: Human Resource Development Press.

Atwood, M. S. (1964). Small scale administrative change: Resistance to the introduction of a high school guidance program. In M. B. Miles (Ed.), *Innovation in Education (pp.49–77).* New York: Bureau of Publications, Teachers College, Columbia University.

Baker, S. B., & Cramer, S. H. (1972). Counselor or change agent: Support from the profession. *Personnel and Guidance Journal, 50,* 661–665.

Baldridge, J. V. (1972). Organizational change: The human relations perspective versus the political systems perspective. *Educational Researcher, 1 (2),* 4–15.

Baldridge, J. V., Curtis, D. V., Ecker, G., & Riley, G. L. (1978). *Policy making and effective leadership: A national study of academic management.* San Francisco: Jossey–Bass.

Bennis, W. (1966). *Changing organizations.* New York: McGraw–Hill.

Berman, P., & McLaughlin, M. W. (1978). *Rethinking the federal role in education.* Santa Monica, CA: Rand.

Ciavarella, M. A., & Doolittle, L. W. (1970). The ombudsman: Relevant role model for the counselor. *School Counselor, 17,* 331–336.

Cook, D. R. (1973, February). The counselor and the power structure. *Focus on Guidance.*

Ein-Dor, P., & Segev, E. (1978). *Managing management information systems.* Lexington, MA: Lexington Books.

House, E. R. (1978). Assumptions underlying evaluation models. *Educational Researcher, 7 (3),* 4–12.

Lewis, M. D., & Lewis, J. A. (1974). A schematic for change. *Personnel and Guidance Journal, 52,* 320–323.

Orlich, D. C. (1979). Federal educational policy: The paradox of innovation and centralization. *Educational Researcher, 8* (7), 4–9.

Penny, J. F. (1969). Student personnel work: A profession stillborn. *Personnel and Guidance Journal, 47,* 958–962.

Rapaport, A. (1968). The promise and pitfalls of information theory. In W. Buckley (Ed.), *Modern systems research for the behavioral scientist (pp. 137–140).* Chicago: Aldine.

Rappaport, J., Davidson, W. S., Wilson, M. N., & Mitchell, A. (1975). Alternatives to blaming the victim or the environment: Our places to stand have not moved the earth. *American Psychologist, 30,* 525–528.

Rousseve, R. J. (1968). The role of the counselor in a free society. *School Counselor, 16,* 6–10.

Ryan, W. (1971). *Blaming the victim.* New York: Random House.

Shaw, M. C. (1973). *School guidance systems.* Boston: Houghton Mifflin.

Shaw, M. C. (1977). The development of counseling programs: Priorities, progress and professionalism. *Personnel and Guidance Journal, 55,* 339–345.

Shaw, M. C., & Rector, W. H. (1968). *Modification of the school environment through intervention with significant adults.* Chico: California State University, Interprofessional Research Commission on Pupil Personnel Services, Western Regional Center.

Stolz, S. B. (1981). Adoption of innovations from applied behavioral research: "Does anybody care?" *Journal of Applied Behavior Analysis, 14,* 491–505.

A MENU OF SUGGESTIONS FOR K–12 PRIMARY PREVENTION PROGRAMMING

The proposals made in this chapter are offered somewhat tentatively because a task of this nature requires that the proponents meet several assumptions that we are unable to address. In the real world, planners will understand the communities in which they are working, the faculty and staff in the educational institutions, the existing instructional goals, and the needs of the student population.

While realizing that the suggestions made are not founded on assessments of local conditions, we still think that the content of this chapter can serve a useful purpose. The suggestions represent a prototype of how primary prevention programming might be accomplished; and, as such, can serve as a resource for readers. This structure may provide food for thought, raise questions that require resolution before programming is initiated, and suggest strategies for making operational the information found in earlier chapters.

An alternative to the menu presented herein that we considered was to offer the readers our own K–12 prevention program proposal. That idea was abandoned when we realized that the results of our efforts would be a prescription that represented only the biases of the authors of this book. To do so would saddle our readers with a singular program design and restrict their thinking. Table 10-1 presents all of the programmatic ideas that were reviewed in earlier chapters in a manner designed to enhance reader decision making while promoting a process of selecting programs according to one's own needs and interests.

ASSUMPTIONS FOR THE PROTOTYPE

Although unable to conceive of assumptions for specific institutional settings, we were able to derive assumptions on which a generalized prototype for primary prevention programming might be designed. First, we are assuming that basic education is founded on the principle that there should be a balance between emphases on cognitive and affective goals. As such, students need classroom instruction that enhances both their cognitive and affective development. Of course, the primary prevention prototype developed in this chapter focuses the reader's attention on affective goals and programming. We assume that the traditionally strong emphasis on cognitive goals from other sources will continue and are not concerned about an overemphasis on the affective domain. In fact, given the national state of mind in the mid-1980s, we are indeed concerned about an overemphasis on the cognitive domain, viewing our effort as a timely reminder of the necessity for a balanced approach to curriculum design.

Second, it is assumed that there is an interactive effect between the characteristics of the learning environment in the school and home and the amount and quality of cognitive learning that occurs. Learning environments can facilitate or inhibit learning. A facilitative learning environment will result in more and better cognitive learning; an inhibiting learning environment will actually retard cognitive development. The intent of indirect, primary-preventive approaches is to improve the learning environment. This may be done through attempts to change parent and teacher behaviors by providing them with improved skills (see chapters 2, 3, 4, 5, & 6) or by changing the organization of learning and the structure of the environment (see chapter 7).

Third, it is assumed that much of what constitutes a facilitative learning environment depends on the affective characteristics of that environment that are created by teachers and parents. It is a fundamental responsibility of guidance specialists to assist teachers and parents to develop skills and behaviors that will promote the positive conditions leading to maximum cognitive and personal growth in children. This requires a positive, effective, cooperative relationship between guidance personnel and both teachers and parents.

A fourth assumption is that administrators will attempt to create an environment in which both affective and cognitive goals can be achieved. For example, curriculum planning and master scheduling will be conducted in a manner such that both cognitive and affective goals can be achieved. In addition, administrators will attempt to create an environment in which a balanced curriculum and cooperative programming are encouraged and supported. Finally, administrators will treat instructional and guidance personnel as unique yet equally important professionals.

A fifth assumption is that guidance programs can and should operate in a balanced manner. It cannot realistically be expected that all energies of guidance personnel could be expended in primary-preventive efforts. On the other hand, responding only to immediate demands will result in the provision of services that are remedial at the expense of those that are preventive. To achieve a balance across primary, secondary, and tertiary preventive efforts, it will be necessary to plan primary prevention programs conscientiously with teaching and administrative colleagues. Unless such deliberate plans are made, reserving time for primary-preventive functions, the immediate pressure for the delivery of remedial functions will absorb all of the time of competent professionals.

BASIC STRATEGY

Program planning from a kindergarten through grade 12 (K–12) perspective requires a master design. The master design should include goals and corresponding objectives that can be measured by outcome data. Then, specific tactics may be selected and implemented in order to achieve desired goals.

The suggested program design includes both horizontal and vertical planning and provides for direct and indirect primary prevention services. Horizontal planning efforts are focused on providing continuous programming across grade levels in order to build on efforts that were initiated earlier. This approach is used for several reasons. First, as children and adolescents age, they pass through psychological developmental stages. Although life is indeed a continuous process, the stages can be grossly identified by developmental tasks or challenges that confront us all (e.g., being able to trust others, learning to count and write, and learning to express feelings in an socially acceptable manner).

A second reason is that human development is cumulative. What is accomplished at one level establishes a foundation for future accomplishments and thus enhances the probability of continuous development. Thus, goals and programs cannot be viewed idiosyncratically. Achievement of one goal may be dependent on success with tasks associated with other goals. In addition, goal achievement does not always occur immediately. In fact, it often takes place over time and may be analogous to a series of baby steps. As a result, horizontal planning is needed in order to provide opportunities for the stepped growth process to bear fruit.

Third, it is possible to achieve the same goals across various age groups. The key to accomplishing this is identifying tactics and materials that are attuned to an appropriate level of student sophistication. Thus, while a goal may remain constant across time, the tactics used in order to achieve that goal will vary according to the developmental level of the group being served.

Vertical planning efforts are focused on identification of tactics for each of several goals that are important at any specific time or stage (e.g., primary, intermediate, junior high school, and senior high school levels). Consequently, planners may design several primary prevention programs at each

grade level in order to provide opportunities for students to progress toward achieving different developmental goals.

Two different modes of service delivery are available to guidance personnel. Through a *direct service* mode, they deliver primary prevention programs to children and adolescents via direct contact with them. The *indirect service* mode adds third parties to the process (e.g., teachers, parents) who deliver the services directly after receiving necessary instruction and/or motivation from a guidance professional. Both modes are appropriate and each presents both advantages and disadvantages. For instance, a direct service approach brings the consumers into direct contact with the professionals assumed to be knowledgeable about affective programming. However, the direct service approach imposes severely on the time of professionals involved in service delivery and, thus, limits the availability of services. While the indirect service approach offers the advantage of making more services available, more students miss an opportunity for direct contact with guidance professionals.

Both direct and indirect services have a purpose at all developmental levels since each mode has clear advantages. Circumstances peculiar to specific developmental stages and to the manner in which schools are organized make it likely that the indirect service approach will be the most prevalent one in the primary and intermediate levels, with the direct service approach becoming the dominant mode during the secondary school years. As such, consulting and inservice program delivery skills will be the most important ones for elementary school guidance personnel. On the other hand, program design and training/teaching skills will be the most important ones for secondary school guidance personnel where primary prevention programming is involved.

THE PROTOTYPE

Table 10-1 contains a suggested prototype for K–12 primary prevention programming. It is organized both horizontally and vertically. Grade levels are grouped into five categories: Preschool, K–3, 4–6, 7–9, and 10–12; and the presentation begins with suggestions for preschool, proceeding horizontally through the K–3, 4–6, 7–9, and 10–12 clusters. Each cluster contains several affective goals with corresponding tactics (i.e., vertical planning) which have been derived from programming ideas that were suggested in previous chapters. Finally, where tactics are presented, an attempt is made to suggest whether direct and/or indirect services are the most appropriate delivery mode. We recognize that much more is presented in this model than could possibly be carried out, even if all time were spent in primary prevention. The suggestions included in table 1 should be regarded as a menu from which specific functions may be selected that are appropriate and relevant to specific situations and specific objectives.

EVALUATION OF PRIMARY PREVENTION PROGRAMS

An important ingredient of all programming efforts is to plan in advance for evaluation of the programs once they are designed and implemented. Simply stated, evaluation activities provide information that helps programmers to assess the effects of their efforts and improve services to their constituents. In addition, evaluation data serve as a foundation on which guidance professionals may respond to expectations that they be accountable to their immediate supervisors and eventually to those who fund their services.

Whatever the services are that are being rendered, there are challenges that must be met in order to evaluate individual and programmatic efforts

Table 10-1
A Prototype for K–12 Primary Prevention Programming
D = Direct services; I = Indirect services

GOALS	TACTICS
Preschool	
Children will . . .	
develop higher levels of competence (chap. 6)	Parent workshops for new parents and parents-to-be (I)
be developmentally ready to learn to their maximum (chap. 6)	Preschool screening programs to identify children at risk (D, I)
Grades K–3	
Students will . . .	
become more aware of the world of work and the place of work in life (chap. 5)	Interest centers (I) Field trips (I) Visits by role models (I) Integrate related materials into school curriculum (I) Parent workshops (I)
become more aware of nontraditional careers (chap. 5)	Integrate nontraditional materials into the school curriculum (I) Parent workshops (I)
improve interpersonal communications in the schools and, it is assumed, in the mental health climate (chap. 2)	*Communication skills training for teachers, administrators, and paraprofessionals (I) e.g.,* Human Resource Development Training Person-Centered Education Relationship Enhancement Training Teacher Effectiveness Training Interpersonal Process Recall
improve social and interpersonal skills (chap. 8)	Intervention Analysis Interpersonal Cognitive Problem Solving (D, I) Sociometric Analysis (D, I)
learn the valuing processes and apply them to their own lives (chap 3).	Values Clarification (D, I)
become more aware of their feelings, thoughts, and actions; have greater self-confidence in their abilities, and understand others better (chap. 3)	Human Development Program—Magic Circles (I)
experience an understanding and encouraging environment at home (chap. 3)	Children: The Challenge Program for Parents (I)
be able to develop personal goals and future plans, trust selves and others, feel competent, and possess adequate levels of self-esteem (chap. 3)	The Salem Guidance Curriculum (I)
explore their feelings, values, and attitudes (chap. 3)	Developing Understanding of Self and Others Program—DUSO I (D, I)
learn ways to cope with stressful situations when they occur (chap. 4)	Progressive muscle relaxation training (D, I)
learn to relax by becoming aware of the sensations of tensing and relaxing major muscle groups and through use of guided imagery (chap. 4)	Progressive muscle relaxation training (D, I) Guided imagery training (D, I)

Table 10-1, continued

GOALS	TACTICS

Grades 4–6

Students will . . .

GOALS	TACTICS
become more aware of the world of work and the place of work in life (chap. 5)	Continue field trips, classroom visits by role models, and integration of related materials into the classroom curriculum (I) Continue parent workshops (D)
become more aware of nontraditional careers (chap. 5)	Continue to integrate nontraditional materials into the school curriculum (I)
improve interpersonal communications in the schools and, therefore, in the learning environment (chap. 2)	Continue communication skills training for teachers, administrators, and paraprofessionals (I) Continue Interaction Analysis
improve interpersonal communications in family relationships and, therefore, in the learning environment (chap. 2)	Continue communications skills training for parents and guardians (I)
be able to understand and acknowledge their own emotions and desires; communicate that understanding to others; generate understanding, appreciation, trust in others; and mutually solve problems and resolve conflicts (chap. 2)	Pupil Relationship Enhancement Program (D)
learn the valuing processes and apply them to their own lives (chap. 3)	Continue Values Clarification (D, I)
become more aware of their feelings, thoughts, and actions; have greater self-confidence in their abilities; and understand others better (chap. 3)	Continue Human Development Program—Magic Circles (I)
experience a democratic, supportive classroom environment (chap. 3)	Reality Therapy Training for Teachers (I)
experience an understanding and encouraging environment at home (chap. 3)	Continue Children: The Challenge Program for Parents (I)
be able to develop personal goals and future plans, trust selves and others, feel competent, and possess adequate levels of self-esteem (chap. 3)	Continue the Salem Guidance Curriculum (I)
explore their feelings, values, and attitudes (chap. 3)	Continue Developing Understanding of Self and Others—DUSO II (D, I) Assertiveness training (D, I) Social problem–solving training (D, I)
learn ways to cope with stressful situations when they occur (chap. 4)	Continue progressive muscle relaxation training (D, I) Assertiveness training (D, I)
acquire greater self-confidence, awareness, self-respect, and respect for others (chap. 4)	*Social problem–solving training* (D, I) *e.g.,* Galvin's Alternative Interactive Network program

improve social and interpersonal skills (chap. 4)	Continue Interpersonal Cognitive Problem Solving program
	  Rochester Social Problem Solving program
	  Continue use of sociometry (D, I)

learn to relax by becoming aware of sensations of tensing and relaxing major muscle groups and through use of guided imagery (chap. 4)	Continue progressive muscle relaxation training (D, I) Continue guided imagery training (D, I)

Table 10-1, continued

GOALS	TACTICS

Grades 7–9

Students will . . .

learn about jobs, satisfactions to be derived from work, requisite skills, and interests for different occupations and the variety of job functions involved in different occupations (chap. 5)

Vocational Exploration Groups (D, I)
Simulations (D, I)
Continue parent workshops (I)

learn the steps in rational decision making (chap. 5)

Rational decision making training (D, I)
Simulations (D, I)
Integrate related units into courses in the school curriculum (I)

become more aware of nontraditional careers and the eventual necessity to decide (chap. 5)

Values Clarification exercises (D, I)
Opening Career Options workshop (D)
Career development courses (D)
Continue parent workshops (D)

improve interpersonal communications in the schools and, therefore, in the learning environment (chap. 2)

Continue communications skills training for teachers, administrators and paraprofessionals (I)
Continue Interaction Analysis

improve interpersonal communications in family relationships and, therefore, in the learning environment (chap. 2)

Continue communication skills training for parents and guardians (I)

be able to generate multiple alternative communication responses in given situations (chap. 2)

Microcounseling training (D)
Peer helper training programs (D)
Continue Pupil Relationship Enhancement Program (D)

be able to understand and acknowledge their own emotions and desires; communicate that understanding to others; generate understanding, appreciation, and trust in others; and mutually solve problems and resolve conflicts (chap. 2)

accept ownership of problems and responsibility for resolving them (chap. 2)

Youth Effectiveness Training (D)

learn to think nonstereotypically about selves and others and to think increasingly about the thoughts and feelings of others (chap. 3)

Deliberate Psychological Education (D, I)

acquire cognitive skills indicative of Kohlberg's Conscientious, Autonomous, and Integrated stages (chap. 3)

Planned Moral Education (D, I)

learn the valuing processes and apply them to their own lives (chap. 3)

Continue Values Clarification (D, I)

experience a democratic, supportive classroom environment (chap. 3)

Continue Reality Therapy training for teachers (I)

experience an understanding and encouraging home environment (chap. 3)

Continue Children: The Challenge Program for Parents (I)

learn ways to cope with stressful situations when they occur (chap. 4)

Continue assertiveness training (D, I)
Continue social problem–solving training (D, I)
Cognitive-restructuring training
Emotive imagery training (D, I)
Continue progressive muscle relaxation training (D, I)
Continue guided imagery training (D, I)

acquire greater self-confidence, awareness, self-respect, and respect for others (chap. 4)

Continue assertiveness training (D, I)

learn to reduce trial-and-error problem-solving behaviors (chap. 4)

Continue problem-solving training (D, I)

recognize self-defeating thoughts and replace them with self-enhancing thoughts (chap. 4)

Cognitive-restructuring training (D, I)

Table 10-1, continued

GOALS	TACTICS

Students will . . .

learn to relax by becoming aware of the sensations of tensing and relaxing major muscle groups and through use of guided imagery (chap. 4)

Continue progressive muscle relaxation training (D, I)
Continue guided imagery training (D, I)

Grades 10–12

learn about jobs, satisfactions to be derived from work, requisite skills and interests for different occupations, and the variety of job functions in different occupations (chap. 5)

Continue Vocational Exploration Groups (D, I)
Continue simulations (D, I)
Career development courses (D)
Continue parent workshops (D)
Persuasion skills training (D, I)

learn job seeking skills (chap. 5)

learn steps in rational decision making (chap. 5)

Continue rational decision making training (D, I)
Career development course (D)
Simulations (D, I)

become more aware of nontraditional careers and the eventual necessity to decide (chap. 5)

Continue classroom career awareness units (D, I)
Continue career development courses (D)
Continue parent workshops (D)

improve interpersonal communications in the schools and, therefore, in the learning environment (chap. 2)

Continue communication skills training for teachers, administrators, and paraprofessionals (I)
Continue Interaction Analysis (I)

improve interpersonal communications in family relationships and, it is assumed, in the mental health climate (chap. 2)

Continue communication skills training for parents and guardians (I)

be able to generate multiple alternative communication responses in given interpersonal situations (chap. 2)

Continue microcounseling training (D)
Continue peer helper training

be able to understand and acknowledge their own emotions and desires; communicate that understanding to others; generate understanding, appreciation, and trust in others; and mutually solve problems and resolve conflicts (chap. 2)

Continue Pupil Relationship Enhancement Program (D)

accept ownership of problems and responsibility for resolving them (chap. 2)

Continue Youth Effectiveness Training (D)

learn to think nonstereotypically about selves and others and to think increasingly about the thoughts and feelings of others (chap. 3)

Continue progressive muscle relaxation training (D,I)

acquire cognitive skills indicative of Kohlberg's Conscientious, Autonomous, and Integrated stages (chap. 3)

Continue Planned Moral Education (D, I)

learn the valuing processes and apply them to their own lives (chap. 3)

Continue Values Clarification (D, I)

experience a democratic, supportive classroom environment (chap. 3)

Continue Reality Therapy training for teachers (I)

experience an understanding and encouraging environment at home (chap. 3)

Continue Children: The Challenge Program for parents (I)

learn ways to cope with stressful situations when they occur (chap. 4)

Continue assertiveness training (D, I)
Continue social problem–solving training (D, I)
Continue cognitive restructuring training (D, I)
Continue emotive imagery training (D, I)
Meditation training (D)
Continue progressive muscle relaxation training (D, I)

acquire greater self-confidence, awareness, self-respect, and respect for others (chap. 4)

Continue assertiveness training (D, I)

Table 10-1, continued

GOALS	TACTICS
Students will . . .	
learn to reduce trial-and-error problem-solving behaviors (chap. 4)	Continue social problem-solving training (D, I)
recognize self-defeating thoughts and replace them with self-enhancing thoughts (chap. 4)	Continue cognitive restructuring training (D, I)
become more calm, more aware, and more in control of themselves (chap. 4)	Meditation training (D)
learn to relax by becoming aware of sensations of tensing and relaxing major muscle groups (chap. 4)	Continue progressive muscle relaxation training (D)
learn to raise competent children (chap. 6)	Training in the importance of the first three years of life (D, I)

successfully. Presenters of primary prevention programs are beset with common evaluation problems and with challenges that are peculiar to the type of activity in which they are engaged. For instance, when prevention programming is offered, how can it be determined whether or not problems were prevented? On the other hand, immediate impact of remediation and treatment services can be more readily discussed by assessing client levels of functioning before, during, and after efforts to treat and/or remediate specific problems.

Recognizing primary prevention programming as being susceptible to both unique and common evaluation challenges, we will attempt to address our comments in this section accordingly—in a balanced fashion. In so doing, we also realize that the readers may possess varying levels of sophistication about evaluation and research methods. Consequently, an effort has been made to offer a menu of evaluation as well as programming suggestions.

Outcome, Opinion, and Enumerative Data

It is possible to distinguish three major types of data important in the evaluation of a guidance program. The first of these is outcome data. In their ultimate form, outcome data describe how children are different as a result of the fact that guidance services of a particular kind have been provided. . . . Opinion data reflects the subjective attitudes of the respondent. . . . Enumerative data . . . reflects such facts as the number of tests given, the number of individual interviews held, the average length of interviews, and other objective types of data. . . . A thorough evaluation of a guidance program requires the collection of all three types of data. (Shaw, 1973, pp. 279-280)

This quotation reflects our current position and summarizes our recommendation to all guidance program evaluators. Our recommendation is that they attempt to collect a blend of outcome, opinion, and enumerative data. Such a strategy provides comprehensive coverage. If less than this is done,

Such a strategy provides comprehensive coverage. If less than this is done, evaluators increase the probability of having incomplete coverage, which may lead to inadequate accountability information and inappropriate planning decisions.

■ *Outcome data.* Outcome data are dependent upon measurable goals and objectives. Given a set of measurable goals and objectives, evaluators must identify measures that determine whether the objectives were achieved and specify procedures for applying the measures, scoring them, and reporting the results. Obviously, outcome data cannot be acquired where there are no measurable program goals and objectives. Therefore, the first step in acquiring outcome data is to establish goals or purposes for primary prevention programming and derive measurable objectives from those goals.

Look at table 10-1 for example. In the Grades K–3 cluster, one of the goals is that children become more aware of nontraditional careers. One objective of a subsequent classroom unit designed to integrate materials and activities about nontraditional careers into the curriculum might be that male and female children involved in the classroom unit will similarly identify more career options as appropriate for them to consider then they did prior to the curriculum intervention. This is only one example of many possible goals, even more objectives, and also more outcome measures that could be identified from the material in table 10-1. The variety of different forms that outcome data may take is quite comprehensive (e.g., behavioral observation counts, surveys of attitudes, objective achievement or knowledge tests, and self-reports), and an inventory cannot be provided in the space available here. The fact that there is such a variety of choices available is advantageous to evaluators because it means that they are not excessively limited when attempting to evaluate program outcomes. One aspect of measuring outcome data does remain constant, however, and that is the process: design programs based on goals that lead to measurable objectives and find or develop valid and reliable measures for assessing the outcomes.

■ *Opinion data.* Constituent attitudes about the programs and services rendered are important to know because satisfied consumers are more likely to be motivated to respond positively to program content and achieve desired goals than are dissatisfied ones. Opinion data are also a source of information about inappropriate program content, goals, and objectives. In an extreme example of differences between outcome and opinion data, we cite a hypothetical situation in which the outcome data indicates that recipients of a preventive program achieved high scores on a test of knowledge about the information presented to them, while results of a survey of attitudes toward the program indicates that participants did not like the methods used, were bored by it all, and do not think it will influence their behaviors and attitudes significantly in the future.

If either the outcome or opinion data had not been collected, important evaluative information would have been overlooked. Without the outcome data, the program would have appeared to be a complete failure. Without the opinion data, the program would have appeared successful, and it is doubtful that any changes would have occurred. Yet, it appeared as if modifications were desired and needed. By collecting both opinion and outcome data, the evaluator would have been in a better position to assess program effects objectively and plan necessary modifications. Thus, we strongly advocate using outcome and opinion measures when evaluating all guidance programs, including primary prevention programs.

Unlike the situation evaluators encounter when planning to collect outcome data, opinion data may be acquired by using a relatively common set of procedures requiring levels of sophistication that we believe all readers of this book possess or may possess with sufficient motivation on their part. In our opinion, the key ingredients are to design survey questions that allow respondents to state exactly the information about which evaluators are inquiring and to provide a scoring system that translates opinions and attitudes into useful data.

Others such as Brown, Hartman, and Fuqua (1981) and Hackett (1981) have devoted entire journal articles to suggestions about the design and use of surveys and questionnaires by working professionals, and we recommend that such resources be read. Two approaches to scoring opinion data are presented here in order to elaborate on a point made in the previous paragraph—the importance of acquiring useful data.

Some items may be stated in such a way that results are idiosyncratic to that particular item. Thus, a scoring system and total is assigned to that item independent of the scoring system and totals assigned to other items. If a survey consists of many or all items designed similarly, then results have to be recorded and reported independently rather than in a cumulative manner. To do otherwise, would lead to a loss of important information and acquisition of potentially misleading data. An example follows.

Two idiosyncratic items on the same survey may appear as follows:

	Circle One
I learned important information about my attitudes toward non-traditional careers in this program.	Yes No
The group leader was knowledgeable about the information presented in this program.	Yes No

Each item provides important information about different aspects of the program and the results will lose impact if combined. Thus, each needs to be scored and reported independently of the other. In this case, similar scoring and reporting methods are used. Total up the number of Yes and No responses to each item and determine the percentage of each. For example, 75% of the respondents thought the information was important (responded yes), while 90% thought the leader was knowledgeable (responded yes). Both summaries of opinions are important but for differing reasons.

Where evaluators wish to assess general attitudes about a program, it is possible to design an instrument in which several items reflect various response levels toward the same event. In this case, the item scores are blended into a single total score. An example follows.

	Never	Sometimes		Always	
The ideas presented were useful.	1	2	3	4	5
The reading materials were interesting.	1	2	3	4	5

If a respondent circled a 1 for the first item and a 5 for the second item, the total score would be 6, and the average would be 3, leading to a conclusion that the summative program ingredient being assessed was successful "sometimes" or for some of the participants some of the time. Of course, a survey of this nature would need more than two items in order for this approach to be a useful one.

Opinion surveys are directed to the participants in primary prevention programs. Thus, they must be designed with clear directions, a format that can be understood, and at a language level that the recipients can be expected to understand. Not all respondents in a K–12 system can be surveyed by the paper and pencil technique. Other methods such as the interview or observational strategies will have to be employed with some participants, especially the youngest ones.

■ *Enumerative data.* Perhaps the most common format used in evaluating guidance programs is counting or tallying information about the amount of time devoted to delivering services, how many persons received the services, and the cost of the services delivered. These are examples of enumerative data—counting or tallying the number of times an event or service occurred.

Enumerative data supplements outcome and opinion data by providing information that can eventually lead to evidence of cost-effectiveness for the services being delivered. Krumboltz (1974) suggested a useful format for linking outcome and enumerative data and achieving estimates of cost-effectiveness while also providing an intelligent rationale for the accountability procedures he suggested.

Enumerative data may also be used for making decisions about programming efforts. Guidance personnel can use enumerative data to determine how much time they spend delivering primary prevention services in comparison to the amount of time devoted to treatment and remedial services. They also are able to determine how many constituents were served by primary prevention, treatment, or remedial programming. The aforementioned information is then available for planning purposes where guidance personnel and their colleagues wish to decide how best to use their time—a limited resource—or justify previously determined decisions about time usage.

The type of information normally classified as enumerative data is relatively easy to identify, collect, and analyze. Difficulties occur during the collection stage because doing so can become an annoyingly time-consuming activity. Having continuously and laboriously to keep records of one's professional activities is in itself a wastefully inefficient use of time. Thus, enumerative data should be collected efficiently in order to be useful.

Baker (1981, 1983) has offered suggestions for alleviating this problem. Figures 10-1 and 10-2 present examples of summative data collecting strategies designed by school district personnel. The six cards in Figure 10-1 were developed for data collection purposes in Erie, Pennsylvania and were each of a different color. Users conveniently reached in a desk drawer for a card of the desired color, circled the appropriate information, entered in a number, and placed the card in a repository. The tally sheet in Figure 10-2 developed by the State College, Pennsylvania school district may be used in a similar fashion with the desired information all being entered on the same form.

A somewhat different approach has been suggested by Shaw (1973) and is reflected in Figure 10-3. A card reflecting all major activities of a counseling staff was developed cooperatively with the staff of a school district. Each counselor received a set of cards for each school day, preprinted with the date. At the end of each day, each counselor completed a card for that day by filling in appropriate bubbles. Daily completion of the card took about one minute. The cards used a mark sensing format and data were aggregaterd monthly in the computer.

These approaches were developed to provide certain kinds of information in a specific situation. It is unlikely that any one approach can meet the needs of every situation, and it will be necessary to develop materials to meet local needs. Any such instrument must take a minimum of time to complete and to analyze. The use of mark sensing approaches with potential for computer aggregation and analysis is recommended.

Evaluation or Research?

Do professionals in the field have to be sophisticated in the nuances of research design in order to evaluate primary prevention program successfully? Our answer is a qualified no. Most, if not all, professionals in the field are logistically unable randomly to assign participants to treatment and control groups and attend to the other facets of experimental research design—nor are they inclined to do so. This does not mean that they cannot acquire meaningful evaluation data.

Primary prevention programs that have been designed from clearly stated goals and objectives provide evaluators with a foundation for finding and developing outcome measures that will provide evidence of the effects of the program on the recipients. Pretesting and posttesting of the participants on the outcome measures or the use of preexisting baseline data will provide information about how they performed at the beginning and at the closing of the program. Of course, if the participants are achieving relatively high performance on program objectives at the outset, the probability of discovering improvement upon completion of the program is lessened greatly.

We qualified our answer to the opening question because of our belief that the validity of evaluation results can be enhanced by attending to some of the canons of experimental research. To do so will require some additional planning and may require programmers to increase their existing level of competence in and knowledge about research designs. For example, if one

Figure 10-1. *Erie Data Cards*

INDIVIDUAL STUDENT COUNSELING 1	INDIVIDUAL STUDENT INFORMATION/SERVICE 2
SCHOOL _____	SCHOOL _____
COUNSELOR _____	COUNSELOR _____

0	Less than 10 minutes	0	Less than 10 minutes
1	10–19 minutes	1	10–19 minutes
2	20–29 minutes	2	20–29 minutes
3	30–39 minutes	3	30–39 minutes
4	40–49 minutes	4	40–49 minutes
5	50–59 minutes	5	50–59 minutes
6	60–69 minutes	6	60–69 minutes
7	70–79 minutes	7	70–79 minutes
8	80–89 minutes	8	80–89 minutes
9	90 or more	9	90 or more
01	Attendance	01	Attendance
02	Behavior	02	College Guidance
03	Career Counseling	03	Discipline
04	Career Decision-Making	04	Employment, Full Time
05	College Counseling	05	Employment, Part Time
06	Drop-Out	06	Enrolling
07	Drug Counseling	07	Financial Aid, College
08	Employment Counseling	08	Financial Aid, Current
09	Finances	09	Free Lunch
10	Home Problems	10	Military Information
11	Personal Social Adjustment	11	Occupational Information
12	School Program Choice	12	Program Change
13	Sex	13	Program Information
14	Subject Change	14	Sick Calls
15	Teacher–Student Problem	15	Summer School
16	Value Counseling	16	Test Information
17	Other	17	Test Interpretation
		18	Transportation
		19	Withdrawing
0	Problem Identified	20	Work Permit
1	Solution Implemented	21	Other
2	Problem Solved		

Figure 10-1. *Erie Data Cards,* continued

INDIVIDUAL ADULT CONFERENCE IN–SCHOOL 3	ADULT GROUP AND OUT–OF–SCHOOL ACTIVITY 4
SCHOOL _____	SCHOOL _____
COUNSELOR _____	COUNSELOR _____

	INDIVIDUAL ADULT CONFERENCE IN–SCHOOL		ADULT GROUP AND OUT–OF–SCHOOL ACTIVITY
0	Less than 10 minutes	0	Less than 10 minutes
1	10–19 minutes	1	10–19 minutes
2	20–29 minutes	2	20–29 minutes
3	30–39 minutes	3	30–39 minutes
4	40–49 minutes	4	40–49 minutes
5	50–59 minutes	5	50–59 minutes
6	60–69 minutes	6	60–69 minutes
7	70–79 minutes	7	70–79 minutes
8	80–89 minutes	8	80–89 minutes
9	90 or more	9	90 or more
01	Administrator, Central Office	01	Case Conference
02	Administrator, Own School	02	Meetings
03	Administrator, Other School	03	Other Adult Groups
04	Business Representative	04	Case Conference
05	College Representative	05	Classes Attended
06	Community Representative	06	Meetings
07	Counselor Own School	07	Other Adult Groups
08	Counselor Other School	08	Clerical Routine
09	Parent	09	Correspondence
10	Professional Non-School	10	Information, Looking Up
11	Psychologist, School	11	Recommendations, College
12	Referral Agency	12	Recommendations, Job
13	Social Worker	13	Phone Calls
14	Teacher	14	Transcripts
15	Visiting Teacher	15	Other
16	Other		

_____ Units Counted

_____ Units Estimated

Figure 10-1. *Erie Data Cards,* continued

SOLITARY IN-SCHOOL ACTIVITY	5

SCHOOL _____

COUNSELOR _____

0	Less than 10 minutes
1	10–19 minutes
2	20–29 minutes
3	30–39 minutes
4	40–49 minutes
5	50–59 minutes
6	60–69 minutes
7	70–79 minutes
8	80–89 minutes
9	90 or more

01	Bulletins, Writing
02	Correspondence, Miscellaneous
03	Forms, Various
04	Information, Looking Up
05	Listing
06	Mail Handling
07	Program Changes
08	Recommendations, College
09	Recommendations, Job
10	Summons
11	Phone Calls, Parents
12	Phone Calls, School Personal
13	Transcripts
14	Trays, Checking
15	Other

_____ Units Counted

_____ Units Estimated

STUDENT GROUP ACTIVITY	6

SCHOOL _____

COUNSELOR _____

0	Less than 10 minutes
1	10–19 minutes
2	20–29 minutes
3	30–39 minutes
4	40–49 minutes
5	50–59 minutes
6	60–69 minutes
7	70–79 minutes
8	80–89 minutes
9	90 or more

01	Class Visitation
02	Classroom Coverage
03	Group Counseling
04	Enrolling
05	Excuse from School
06	Free Lunch
07	Information, College
08	Information, General
09	Information, Occupational
10	Material Distribution
11	Information, Test
12	Monitoring Activities
13	Orientation
14	Program Choice
15	Tardiness
16	Testing
17	Test Interpretation
18	Transportation
19	Other

_____ Number of Students Served

Figure 10.2. State College Tally Sheet

NAME _____ DATE _____

DISTRICT _____

INSTRUCTIONAL LEVEL

_____ Elementary _____ Junior High _____ Other (explain)

_____ Middle _____ Secondary

STUDENTS
- Individual — 1
- Small Group 2–10 — 2
- Large Group 11+ — 3

PEOPLE
- Parents — 4
- Teachers — 5
- Principal — 6
- Counseling Staff — 7
- IU, PPS, NURSE — 8
- Referral Agency — 9
- Parent(s) and Teacher(s) — 10
- Parent(s) and Principal — 11

TIME
- 0–5 Minutes — 1
- 6–15 Minutes — 2
- 16–30 Minutes — 3
- 31–60 Minutes — 4
- 61–+ Minutes — 5

CONCERNS
- Attendance — 1
- Achievement — 2
- Behavior — 3
- Health — 4
- Home Problems — 5
- Personal/Social Adjustment — 6
- Records/Research — 7
- Scheduling — 8
- Teacher/Student Relationships — 9
- Testing — 10
- Vocational/Career — 11
- Supportive — 12
- Exceptional Students — 13

METHODS
- Classroom Visit/Observation — 1
- Conferences/Consultation — 2
- Group Counseling — 3
- Home Visits — 4
- Individual Counseling — 5
- Phone — 6

OTHER
- Professional Growth — 1
- Assigned Duties — 2

Figure 10.3. *Cards Prepared for Computerized Data Collection*

were to evaluate outcomes of programs in the manner suggested in the previous paragraph, someone could question whether or not any effects discovered through outcome measures were caused by the program or some other circumstances (e.g., natural development, other experiences, and other programs). Such concerns can be attended to where there are enough participants to form more than one group and there is time to delay delivery of the program to half of them without the delay being harmful. Those waiting to be offered the program can then serve as a comparison or control group for those being served, and the outcome measures can be given to both the group receiving the program and those waiting for it. Eventually, everyone is served and the comparison group provides data that may validate significant effects found in the outcome measures given to those who received the program.

This approach is known as a quasiexperimental design, and such designs are applicable to in-the-field evaluation studies while also having the attributes of experimental research. Cook and Campbell (1979) is perhaps the most comprehensive source of information about quasiexperimentation. In summary, we think that the minimum level of adequate evaluation assessment will be achieved by designing outcome measures from measureable goals and objectives and using those measures to evaluate the effects of primary prevention programs. Beyond that, we believe that evaluation efforts can be improved through the use of quasiexperimentation strategies because such strategies will assign greater meaningfulness and validity to outcome data.

Previously Measured Effects of Primary Prevention Strategies

One way to respond to demands for program accountability is to evaluate the programs in question in a manner similar to the suggestions expressed in the previous section, and report the results. Another approach to accountability is to make inferences based on the effects of programs similar to those in the planning stage that have previously been evaluated. The second approach is especially useful where there are no previous local experiences with the programs in question and doubts exist about the appropriateness of said programs.

A traditional method of acquiring information upon which to make such inferences is to search the professional literature for reports of evaluations of programs like the ones in question. If the search uncovers several reports and the results indicate significant effects on the desired populations, then programmers can assert with some confidence that the program in question is a feasible one. On the other hand, the professional literature often contains mixed and qualified information about the apparent effects of the programs being evaluated. Meta-analytic integration of research studies into a summary statistic offers a solution to this problem.

▪ *Meta-analysis procedures.* We do not suggest that all programmers should synthesize research from independent studies in the professional literature. Our purpose in this section is to inform readers about a procedure for synthesizing research known as meta-analysis and to report that the professional literature now contains meta-analysis studies that may provide useful information.

There are several statistical techniques that are used in meta-analysis studies. The one cited here is known as the Effect Size statistic (ES). It is used to summarize results of related experimental studies and can be determined in several ways. The most common technique for acquiring the ES of an experimental treatment is to subtract the arithmetic posttest mean of the control group from the mean of the treatment group and divide the resultant integers by the posttest standard deviation of the control group. The formula for the data transformation is as follows: $ES = (\bar{X}_t - \bar{X}_c)/SD_c$, where $\bar{X}_t =$ posttest mean of the treatment condition; $\bar{X}_c =$ posttest mean of the control condition; $SD_c =$ posttest standard deviation of the control condition).

This technique provides a summary of all comparisons within one study and of comparisons across a group of independent studies in a uniform statistic—the ES. The ES is similar to the Z score which is associated with the normal curve and the normal distribution concept. The mean of the distribution is represented by a Z score of zero and the areas under the curve are divided into standard deviations below or above the mean (i.e., −1, −2, −3 standard deviations below the mean and +1, +2, +3 standard deviations above the mean).

▪ *A Meta-analysis of primary prevention studies.* In the study we are reporting here, the average ES was 0.55, which is analogous to +.55 standard deviations above the mean of a normal distribution. In their report, Baker, Swisher, Nadenichek, and Popowicz (1984) suggested that an ES of 0.55 means that a hypothetical person not having previously received one of the primary prevention programs included in the meta-analysis will, after participating in the program, achieve a gain of 0.55 standard deviations on relevant outcome measures. Cohen's (1969) criteria for judging the magnitude of an ES suggests that 0.55 be considered medium on a scale with three categories: small, medium, and large.

In summary, the meta-analysis by Baker et al. (1984) offers an estimate that the primary prevention programs studied had positive effects of a "medium" nature, which we think should be encouraging information for those preparing to venture into primary prevention programming. Baker et al. (1984) also offer a summary of effects across specific primary prevention categories (e.g., communication skills training, moral education programs). That summary is reproduced here in table 10-2. Readers should be cautious when inspecting the ES in table 10-2 and drawing conclusions because the number of studies in some categories is quite small (e.g., two deliberate psychological education studies, three moral education program studies).

Table 10-2
Summary of Effects of Primary Prevention Strategies

	N_S	N_{ES}	*Range ES*	%(−)	*ES*
Combined group of primary prevention studies	42[a]	308	−.40 to 15.75	9.5	.91
Combined primary prevention studies without outlayer[b]	41[a]	302	−.40 to 1.95	9.8	.55
Programs designed to enhance career maturity	12	62	−.08 to 1.40	16.7	1.33
Coping skills training founded on cognitive-behavior modification principles	8	52	−.40 to 1.02	37.5	.26
Communication skills training programs	5	87	.08 to 15.75	0.0	3.90
Communication skills training programs without outlayer[b]	4	81	.08 to 1.94	0.0	.93
Deliberate psychological education programs	2	3	.90 to 1.95	0.0	1.43
Moral education programs	3	21	.32 to .56	0.0	.43
Deliberate psychological education and moral education programs	5	24	.32 to 1.95	0.0	.83
Substance abuse prevention programs	7	98	.08 to 1.13	0.0	.34
Programs categorized as values clarification in nature	7	44	.29 to 1.13	0.0	.69
Programs in which values clarification strategies were blended with other strategies	9	98	−.08 to 1.41	28.6	.37
All values clarification programs in combination	16	142	−.08 to 1.41	14.3	.51

Key to abbreviations: N_S = number of studies; *N_{ES}* = number of Effect Sizes within the total number of studies; *Range ES* = lowest to highest average Effect Size across the 40 studies; %(−) = percentage of Effect Sizes that are negative; *ES* = estimated Effect Size.
[a]Two of the 40 reports cited by Baker et al. (1984) reported more than a single independent primary prevention variable being investigated.
[b]One study had an Effect Size of 15.75 and was treated as an outlayer because of its significant impact on overall Effect Sizes when entered into a summary statistic.

Note. From "Measured Effects of Primary Prevention" by S. B. Baker, J. D. Swisher, P. E. Nadenichek, and C. L. Popowicz, 1984, *Personnel and Guidance Journal, 62*, pp. 459–464. Copyright 1984 by the American Association for Counseling and Development. Reprinted by permission.

CONCLUSION

In this book, we have attempted to provide a rationale for setting primary prevention goals using related programs to enhance counseling and guidance services to children and adolescents. Clearly, much of what we offer has a school-based flavor. Most of the ideas we presented seem to focus on applications in school settings. One reason for this is that the objects of our attention are children and adolescents who spend much of their time during these formative years in schools, being "educated." A second reason is that the authors are more familiar with schools than with other human service settings. We are familiar enough with other human service settings to believe that many of the programmatic ideas presented in this book can be adapted to settings outside of the schools where groups of children, adolescents, and interested adults gather or can be gathered in order to engage in potentially beneficial primary prevention programs.

There are specific, independently designed primary prevention programs and techniques that are well developed and available for adaptation. A number of the more important ones have been presented here. Evidence is accumulating that many of these programs are effective, and we assume that evidence will continue to accumulate. Thus, there is empirical support for implementing primary prevention programming.

To our knowledge, there are few schools or agencies that provide primary prevention programs in a systematic manner. We think that the dearth of primary prevention programming is an unfortunate circumstance. Primary prevention goals are worthwhile and primary prevention programs are known to be successful. We think that an increased emphasis on primary prevention is long overdue. Our goal, however, is not to eliminate remedial and treatment services. As was stated earlier, our goal is to strike a balance among primary, secondary, and tertiary prevention services by helping human service providers to acquire ideas and resources for the delivery of primary prevention programs.

The potential change agents in this effort to strike a balance are you, the readers. We urge that the challenge presented to you through the ideas in this book be enthusiastically accepted. You represent the means by which needed changes will occur. We have provided a foundation for your efforts by bringing together many useful ideas and weaving a motivational theme into our presentation. In the final analysis, our offerings are modest in comparison to the mental health contributions you will make to those whom we all serve.

REFERENCES

Baker, S. B. (1981). *School counselor's handbook: A guide for professional growth and development.* Boston: Allyn and Bacon.

Baker, S. B. (1983). Suggestions for assessing guidance accountability. *Pennsylvania Journal of Counseling, 2*(1), 52–69.

Baker, S. B., Swisher, J. D., Nadenichek, P. E., & Popowicz, C. L. (1984). Measured effects of primary prevention. *Personnel and Guidance Journal, 62,* 459–464.

Brown, D. F., Hartman, D. W., & Fuqua, D. R. (1981). Guidelines for consumers of survey research. *School Counselor, 28,* 279–284.

Cohen, J. (1969). *Statistical power analysis for the behavioral sciences.* New York: Academic Press.

Cook, T. D., & Campbell, D. T. (1979). *Quasi-experimentation: Design and analysis issues for field settings.* Chicago: Rand McNally.

Hackett, G. (1981). Survey research methods. *Personnel and Guidance Journal, 59,* 599–604.

Krumboltz, J. D. (1974). An accountability model for counselors. *Personnel and Guidance Journal, 52,* 639–646.

Shaw, M. C. (1973). *School guidance systems: Objectives, functions, evaluation, and change.* Boston: Houghton Mifflin.

SUBJECT INDEX

AUTHOR INDEX